Learning Disabilities
From a Parent's Perspective:

What you need to know to understand, help, and advocate for your child

Kim E. Glenchur

pince-nez press
san francisco

Learning Disabilities From a Parent's Perspective:
What you need to know to understand, help, and
advocate for your child

ISBN 1-930074-07-7
Library of Congress Control Number 2002117666, 371.91

Cover design & page design: Idintdoit Design
Layout by Judy Christenson

Pince-Nez Press
San Francisco, CA
(415) 267-5978 fax (800) 579-3614
www.pince-nez.com
info@pince-nez.com

Publisher's Note

During the seven years I've published books on education, one issue is continually raised: learning disabilities. Wherever I speak with parents, no matter in cities or suburban areas, no matter economic level or educational level of the parent, race, or background, I hear about parents having to face issues of learning disabilities. Sometimes it is only a fear or concern that is alleviated by time or by a little extra help. Sometimes it is a full-blown case with the concomitant educational professionals, therapists, and IEP and a morass of public and private resources.

What I hear from parents is frustration, pain (their hearts breaking for their children), confusion, and loneliness. On top of this is the question "How did this happen?" Many parents of children with learning disabilities are extremely bright, highly educated and very successful in their careers. They never dreamed they would have a child who would not have it as easy in school as they did (or who would not be able to overcome difficulties through hard work).

When parents first hear or suspect their child may have a learning disability they enter a different world: one that includes jargon they most likely have never heard, testing, bureaucratic struggles, differing opinions, and controversy. To advocate for their child in this world, they need to know the vocabulary of the LD world, understand the scientific and medical aspects of it and know the roles of the players and the paths to obtain the services their child needs. It's an education.

The area of learning disabilities is controversial and parents, educators, and medical professionals sometimes work together smoothly and sometimes are at odds with each other. Countless parents have told me their stories of how hard they have had to fight to get what their children have needed from "the system" including schools, medical professionals, and insurance companies.

For this reason, I wanted a book written by a parent helping parents acquire the knowledge they need to enter the specialized world. When I met Kim Glenchur, I knew she was the person for this task. She is an educated, intelligent mother of three teenagers who has dedicated herself to doing everything possible to help her children succeed.

And her story is a success story.

Susan Vogel

i

Acknowledgment

I would like to thank the many people who helped me with this book, especially Susan Vogel, who initiated this project. She asked me to write on what I wish I had known when I first suspected something was amiss. Some mothers who wish to remain anonymous also contributed their experiences of woe, regret, hope, and eventual triumph. Many people also helped review this book, among them Mr. Marty Procaccio, Dr. Alin Botoman, Mr. William Lepowsky, and Ms. Lisa Hague. I would also like to thank the Schwab Foundation for Learning for its support of library resources; my father for his medical research assistance; Judy Christenson for her formidable desktop publishing skills; my wonderful husband for his patience and support during the writing of this book; and my children who taught me how to surf the Internet. One is never too old to learn.

The references at the end of the book suggest the many field investigators and authors to whom I am indebted for ideas and information. I am deeply grateful to the many who have granted *gratis* reprint permissions: Academic Therapy Publications, Brother James Dods, Ms. Deidre Hayden, Educators Publishing Service, Free Spirit Press, Ms. Johanna Kroenlein, *Macworld*, Modern Learning Press, Dr. Kathleen Nadeau, Pearson Education, Schwab Learning, *Scientific American*, *Scholastic Parent and Child*, Ms. Shirley Cramer, Springer-Verlag GmbH & Company, *Stanford Magazine*, Dr. Catherine Trapani, Dr. Susan Vogel, and Mr. Colin Whurr.

Submitted excerpts on pages 81 and 189 are from *Patton: A Genius for War* by Carlo D'Este Copyright © 1995 by Carlo E'Este. Reprinted by permission of HarperCollins Publishers Inc. For additional territory, contact Carlo D'Este, C/o McIntosh & Otis, Inc., 310 Madison Avenue, New York, NY 10017. Territory Granted: United States, its dep., Canada, Philippine Islands, Open Market.

Preface

Many parents have asked for a single source unifying the various topics involved in dealing with learning disorders. While this is an impossible ideal, this book highlights the literature and reviews possible resources. The hard part for many parents is researching the choices available, because it requires a steep learning curve. Once you begin to explore reasons for learning problems, you'll be faced with a barrage of often confusing information and terms. The topics are complex, interconnected, subtle, and always being updated with new discoveries and ideas. The material presented here is not a quick study. If it were, resolving learning disabilities would not be such an ordeal. I hope this book will reduce your time in searching for information and guide you toward better decision-making for your child.

Internet addresses in this book begin with "www." and are preceded by "http://" unless otherwise indicated. No punctuation marks exist at the end of the URLs. I have tried to identify noncommercial websites with useful information and good support. The addresses were reviewed for accuracy before press time as many publishers often revamp their material. Some addresses, like government websites, are *case-sensitive*, which means that an upper or lower case letter is a crucial part of the address. Since this book was written, some addresses may have changed. A search engine or the search feature available on many websites can be used to locate a particular reference. Contact information may exist on an organization's web site. Phone numbers, if available, are listed in this book or at such places as www.switchboard.com.

I have not received any gifts or payments in exchange for any products and services mentioned in the book. These are only suggestions, to give you an idea of what has worked for other people. Each child has a unique set of circumstances and available options. Unfortunately, the effectiveness of a course of action may be determined only through trial-and-error. Research before you buy.

That many disciplines are involved in learning disabilities is similar to the fable of the seven blind men who studied an elephant: Each has a different perspective. Many voices from many disciplines are included in these pages. You, as the parent, must integrate them all in order to obtain the most appropriate help for your child. Healing is an interdisciplinary art. So is good teaching and parenting.

Current medical investigations are discovering real physical phenomena underlying learning problems. Treatment, though, mostly lies in education, now guaranteed by antidiscrimination laws. Without proper treatment, bigger psychological and social problems emerge.

The Introduction to this book is a memoir presenting many of the problems families must address: diagnosis, treatment decisions, school interactions, tutoring, special equipment, psychological needs, advocacy, and planning for the future. The personal stories in the text are not from clinical settings, but from ordinary people in everyday life. With minor modifications to ensure privacy, the profiles show the problems of obtaining appropriate help. Although investigators have found that most learning disabilities affect both sexes equally, males are more often identified, perhaps because male manifestations are more disruptive in the classroom. Families, especially mothers, are also affected.

Ignoring the problem will not make it go away. Dealing with learning disorders requires incredible patience, substantial effort, and sometimes therapy. Quite often, however, time, energy, and money are in short supply. Still, with all that is presently known, and given the willingness of families to contribute extraordinary efforts, these problems don't have to be as hard to solve as they are now. Real help is available.

Kim Glenchur

Dedication

To my children, through whom I have learned so much.

TABLE OF CONTENTS

Part II: Getting Help

<h1 style="text-align:center">Introduction</h1>

A Mother's Perspective

[The following true story of a mother's experiences of schooling her son—from first grade through high school—illustrates many of the issues discussed in this book.]

The local private elementary school was the worst place that we ever put our son. We found out from our daughter that the teacher was putting Alex in the corner facing the chalkboard with his back to the class all day long; she moved his desk to have him behind her. He couldn't see her speak. To ask any questions, he had to call out because he was behind her. But this only got him in trouble for disrupting the class, resulting in him being yelled at to be quiet. She referred to him as *stupid* according to both my daughter and my son. The teacher targeted him for punishment. She chose him because he was generally a quiet child who wasn't really confident. She continuously picked on him in class.

Our daughter, Meg, learned this because she had been bumped up two grades from preschool to Alex's combination kindergarten-first-grade class. Meg had problems with the teacher too. To give you an example, one weekend in this first-grade class, Meg brought home a workbook and completed it all by herself. Alex was very proud of her because he said that all of the other students couldn't have done this. Meg took the workbook to class for show-and-tell. She showed the teacher that she had done the whole workbook on the weekend. The teacher told her that she couldn't have done it and that she was a liar, and made her say and write that she was a liar. Meg got so upset with the teacher that she spit at her. And that's when the school called me and declared, "You have unruly children. Come and pick up your child. She can't be in our class." I left work immediately and found her alone on the street corner outside the school.

Later that afternoon, Alex reported that Meg "couldn't control herself, Mom. The teacher made her say in front of the class that she was a liar. And she had done all that work and I had tried to say that she really did all that work and they wouldn't believe her. They should have been proud of her instead of making fun of her."

We thought our son was doing fine until our daughter kept giving us poor reports. We noticed our son getting more emotional and upset over his struggle to learn. I went in to talk to the head of the school over various classroom incidents and asked they check in on the teacher.

They refused to listen and defended the teacher. At this point, I said I'd pull him out of the school. The head of the school stated I couldn't do that because the state law requires that the child be in a school. I replied that this was a terrible school. I'd rather have no school than this school because the damage the school was doing I couldn't reverse. We pulled our children out near the end of the academic year.

After that year in first grade, Alex's desire to learn was deeply set back. What a contrast from his preschool and kindergarten years when he was such a happy student! The person who was the head of the kindergarten school loved the children. She came over to see them. She was just mortified when she saw Alex with his ability, everything stripped away—she remarked she didn't even recognize him. We know her pretty well and she just truly loved him. She loved to teach young people, she took pride in getting them to the next level. To see what someone else had done to her student in one year was more than she could handle. She actually came over to our home during the summer and during the next school year to help him build his self-esteem again.

The sad thing is when we left that private school, parents and other teachers didn't know why we left. We never told them. One of Alex's friends ended up being the child the first-grade teacher bullied in the class the next year. We later found out he suffered through almost the identical problems. He had the same type of personality as Alex, not a real strong personality, but a kind child. The type of person who would be the peace-maker in a quiet way. This teacher had to find someone else to pick on.

The next choice for us was the public school system. We found they just didn't have the ability to deal with the individual needs of so many students. When Alex came to this new school in the second grade he was behind. He had no self-confidence. He couldn't read because the first-grade teacher had put him in the corner most of the time with no reading instruction and no interaction time. We tried continuously to work with him.

At this point, we didn't know that learning disabilities existed to even ask for testing in the first place. We just knew that Alex had lost his self-esteem, that he was just depressed, and that he was completely frazzled trying to study. I kept working with him on things. About half-way through the year, I had the first parent-teacher conference. She began, "Alex is an incredibly bright student but he's failing his math tests." And I replied, "He used to be so good in math. I find that hard to believe." She explained, "The problem is that he can't read the directions." Well, I discovered that nobody would give him the directions. They'd let him fail. They were too busy. They're not in the business of helping individual children beyond a certain level. So the subject in which he excelled and which gave him some self-esteem, he could no longer do because he wasn't able to read. Also the children were making fun of his oral reading.

I started asking people and heard two suggestions about this place called the Reading Game, later known as Britannica Learning Center (now run by Sylvan Learning Center). We met this wonderful woman who really loved to teach children. Alex was there for three hours a week and loved every minute of it. Each session was an hour-and-a-half, scheduled twice a week. My mom would take him one day, and then I would take him the other day. Britannica gave reading instruction and when a child reached certain levels, tokens were awarded, redeemable for prizes. Alex just loved having someone to listen to him, and wanting him to read. He just started reading aloud. He was in small groups with two other children that were not from his school. These children may have had similar problems or not. They became his friends, which was very nice because they were understanding.

So for the first time since kindergarten we had support from a teacher. The second-grade teacher didn't set him up for failure. She realized that he didn't have the ability to read. She wouldn't make fun of him. She'd quietly, tactfully, figure a way to let him perform. At the end of second grade the teacher warned us, "You know, his next teacher is not going to be a teacher that will be very appreciative about Britannica." Sure enough. We continued with Britannica and Alex was feeling successful. In third grade, we were trying to have Britannica and the school teacher coordinate ideas and work together. The Britannica teacher called the school, but was dismissed by the classroom teacher who told me, "I don't approve of that program and I think it's a waste of time and money and I won't contact them." I asked Britannica to continue to contact her. They kept documentation of the number of times that she never returned their calls.

Our first parent conference was around three weeks into the school year. My husband and I walked in and the third-grade teacher declared, "You have a son that's nonteachable, who clearly doesn't belong in my class. He is a nonteachable child." My husband responded, "How do you discover that you have a nonteachable child in less than three weeks?" But all she had to say to us that he was nonteachable and added, "I don't want to teach him." We asked, "How can you say that? He's a very bright child. He hasn't had any help in school." We acknowledged that we knew that he was behind in reading but his math skills were good. I inquired, "Have you ever contacted Britannica?" She responded, "That's not part of my job to deal with that." That's when I suggested if our son was not teachable, then maybe we need him tested. Then the teacher rendered her judgment, "I want him out of my class."

After that, I went to the principal. I stated, "I want him out of her class because she doesn't even care enough about him to respond to his needs." But they wouldn't take him out of her class. They answered, "You'll have to work with her. Whatever she does is the way it will be or he can be held back." And I responded, "Then I want him tested because the teacher said that he was nonteachable." They noted, "Well, we've got a waiting list. He won't get tested until the end of February." I countered, "That's a little over three months. That's so far off, by then, all the damage is done. That's really a problem. And she clearly doesn't want to teach him." I continued, "Aren't you obligated as a school district to help the children that are in need?" And they shrugged, "We have so many children in testing." I said, "He needs help now."

Immediately following this, I went across the street to the district office and spoke to the person in charge and asked about the protocol in this district. "Nobody in this district wants to teach my child. The principal says that I'm on a long, long waiting list. How do you get to the top of the list? Can I pay somebody privately to test my child so I know what's going on in order to help him? Seems to me it makes no sense to wait until he's so discouraged he can't possibly recover."

They got back to the principal. They rearranged the schedule and he did get testing. It took over a month. So meanwhile, nothing's going on. All the negative stuff that could possibly be done was being done by the teacher. She was as mean as possible. She'd yell at him, make fun of him in the class, and he'd come home in tears. He'd sit in his bed and cry his eyes out. And this was the child who used to love to learn, that was a fact. The third-grade teacher would call on him in class and remark, "I guess, Alex, you don't know." And then she would also tell me he was stupid in class. So he really started getting the idea he was stupid because two teachers at this point made reference to it.

The children at this public school were the ones that he was going to grow up with. These were the children he saw at recess. These were the children he saw after school. The problem is that children don't want to play with another child whom they consider stupid. Alex had a couple of friends, but not a lot of friends. So for Alex, childhood mushroomed from the teacher into a kind of lonely experience.

That's when we, as a family, decided that we were going to find something that would help him develop his self-esteem because he had absolutely none. He was growing so fast that he was awkward. If he'd play soccer, the children would make fun of him because he was so gangly and uncoordinated. So we tried to find some sports that he liked. He learned that he could excel beyond anyone else he knew in snow skiing and water skiing. These sports gave him self-confidence because he secretly knew that he was really good at something. It may not be a sport that he could ever show the other students but at least he felt he was good at it. And that was his reward for all the hard work at school and everything else. So we committed ourselves to continue these sports.

To do these sports, Alex worked like a fiend on schoolwork. He worked on a computer, at a very young age, on a laptop—one of the first ones made. I heard it said that a computer could help a child like him. I bought one. Helping Alex took hours and hours of energy on my part. My mom was also dedicated to him. People who don't have similar help and devices available to them are left out because there was nothing comparable in the public school system.

Once Alex was diagnosed by the school system, he received some help. At the evaluation meeting, I was in the room with my mother, who was there because my husband was out of town. All the specialists read their report. Alex had tested years above his class level in technical knowledge. But his processing disorders were extreme. They also felt he had a hearing impairment which might have explained his delayed clarity of speech and other things.

The specialists concluded, "We think that this child will excel because of his genuine desire to learn." They all found him to be a dedicated student with curiosity to learn and not turned off yet. I had told them my perception as a parent was that he could do anything at home as long as we gave him encouragement. He was able to conquer almost anything; he was way beyond a lot of the children in the neighborhood on some of the things he did. I responded, "To me, he seems very bright in a lot of areas that other students are so deficient in. So I don't perceive that he is 'nonteachable' as the teacher said. Maybe something isn't working right. But I don't see, in any fashion, that he is retarded in his learning."

They asked the teacher for her evaluation. She basically said in front of all these people that he was nonteachable, he should be held back a year, and expressed nothing positive about him. Then they quizzed her, and requested to see her assessments and how she came to her conclusions. They asked her if she would rethink her antiquated teaching methods. She replied, "Well, if he is in my class he won't succeed." They advised, "He needs to succeed in your class. This will be a test of you, evaluating your teaching methods."

The learning specialist and a speech therapist worked with him certain days of the week. They pulled him out of class and he would go and work with them in another part of the school. They started to see huge improvements in the one-to-one situations. But when he reentered the classroom environment, he would be just shattered again because the teacher continued her negative ways.

She was a tenured teacher doing the same things she had done for years with all the children. She loved the girls; she hated all the boys in the classes. Weird, because all the boys were always in deep, deep trouble. She didn't handle the boys' energy level very well. We also knew that Alex couldn't sit still.

Finally at the request of the learning specialist, some things did improve. The learning specialist told her, "In the morning when they have their break, let Alex run around and get his energy out and he will be able to focus. And try not to pick on him first thing. Let him process what you've said and maybe call on him after he's heard the assignment." She kept insisting on doing things her way, but at least, when Alex would come home, I'd ask him, "How was your teacher today? Was she nice?" He'd say, "Mom, she's like a different person!" As a parent, my concern was that the teacher would make our son's life as miserable as possible, a way of retaliating after basically being told in front of everybody at the meeting that she was doing things wrong. In the beginning she did. But then the learning specialist made suggestions and monitored her classroom throughout the year. So he'd say, "Mom, Mrs. _____ is being nice to me now." I'd say, "Alex, because you're just so good, everybody loves you!"

During the fourth and fifth grades, Alex was able to hold in there. And despite the system, he was succeeding because of all the energy we put in personally and privately with the tutoring.

The grade school did a reassessment and recommended he be dropped from their special education program. I didn't know a lot about learning disabilities. They told me basically that he was all better. They told me, "You sign this paperwork and he can be released from the program." I reported I didn't know if he's better or not. "I think that just he's coping with it better. I don't want to drop him from the program. I think he still needs to be in the program."

When he began middle school there was absolutely no help at all from the special ed program. He was monitored on an occasional basis. Individual teachers often took the task on themselves with limited resources. The constant complaint was that our son could never finish the tests on time; he'd beg his teachers to let him finish his work. His classmates didn't treat Alex with respect because they felt he didn't know the material being taught. He'd usually have more questions in class and take longer to complete tests than other students.

His frustration grew along with his anxiety level, but we kept working like crazy at making improvements. Alex was so driven to succeed on his own we didn't want to let him down. That's when we decided in middle school he needed to join a ski team to increase his self-esteem. This was not a school ski team but a private team at a resort four hours away. We'd drive up at night. And he'd work on his computer the whole way up and back doing homework or writing stories. He could see the screen in the dark. (We kept doing this through high school.)

In middle school, his history teacher and his English teacher offered recommendations for high school honors classes for anyone who got *A's* in history and English. So Alex worked like a fiend. He even took a higher math class to get the recommendations. And when he went to high school with those *A's* on his transcript, he found that those teachers broke their promise: They didn't recommend him.

I went back to the middle school and complained, "You promised this child honor classes. He doesn't lie. I think this is unfair—he wants to take these classes." He went into the high school and stated, "I really want to be in the honors division." The counselor advised, "You cannot be in there unless you were recommended by your middle school. And they didn't recommend you." So he went back to his middle school, and the teacher responded, "Sorry, we made our recommendations." They didn't care. He was very frustrated. He met these objectives, but the rules changed after he met them. He wouldn't ever hold any anger against the teacher, and he'd say, "Mom, they just can't do it any other way, they just don't keep their word like other people."

He began high school in the regular math, history, and English program. But he found the English class especially boring because his favorite hobby was writing and reading. By this point, he was writing journals on his computer on a daily basis and reading volumes of books. This was the child that they couldn't even get to read in first grade. So it all paid off after we read aloud for I don't know how many years. Also, after finishing his homework during the four-hour commute up to the snow for skiing, his favorite activity was to be on the laptop computer in the dark writing stories. He'd write all the way up in the car. So he just kept reinforcing all the things they believed he couldn't do. His typing skills for a ninth grader were exceptional, in fact, much better than many secretaries.

Alex again visited the high school counselor and implored, "Please, a week has gone by and if I don't get into those honors programs (the joint English and history program and honors math class), I am going to be too far behind the other students. I need to get into them." The counselor responded, "You can't get in there. You've missed it already." Alex explained his situation, "But I went to my middle school teachers and I asked them for the recommendations and they wouldn't give it to me even though they had promised me that if I had gotten an *A*. I really want to be in there. The books they're reading are exciting. I've already read all the books in my class. What good will it do me?"

I went with him to see the counselor. He advised, "We have plenty of parents that come in here and are trying to push their children beyond their child's ability. I think it would be wise of you to let your son make his own choices." I responded, "I'm sorry. The reason I took off work today, the reason I am here, is because my son wants these classes so badly. He has asked you but no one listens. For that reason I am here. He has asked me to do this. It's not my idea. I told him to stay in the easy class, get the easy grade. But no, he wants the challenge." The counselor replied, "I don't think he can get into the class now. He has to go to the individual teachers and try and sign in."

Unbeknownst to me, Alex had been getting the honors assignments since the beginning of the school year from his best friend who was in the classes. Unfortunately, the best friend gave him some wrong assignments. But at least they were assignments. Alex had done all the honors math, English, and history homework as well as all his other class assignments. So he did double duty on these classes.

Alex was able to switch into honors geometry with an excellent teacher. And then he went to the English teacher and begged, "Please, let me into your class." By now, it's almost the second week. The teacher answered, "I'm sorry, son, I can't let you in this class. You're too far behind." Undaunted, Alex explained, "But I've done all the work." And he laid it all out in front of the teacher. "Where'd you get this?" he asked. Alex replied, "I got the assignments from people in the class. I don't know if it's right. I know I had to write a paper. I wrote what I thought." The teacher responded, "Well, son, you kind of did the assignment, but they didn't give you all the instructions. I can't let you redo it." Alex volunteered, "Please let me redo it. I'll do it right this time." Then came the decision. "I can't let you redo it, because you'd never catch up in the class, you're too far behind. I will grade your work hard. And don't take it personally because you didn't have the assignment. I will count it as a grade for my class. And you can be in my class."

The teacher then called us up to his class for a parent conference and warned, "I don't think he can catch up. He's already behind." My appraisal was more optimistic. "The fact that he did all this work—I'm just floored." He explained his position, "Well in all my years of teaching, I've never seen a student do that before. On that merit alone, I'm letting him into the class." Later, this teacher was the one who wrote all the letters of recommendation for college. He wanted to do this because he felt our son could do anything he puts his mind to. He remarked that, as a teacher, Alex was an inspiration for him in all the years he's been in school. "I've taught hundreds of students and nobody's ever done what he did. Alex wanted the honors classes so badly." The history teacher also let him in based on the English teacher's recommendation and explanation of what Alex had done with all the extra work. Alex got a *B* in honors history and was one of the few students who received an *A* in freshman honors English. And he followed with mostly *A's* in these two courses throughout the rest of high school.

The spring of Alex's junior year was a very busy year. The college screening process could stand between admission to a good engineering program and my child's academic success from all those years of work. This was the culmination of all his schooling.

Right before the AP exams, the AP U.S. history teacher advised me, "Alex is an excellent student, knows the material, but will probably not pass the AP test due to the time restriction." I was surprised because I was unaware he could qualify for extended time on the AP exams. Thank goodness this teacher was well informed on standardized test modifications. This event got me started on securing extra time for Alex's AP exams and his SAT tests.

I asked about reevaluating Alex so that he could receive accommodations for standardized testing. (He was last tested in elementary school.) The school wouldn't retest him. They told me, "Can't do it." Essentially, they had dropped him from the special education program without ever informing me of his options for testing accommodations, and now I was up against a deadline. I decided to get private testing and then tried to find someone who'd do it under the gun. I didn't care. I just wanted to do what I could. I finally found a person who was very sympathetic. She completed his testing with a written report over the weekend (her testing usually takes two weeks) and advised, "Alex's difficulties will never go away. What's important is how he perceives himself and how he learns to manage with his disability, which is what he's already done. He's tremendously compensated." By Tuesday, the pediatrician—who specializes in learning disabilities—had written a request to the school to give him extended time on the AP exam and any other testing like the SATs. I hand-carried these documents to the school.

The head of the school district decided which students get extended time, based on their records and supporting evidence. (The district's coordinator for learning disabilities would then forward the paperwork to testing centers like the College Board to get extended time.) But for weeks the man wouldn't read Alex's paperwork; "Too busy," I thought to myself, and vowed to camp out at his office. I canceled my work; this was crucial. He was somewhere on the surrounding school grounds. I waited for hours. The secretary advised, "You know, he's not going to see you without an appointment." I responded, "That's fine. He's got to walk in and out of his office eventually and I can just look at his face. I'm not leaving until he reads these crucial testing results on my son." But he refused to read the documents even though I sat there. He did walk by me with his coffee explaining he had a very busy schedule and would try to review them *if* he had time.

I went to the counselor, the fellow we originally went to see about the honors classes, because by now he really knew me and showed concern for Alex. He greeted me, "Mrs. _____, you're back again!" I delivered a letter to him and stated, "I will hold you personally liable if my son does not get extended time knowing you had his psychoeducational test results four weeks prior to this deadline. You can't mean to tell me your school is so large that you can't walk down to the other end of the corridor and make sure he reads that material?" He answered, "Well, I can't. He won't do it." I replied, "Well, I'm telling you, you have more power than I do. If you can't make him do it, and he's your co-worker, something is really wrong in this district."

After that, I called the SAT center, got a woman on the phone, and explained, "I'm desperate. I don't know what to do. My son is not going to get into college, not because he is not qualified, but because of protocol. This is the situation." The lady responded, "Sorry, you're going to be past the deadline." I persisted, "This has to happen," and then I just fell apart on the phone. The woman tried to comfort me. "Calm down, calm down." I said, "You don't understand. I have been battling this since he's been in first grade. And I am sick of protocol. There is not one person in all of your whole organization back there that gives a ____ ! There's a student out here. I can't find anybody here that gives a darn either. For me, it's frustrating. I have an A-student here who struggles on standardized tests without extended time. And you're telling me that you're not going to accommodate him when there's multiple, multiple, pages of documentation since third grade that says what he's got will never go away?"

She then thought. "Hold on. They're having a meeting about the students right now. Will you fax me what you have?" I became hopeful. "You bet! I'll fax you everything." So I faxed it. The SAT center mandated back to the school district, which then got to the head of the school district LD center—the same person I had called and tried in person to deal with—and stated he'd better have read that paperwork because it should have been on their desk weeks ago. And they were authorizing extended time from the SAT center in time for the upcoming SATs. And if they didn't give extended time to Alex at the test place because the paperwork didn't get there quick enough, that was a major problem. So Alex was able to take the AP exams and the SAT with extended time. Alex passed all five AP exams and received the designation of *AP Scholar with Honors* from the AP Program of the College Board. He received almost enough credits to enter college with sophomore standing. He went up 140 points in the SAT math section and 90 in the verbal portion, which was the difference for him to get into some top colleges. He eventually graduated as one of the 35 teenagers recognized for high academic honors out of his class of 313 students, and, of the 35 students, only a few had taken AP classes.

The high school could be in trouble legally for not sending the paperwork to the SAT center. They had refused to read the material I privately paid for. They had denied him access to being evaluated through the district. And they had dropped him from the learning disabilities program when they should have informed him and me of his rights and options.

The school district wouldn't read his paperwork because, as they explained, "He was a success in class and didn't need extra help or provisions. How can you say that one of our top students can perform so well with all those problems?" I replied, "Because he worked relentlessly, even late at night. He's missed a lot of the sports events. He's missed a lot of the social activities. He made that effort, even stressing his health. So you're going to penalize him because he succeeds against all odds? That is lopsided. No wonder no other child succeeds. It's your philosophy that's way off."

Managing all this in addition to other family responsibilities and work obligations made us a wreck. It's hard on your marriage. It's hard on your family friends because there isn't time for them. People don't see you. You have to realize what's important and you have to be willing to choose. I had to make sure that, most of all, my children were okay. They were my top priority. Other things had to go on the back burner. People who have done it understand it. People who haven't gone through the experience will never understand it.

Later when my daughter graduated after Alex, the counselor remarked, "I only saw you the day she came into school and the day she left!" I explained, "The needs were different. You saw my daughter was always organized and able to tackle everything in school." He responded, "I understand." Then he asked, "How is Alex?" I answered, "You'd be proud of him. He's hanging in there in engineering and he's trying to graduate with a double degree." The second degree may be in business. I think he's going to be able to do it. He says most other classes are like a little walk in the park after the engineering classes.

And that's how it goes. Things will change. It's going to take a while. The person who was responsible for reviewing Alex's school district's LD evaluations is no longer there. Maybe other students he could have helped, but he didn't. To me, if that's your main job, you need to address learning issues without putting people off or at least by giving them some kind of hope.

The school district as a whole has been a kind of a failure in responding to our son's learning disabilities. The only thing that has helped us through it all were the understanding people along the way and the many individual teachers who really did care, like the freshman honors English teacher and the honors U.S. history teacher. There was one math teacher who was fabulous. He was the one math teacher who held office hours every day before school for every student in his class. He said Alex was the only student who showed up almost every day with a smile on his face always wanting to learn more. When Alex decided to go into engineering, he cautioned, "Alex, it's going to be hard. Really hard. But you can do it! Just stick in there." Those are the good teachers who open themselves up to the students or for anybody who needs help.

And then there was a calculus teacher who told me at the beginning of the class he didn't care that the school mandated that Alex get extra time on exams. He felt it was an AP class and should be run as a college course because "your lesson in life is if you can't make it here, you're not going to make it in the real world." I had a talk with the teacher. His job as an educator is to follow the specifications for accommodations I had sent to the counselor to be delivered to all his teachers. (This was so the teachers could have a better understanding of what Alex was dealing with.) I made it clear we were not at that point of Alex's crossroads where we get to decide whether he's going to fail or succeed in life. We were at the point where the educator has to make it accessible for him to at least learn the material and give him adequate time to respond in a testing situation. This teacher actually came around in the end—maybe he finally understood that Alex didn't want anything extra, he just wanted the same opportunity to be able to perform academically without constraints.

In retrospect, our family has been elevated by these shared experiences overcoming adversity. Most people look at the situation as a real downer. It is, if you look at just the basics. But if you look beyond it, you see how enriching it is because it gives you one-on-one interactions with your child—my son and I have this tremendous bond that no one will ever take away. My mother, a grandparent, also has this wonderful bond with him. My husband doesn't have this bond. Most people don't get that. My son and daughter are each other's very best friends, and are also each other's best advocates. They have never had one fight in their whole lives because as my daughter said, "There are much bigger issues, mom. Way bigger issues. Fighting is a trivial thing. It brings somebody down. He spends every day trying to be up." So we've really been blessed. People don't understand it.

Some days, I dreaded having to deal with a discouraging situation. I might say to myself, "One more battle … one more battle. I don't think I can do it." And half of those battles were the teachers and the educational system because they weren't taught to deal with students with learning disabilities. And they can't deal with all these students. They need more support. They should at least give the parents a place to turn to or a place to go. The only place I ever found any support was another parent who had been through it. I'd try to read here and there a little article on something. Back then, there wasn't enough out there.

PART I:
UNDERSTANDING THE PROBLEMS

Chapter One

How do parents first learn that their child may have a learning disability?

"They're fighting on me!" My (then) four-year-old son was good-natured, knew his alphabet and colors before age two, could sight-read some words, liked playing ball, and yet was the target of bullies in his private preschool. Maybe there were some overly aggressive boys at the school. Maybe some families were going through a stressful time and the kids were acting up. Maybe Max didn't like rough-and-tumble play. It's easy to disregard preschoolers' tussles.

Underneath it all, however, there were disquieting signs. He had had chronic ear infections requiring two surgeries by age three. His use of language was awkward. He mispronounced words. His pediatric medical exams and hearing tests were normal though. A parochial kindergarten—connected with the church where he was baptized—that professionally screened applicants sent us a postcard of summary rejection with "70 IQ" scrawled across it. I thought my child was bright but some psychologist who had met my son for less than an hour thought otherwise. The preschool teacher who knew the psychologist recommended that I ignore this appraisal. Nothing made sense.

Children mature at different rates physically, mentally, and emotionally. Environmental, cultural, or economic disadvantages can also delay development. Misdiagnosing a child can affect parental and teacher expectations. Some problems can be resolved by delaying school entrance by a year, hiring tutors, switching teachers, or enrolling at another school. One of the toughest jobs in raising children is identifying whether a problem exists, whether it will resolve itself without intervention and, if not, what actions may be required to improve the situation.

Pediatricians identify severe developmental lags early in a child's life. Mild developmental problems have subtle signs that may appear before the child enters school, but more often when the child is actually in school, thus the term *learning disability*. This identification problem is like a new car: The problems have been there all along, but will remain undiscovered until tested on the road.

One real problem of a good school system is to match curriculum standards—what is to be specifically learned at each grade level and in each subject area—with the neurodevelopmental abilities of the student population. The University of Michigan Health System offers a website, "Your Child: Development & Behavior Resources" at www.med.umich.edu/1libr/yourchild/devmile.htm, which links to many other resources on early childhood development. Yahoo! provides a directory of the curriculum standards for most states at http://dir.yahoo.com/Education/K_12/Curriculum_Standards.

Girls and boys develop differently

Male and female brains are organized differently. Male brains are more compartmentalized, with verbal, analytical, and sequential thinking located on the left side and spatial ability located on the right side. Female brains are more generalized, and have more connections (the corpus callosum) between the right and left hemispheres. In short, real differences exist when comparing a typical boy to a typical girl.

Elementary school curricula stress verbal and fine motor skills, skills at which girls excel. For example in 2001, an average eighth-grade girl wrote as well as an average eleventh-grade boy.[1] Boys are more physically active and demonstrate better spatial and gross motor skills than girls. Many male students later do well in secondary school courses such as physics which require three-dimensional visualization, a skill at which boys excel.

Boys in particular have trouble in school. A few schools are eliminating recess altogether, which is an opportunity especially for boys to blow off steam. Some educators suspect that many elementary and secondary teachers (70 percent of them are female) prefer neater, compliant girls over messy, physically active boys.[2] One study tracked

---

1 Anna Mulrine, "Are Boys the Weaker Sex?" *U.S. News & World Report*, 30 July 2001, p. 42.

2 Brendan I. Koerner, "Where the Boys Aren't," *U.S. News & World Report*, 8 February 1999, p. 50.

the erosion of male academic self-confidence. A 10-year longitudinal study of 761 middle-class white public-school students found boys' feelings of academic confidence dropped from being at least equal to that of girls in elementary school to below that of girls by the twelfth grade.[3] Boys account for 70 percent of Ds and Fs, two-thirds of diagnosed learning disabilities, 90 percent of substance abuse violations, 80 percent of criminal juvenile court cases, and 80 percent of high school dropouts and diagnosed attention deficit disorders.[4] Additional information can be found in an article by Anna Mulrine, "Are Boys the Weaker Sex?" (*U.S. News & World Report*, 30 July 2001) and in books by Michael Gurian (www.michael-gurian.com). Many parents have found that problems disappear or are dealt with more effectively when their children are switched to a single-sex school.

Waiting to see if the problems will go away

Throughout childhood and adolescence, the brain makes new neural connections and undergoes maturational spurts. Learning problems are often somehow addressed, sometimes by the child, sometimes with adult intervention. Improved school performance may result from natural brain development, the brain's plasticity in response to treatment, or a combination of both. Sometimes after overcoming one problem, another problem will appear. For example, a child who has learned how to read lines of text may not necessarily be able to *read between the lines* and make inferences. There is also the possibility that problems will not improve. Individuals face three choices:

Figure 1.1

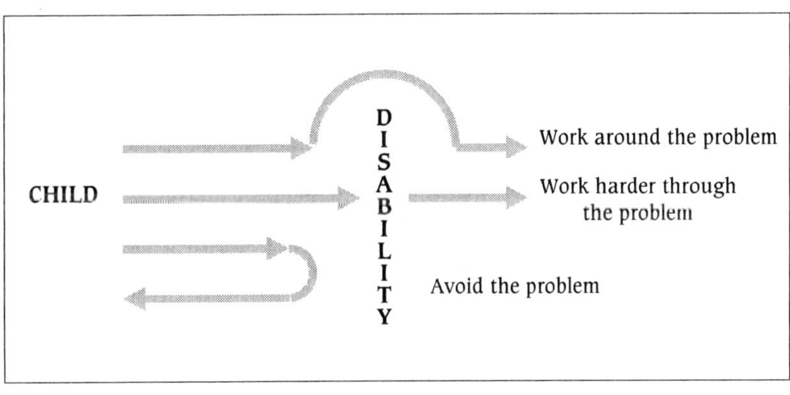

---

3   Bruce Bower citing a study by Janis E. Jacobs of Pennsylvania State University in "Boys Take a Tumble," *Science News*, 11 May 2002, p. 301.

4   Mulrine, p. 42.

There are many explanations for academic troubles unrelated to learning disabilities, but these developmental disorders really do exist. Learning disorders are neurological problems and may not be remedied with repeated practice, or at least not in the time allocated within the typical curriculum. Denying problems can be tantamount to denying opportunities for your child.

At this point, one must consider what constitutes a successful education. Acquaint yourself with available options. While reading or handwriting skills are important, they should not become an end in themselves. Too many children grow up unhappy because their capabilities do not match the pace of the standard curriculum which sequences tasks to be mastered. Far more important is critical thinking, especially in an age when more people obtain news from television than from newspapers. Chapter 6 lists famous folks who have accepted their disability and moved on to extraordinary achievements despite significant odds against them. The latter half of this book will review many methods to deal with difficulties.

What to look for

Forty percent of parents have considered at one time or another the presence of a learning problem in their child; 70% of these parents—or 27% of all parents—suspect that a serious problem exists.[5] Sometimes, parents will be the first to notice something amiss; at other times, teachers will observe that the child is not progressing at the same pace as most other children. Problems may be reminiscent of those seen in a relative. Troubles also seem to appear at above-average rates in adopted children (see "Identifying Learning Differences in Adopted Children," by Annie Stuart, available at www.schwablearning.org/articles.asp?r=689). Early warning signs of potential academic problems usually present themselves in subtle ways, not necessarily the uncontrollable behavior or letter reversals often cited in media accounts.

Many publications and websites list symptoms that may indicate a need to investigate whether your child has a learning disability.
*   *Symptoms and Treatment of a Child's Learning Disorders and Academic Disorders* by Morrison F. Gardner (1990) provides lists of warning signs often seen in elementary school. Psychological and Educational Publications (800/ 523-5775) offers it at a nominal fee.

---

5   Roper Starch Worldwide, *Measuring Progress in Public & Parental Understanding of Learning Disabilities* [Internet], March 2000, p. 17, available from: http://www.ldonline.org/news/roper_poll_2000.pdf

- Medline Plus (www.nlm.nih.gov/medlineplus/learningdisorders. html) links to a number of websites with lists of symptoms, explanations of symptoms, and organizations with information for parents.
- *Educational Care: A System for Understanding and Helping Children with Learning Problems at Home and in School*, second edition (2002), by Mel Levine, provides a diagnostic approach for identifying problems and methods for dealing with them. It is not a substitute for a professional assessment of your child, however. This book can be ordered from the publisher, Educators Publishing Service, at 800/ 435-7728 or through retailers.

In the larger middle school environment, children can fall through the cracks if they have problems organizing their work, time, and materials for many classes. Some students may have trouble with time or confuse the directions left and right. Others may have unusual trouble following formal rules of logic, or inferring, analyzing, and synthesizing abstract concepts. In high school, behavioral problems may overshadow the learning disability itself.

Evaluating mental health news

With so much material available on the Internet, and because it is used by the media as a resource, you must consider the source of the information. You can find tips for appraising website information from "How to Be an Educated Consumer of Mental Health News," by the New York University Child Study Center (www.aboutourkids.org/articles/educatedconsumer.html), or "Tips for Evaluating a World Wide Web Search," by the University of Florida (www.uflib.ufl.edu/hss/ref/tips.html). Bad research studies or flawed interpretations of significant findings can mislead you, causing needless expense and real harm to your child. Specifically consider:
- How was the information developed?

The best studies emerge from a rigorous peer-reviewed process in which experimental and statistical methods are scrutinized. For example, field professionals may have concerns over control groups or population characteristics. Alternatively, information may be derived from some observable pattern like an extrapolation of known data, an opinion based on long clinical experience, or the collected anecdotes or impressions of people gathered in a certain area or by certain means.
- Was the result replicated by others or consistent with another body of information?

For any new information to be accepted as fact, true science requires that experimental findings be verified and replicated. Parents of children with learning disabilities should be wary of information and therapies that are too good to be true, can treat a wide variety of

problems, and that can't be duplicated by others using similar methods. Furthermore, misleading information on one website can easily pop up on other websites. Reports of unusual findings should be explored with licensed professionals in relevant fields or reputable information groups knowledgeable about learning disabilities.
- What was the source of the information?

Many parents must rely on layman interpretations of professionally published research articles. The best sources examine submitted material for their integrity and have no financial interest in publishing the results. Sometimes authors of professional articles publish review articles for the general public summarizing up-to-date information. Often your only clue is the reputation of the website publisher.

Understanding terminology: What's in a name?

Many terms describing developmental deficits are confusing. Part of the problem is that many designations have emerged from different disciplines such as education, psychology, and medicine. Some very different terms may have the same meaning, while the very same term may have very different meanings depending on the situation. You should not hesitate to ask questions if you are not exactly clear on what a person means.

Some terms characterize the problem as a specific isolated exception in an otherwise normal individual:
- dyslexia: Difficulties in reading
- dysgraphia: Difficulties in writing
- dyscalculia: Difficulties in math calculations
- dysfluency: Difficulties in producing smooth fluent speech
- developmental dysphasia: Difficulties in language development, particularly in speaking and comprehending words
- expressive aphasia: Difficulties in speaking or writing
- receptive aphasia: Difficulties in understanding speech or text
- dysnomia: Difficulties in retrieving words
- dysmnesia: Difficulties of memory
- dyspraxia: Difficulties in coordinating movement.

These labels stem from Greek and Latin words, and may sound quite scientific to many people. These terms, however, only indicate that a general functional difficulty exists; they don't indicate how it affects the individual nor how to solve the problem. *An observation is not a solution.*

Other labels are derived from descriptions of mental processes. *Language disability* denotes an individual having unspecified difficulties with receiving, processing, or expressing language. Each of these three stages of communication may themselves become descriptors as well, for example, *receptive language*, *auditory processing*, or *expressive language* problems. Precise anatomical or physiological designations may yet emerge from ongoing medical research.

The term *learning disability* was first introduced by special educators in the 1960s. Learning disability can either specifically refer to the above disorders, or may be more generalized to encompass attention deficit disorders as well. This broad brush of a description paints an unduly harsh characterization about a child's abilities that the general public little understands. People, including teachers, generally respond to labels depending on their own personal knowledge about them.

An individual identified with a learning disability is commonly stigmatized by others. Researchers have found that when a group conforms to a notion that a difference is undesirable, stereotypes based on this difference harden into *them* versus *us*, and the stigmatized individual experiences discrimination, shame, guilt, and a loss of social standing.[6] For these reasons, *labeling* or using information irrelevant to actual performance as an inference of ability is a form of discrimination, as much as inferring ability by the color of one's skin or gender:

> "In testing individuals with disabilities, test developers, test administrators, and test users should take steps to ensure that the test score inferences accurately reflect the intended construct rather than any disabilities and their associated characteristics extraneous to the intent of the measurement."[7]
>
> *— U.S. Department of Education Office for Civil Rights*

Indeed, special education law acknowledges the stigma of a disability label by allowing states to substitute *child experiencing developmental delays* for *child with a disability*.

Many practitioners use *learning differences*, or *learning exceptionalities*, because *learning disabilities* is a generalized term emphasizing a person's weaknesses. These terms, however, have a euphemistic quality to them in that they could describe almost any divergence from the norm. *Learning disabilities* has also become somewhat controversial with connotations of educational rights being demanded for a certain group of individuals. Clearly, current

---

6   Bruce Bower citing a hypothesis by Link and Phelan, "Plight of the Untouchables: Stigmas Harm Public Health in Unexplored Ways," *Science News*, 27 October 2001, p. 270.

7   U.S. Department of Education Office for Civil Rights, "The Use of Tests as Part of High-Stakes Decision-Making for Students: A Resource Guide for Educators and Policy-Makers" [Internet], December 2000, p. 40, available from: http://www.ed.gov/offices/OCR/testing/TestingResource.doc

terminology is unsatisfactory. In this book, however unsettled, I use *learning disabilities* because it is the most commonly used term. Similarly, *LD* in this book refers to *learning disabilities*, although many people use *LD* to refer to *learning differences*. I also use *parents* to refer anyone who is a primary caregiver of a child, such as biological parents, adoptive parents, foster parents, stepparents, grandparents, and legal guardians. *Private school* means a nonpublic school, whether secular or religious, unless otherwise stated.

The possibility of stigmatization deters many individuals from seeking treatment. Some parents find it difficult to reconcile themselves to a professional confirmation of a suspected malady in their child, but a diagnosis of a disability is necessary for receiving classroom accommodations and publicly funded special education services. (Chapter 14 discusses privacy issues pertaining to school records, including their destruction.) Other parents are relieved to understand that the problems can be identified and appropriately managed. The second big decision is whether the best course is through public agencies or through privately engaged service providers. The first big decision is whether to investigate your child's difficulties.

Chapter Two

Why are children with learning disabilities taught in regular classrooms?

Full educational opportunity: A legal overview

Learning disability is a generic term encompassing a variety of conditions that impair the mental processes needed for learning, not due to a lack of opportunity (absenteeism, impoverishment, or chaotic living environments), poor teaching, cultural circumstances, mental retardation, or sensory deficits. A body of civil rights legislation governs the education of children with learning disabilities.

For most of the last century, public schools could legally exclude certain types of children. A child deemed *unteachable* was unlikely to be schooled at all. *Something's Not Right: One Family's Struggle with Learning Disabilities*, by Nancy Lelewer (VanderWyk & Burnham, 1994), chronicles the educational obstacles as recent as the 1960s. This situation began to change with the 1954 landmark case of *Brown v. Board of Education of Topeka*, which established the right of minority children to an equal educational opportunity. In 1972, the federal court in *Mills v. Board of Education of the District of Columbia* held that a lack of funds was no reason to deny a beneficial publicly-supported education for children with disabilities.

Section 504 of the Rehabilitation Act of 1973 mandates reasonable accommodations and prohibits discrimination against individuals with disabilities—including children with learning disabilities—by organizations receiving federal financial assistance, such as public schools and universities. The Americans with Disabilities Act (ADA) of 1990 extended the 1973 law and prohibited discrimination against individuals with disabilities by private organizations not receiving federal assistance. A government website entitled "Disability Discrimination: Overview of the Laws" gives some basic information and is found at www.ed.gov/offices/OCR/disabilityoverview.html.

In 1969, Public Law (PL) 91-230 first defined learning disabilities. In 1975, PL 94-142, the Education for All Handicapped Children Act, recognized learning disabilities as a category eligible for special education. It has been amended several times since then, and now exists as the 1997 Individuals with Disabilities Education Act (IDEA). At the time of this writing, Congress is amending IDEA.

Unlike Section 504 and the ADA, IDEA provides *services* such as specialized instruction and therapy to improve school performance. Enforcement is through the U.S. Office of Special Education Programs. Schools, however, are often underfunded for the services mandated by both federal and state laws. Consequently, services are rationed.

Parents must become familiar with the legal rights of their children in order to effectively advocate for them. The website, www.ed.gov (click on *Visit the U.S. Department of Education website*, at the next screen click on *Other preK-12 topics* listed under *Education Resources*, then scroll down to *Special education*) offers recent news, documents, and free publications. Other legal sources are listed in the Resources section at the back of this book. The laws summarized above are discussed in more detail below.

Section 504 of the Rehabilitation Act of 1973 and the Americans with Disabilities Act (ADA) of 1990

Section 504 of the Rehabilitation Act of 1973, also known as the Civil Rights Act for the Handicapped, and the Americans with Disabilities Act (ADA) of 1990 are both used as the basis for securing *reasonable* educational accommodations for students with disabilities, regardless of whether they are eligible for special education services under IDEA. Section 504 and Title II of the ADA are similar in many of their provisions; indeed "the U.S. Department of Education generally uses Section 504 regulations to interpret Title II of the ADA."[1] "Questions and Answers on Disability Discrimination under Section 504 and Title II" (www.ed.gov/offices/OCR/qa-disability.html) discusses how these laws apply to public organizations or those receiving federal funds. With respect to private schools not receiving federal funds, Title III of the

---

1   Winifred Anderson, Stephen Chitwood and Deidre Hayden, *Negotiating the Special Education Maze: A Guide for Parents and Teachers*, 3rd Edition (Bethesda, Maryland: Woodbine House, 1997), p. 185.

ADA (www.usdoj.gov/crt/ada/statute.html) has defined places of education—"a nursery, elementary, secondary, undergraduate or post-graduate private school"—as public accommodations *(Sec. 301)* that must observe the general rule prohibiting discrimination "on the basis of disability in the full and equal enjoyment of the goods, services, facilities, privileges, advantages, or accommodations" unless demonstrated to be not "readily achievable" *(Sec. 302)*.

Enforcement is through the U.S. Office for Civil Rights (OCR). The ADA *(28 CFR § 35.134* and *28 CFR § 36.206*[2]) prohibits private or public entities from retaliating against an individual who is opposing "unlawful" discriminatory practices, participating in their investigations, or assisting someone in exercising "any right granted or protected" under the ADA. Unlike IDEA and the Rehabilitation Act, which focus on government entities, Title III of the ADA *(28 CFR § 36.504)* allows monetary relief and civil penalties, but not punitive damages.

An example of possible educational benefits is seen in this accommodation plan for a high school student who was not receiving special education services:

Subject: Accommodation for a disabled mainstream student

According to the <u>American Disabilities Act</u>, *and* <u>Section 504</u>, *a student who is professionally identified as disabled* **is entitled** *to modifications and accommodations to the regular school program. The purpose of these laws is to provide an identified student with a successful educational experience. Subsequent to appropriate testing, this student is qualified for special accommodations. The student has been diagnosed as extremely hard working with above-average cognitive abilities, but whose performance in timed situations is compromised by the presence of processing problems. The student is unable to show knowledge under time pressure; thus, this student is unfairly handicapped. If given enough time both in the classroom and in a testing situation, then the student is very capable of demonstrating both innate intelligence as well as learned knowledge. The modifications requested are:*
1. Training in mnemonic devices
2. A multi-sensory approach to preparing for tests
3. An opportunity to physically manipulate materials
4. Provision of syllabi and lesson previews prior to class
5. Teachers need to repeat information at least three times and offer visual stimuli to support verbal communication.

---

2   *CFR* means *Code of Federal Regulations*. Regulations are developed from the original legislation and are the specific rules requiring compliance. "§" means *Section*. The Resource section of this book offers suggestions for obtaining a copy of these regulations.

6. Allowing at least 45 seconds to process questions before requiring responses.
*7. **Mandatory** extended time in testing situations*
8. Announcements of assignments and tests well before due dates.

Section 504 and the ADA prohibit discrimination against individuals with disabilities *if these individuals are qualified to participate*. For example, students with learning disabilities can take an AP high school course if they can learn the material, not if they can take an exam as fast as other students without disabilities. The student profiled in the Introduction of this book had met the qualifications for freshman honors classes in high school, but suffered discrimination when his middle school teachers denied him recommendations for these classes.

For more information on Section 504, see "Section 504: What Teachers Need to Know," by Tom Smith, available at www.ldonline.org/ld_indepth/legal_legislative/section_504_for_teachers.html. A fact sheet entitled "Myths and Facts about the Americans with Disabilities Act" is provided by the Albert Einstein Healthcare Network in Philadelphia, Pennsylvania at www.mossresourcenet.org.

Individuals with Disabilities Education Act (IDEA)

IDEA is the basis for special education services and is predicated on providing a full educational opportunity for children with disabilities from birth to age 21 (*34 CFR § 300.123*). Two of the purposes of IDEA are to 1) prepare children with disabilities for employment and independent living and 2) protect their rights as individuals with disabilities (*34 CFR § 300.1*). The U.S. Supreme Court has interpreted IDEA as requiring a level of services so that a student would educationally benefit from instruction, evident in passing marks *and* (not *or*) grade advancements.[3] By definition,

> "... *special education* means specially designed instruction, at no cost to the parents, to meet the unique needs of a child with a disability, including ... [i]nstruction conducted in the classroom, in the home, in hospitals and institutions, and in other settings .... *Specially-designed instruction* means adapting, as appropriate ... the content, methodology, or delivery of instruction ....
>
> —*34 CFR § 300.26*

---

3   Allan G. Osborne, Jr., *Legal Issues in Special Education* (Needham Heights, Massachusetts: Allyn & Bacon, 1996), p. 20.

If a child needs professional services beyond specialized instruction, additional support is provided by related services, not limited to those listed in the following definition:

> "... *related services* means transportation and such developmental, corrective, and other supportive services as are required to assist a child with a disability to benefit from special education, and includes speech pathology and audiology services, psychological services, physical and occupational therapy, recreation, including therapeutic recreation, early identification and assessment of disabilities in children, counseling services, including rehabilitation counseling, orientation and mobility services, and medical services for diagnostic or evaluation purposes. The term also includes school health services, social work services in schools, and parent counseling and training."
>
> *—34 CFR § 300.24*

Related services are *not* medical services, as defined by the laws of each individual state.[4] That is, school districts provide educational services, not medical treatment. Hence, related services could include dance therapy but not psychotherapy provided by a psychiatrist. A pediatrician, attorney, or parent information center can help you find more definitive information in your area. (Any medical diagnostic services required for determining IDEA eligibility are part of a free evaluation.)

Limitations have been placed on other related services. Parent counseling and training refers to teaching parents any necessary skills so they can reinforce the child's special education program at home. Transportation is provided for students placed in facilities by the school district, not necessarily for students unilaterally placed in private schools by their parents.[5]

Some school systems request parents to use their health insurance to cover costs, but related services are included as part of FAPE (defined below) and provision of these services should not depend on whether private resources are used to defray costs. Specific regulations apply when a public agency must provide informed consent for accessing a parent's private insurance (*34 CFR § 300.142 (f)*), or must not require public insurance payments that affect a child's lifetime benefits or out-of-pocket expenses (*34 CFR § 300.142 (e)*).

---

4   Osborne, pp. 141-142.
5   Osborne, p. 149.

Free Appropriate Public Education (FAPE)

FAPE is the civil rights portion of IDEA and is permanently authorized by the federal government. It states:

> "... *[F]ree appropriate public education* or *FAPE* means special education and related services that—(a) Are provided at public expense, under public supervision and direction, and without charge; (b) Meet the standards of the SEA [state education agency] ... (c) Include preschool, elementary school, or secondary school education ... (d) Are provided in conformity with an individualized education program ...."
>
> *—34 CFR § 300.13*

Eligible children can neither be denied a FAPE based on the severity of the disability, nor be required to demonstrate the potential to benefit from services.[6] FAPE is also defined in Section 504 (*34 CFR § 104.33*). The critical issue then is defining what constitutes a learning disability in order to determine eligibility for FAPE.

Federal funding for special education is annually budgeted as are other federal programs. Every five years, however, statutory sections of IDEA related to what gets funded—such as public information, personnel development, and parent training—must be *reauthorized* in new federal legislation.[7] Congress can modify—and has done so in the past—permanent sections pertaining to FAPE. FAPE is further reviewed in Chapter 16.

Defining learning disabilities: Costs and politics

The lack of common, well-defined physical evidence such as a medical diagnostic test has led some people to conclude that learning problems don't exist. Others erroneously believe that individuals with learning disabilities can't be helped. Many more fault the parents for not encouraging the child to read, for letting the child give up too easily, for not appropriately interacting with the child, or for not applying more discipline. The notion of what constitutes a learning disability is further confused when schools direct low-achieving, culturally disadvantaged, or disruptive students who are not identified as having learning disabilities, into special education programs.

---

6   Osborne, p. 18.

7   Matthew Cohen, "Legal Briefs from Matt Cohen, Esq." [Internet], accessed 11 October 2002 from: http://www.ldonline.org/legal/index.html

Many controversies surround the definitions of learning disabilities. Since children diagnosed with LD can receive extra time on exams and other accommodations, many parents of normal children perceive these measures as providing an undue advantage. In addition, some unscrupulous parents have sought diagnoses of learning disabilities for their normal children to gain them more time on college entrance tests. Says Robert Sternberg, a professor of psychology and education at Yale, "people are fighting for the label."[8] The result has been to cast a cloud of suspicion on all children who seek help for learning disabilities. Cecil Mercer, author and professor of special education at the University of Florida, has outlined the problems resulting from this identification uncertainty and a large national demand for services:

> "Underidentification deprives them of services, whereas overidentification results in inappropriate placements and drains resources from other programs and students .... [E]vidence of a backlash against learning disabilities can be found in some local school services. For example, some school districts are making the criteria so stringent that students with learning disabilities who need services are not receiving them."[9]

Special education costs can be controlled by reducing eligibility. Although the difference between *disorder* and *disability* may be negligible in many cases, a chasm of difference exists in whether a child receives services and/or accommodations. Meanwhile, parents and advocacy groups who are dealing with a child's ever-worsening classroom performance seek relief through more favorable eligibility standards. Says Larry Silver, Clinical Professor of Psychiatry at the Georgetown University School of Medicine, "We have a tug of war. What should be a clinical or educational diagnosis of learning disabilities has become a political diagnosis of learning disabilities."[10]

Past reauthorizations of IDEA have expanded eligibility for special education services as new information emerged about disabilities in children. The 2003 reauthorization, however, may continue another trend of limiting services for eligible children. Beginning in the 1990s, inclusion programs (Chapter 16) have had the *de facto* effect of

---

8   Eben Carle, "ADHD For Sale," *Psychology Today* [Internet], May/June 2000, accessed 31 August 2002 from: http://www.psychologytoday.com/HTDocs/prod/PTOhome/home.asp

9   *Students with Learning Disabilities* 4/E by Mercer, Copyright © 1992 by Macmillan Publishing Company. Reprinted by permission of Pearson Education, Inc., Upper Saddle River, NJ.

10   Larry B. Silver, "Introduction," in *The Assessment of Learning Disabilities: Preschool Through Adulthood*, ed. Larry B. Silver (Austin, Texas: PRO-ED, 1989), p. viii.

excluding non-public school students from services. The 1997 reauthorization allowed the *de jure* exclusion of non-public school children from services. In 2003, legislation by the House of Representatives included a new federal special education spending cap of 13.5% for a state's student population, *optional* not *mandatory* annual reviews of a student's progress, and easier suspension or expulsion of students with disabilities for non-major behavioral violations. A lack of common understanding is evident in ongoing legislation as seen in:

• "Rewrite of Spec. Ed Law Passes the House," by Lisa Goldstein, available at www.edweek.org/ew/ewstory.cfm?slug=34idea.h22

• "IDEA Update: 'Reforms' in H.R. 1350 Undercut Parent Involvement," by Candace Cortiella, available at www.schwablearning.org/articles.asp?r=711

• "Spec. Ed. Growth Spurs Cap Plan in Pending IDEA," by Lisa Goldstein, available at www.ldonline.org/news/pending_idea.html

• "House Passes Special Education Bill While Senate Continues to Work on Bi-Partisan Alternative," available at www.chadd.org/press.cfm?cat_id=10&subcat_id=29&press_year2003&press_id=73.

New technologies may yet redefine learning disabilities and so could clear the present confusion. Problems underlying school difficulties may soon be reliably identified through medical tests instead of being inferred through psychological testing. (Such medical testing would not be cheap, however, and psychological testing would still be an invaluable tool to understand the performance limitations of an individual's LD.) With better methods to validate the presence of learning disabilities, their prevalence can be better known, and society can then engage in a more meaningful discussion about providing what kind of services and for what degrees of impairment, and the expected consequences for providing or not providing help.

That day may not be far off. In February, 2002, a federal judge ruled that problems that are usually considered a *mental* disorder could be considered a *physical* disorder, based on brain scan characteristics, evidence of brain chemical imbalances, and possible genetic causes. He noted that the *Diagnostic and Statistical Manual of Mental Disorders*, published by the American Psychiatric Association and based on World Health Organization standards, "posits that the distinction between mental disorders and physical illnesses is a false one," and cited Alzheimer's disease and anorexia nervosa as examples.[11] Indeed, medical research has discovered some physical distinctions associated with learning disabilities already.

---

11 Michael Orey, "Bipolar Disorder Is a Physical Ill, U.S. Judge Rules," *The Wall Street Journal*, 12 March 2002, pp. B1 and B4.

Chapter Three

What are specific learning disabilities?

"I should see the garden far better," said Alice to herself, "if I could get to the top of that hill: and here's a path that leads straight to it—at least, no, it doesn't do that—" (after going a few yards along the path, and turning several sharp corners), "but I suppose it will at last. But how curiously it twists! It's more like a corkscrew than a path! Well this turn goes to the hill, I suppose—no, it doesn't! This goes straight back to the house! Well then, I'll try it the other way."

And so she did: wandering up and down, and trying turn after turn, but always coming back to the house, do what she would. Indeed, once, when she turned a corner rather more quickly than usual, she ran against it before she could stop herself.

"It's no use talking about it," Alice said, looking up at the house and pretending it was arguing with her. "I'm not going in again yet. I know I should have to get through the Looking-glass again—back into the old room—and there'd be an end of all my adventures!"

So, resolutely turning her back upon the house, she set out once more down the path, determined to keep straight on till she got to the hill. For a few minutes all went on well, and she was just saying, "I really shall do it this time—" when the path gave a sudden twist and shook itself (as she described it afterwards), and the next moment she found herself actually walking in at the door.

"Oh, it's too bad!" she cried. "I never saw such a house for getting in the way! Never!"

However, there was the hill in full sight, so there was nothing to be done but start again.

—Through the Looking-Glass

To show evidence of learning, a child must perceive sensory information (input), understand it (integration), prepare it for storage and later recall (memory), and produce a motor response to the information when prompted like speaking or writing (output).[1] A learning disorder interferes with this process, similar to Alice's experience in trying to get to the top of the hill. LD diminishes a person's ability to interpret what is seen and heard, and/or connect information between different parts of the brain.

IDEA has defined *specific learning disability* as:

> "… a disorder in one or more of the basic psychological processes involved in understanding or in using language, spoken or written, that may manifest itself in an imperfect ability to listen, think, speak, read, write, spell, or to do mathematical calculations, including conditions as perceptual disabilities, brain injury, minimal brain dysfunction, dyslexia, and developmental aphasia. … The term does not include learning problems that are primarily the result of visual, hearing, or motor disabilities, of mental retardation, of emotional disturbance, or of environmental, cultural, or economic disadvantage."

> *—34 CFR § 300.7 (10)*

A disorder can be quite mild to quite severe. Section 504 first established in 1973 when a disorder is a disability. A disability exists when a disorder "substantially limits one or more major life activities …. such as … learning …" (*34 CFR § 104.3*). In general, having a *disorder* will not secure your child services. Having a *disability* will provide access to special education. This legal requirement for a disability is not like diabetes, in which all cases are treated. Currently, psychological tests determine the presence and significance of learning disorders.

Public policy toward learning disabilities developed from expediency as civil rights laws—which placed children in schools rather than in institutions—outpaced neurological understanding and accommodative educational practices. Medical technology has only recently enabled live studies of phenomena that are currently inferred from psychological tests. Field research is identifying the best teaching methods and environments. Chapter 13 reviews the legal criteria for determining the presence of a specific learning disability.

---

1   Larry B. Silver, *The Misunderstood Child: Understanding and Coping with Your Child's Learning Disabilities*, 3rd Edition (New York: Three Rivers Press, 1998), p. 39.

"... I'll tell you all my ideas about Looking-glass House. First, there's the room you can see through the glass—that's just the same as our drawing-room, only the things go the other way. ... the books are something like our books, only the words go the wrong way .... now we come to the passage. You can just see a little peep of the passage in Looking-glass House, if you leave the door of our drawing-room wide open: and it's very like our passage as far as you can see, only you know it may be quite different on beyond."

—*Through the Looking-Glass*

Reading, writing, and arithmetic are complex skills requiring the coordination of many distinct or *specific* processes. Among them:

Auditory perception. Oral comprehension is understanding speech quickly and easily. A child with auditory processing problems may respond slowly, misinterpret meaning, mispronounce words, read aloud poorly, prefer individual over group interactions, and lack confidence from not being able to respond as quickly as others. Apparent inattention may mean that the listener has been unsuccessful in trying to understand the speaker. It would be like watching a foreign film without the subtitles; after a while, one gives up trying to understand the movie. The child's behavior may be defensive so as not to appear unintelligent, shy and retiring, verbose and obstinate, awkward, inappropriate, or even antisocial. Because they only partly understand verbal exchanges, their recounting of events can differ from others', and so they can be accused of untruthfulness. Not understanding oral directions may mean that the child looks at a classmate's work, or talks to an adjacent child for clues, and so can be accused of cheating or disrespectful behavior. The logical order of a class lecture can be lost when note-taking becomes a scramble for capturing all the material presented: The note-taker can't determine in real time what is important to know. The student may be overwhelmed with listening, writing, and prioritizing simultaneously.

Auditory processing disorders can result in misunderstood pronouns, homonyms, multiple instructions, and social exchanges. I had to wonder what my son's world is like when he once wrote about *rose and rose of houses*. They may have difficulties understanding temporal or causal connections between events in a story or a history lesson because they may miss little prepositional word-clues explaining which one (*immigration from* Europe), when (*in* the 1700s), where (*to* North America), how (*by* sailing ships), and why (*for* a better life).

Phonemes. The word *bat* is composed of the sound elements—or phonemes—*buh*, *aah*, and *tuh*. In a phonological model presented by Sally Shaywitz of the Yale School of Medicine, the brains of most young children automatically break down words into phonemes, which are then auditorily processed for word identification, understanding, and memory storage or retrieval.[2] Normal children can process phonemes in less than 40 milliseconds; a child with a language processing problem may require 500 milliseconds.[3] Phonological processing problems can occur despite normal hearing and vision and can lead to difficulties in word identification, verbal comprehension of sentences and discourse, and phonetic decoding of alphabetic text (or *phonics*).

Moreover, English is not an easy language to learn. *Bough*, *cough*, *dough*, *rough*, and *through* are spelled similarly but pronounced differently. *Ate* and *eight* are spelled differently but sound the same. *Polish*, *read*, *arithmetic*, *learned*, *wind*, and *sake* have different pronunciations depending on the context. In a phonetically ideal language, only one spoken sound corresponds to only one letter. No language fits this ideal, but some languages are much easier to learn than others. Russians learn reading by the end of first grade. English, however, takes years to master: it is a Teutonic language with numerous vowel sounds, but uses a five-vowel Latin alphabet and applies French spelling rules to what may be the largest vocabulary in the world.

English uses 1,120 letter combinations to represent 40 different *phonemes*; in contrast, Italian uses 25 letter combinations for 33 different sounds.[4] A University of Milan Bicocca study compared the reading skills of English, French, and Italian native speakers, with and without language disorders, and found that the Italians had a significantly higher reading performance than either the English or the French.[5] In other words, the inconsistent English and French reading and writing systems are more likely to impede reading fluency for individuals with language disorders, as compared to more uniform alphabetic systems.

Visual perception. Young children commonly cannot differentiate between *if* and *of*, between *v* and *x*, or between *d, b, p, q, 6, and 9;* if this confusion persists, a child could have trouble with reading or math. Words and lines are often skipped when she or he can't decode (match visual alphabetic symbols to known sounds) easily. Typically, reading

---

2   Sally E. Shaywitz, "Dyslexia," *Scientific American*, November 1996, p. 99.

3   John Horgan citing the work of Paula Tallal of Rutgers University, "Playing Past Learning Disabilities," *Scientific American*, November 1996, p. 102.

4   American Association for the Advancement of Science, "Study Examines Impact on Dyslexia of English, French and Italian Spelling" [Internet], 2002, available from: http://www.aaas.org/news/releases/dyslexia/shtml

5   Bruce Bower citing the 2001 Paulesu study, "Dyslexia Gets a Break in Italy," *Science News*, 31 March 2001, p. 205.

is quite labored and extremely slow. To understand, try reading the text of Figure 3.1 and answer the questions under time pressure:[6]

Figure 3.1

E ach ad ut mitha ie ar mimp bisadility is am iubiubnal, het someg ene ral charact eristic s ho exist

He or sve has aver ape or adove averape iwtellipence; so me of thw wore quenalvet sywgto ws appear to de—bis or hers of wotor ac tivity; bisorder sof ewotionalith; bisorbeRs of berceb tiou; bisorb era of coucegtion; d. sorner s of attentiow; bisorders of wewory.

NOM let, s biscus s sowe of your "percegtual brodlews."

1. Lis t swe o f tye things tyat wabe yonr reabinp tash wor e biff i cnlt.

2. Li st sowe oft he tying s yon bib th at enadled yon to reab tyis gaper.

What mere so we of you r jeelings or tho ug ts mylie a ttemgting tor ea b tyis?[7]

Other types of visual perception disorders exist. A child having *figure-ground* perceptual problems may lose track because reading requires focusing on each letter, word, and line of text from left to right, one by one, down the page. Comprehension is lost because text is skipped. A page loaded with print may overwhelm a student. Visual details can be missed when reading or plotting maps and graphs. Poor *depth perception* results in poor hand-eye coordination or awkward movement. Misperception of facial expressions or body language undermine social skills. The biology of visual perception is very complex and not as well understood as auditory language perception.

---

6   From *Success for College Students with Learning Disabilities,* ed. Susan A. Vogel and Pamela B. Adelman, "Faculty Development: Changing Attitudes and Enhancing Knowledge About Learning Disabilities," by Ernest Rose, p. 136, Figure 7.1, 1993. Copyright © 1993 by Springer-Verlag New York, Inc. All rights reserved. Reprinted with permission of Springer-Verlag GmbH & Co.KG and Susan A. Vogel.

7   Translation is as follows:
Each adult with a learning disability is an individual, yet some general characteristics do exist.
He or she has average or above average intelligence; some of the more prevalent symptoms appear to be —disorders of motor activity; disorders of emotionality; disorders of perception; disorders of cognition; disorders of attention; disorders of memory.
NOW, let's discuss some of your "perceptual problems."
1. List some of the things that make your reading task more difficult.
2. List some of the things you did that enabled you to read this paper.
What were some of your feelings or thoughts while attempting to read this?

Memory. Over the past two decades, new concepts on memory have emerged. Instead of stores of short-term and long-term information, memory may exist in several forms intrinsic to a dynamic learning process. These new theories allow a better understanding of many perplexing behaviors observed in individuals with learning disabilities. Evidence from some behavioral and anatomical investigations support these new theories.

Learning captures experiences, which alter memory. In the conceptual learning model pictured in Figure 3.2, various separate systems have been unified as one gray box for purposes of diagrammatic simplicity. Sensory input is uniquely *encoded* into each information system, such as phonemes. The coded information is then stored briefly as a prolonged memory trace for recognition and further processing. During processing, either working memory attends to the information or the information is categorized and stored as a more durable memory.[8]

Figure 3.2

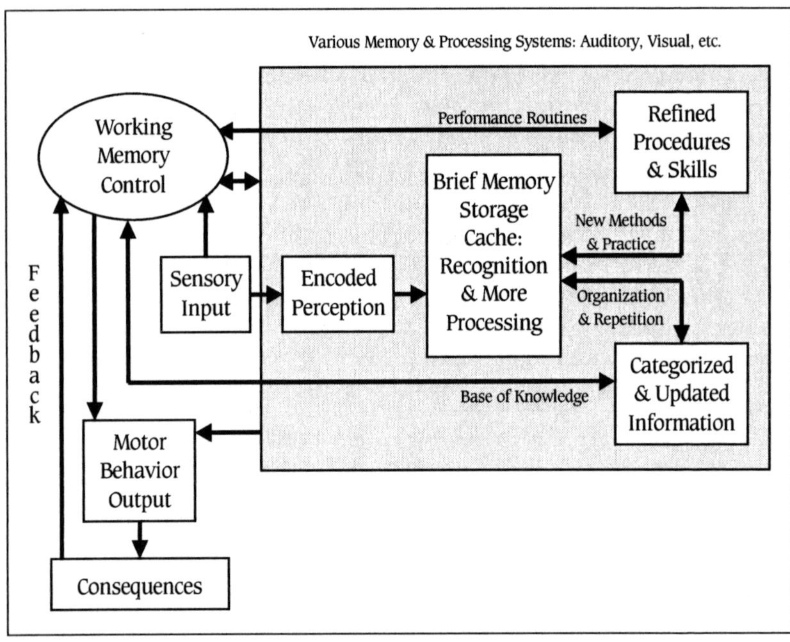

8 Joseph K. Torgesen, "A Model of Memory from an Information Processing Perspective: The Special Case of Phonological Memory," in *Attention, Memory and Executive Function*, ed. G. Reid Lyon and Norman A. Krasnegor (Baltimore: Paul H. Brookes Publishing, 1996), p. 158.

Auditory memory is remembering what was spoken. A child with auditory memory problems may have trouble following oral directions. One mother successfully reminded her son of the three steps for bedtime preparation by just saying "1, 2, 3," instead of a litany of specific directions. Auditory memory has also been described as a *phonological loop*, a recycling length of mental recording tape of finite capacity. A person with a shorter phonological loop will have more memory trouble than someone with a longer loop or mnemonic strategies. Other linguistic memory problems include recalling a word out of context (*naming difficulty*) or remembering which direction is named *left* and which direction is named *right*.

Visual memory is remembering what was seen. People with faulty visual memory have problems with copying, spelling, recognizing familiar acquaintances, or finding routes to destinations. There is also the possibility that they can see the difference between letters, but cannot associate any meaning to the symbols. Differences in visual memory have been linked to variations in a brain chemical.[9]

Episodic memory is remembering what happened.[10] An individual with this type of trouble will have poor recall of details after experiencing the event. Verbal interpretations of an event can interfere with the original memory of the event.[11]

Long-term memory which is an archival function and therefore retrospective in nature. The capacity for long-term memory is unlimited.[12] A student may comprehend language quite well, but be at a loss remembering clearly what or how something was said.[13] A child with significant memory deficits could require 10-15 repetitions each day for several days to remember what a normal child would grasp after 3-5 rehearsals in one day.[14] Some students may be able to absorb only small bits of information at a time. Others may remember information while concentrating on it, but cannot recall it later.

Working memory is transient, is prospective in nature, and has several roles:

---

9   John Travis reviewing 2002 Hariri study, "Gene Change Linked to Poor Memory," *Science News*, 23 November 2002, p. 334.

10 Mel Levine, *A Mind at a Time* (New York: Simon & Schuster, 2002), p. 114.

11 Bruce Bower, "Words Get in the Way: Talk is Cheap but It Can Tax Your Memory," *Science News*, 19 April 2003, pp. 250-251.

12 H. Lee Swanson, "Information Processing: An Introduction," in *A Cognitive Approach to Learning Disabilities*, 2nd Edition, ed. D. Kim Reid, Wayne P. Hresko, and H. Lee Swanson (Austin, Texas: PRO-ED, 1991), p. 143.

13 Richard K. Wagner, "From Simple Structure to Complex Function: Major Trends in the Development of Theories, Models, and Measurements of Memory," in *Attention, Memory, and Executive Function*, ed. G. Reid Lyon and Norman A. Krasnegor (Baltimore: Paul H. Brookes Publishing, 1996), p. 149.

14 Silver, *The Misunderstood Child*, p. 51.

- Has a limited capacity, but is the primary workspace for processing information relevant to a current task.
- Is associated with *executive function,* a self-regulatory mechanism that is key to "checking, planning, monitoring, testing, revising, and evaluating during an attempt to learn or solve problems."[15] (Executive function will be explained in further detail later.)
- Is connected to multiple memory and processing systems; auditory, visual, and other systems are believed to exist. These systems have various coding operations and linkages to each other.

Short-term memory is the temporary activation of a portion of long-term memory by working memory in order to execute a task.[16] In other words, memory is not passive storage but involves the selective activation of relevant neurons. One model has hypothesized the immediate memory requirements of working memory to be a subset of short-term memory, and short-term memory to be a subset of long-term memory.[17] This model is analogous to a theater production in which the main action is spotlighted (working memory), lesser lighting shines on the rest of the cast (short-term memory), and the least lighting illuminates the rest of the stage (long-term memory) at any time. Deficits of short-term memory do not limit language comprehension but appear to impair verbatim recall and the ability to pair known words with new vocabulary or foreign words.[18]

Trouble in one processing system and its associated memory functions may not affect other processing systems. For example, some people might learn quite easily by viewing a demonstration rather than receiving a written description of it. Einstein once said, "I very rarely think in words at all .... A thought comes, and I may try to express it in words afterwards."[19]

Executive function. Many students with learning disabilities have inefficient methods of learning. Thus help is required not only for learning the actual subject material, but also for learning systematic methods for understanding, remembering, recalling, manipulating, and expressing the material in a class discussion, essay, or exam. These latter methods of knowing how to learn are associated with working memory and are controlled by *executive function.* Executive function provides a temporal awareness of past, present, and future, and enables the student to oversee all phases of a task for its completion, as diagrammed in Figure 3.3:

---

15   Swanson, "Information Processing," p. 149.
16   Wagner, "From Simple Structure to Complex Function," p. 148.
17   Wagner, p. 149.
18   Wagner, p. 147.
19   Bower, "Words Get in the Way," p. 251.

Figure 3.3

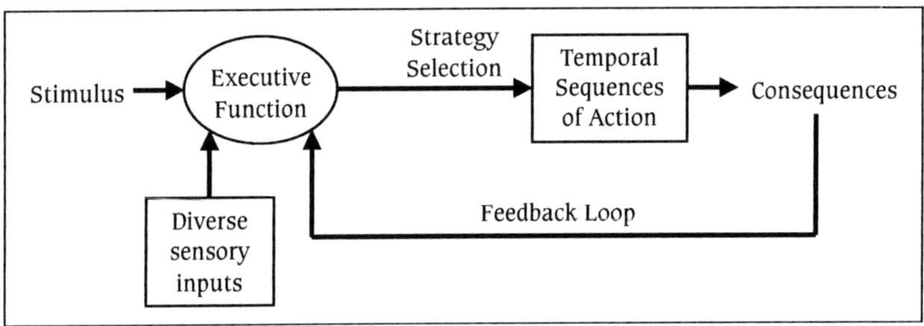

The diverse sensory inputs include physical and emotional states, verbal rules governing behavior, and visual perceptions and memories. Executive function then activates or inhibits behavior.

Executive function matures with language competence and over time. An underdeveloped executive function creates an unawareness in students who *don't know that they don't know* what to do, or uninhibited behavior in students who know better but do it anyway.

Organizing. Individuals with learning disabilities might have trouble breaking down tasks into action steps, or concepts into concrete details. Some of these thought processes might be reflected in poor management of time, priorities, and materials. H. Lee Swanson, an education professor at the University of California at Riverside, has reinterpreted these students, commonly called *passive* or *inactive learners*, as instead being actively engaged in searching for alternative strategies. Rather than using systematic linear step-by-step integrated strategies to solve problems, students with LD resort to opportunistic, though often inefficient, experimentation. There is a focus on the end product and not on the linear steps to finish the task. They appraise *"multiple"* methods and facts during the problem-solving process somewhat like brainstorming. Given the presence of a disorder interfering with normal information processing, he recommends instruction of appropriate strategies to smooth task performance.[20]

Sequencing. Sequencing difficulties occur when individuals have trouble organizing the order of things that they've seen, heard, or want to talk about to others. One man described this to me as being tongue-tied because all his thoughts flooded to him at the same time, and so he didn't know how to begin. Students can have trouble telling time, following procedures, recounting events in a story, or understanding historical progressions.

---

20   Swanson, "Information Processing," pp. 140-141.

"Well, in our country," said Alice, still panting a little, "you'd generally get to somewhere else—if you ran very fast for a long time as we've been doing."

"A slow sort of country!" said the Queen. "Now, here, you see, it takes all the running you can do, to keep in the same place. If you want to get somewhere else, you must run at least twice as fast as that!"

—Through the Looking-Glass

Verbal expression. Verbal expression skills are required for almost any social interaction. A child with difficulties in oral comprehension, auditory memory, word retrieval, and sequencing will have trouble understanding speech, remembering all parts of the message, and gathering words together in the right order for a response. Beyond the actual language problems are emotional problems when the child perceives himself or herself as inadequate in everyday social interactions. (Augusta Gross addresses issues of self-confidence and offers help in "Supporting a Sense of Learning Competency for Children with Language Related Learning Disabilities," available at www.ldonline.org/ ld_indepth/self_esteem/learning_competency.html.)

Verbal problems appear in several forms. One difficulty may be a *tip-of-the-tongue* phenomenon, in which different brain regions try to reconcile conflicting knowledge when searching for the correct memory.[21] Only word retrieval is blocked, but not the related higher-level processes like comprehension, connotations, and word usage.[22] Other common difficulties include incorrect use of pronouns, verb tenses, and plurals; tangled sequences of word syllables such as spoonerisms (*bandy car* instead of *candy bar*); and trouble in getting to the point when speaking.[23]

In school, students with learning disabilities may use simpler words and sentences than normal classmates; however, they can use more complex sentences with adults indicating social awareness.[24] Under time pressure, a student with an expressive language disorder

---

21   Bruce Bower citing the 2000 Maril study, "A Tip of the Tongue to the Brain," *Science News*, 8 September 2001, p. 155.

22   Shaywitz, "Dyslexia," *Scientific American*, p. 102.

23   Priscilla Vail, "Detecting Problems," *The Expert Answers: Priscilla Vail on Learning Styles and Emotions* [Internet], 22 March 2002, p. 3, available from: http://www.schwablearning.org/pdfs/expert_vail.pdf

24   William N. Bender citing Boucher's 1984 and 1986 studies, *Learning Disabilities: Characteristics, Identification, and Teaching Strategies*, 2nd Edition (Needham Heights, Massachusetts: Allyn and Bacon, 1995), p. 130.

may copy another person's words. In group projects, a child with a learning disability would learn tasks more slowly and be less capable in communicating information and instructions than normal children. Compared to normal peers, a student with a verbal disorder tends to make statements that are more instructive (*know-it-all*), inventive (*silly, stupid*), controlling (*bossy*), and inappropriate (*strange, insensitive*).[25] While these statements may reflect the children's actual language environment (after all, they are intensively instructed, highly directed, and often insulted), such verbalizations can lead to ostracism and further deficits in social skills.

Remedial attention is usually given to articulation and decoding (phonetic reading) problems. But school and social success is more dependent on language skills at higher levels. *Syntax* refers to the sequence of words, verb usage, and the relationships among words. *Semantics* is the meaning of words, not just vocabulary. *Pragmatics* is the use of language for communication, and is affected by the social roles and cultural backgrounds of the people conversing. Problems at these higher levels may be overlooked and the child may never rise above a basic proficiency level. To smooth performance, many students require explicit instructions, rehearse anticipated situations, and *overlearn* items for later recall. Often, comprehension is improved if words can be visualized (text or images) as well as heard.

The neural pathways for hearing, reading, and speaking have been most studied in the brains of right-handed males (Appendix 1); females and left-handed people have different brain organizations. In the typical right-handed male brain, verbal ability generally exists in the left hemisphere, and nonverbal abilities generally lie in the right hemisphere. These left and right brain areas are intricately linked, however, and a normal person does not function exclusively *left-brained* or *right-brained*.

Adult females may be able to compensate for language disabilities more than adult men. Brain scans show phonological processing centers on both sides of the normal female brain, the development possibly occurring during adolescence,[26] while the male brain continues to process language on one side. One woman remembers that the only sentences she could write during third grade as being those she copied from books. Around the sixth grade, school started to become easier. Another parent remembers his daughter's language troubles alleviating during adolescence as well.

---

25 Bender, p. 131.

26 Sally E. Shaywitz and Bennett A. Shaywitz, "Unlocking Learning Disabilities: The Neurological Basis," in *Learning Disabilities: Lifelong Issues*, ed. Shirley C. Cramer and William Ellis (Baltimore: Paul H. Brookes Publishing, 1996), p. 259.

Abstractions. Some individuals may have trouble making generalizations, reconciling ambiguities, inferring meaning, or comprehending metaphors, idioms, puns, and jokes. A student might correctly identify people, places, and dates on an exam, but erroneously define *social upward mobility* as *walking around with an upright posture*. Many of these difficulties are related to language problems. However, any abstraction difficulties existing in children with learning disabilities are usually "mild"[27] and can improve with maturation and education.

Reading. Reading integrates many processing skills: written symbols are decoded into sounds, and the sounds are translated into words with meaning. In the first and second grades, children are learning to read. Around the third or fourth grade, children are reading to learn. This change in emphasis requires a shift from pattern recognition in early reading to language interpretation in later reading. Reading skills include the following:[28]

WORD ATTACK
- *Phonics:* letter symbols are decoded into sounds
- *Sight words*: words recognized immediately by sight

WORD COMPREHENSION
- *Vocabulary:* collection of words known to the reader
- *Morphology:* structure of words derived from word roots, with prefixes, suffixes, plural forms, or verb tenses
- *Semantics:* the meaning of a word within its context (e.g., irony, understatement, exaggeration, or multiple meanings as in a pun)

SENTENCE COMPREHENSION
- *Syntax:* rules for forming sentences and phrases
- *Context clues:* comprehension through readings of passages

COMPREHENSION OF LONGER TEXTS
- *Literal comprehension:* concrete interpretation of text statements
- *Inferential comprehension:* conclusions gathered from clues in text
- *Evaluation:* comparison of a text's accuracy and supporting arguments to other readings
- *Appraisal:* comparison of the text's quality to similar works

Over the course of reading instruction, decoding or comprehension difficulties may appear.

Decoding or phonetic reading. Skilled readers do two things: 1) they process every letter of every word rapidly and effortlessly, and 2) they familiarize themselves with new vocabulary through repeated

---

27 Silver, *The Misunderstood Child*, p. 48.
28 Bender, pp. 201-209.

phonological decoding, so that words are eventually recognized accurately and fluently by sight.[29] The more they read, the better they read.

Sally Shaywitz of the Yale School of Medicine found in her Connecticut Longitudinal Study that reading difficulties of neurological origin affect up to 17.5% of the U.S. school population, are a lifelong condition not a transient developmental phase, have genetic influences, and occur equally in both boys and girls.[30] However, males account for 60-80% of diagnosed reading disorders.[31] G. Reid Lyon, a research psychologist and Chief of the Child Development and Behavior Branch at the National Institute of Child Health and Human Development within the National Institutes of Health in Bethesda, Maryland, has described reading problems at the individual level:

> "Most reading problems can be observed when the child (or adult) attempts to read the words on a page of print out loud. In most cases you will quickly notice a labored approach to decoding or 'sounding out' unknown or unfamiliar words. Reading is typically hesitant and characterized by frequent starts and stops. If asked about the meaning of what was just read, the individual frequently has little to say. Not because he or she isn't smart enough. In fact, many people with reading problems are very bright. The poor comprehension occurs because they take far too long to read the words, leaving little energy for remembering and understanding what they have read."[32]

Three reading perceptual disorders have been identified: 1) deficits in phonological processing of the printed words into recognizable phonemes (*auditory-linguistic type*), 2) visual processing of the sequence of the letters into recognizable words (*visual-dysphonetic type*), or 3) a combination of these two types.[33] Reading disorders are rarely diagnosed before formal reading instruction begins, around first grade. All

---

29 Joseph K. Torgesen, "Instructional Interventions for Children with Reading Disabilities," in *Specific Reading Disability: A View of the Spectrum*, ed. Bruce K. Shapiro, Pasquale J. Accardo, and Arnold J. Caputo (Timonium, Maryland: York Press, 1998), pp. 200-202.

30 Sally E. Shaywitz, "Dyslexia," *The New England Journal of Medicine*, 29 January 1998, p. 307.

31 *Diagnostic and Statistical Manual of Mental Disorders*, 4th Edition, Text Revision (Washington D.C.: American Psychiatric Association, 2000), p. 52.

32 Reid Lyon, "Developing Reading Skills in Young Children," *LD Matters*, Winter 1998, p. 2. © Copyright 2002 Schwab Learning. Reprinted with permission of Schwab Learning. For more information please visit www.schwablearning.org.

33 Carol Sullivan Spafford and George S. Grosser, *Dyslexia* (Needham Heights, Massachusetts: Allyn and Bacon, 1996), p. 9.

too often, reading disorders may not be identified until at least the fourth grade. "But," says Shaywitz, "our experience at the Yale Center suggests that many compensated dyslexics have a distinct advantage over nondyslexics in their ability to reason and conceptualize and that the phonological deficit masks what are often excellent comprehension skills."[34] Thus the problem for the student may be how to learn academic content despite decoding difficulties.

Text comprehension. Fluent decoding does not always lead to good reading comprehension. In *Children's Problems in Text Comprehension: An Experimental Investigation* (Cambridge University Press, 1991), Nicola Yuill and Jane Oakhill present the cases of two girls, one who is one month above her chronological age in decoding but 16 months below in comprehension, the other six months below in decoding but average in comprehension. Thus, the possibilities of reading skills can be described, though not explained, as shown in Figure 3.4:

Figure 3.4

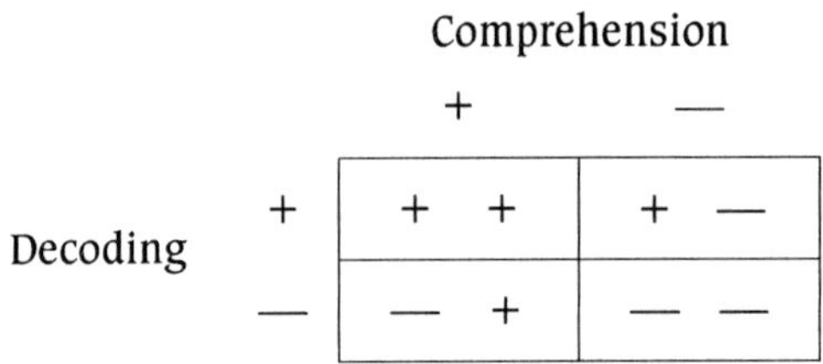

Yuill and Oakhill identified seven- to nine-year-olds in Brighton schools (near London) who demonstrated both fluent decoding and comprehension skills at least six months below their levels of reading accuracy. The investigations ruled out possible deficiencies in decoding speed, vocabulary, background knowledge, or short-term memory as the underlying cause. Typically, these students retained a text's verbatim language, and so could understand isolated facts of literal concrete information. However, these children failed to build an overall mental representation of the information from the reading material irrespective of the exact words used in the text. In other words, the children saw each individual tree but not the forest. For them, a how-to technical manual would be much easier to understand than an evocative work of literature.

---

34 From "Dyslexia," by Sally E. Shaywitz, *Scientific American*, November 1996, p. 104. Reprinted with permission of *Scientific American*.

Yuill and Oakhill described deficits in the following list as reading difficulties of *poor comprehenders*:

TEXT INFERENCES
* Linking pronouns, noun phrases, synonyms, and other word substitutes to their corresponding antecedents
* Scanning text to answer questions
* Appropriately applying personal experiences to text passages
TEXT INTEGRATION
* Grasping the main idea versus, for example, the main event
* Using conjunctions, prepositions, and inferences to effectively understand the relationships (e.g., causation) between characters, events, and ideas
* Prioritizing and applying explicit or implicit reading clues in terms of relevance or materiality
COMPREHENSION MONITORING
* Realizing that text has not been adequately understood
* Fulfilling the purposes for the reading activity: What's important to know?
* Incrementally composing the mental representation *while* reading by reviewing, rehearsing, self-testing, and predicting material
* Identifying and resolving inconsistencies in the text
WORKING MEMORY
* Building the mental model of the text message if reading has both high processing and memory demands
LISTENING COMPREHENSION
* Understanding the meaning of the entire oral presentation; problems are similar to those seen in reading comprehension
WRITTEN EXPRESSION
* Writing elementary school narratives as a running series of present-tense events, instead of an integrated sequence of statements.

Children with these generalized language problems find academics frustrating because almost all school learning is based on language skills. With each passing year, a higher language skill level is presumed, and a child can easily fall farther and farther behind. A cumulative deficit occurs when a child does not master each grade's reading curriculum. For example, a child progressing at two-thirds the normal rate would have achieved a second-grade reading level by the beginning of fourth grade. Tenth-graders with a fifth-grade reading level will need instructional modifications to learn academic material. College students can demonstrate normal understanding of literal text material but may show difficulties in making inferences, the problems unrelated to decoding skills.[35]

Yuill and Oakhill did not expect their research to uncover such "an educationally significant problem" that constituted 10-15%[36] of the school populations studied. Moreover, they surmised that their results were not atypical of students in general. As many of their investigations drew on previous findings of adults with and without similar problems, the researchers suggested longitudinal studies on reading comprehension difficulties.

Writing. Writing is a form of communication, with content relevant to both the writer and the reader. Similar to good reading comprehension, good writing integrates a wide variety of abilities and skills. Figure 3.5 graphically interprets Levine's ideas[37] of a writing *reinforcement* cycle. A child's abilities and skills are coordinated to enable writing, and, through practice, enhance better writing the next time around:

Figure 3.5

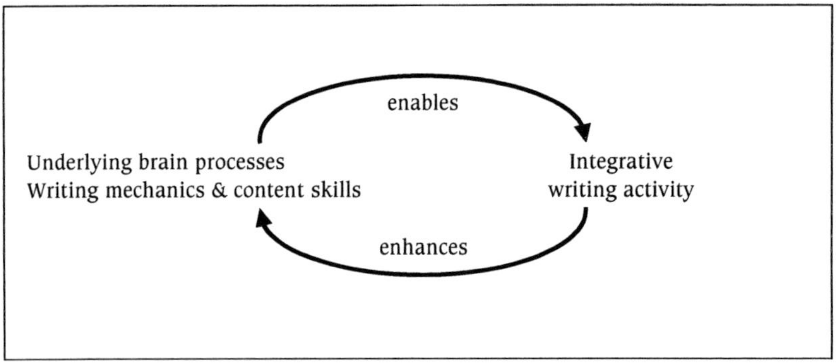

According to Levine, writing demands both innate abilities and academic skills, some of which are:

• Underlying brain processes: language ability, various types of memory, sequencing, conceptual thought, and motor skills

• Problem-solving skills: Topic selection, resource identification, and presentation strategy

---

35   F. Simmons and C. Singleton, "The Reading Comprehension Abilities of Dyslexic Students in Higher Education," *Dyslexia* [Internet], July-September 2000, available from: http://www.ncbi.nlm.nih.gov/entrez/query.fcgi?cmd=Retrieve&db=PubMed &list_uids=10989566&dopt=Abstract

36   Nicola Yuill and Jane Oakhill, *Children's Problems in Text Comprehension: An Experimental Investigation* (Cambridge: Cambridge University Press, 1991), p. 217.

37   Melvin D. Levine, "What's Riding on Writing," Foreword to *The Writing Dilemma: Understanding Dysgraphia* by Regina G. Richards (Riverside, California: RET Center Press, 1998), p. vii.

• Social skills: assessment of the prospective reader's expectations, preferences, and background.

Writing failure may begin in little ways. Handwriting may be especially labored. Spelling errors made by students with learning disabilities are similar to those made by younger students, but occur more frequently than in normal peers.[38] Children with language difficulties show problems with grammar and paragraph organization. In short, most writing failures cannot be globally attributed to any single deficit of neuromuscular coordination, language, attention, or effort. Disorders of written expression usually coexist with other learning disorders, and are generally apparent by second grade.[39]

Learning disabilities create a writing *avoidance* cycle in Figure 3.6. The student writes "as little and as passively" as possible:[40]

Figure 3.6

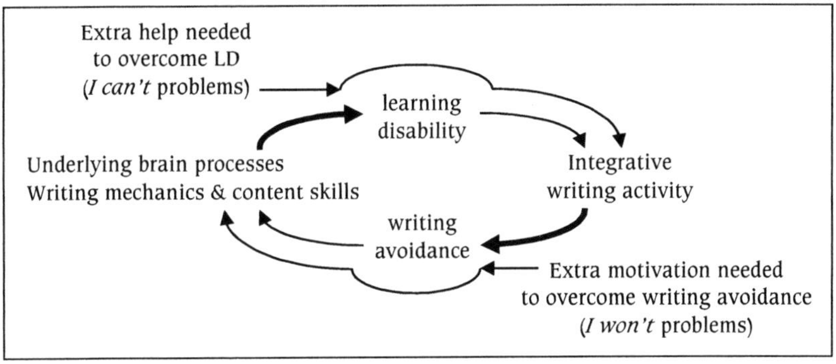

In this model, proper identification of specific problems can lead to appropriate interventions. Learning disabilities can be remediated, compensated, or accommodated in various ways. Motivation requires positive attitudes, not tough-love remarks, humiliation, or penalties. Learning to write should be heartfelt positive experiences, not chores to be undertaken with grim determination.

A discouraged student will understandably try to minimize writing practice. Your job, however difficult, is to see that writing practice continues. All too often, performance anxieties and negative experiences compound a *can't* problem into a *can't and won't* problem. Helping a student with learning disabilities to write is tough; motivating a noncompliant student is tougher.

---

38 Bender citing the 1987 Gerber and Hall study, *Learning Disabilities*, p. 216.
39 *Diagnostic and Statistical Manual of Mental Disorders*, p. 55.
40 Levine, "What's Riding on Writing," pp. vii-viii.

Spelling and handwriting problems alone do not constitute a diagnosis of a written expression disorder. A diagnosis may require comparisons between expected performance and actual writing samples.[41] While little is known about remediation and long-term outcome,[42] many individuals have persevered and even have established professional writing careers, as seen in Chapter 6.

Foreign languages. Foreign language study, commonly required in school and for college admissions, is difficult for many students with language learning disabilities. In 1971, Kenneth Dinklage, a counselor at Harvard University, found that students failing foreign language courses exhibited the same types of problems typically seen in students with language learning disabilities: poor reading and spelling skills, poor auditory discrimination skills, and poor auditory memory.[43] Indeed, students with subtle language disorders who have been able to successfully compensate in their native language may not recognize their learning disability until "confronted with a foreign language and its new and unfamiliar linguistic coding system."[44]

Pronunciation and sound discrimination problems, interference with the individual's native language, word formation (morphology) patterns, vocabulary acquisition, and thinking in a new grammatical (syntactical) system require abilities of phonetic coding, grammatical sensitivity, rote memory, and an innate sense of how language works.[45] Some U.S. immigrants with language disorders also have problems learning a foreign language—English—even with good instruction. The Department of Education has raised concerns that these students are not being appropriately assessed and schooled.[46]

Math. *Claire was born approximately nine weeks premature and was released after four weeks of hospitalization. In preschool, she was*

---

41 *Diagnostic and Statistical Manual of Mental Disorders*, p. 55.

42 *Diagnostic and Statistical Manual of Mental Disorders*, p. 55.

43 Lenore Ganschow and Richard Sparks, "'Foreign' Language Learning Disabilities: Issues, Research, and Teaching Implications," in *Success for College Students with Learning Disabilities*, ed. Susan A. Vogel and Pamela Adelman (New York: Springer-Verlag, 1993), p. 289.

44 From *Success for College Students with Learning Disabilities*, ed. Susan A. Vogel and Pamela Adelman, " 'Foreign' Language Learning Disabilities: Issues, Research, and Teaching Implications," by Lenore Ganschow and Richard Sparks, p. 292, 1993. Copyright © 1993 by Springer-Verlag New York, Inc. All rights reserved. Reprinted with permission of Springer-Verlag GmbH & Co.KG and Susan A. Vogel.

45 Melvin D. Levine, *Developmental Variation and Learning Disorders* (Cambridge, Massachusetts: Educator's Publishing Service, 1987), pp. 375-378.

46 U.S. Department of Education, "Twenty-third Annual Report to Congress on the Implementation of the Individuals with Disabilities Education Act" [Internet], 2001, p. II-36, available from: http://www.ed.gov/offices/OSERS/OSEP/Products/OSEP 2001AnlRpt/Section_II.pdf

*slightly shy, but made friends with boys and girls and loved her teach-
ers. We enrolled our daughter in a Montessori kindergarten at a K-8
parochial school. She liked going to school, liked the teachers, made
friends, played any sport that was available to her, and developed strict
study habits by herself. Beginning in the first grade, she exhibited the
first signs of test anxiety, especially with math and reading aloud. This
struggle with schoolwork continued through the eighth grade.*

*All through grammar school Claire played two sports simulta-
neously in fall, winter, and spring. She got mostly Bs and Cs on report
cards and an occasional D in math, which would devastate her. We let
her continue in sports because she managed her time so very well and
felt so good about herself in athletic endeavors.*

*From first grade on, we inquired about having her tested and were
told it wasn't necessary—over and over. At every parent-teacher conference, we were told Claire was a teacher's dream student. She paid
attention in class, turned in assignments on time, was well-behaved,
put great effort into projects, made friends easily, and managed her
time very efficiently in school and at home. We were informed that she
lacked self-confidence in school, but was very confident in sports activities. The teachers told us her good habits would help her in high school
and her confidence would probably emerge in high school. In the second
grade, she began receiving tutoring in math; this continued on through
high school. We had a long conference with her eighth-grade teacher
and was told that LD testing was not necessary.*

*She wanted to take AP classes along with her other classes in high
school. However, she still struggled desperately with math and would
not sleep before big tests, especially SAT testing. She continued with
sports activities, made good choices with friends and activities, did
extra credit assignments to make up for her test scores, and went to
teachers in her free time for extra help.*

*In the spring of her junior year, her math teacher called to inform
us that she was getting a D and was the hardest working student she
had every seen. The teacher suggested LD testing. My daughter was
diagnosed with dyscalculia. We were warned to take care in discussing
this finding with her. Sure enough, Claire was devastated and
lamented, "I am mentally retarded after all!" We found out that since
grade school, she had been tormented by a classmate about her problems in school.*

*We looked for a college with a good LD program. Claire is now a col-
lege sophomore, on the cross-country team. She still works very hard on
her school work. As parents, we wish she would utilize the LD department more than she does, but we believe she is still somewhat in denial
about her LD. The LD department offers many opportunities for help
and seems to be a group of considerate and caring professionals.*

Math has its own language, thinking processes, grammar, and symbols. Math learning disabilities are less common and less understood than language learning disabilities, and usually not diagnosed at all. Difficulties in math readiness skills like sorting, matching, sequencing, and numbering can be identified before a child enters first grade. Math disorders are usually apparent in the second or third grade, but may not raise concerns until the fifth grade when children must use math facts to solve multi-step word problems.[47]

About 2% to 6.5% of elementary school age children have dyscalculia,[48] or arithmetic difficulties. Children seem to be less able to compensate for dyscalculia, a type of nonverbal disorder, than for reading disorders.[49] Girls more than boys are affected by dyscalculia.[50] Not much is understood about any specific disorders affecting higher levels of mathematics like algebra or geometry.[51]

Other math troubles are associated with language disorders. A naming difficulty can occur when referring to mathematical labels, terms, and symbols. Some students may have problems reading or writing math symbols and equations. These types of math impairments are observable:

• Language skills	Understanding or naming mathematical terms, operations, or concepts: *the numeral 9 means a quantity of nine*. Some symbols may represent more than one concept; "+" can indicate *add, more, plus*, or *positive* Following directions Accurately interpreting word problems into mathematical symbols and thought.
• Visuomotor skills	Numbers written backwards: $\mathsf{2}$ instead of 2 $\mathsf{3}$ instead of 3 $\mathsf{4}$ instead of 4

---

47 *Diagnostic and Statistical Manual of Mental Disorders*, p. 54.

48 Ruth S. Shalev, Orly Manor, Judith Auerbach, and Varda Gross-Tsur, "Persistence of Developmental Dyscalculia: What Counts?" *The Journal of Pediatrics*, September 1998, p. 358.

49 Shalev, Manor, Auerbach, and Gross-Tsur, pp. 359 and 361.

50 R.S. Shalev, J. Auerbach, O. Manor, and V. Gross-Tsur, "Developmental Dyscalculia: Prevalence and Prognosis," *European Child & Adolescent Psychiatry* [Internet], 2000, available from: http://www.ncbi.nlm.nih.gov/entrez/query.fcgi?cmd= Retrieve&db=PubMed&list_uids=11138905&dopt=Abstract

51 David C. Geary, "Mathematical Disabilities: What We Know and Don't Know" [Internet], accessed 24 February 2002, available from http://www.ldonline.org/ ld_indepth/math_skills/geary_math_dis.html

Confusion of similar or poorly written symbols:

1, 7, and lowercase l	5 and s	addition + and
2 and z	6, 0, and lowercase b	division ÷ signs
3 and 5; 4 and 9	8, 13, &, and uppercase B	addition sign + and
4 and lowercase t, x, and y	9 and lowercase g and q	lowercase t

One way to improve legibility is to use European symbols:

Ø instead of 0	7̶ instead of 7	z̶ instead of z

Other small handwriting disciplines are to hook the bottom of the lowercase *t:*

t instead of t

and loop the lowercase *l*:

ℓ instead of l

- Spatial skills

  Matching corresponding items one-to-one
  Clustering objects into groups
  Copying numbers or figures correctly
  Keeping one's place on a page
  Proper alignment of numbers and symbols
  Translating 2-dimensional figures into 3-dimensional concepts and vice-versa

- Quantitative skills

  Counting objects
  Calculating
  Understanding place value

- Understanding time

  Events happen in a linear sequence, but the analog clock face is a number line in the shape of a circle.
  Time measurement uses the unfamiliar number bases of 12, 24, and 60 instead of the familiar base 10.
  Minutes are counted after the current hour and before the next hour.
  Fractions of an hour are used, not apparent on digital clocks.

- Procedures

  Working right to left, not left to right:

addition	subtraction	multiplication
894	237	47
+ 756	− 162	x 53

  Working left to right, not right to left:
  division 6)84332

- Sequencing problems are apparent in transposition errors (29 instead of 92), improper execution of steps in an algorithm (adding fractions with uncommon denominators), or not identifying the pattern in a number series (1, 2, 4, 8, 16, 32, 64, 128).

- Working memory is similar to RAM (random access memory) in a computer, and temporarily stores data for mental manipulation. For example, a child mentally adding 67 and 89 must hold both of these numbers in memory, recall math facts from long-term memory, add the 7 and 9 together, place a 6 in the units position, regroup or carry a 1 to be added to the 6 and 8, recall math facts again, add the 1 and 6 and 8 to make 15, recall the 6 in the units position, and finally sequence these elements into the sum of 156. Problems with memory can thwart this addition process at any one of these steps, perhaps even undermining memory of the teacher's instructions altogether. Other problems may include remembering instructions or counting forwards and backwards.
- Long-term memory is the repository of a person's base of knowledge and procedural knowledge. If memory processes are weak, learning math facts, algorithms, and multi-step procedures for solving problems will be severely compromised. Some students may flounder in the rote learning of basic facts, but easily comprehend advanced math topics. Other students may retrieve not only the correct math facts when solving a problem, but also other math facts as well. For example in response to the question $4 + 5 =$, the child could summon from memory *9, 20* (the answer to 4 x 5), or *6* (which follows the series 4, 5, ?). These choices could confuse a child, who would require more time to select the correct answer.

Higher levels of math are not about calculating big numbers in complicated formulas, but about developing and applying universal formulas. Math requires an understanding of procedures, postulates, and theorems in order to logically manipulate symbolic quantities, equations, and proofs. Problems with working memory, deductive reasoning, and conceptual thinking will hamper mathematical performance. Professional mathematicians regard their discipline as a creative process requiring intuition and ingenuity in order to construct universal concepts, not an archival function of various facts and figures. Hence, one can be a mathematician yet be unable to do arithmetic. For example Einstein confessed to having a poor memory, but his equation $E=mc^2$—a quantitative relationship between energy and mass—was derived through mathematical proofs.

Nonverbal learning disability. Less well-known than language disorders which are primarily problems in *left*-brain functioning (using the model of a right-handed male brain), are nonverbal learning disabilities (NLD) which are dominated by disorders in *right*-brain functioning. Behaviors vary but generally include:
- Competence in auditory perception, word decoding, auditory memory, and spelling

- Difficulties in reading comprehension, and arithmetic; visual and spatial perceptions; and nonverbal social cues, like stances and gestures, or *body language*
- Poor adaptation to novel situations and poor social relationships.

Identification requires a differential diagnosis because the symptoms could be those of other conditions. More information can be found in a review article published in "Nonverbal Learning Disabilities," by Stephen Sands and Susan Schwartz, available at www.aboutourkids. org/letter/mayjun00.pdf; *Developmental Variation and Learning Disorders*, by Melvin Levine (Educators Publishing Service, 1998); and in *Children's Psychological Testing: A Guide for Nonpsychologists*, by David Wodrich (Paul H. Brookes Publishing Co., 1997).

Cause. Brain scans show activity differences between normal brains and brains of those diagnosed with a learning disorder. Galaburda and colleagues demonstrated unusual neural connections in the cerebral cortex, which could account for the variable pattern of language and visual processing difficulties.[52] Language developmental delays have been associated with genetics, premature birth, prenatal exposure to drugs and alcohol, asphyxiation at birth, and chronic middle ear infections (*otitis media*). Disorders of language have been estimated to account for 85% of children identified as having learning disabilities.[53] Problems in detecting visual motion may be associated with visual-dysphonetic reading disorders.[54] Childhood cancer treatments have been linked to learning and attention difficulties.[55] Nonverbal learning disabilities may be caused by some problem in the brain's right hemisphere or in the fibers that connect the two brain hemispheres together.[56] In short, a diagnosis of a specific learning disability neither specifies an exact problem, nor points to any particular cause. A general discussion on the neurology relevant to LD is presented in "The Expert Answers: Dr. Gordon Sherman on Brain Research and Reading," available at www.schwablearning.org/pdfs/expert_sherman.pdf.

---

52 Judith M. Rumsey and Guinevere Eden, "Functional Neuroimaging of Developmental Dyslexia: Regional Cerebral Blood Flow in Dyslexic Men," in *Specific Reading Disability: A View of the Spectrum*, ed. Bruce K. Shapiro, Pasquale J. Accardo, and Arnold J. Capute (Timonium, Maryland: York Press, 1998), p. 41.

53 Louisa Cook Moats, "Implementing Effective Instruction," in *Learning Disabilities: Lifelong Issues*, ed. Shirley C. Cramer and William Ellis (Baltimore: Paul H. Brookes Publishing, 1996), p. 87.

54 Rumsey and Eden, "Functional Neuroimaging of Developmental Dyslexia," p. 40.

55 Mary Duenwald and Denise Grady, "Young Survivors of Cancer Battle Effects of Treatment" [Internet], 8 January 2003, p. 1, available from: http://www.nytimes. com/2003/01/08/health/08CANC.html

56 Stephen A. Sands and Susan J. Schwartz, "Nonverbal Learning Disabilities," *Child Study Center Letter* [Internet], May/June 2000, p. 3, available from:http://www. aboutourkids.org/letter/mayjun00.pdf

Chapter Four

What are other types of learning problems?

Attention deficit/hyperactivity disorder (AD/HD)

My daughter ran early, talked early, and began reading in preschool. Kindergarten was disappointing; all reading stopped because the teacher didn't feel it was "age appropriate." Her teacher was very structured and determined to be right about each and every conclusion.

The first grade teacher had a big wedding to plan. When I voiced a concern about my daughter's inability to sit, I was reminded that indeed it was too early to be concerned. What should I do, wait and let it get really bad first? I started talking to other mothers. I observed my child. Visits to at least two doctors resulted in AD/HD diagnoses, at least one recommending medication. I was violently opposed as a result of bad memories of my brother's history of drug abuse. I did not understand much but I was sensing failure because a drug was being recommended. I was devastated.

In second grade, Tessa's teacher was convinced that my child could not settle down and suggested special education. My child often went to the pencil sharpener in a pirouette, always moving, always spinning. The teacher wondered why nothing had been done in first grade. Now I was beginning to twirl.

My family has a history of both learning disabilities and AD/HD. My parents were quite strict, so when the rules were broken, the consequences were immediate. I myself have attention deficit disorder, but I managed, learned how to take tests, and prospered. In the 1950's, girls were expected to be active and change their minds. My hyperactivity wasn't noticed much. But my younger brother, now 40, is illiterate, unemployed, and vastly out of step with his peers and his world. His struggles and failures formed the basis of my knowledge and instincts, and were the motivation of my aggressive pursuit of solutions for my child.

You may have seen different names for attention-deficit disorders. To reduce confusion, the American Psychiatric Association standardized terminology in 1994. Its *Diagnostic and Statistical Manual of Mental Disorders, Fourth Edition* (abbreviated as *DSM-IV*), unified Attention-Deficit Hyperactivity Disorder (ADHD) and Attention-Deficit Disorder (ADD) into the single term, Attention-Deficit/Hyperactivity Disorder (AD/HD).

Attention-deficit/hyperactivity disorder (AD/HD) affects the ability to learn and so has been commonly called a learning disability. AD/HD can be misinterpreted by others as "laziness, a poor sense of responsibility, and oppositional behavior."[1] Individuals may be described as *ditsy, forgetful, distractible, unreliable,* or a *screw-up,* and be constantly reminded to *dig in, stay on track, concentrate, focus,* or *pull your life together.* Hyperactivity is a physical restlessness more often pronounced in males than in females. Family and school conflicts, and school and vocational underachievement are common troubles.

AD/HD is not a knowledge deficit about what to do, but a performance deficit in using the knowledge in order to get the task done.[2] Applying a *should have* (knowledge of what task needs to be done), *could have* (ability to do the task), *would have* (mobilizing the will to get it done) analogy, attention-deficit is a *would have* problem:

> "ADHD is not a *learning* disability, it is a *behavioral*
> disorder. ... Many children with learning disabilities
> have attention problems, but this does not mean that
> they have ADHD."[3]

Russell Barkley, Professor in the College of Health Professions at the University of South Carolina in Charleston calls AD/HD an *in*tention deficit because there is no follow-through;[4] it is a disorder of executive

---

1   *Diagnostic and Statistical Manual of Mental Disorders*, p. 88.
2   Russell Barkley, "ADHD: Theory, Diagnosis, and Treatment" [Internet], 17 June 2000, p. 65, available from: http://www.schwablearning.org/pdfs/2200_7-barktran.pdf
3   Fletcher, J.M. and Shaywitz, B.A. (Copyright © 1996). "Attention-Deficit/Hyperactivity Disorder." In Editors Cramer, S.C. and Ellis, W. *Learning Disabilities: Lifelong Issues* (pp. 265-266). Baltimore: Paul H. Brookes Publishing Co. Reprinted with permission of Paul H. Brookes Publishing Co. and Shirley C. Cramer.
4   Barkley, "ADHD: Theory, Diagnosis, and Treatment," p. 71.

function (discussed in Chapter 3), resulting in age-inappropriate self-control. Impulsive behavior is at cross-purposes with temporal organization, self-governance, emotional and motivational control, and problem-solving. Motor coordination problems can exist as well. Barkley estimates a 30% developmental lag in self-control in children with AD/HD; for example, a 16-year-old with a driver's license may only have the self-control of an 11-year-old.[5] His studies have found higher rates of traffic accidents and teenage pregnancies among groups with AD/HD than in normal populations. The disorder affects perhaps 4%-12% of school-age children.[6] Some other statistics relevant to children with AD/HD:[7]

- 25-50% have specific learning disabilities
- 70-80% of young children still show symptoms in adolescence, and 60-70% of these adolescents will continue to have symptoms in young adulthood
- Up to 90% underachieve in school
- 25-30% may suffer major depression by young adulthood
- Over half develop oppositional defiant disorders (hostile behavior defined in *DSM-IV-TR*)
- 24-35% develop conduct disorders (aggressive, destructive, deceitful behaviors, criteria provided in *DSM-IV-TR*).

AD/HD is a serious condition. People were once bemused with seniors having declining memories until the full effects of Alzheimer's disease were understood. Being distractible and impulsive is not a desirable state-of-being either. In 2002, an International Consensus Statement on AD/HD was released to the public. The opening paragraph is as follows:

> "We, the undersigned consortium of international scientists, are deeply concerned about the periodic inaccurate portrayal of attention deficit hyperactivity disorder (ADHD) in media reports. This is a disorder with which we are all very familiar and toward which many of us have dedicated scientific studies if not entire careers. We fear that inaccurate stories rendering ADHD as myth, fraud, or benign condition may cause thousands of sufferers not to seek treatment for

---

5   Barkley, "ADHD: Theory, Diagnosis, and Treatment," p. 37.
6   American Academy of Pediatrics, Subcommittee on Attention-Deficit/Hyperactivity Disorder and Committee on Quality Improvement, "Clinical Practice Guideline: Treatment of the School-Aged Child with Attention-Deficit/Hyperactivity Disorder," *Pediatrics*, 4 October 2001, p. 1036.
7   Russell A. Barkley, "Attention Deficit Hyperactivity Disorder (ADHD)," *LD Matters*, a Schwab Learning Publication, Spring 2000, pp. 1-2.

their disorder. It also leaves the public with a general
sense that this disorder is not valid or real or consists
of a rather trivial affliction."

For the rest of this statement, refer to www.chadd.org/webpage.
cfm?cat_id=10&subcat_id=67&sec_id=0. For general comments about
this statement, CHADD's press release is available at www.chadd.org/
press.cfm?cat_id=10&subcat_id=29&press_year=2002&press_id=27.

Diagnosis. AD/HD is difficult to diagnose in children under five
years of age, and is typically more prominent in elementary school than
in later ages.[8] Some teachers may be too quick to recommend a school
behavioral evaluation which would set into motion an unneeded stig-
matizing process and involve your child's school records. A child may
be active, but it doesn't mean that he or she has AD/HD. Many parents
who have gone through the evaluation process can sense beforehand
when something is *definitely* wrong with their child's behavior. Go with
your feelings. If in doubt, one solution is to have your child evaluated
privately, then decide what to do.

Although medical evidence is gathering that AD/HD has a neurological basis, its existence in a person is determined through criteria
established in the *Diagnostic and Statistical Manual of Mental Disorders, Fourth Edition, Text Revision (DSM-IV-TR)* published in 2000.
Tests typically gather systematic and quantitative information to be
used with the DSM criteria. Subjective rating forms or rating scales are
questionnaires about behavior filled out by teachers and parents.
A continuous performance task (CPT) measures attention to a task,
such as responding to a number appearing on a screen over 10 minutes.
The *DSM-IV-TR* diagnostic criteria are reprinted in Silver's *The Misunderstood Child* and reviewed in "Attention Deficit/Hyperactivity
Disorder," by Mary Fowler, available at www.ldonline.org/ld_indepth/
add_adhd/add_nichcy.html.

The *DSM* diagnostic criteria have been criticized as vague and providing no quantitative guidelines on psychological test performance.[9]
Many tests quantifying attention, such as vigilance tests or reaction
time tests, are also controversial because it's not clear what is being
measured: perception, an accurate response, or the processes that link
perception to response. Indeed, *attention* itself is an interpretation of
the observer, not a diagnosis. Problems with attention are nonspecific,
and can result from issues of perception, emotion, or boredom. In contrast, attention-deficit is an issue of executing an appropriate response.

---

8   *Diagnostic and Statistical Manual of Mental Disorders*, p. 89.
9   David L. Wodrich, *Children's Psychological Testing: A Guide for Nonpsychologists*,
    3rd Edition (Baltimore: Paul H. Brookes Publishing, 1997), p. 290.

For these reasons, many diagnosticians have established their own preferences for determining the significance of symptoms. Silver's *The Misunderstood Child* and Barkley's *ADHD: Theory, Diagnosis, and Treatment* lecture (www.schwablearning.org/pdfs/2200_7-barktran.pdf) provide more extensive explanations on diagnostic issues. The American Academy of Pediatrics published diagnostic guidelines for clinicians, "Diagnosis and Evaluation of the Child with Attention-Deficit Hyperactivity Disorder (AC0002)," which is available at www.aap.org/policy/ac0002.html. "Inattentive AD/HD: Overlooked and Undertreated," by Mary Solanto is offered at www.schwablearning.org/articles.asp?r=683&g=1. Other sources of diagnostic information can be found at www.aboutourkids.org, www.chadd.org, www.ldonline.org, and www.schwablearning.org. Stephen Sands and Susan Schwartz provide some comparisons between AD/HD and nonverbal LD in "Nonverbal Learning Disabilities," available at www.aboutourkids.org/letter/mayjun00.pdf. Initial diagnostic efforts through brain scans are reviewed in a *Wall Street Journal* article, "Hyperactive or Just a Kid? New Tests Claim to Get Rid of the Guesswork," by Tara Parker-Pope (10 December 2002, page D1).

Gender differences. Boys tend to be diagnosed thrice as often as girls because boys, in general, are more difficult to manage. In *Understanding Girls with AD/HD*, authors Kathleen Nadeau, Ellen Littman, and Patricia Quinn compare male and female AD/HD behavior patterns:

> "... male AD/HD patterns may be overemphasized because they are easier to observe. Girls, through biology and socialization, tend to be less active, more compliant, and less aggressive .... Girls who are distracted, disorganized, quiet day dreamers receive less attention from parents and teachers than do boys who are more active, disruptive, and defiant."[10]

Girls are less likely to be diagnosed for the primary problem of AD/HD and more likely to be diagnosed for secondary problems of anxiety, depression, or LD. Many reasons exist for misdiagnosis:

• Teachers may overlook social withdrawal, disorganization, and inconsistent performance in a coed class; parents of female students with AD/HD will more often notice subtle symptoms by comparing their daughters to other girls.[11]

---

10   Kathleen G. Nadeau, Ellen B. Littman, and Patricia O. Quinn, *Understanding Girls with AD/HD* (Silver Spring, Maryland: Advantage Books, 1999), p. 18. Copyright © by Advantage Books. Reprinted with permission of Kathleen Nadeau.

11   Nadeau, Littman, and Quinn citing 1991 McGee and Feehan study, p. 22.

•   Tests may be biased toward detecting evidence of male AD/HD. For example, of the 59 items listed on the *Connors Teachers Rating Scale—Revised (L)*, 23 items described typical *externalized* male behaviors (hyperactivity, impulsivity, defiance) and only seven items described typical *internalized* female behaviors (depression, timidity, anxiety).[12]

•   Girls, who are usually more verbally competent than boys, also have a lesser degree of executive function disorders.[13] Executive function development is linked to language competence.

Eligibility for special education. AD/HD is mentioned as a disability under the IDEA category of *other health impaired*:

> "*Other health impairment* means having limited strength, vitality or alertness, including a heightened alertness to environmental stimuli, that results in limited alertness with respect to the educational environment, that—
>
> (i) Is due to chronic or acute health problems such as … attention deficit disorder or attention deficit hyperactivity disorder … and
>
> (ii) Adversely affects a child's educational performance."
>
> *—34 CFR § 300.7 (c) (9)*

Matthew Cohen offers more information on eligibility criteria in "What You Need to Know About AD/HD under the Individuals with Disabilities Education Act," available at www.ldonline.org/ld_indepth/legal_legislative/q_and_a_idea99.html. Children with AD/HD may also be eligible if they meet the meet the criteria for *specific learning disability* (covered in Chapter 3) or *serious emotional disturbance*, defined in IDEA:

> "*Emotional disturbance* is defined as follows:
>
> (i) The term means a condition exhibiting one or more of the following characteristics over a long period of time and to a marked degree that adversely affects a child's educational performance:
>
> (A) An inability to learn that cannot be explained by intellectual, sensory, or health factors.
>
> (B) An inability to build or maintain satisfactory interpersonal relationships with peers and teachers.
>
> (C) Inappropriate types of behavior or feelings under normal circumstances.

---

12   Nadeau, Littman, and Quinn, p. 21.
13   Nadeau, Littman, and Quinn citing 1997 Seidman study, pp. 44-45.

(D) A general pervasive mood of unhappiness or depression.

(E) A tendency to develop physical symptoms or fears associated with personal or school problems.

(ii) The term includes schizophrenia. The term does not apply to children who are socially maladjusted, unless it is determined that they have a serious emotional disturbance.

—34 CFR § 300.7 (c) (4)

Cause. AD/HD appears to have no single cause which may explain the variety of responses to any single medication. Hyperactivity and restless sleep can occur together in an individual.[14] Brain studies have identified biochemical, structural, and activity differences between the brains of normal people and those in whom AD/HD has been identified. Different mechanisms appear to underlie AD/HD and involve the prefrontal cortex, the basal ganglia, the cerebellum, or the brain chemicals, norepinephrine and dopamine. Structures enabling behavioral self-control are located in these brain regions. Sources of these problems are:[15]

Familial factors of heritability, different genes involved	80%
Prenatal injury: cigarette and alcohol exposure, birth complications	10–15%
Postnatal brain injury from head trauma	3–5%

AD/HD is caused neither by diet nor bad parenting,[16] but "family, school, and peer influences are … crucial in determining the extent of impairments" and the development of other disorders.[17] Sal Mannuzza reviews studies on adolescents and adults with AD/HD in "Long-Term Outcome of Attention-Deficit/Hyperactivity Disorder," available at www.aboutourkids.org/articles/long_term_outcome_adhd.html. For more information refer to Chapter 21 or the Resources Section. CHADD (Children and Adults with Attention Deficit Disorder) offers brief *fact sheets* at www.chadd.org/webpage.cfm?cat_id=24.

---

14 Ronald D. Chervin, Kristen Hedger Archbold, James E. Dillon, Parviz Penahi, Kenneth J. Pituch, Ronald E. Dahl, and Christian Guilleminault, "Inattention, Hyperactivity, and Symptoms of Sleep-Disordered Breathing," *Pediatrics,* 3 March 2002, p. 455.

15 Barkley, "ADHD: Theory, Diagnosis, and Treatment," p. 27.

16 Barkley, "ADHD: Theory, Diagnosis, and Treatment," p. 31.

17 *Diagnostic and Statistical Manual of Mental Disorders,* p. 90.

I waited until my mid-thirties before having my first child and felt very confident that I was ready for motherhood when my son was born. I am in the health care profession and treat many children in my practice and that fact reassured me, but perhaps gave me false confidence. Unfortunately, so much about parenting cannot be formally taught.

The first few years of Kyle's life were fairly typical. He was a very happy, giggly baby/toddler. I nursed him for five months and we bonded well, at least I thought. Before he could even walk, I had him involved in play groups with children of various friends of mine. At that time, he seemed to socialize well, though he did have trouble separating when it was time to go home.

Our pediatrician recommended that I start him in a "therapeutic" type of toddler group at age two because he was not talking very much. That turned out to be a very intense experience for me. The emphasis of this group was on getting kids to express their feelings. That was all well and good, but the method they used required me to take him to his toddler group sessions twice a week. I, as his primary caretaker, had to take him—not dad, not nanny.

I also had to attend a weekly counseling session addressing what were perceived to be my son's needs. I think the main purpose of the latter was to lay a heavy guilt trip on me because I was a "working mom." I should also note here that in order to maintain this schedule, I started working straight nights in order to keep myself available "for my son." This became a strain in itself while I was still trying to work full-time, but I was determined to do what I was led to believe was the best thing for Kyle. But in any event, I did get to spend some regular quality time with him.

Often, I would come straight home after working all night at the hospital, get my son and go straight to toddler group, and try to keep going until early afternoon when I could grab a couple of hours of sleep when the nanny came in, then get up for dinner, try to stay up long enough to put him to bed, and then grab another hour of sleep before I went back to work. Needless to say, eventually chronic fatigue began to set in and I started to wear myself out. Finally, I, the physician, "the healer," the mom (remember, moms are never allowed to get sick), started getting sick and chronically debilitated with new onset asthma. When my son's behavior started getting increasingly bizarre, I became convinced that somehow this behavior was my fault because, although I was there, I was so often not available to him as I was struggling so hard just to breathe.

In any event, Kyle did seem to progress well at toddler group, which he continued through his preschool years. His verbal skills began developing quickly after he really started talking (around age three). He began reading without difficulty and his vocabulary grew rapidly, far above the expectations for his age. He never really did learn to express his feelings well though.

Somewhere between ages three and four however, his whole demeanor seemed to change. He started to exhibit unusual physical behavior, like head bobbing, arm flapping, and eye rolling, whenever he felt uncomfortable in a situation. He became increasingly withdrawn, sullen, and serious. Generally speaking, he became a very somber child. Even in photographs taken of him after age three, there was an obvious difference. This giggly, happy-go-lucky child suddenly started taking life so seriously, and consequently there were no further pictures of him smiling, not to mention laughing. Don't get me wrong, with some effort I could get him to laugh, but that was no longer his "natural state" as it had been before. Strangely enough, he developed a very mature, dry, sarcastic sense of humor which his teachers from kindergarten through second grade commented on repeatedly in a pleasingly, surprised way.

Kyle developed strange idiosyncrasies. He had almost a photographic memory when it came to his areas of interest, which included things like dinosaurs and sea creatures, and gradually expanded to include almost all of the animal kingdom. He became more and more drawn to solitary and sedentary activities. He was not at all athletically inclined, but did enjoy watching television, playing video and computer games, and also drawing. His art work improved dramatically and it soon became a very effective means of calming him down when he would get agitated. He especially got very skilled at drawing animals, but seemed to have a penchant for drawing scarier creatures like vicious dinosaurs, dragons, and various types of monsters.

Because of his interest in animals (and apparent lack of interest in people), I put him in a horseback riding camp where he seemed to flourish as soon as he realized that he could control these animals that were so much bigger than himself. He developed quite a rapport with his horse and at the same time, acquired a great degree of confidence as he learned that he could gain some expertise in an area that others admired. He actually won a few ribbons for his riding. Though he never outwardly showed much excitement, I could tell that he was very proud of them.

Kyle started becoming more easily distracted by minutia. Small details would attract his attention inappropriately, even if something important was going on simultaneously. He would end up playing with little things and get fully absorbed so that his teacher would have trouble redirecting his attention.

Other behavior became increasingly noticeable, especially in school. He began having periods when he would sort of "zone out," particularly when he was involved in situations that he didn't really care for. In those settings, he would start with arm flapping and head rolling and then progress to rocking his whole body. He would physically invade other people's space and consequently other kids would pull away from him. That fact, however, never seemed to bother him. His behavior became increasingly disruptive in the classroom. Other kids wanted to move their seats away from him. Finally, it got to the point that the teacher and I had to concentrate on modifying that behavior before we could even begin to focus on his academic performance.

Now unfortunately, all of these manifestations occurred with the backdrop of considerable domestic turmoil. His father and I were having escalating disagreements, including a lot of differences of opinion regarding our son. As far as his father was concerned, there was nothing "wrong" with his son. I, on the other hand, didn't know exactly what was going on, but I recognized the fact that there was a reason for concern and something more needed to be done—the question was what. In addition to his parents being at odds with each other, there were also the complications of a new baby sister and an acute change in nannies on the home front. These events occurred when he was around five years old, and by age seven (in second grade) his behavior had escalated to the point that I requested outside help for him. Consequently, I had Kyle put in individual counseling, thinking that much of his inappropriate behavior and inattention had to do with him not dealing well with what was going on at home.

Counseling seemed to help only minimally, and it was getting increasingly more difficult to manage him and keep him on task. Most of third grade was spent trying to get his physical behavior (i.e., arm flapping, head rolling, inability to hold still at times) under control. With a concerted effort, his teacher and I, using a tracking system punctuated with positive rewards for acceptable actions, were able to pretty much get his body movements down to a nondisruptive, socially-acceptable level.

But then math became a serious problem—it got to the point where both he and I dreaded homework time. I couldn't understand why a kid who was so bright in other areas seemingly couldn't even grasp the simplest of math concepts. Almost inevitably, math homework sessions would end with him crying, screaming, breaking pencils, tearing up papers and saying "I'll never be able to get this, just do it for me!" Of course, I couldn't "just do it" for him, another concept that at the time he couldn't grasp. This became increasingly frustrating for both him and me. I even tried a tutorial service thinking that he might respond better to someone other than me. It soon became apparent that I was wasting their time and my money because he would get to the tutorial sessions and then just tune them out. He was still in counseling at that time, but there seemed to be nothing that we could do that would motivate him. Even trying to be a strict disciplinarian didn't help and sometimes made matters worse. When he decided not to cooperate, nothing, not stripping him of privileges, not promising rewards, nothing seemed to work to get him going. By age eight, I had a stubborn little rebel on my hands who was content being left alone most of the time.

Of course to the outside world, I was just a weak mother who obviously had not taken control over her son. There was no way I could possibly explain, nor did I feel it necessary, that things were not that simple. Kyle just didn't respond in a typical fashion, for reasons that were unknown at that time. Also, by this time his father had left our household, which also left me in the precarious position of trying to work with my son, manage the household, take care of his younger sister, and still work full time (not to mention dealing with my own worsening health issues) all by myself. Needless to say, by the time his school came to me near the end of his third grade year, suggesting that he be evaluated for autism based on the observations they had made of him during the school year, I was almost relieved. I knew that something had to be done, and I was nearing my wit's end.

That summer, I had him evaluated by a child psychologist and he was diagnosed with "Asperger's syndrome." People were very concerned that I would be distressed that my son was now carrying such a diagnosis. In actuality, I considered it a blessing because finally I could see some potential for help for both him and me.

Some, including his pediatrician, and certainly his father, were not readily convinced about the diagnosis. Evidently, one of the main hallmarks of the syndrome is an inability to establish and maintain relationships. My son seemingly had established friendships that dated back as far as toddler group days. But when these relationships were analyzed, they were all "Mommy driven" and maintained. Most of them were kids of my friends and though he enjoyed playing with them, and didn't want to leave once he was playing, he rarely expressed interest in initiating contact himself. As I said before, he was perfectly content by himself. Also by this time his younger sister was expressing her own personality (age three) and was totally different, very talkative and very sociable. The juxtaposition of her against her brother made her brother's behavior seem even more aberrant.

Now finally with this diagnosis, help became available on several fronts. He now was eligible for all sorts of assistance, including being put in a special needs class for math and getting modified testing environments for standardized tests. (Before modifications, he would get to the middle of a test and get distracted. Then, when his attention was called back to finishing the test, he would just haphazardly fill in answers without even reading the questions because he just didn't care.) An aide worked with him during the day to help keep him organized and focused, and provided a constant communication link between school and home. He also had a very detailed IEP (Individualized Education Plan), which included a whole team of providers including the teachers, counselors, occupational therapists (to help with his atrocious handwriting and fidgeting in class, like special seat cushions, weighted vests, and little gizmos to keep his fingers occupied), speech therapists, and even the principal.

Later I found out that our particular public school system was very well staffed with a wealth of resources. In further investigations, I learned that public schools generally had more adaptive resources than private schools—which at first surprised me because I guess I assumed that if you were paying for it, anything should be available. In actuality, the private schools often end up referring children with "special needs" to the public school system for special services. Public schools must provide services for "handicapped" children by law.

So now my son has all of these services in place. In addition I got him involved in a "socialization" group with kids of his age level and similar "lack of socialization skills," all under the auspices of a child psychologist. Kyle has been involved with this group for a couple of years now, and has become comfortable in it. It is a "kid driven" group where the kids discuss their own issues and the psychologist merely facilitates the discussion. The kids actually get advice from their peers, to which for the most part, they are quite receptive. There are even summer out-of-town camping trips with this psychologist, which provide a therapeutic environment for the kids to learn how to interact appropriately with other kids. The older kids watch out for the younger kids. My son really enjoyed this experience when he was almost 11 years old. He reportedly did very well and even won an award for being the most "cooperative camper" in his group (which came as a pleasant shock to me). The next year he went back again to this summer camp and enjoyed it, but decided afterwards that that was enough.

As he gets older, Kyle is learning to act more appropriately across the board. His IQ tests have scored him in normal range and he still excels in the life sciences. He even won the Science Olympiad award for his middle school in sixth grade. Math is coming slowly, but we're making steady progress. The household has been greatly defused since he's been in the modified math class. He is able to learn appropriate social behavior, though it doesn't seem to come naturally. He's getting better at little things like looking people in the eye when talking to them and not abruptly walking away in the middle of a conversation. He still doesn't consider these courtesies important but he understands that other people do, and if he wants to get the desired reaction from other people it's necessary to "play the game." Sometimes he just doesn't feel like playing and doesn't care about the consequences. I've been told that this will probably continue to some extent his whole life.

I will consider my job done if I can just get him through school successfully and help him find his niche so that he can become a contributing member of society. He'll have to take it from there. And I know that may not seem like much, but there was a time when I wasn't sure if that would be possible. Now at least, I can see some light at the end of the tunnel.

Asperger's syndrome (AS) is new to U.S. mental health professionals and educators; it first appeared in *DSM-IV* (1994) and is now described in *DSM-IV-TR* (2000). The disorder is named after an Austrian physician, Hans Asperger, who, in 1944, published findings on children with normal intelligence and language ability but poor communication and social skills. People with Asperger's syndrome exhibit an unawareness of nonverbal social cues and conventional rules for conversation. Self-monitoring is limited.[18] The prevalence of the disorder is unknown, but it is diagnosed at least five times more in males than in females.[19] The criteria are available at:

- "Asperger's Disorder Homepage," by R. Kaan Ozbayrak, M.D. available at www.aspergers.com. This web site also provides information on treatment and medical specialists.
- Asperger-Syndrome.com by Ben, is available at www.asperger-syndrome.com. This British-based site offers "friendly" information for both adults and children.

Stephen Sands and Susan Schwartz provide some comparisons between AS and other nonverbal disorders in "Nonverbal Learning Disabilities," available at www.aboutourkids.org/letter/mayjun00.pdf.

Mental retardation is unusual in those with Asperger's disorder or syndrome. Asperger's syndrome is not associated with cognitive delays in early childhood, but it is a lack of social reciprocity like a one-sided conversation. In contrast, autism has a pattern of developmental delays and social and emotional indifference. Like autism, however, children with AS persist in repeating certain behavior patterns and activities. Learning is difficult beyond favorite pursuits because of the social deficits (pleasing a teacher is not important) and limited interests (no interest means no reason to learn). A British study claims some

---

18 *Diagnostic and Statistical Manual of Mental Disorders*, p. 81.
19 *Diagnostic and Statistical Manual of Mental Disorders*, p. 82.

success in improving emotional sensitivity in children with AS with an experimental computer program.[20]

In children with AS, early childhood seems normal although some behavior may seem odd in retrospect. Toddlers may be described by parents as *talking* before *walking*.[21] Subtle social problems can exist before preschool, but once in school, peer difficulties highlight the problem, as with other learning disabilities. Adults may misinterpret the presence of verbal skills and the lack of social skills as disobedience (see Kohlberg's theory at the end of Chapter 8). Deficits also appear in language skills beyond concrete expression, nonverbal skills, and sometimes gross motors skills. Routines and familiar circumstances are preferred. Victimization and social isolation by others, and some later development of self-awareness can lead to anxiety and depression by adolescence.[22] One University of New Hampshire survey of middle-class mothers of children with Asperger's syndrome reported in 2002 that 94% of these students had been victimized by peers, 75% had been emotionally bullied, and peer shunning was common.[23]

The severity and pattern of the disorder varies in each individual. For example, media stories have lately appeared about students with AS having extraordinary math abilities, but the child in the profile has great difficulties in math. A person can be preoccupied with learning all aspects of a subject, reminiscent of a stereotypical absent-minded professor. Social interaction may consist of only simple answers to questions, respectfully spoken. A person with AS may sit quietly through family dinner conversation, then unexpectedly make an incisive relevant remark. A seemingly inattentive and overactive child can be misdiagnosed as having AD/HD, or it is possible for an individual to have both disorders. Adults with AS can be self-sufficient and productively employed.

Eligibility for special education. Asperger's syndrome is listed in *DSM-IV-TR* under Pervasive Developmental Disorders (PDD), a category that also includes autism and other disorders not currently well

---

20   M. Silver and P. Oakes, "Evaluation of a New Computer Intervention to Teach People with Autism or Asperger Syndrome to Recognize and Predict Emotions in Others," *Autism: The International Journal of Research and Practice* [Internet], September 2001, available from: http://www.ncbi.nlm.nih.gov/entrez/query.fcgi?cmd=Retrieve&db=PubMed&list_uids=11708589&dopt=Abstract

21   *Diagnostic and Statistical Manual of Mental Disorders*, p. 81.

22   *Diagnostic and Statistical Manual of Mental Disorders*, p. 82.

23   L. Little, "Middle-class Mothers' Perceptions of Peer and Sibling Victimization Among Children with Asperger's Syndrome and Nonverbal Learning Disorders," *Issues in Comprehensive Pediatric Nursing* [Internet], January-March 2002, available from: http://www.ncbi.nlm.nih.gov/entrez/query.fcgi?cmd=Retrieve&db=PubMed&list_uids=11934121&dopt=Abstract

understood. Often, Asperger's syndrome has been called *high-function-ing autism.* Children with autism are eligible for special education:

> "*Autism* means a developmental disability significant-ly affecting verbal and nonverbal communication and social interaction ... that adversely affects a child's educational performance. Other characteristics often associated with autism are engagement in repetitive activities and stereotyped movements, resistance to environmental change or change in daily routines, and unusual responses to sensory experiences."
>
> *—34 CFR § 300.7 (c) (1)*

The National Library of Medicine lists resources for general information and management tips (at http://medlineplus.gov, type in *Asperger's syndrome* in the white box and click on the *Search* button) and abstracts of research discoveries (at www.ncbi.nlm.nih.gov/entrez/query.fcgi, type in *Asperger's syndrome* in the white box following the words *Search PubMed for* and click on the *Go* button). To obtain articles and books, refer to "Frequently Asked Questions" at www.nlm.nih.gov/services/faq.html. More websites related to AS include the following:

- "Pervasive Developmental Disorder: Asperger Syndrome" (www.emedicine.com/ped/topic147.htm) is an updated, well-researched, comprehensive review of identification and treatment issues by physician James Brasic of the Johns Hopkins University School of Medicine.
- Asperger's Syndrome Parent Information Environment (www.aspie.org, requires registration) links to two articles. "The Little Professor Syndrome" by Lawrence Osborne, was published in *The New York Times* on 18 June 2000. "Struggling with Life: Asperger's Syndrome Makes Fitting In a Complicated Challenge" is the website article accompanying the ABC PrimeTime News broadcast of 26 October 2000. Alternatively, you can directly access these articles online. "Little Professor" can be purchased for a nominal fee at http://query.nytimes.com/gst/abstract.html?res=F20811FE3F5A0C7B8DDDAF0894D8404482. "Struggling with Life" is available at http://abcnews.go.com/onair/2020/Primetime_001026_aspergers_feature.html.
- Asperger Syndrome Education Network or ASPEN (www.aspennj.org) links to local support groups and related web sites.
- www.tonyattwood.com links to international resources.

Cause. The cause is unknown. Asperger's syndrome seems to occur more frequently in family members of individuals with the disorder.[24] Some unusual findings of brain anatomy have been reported.[25] Brain imaging studies have shown unusual brain patterns in which faces elicit the same response as an inanimate object,[26] and emotions on faces did not activate normal brain processing areas.[27]

---

24 *Diagnostic and Statistical Manual of Mental Disorders*, p. 82.

25 G.M. McAlonan, E. Daly, V. Kumari, H.D. Critchley, T. Van Amelsvoort, J. Suckling, A. Simmons, T. Sigmundsson, K. Greenwood, A. Russell, N. Schmitz, F. Happe, P. Howlin, and D.G. Murphy, "Brain Anatomy and Sensorimotor Gating in Asperger's Syndrome," *Brain* [Internet], July 2002, available from: http://www.ncbi.nlm.nih.gov/entrez/query.fcgi?cmd=Retrieve&db=PubMed&list_uids=12077008&dopt=Abstract

26 R.T. Schultz, I. Gauthier, A. Klin, R.K. Fulbright, A.W. Anderson, F. Volkmar, P. Skudlarski, C. Lacadie, D.J. Cohen, and J.C. Gore, "Abnormal Ventral Temporal Cortical Activity During Face Discrimination Among Individuals with Autism and Asperger Syndrome," *Archives of General Psychiatry* [Internet], April 2000, available from: http://www.ncbi.nlm.nih.gov/entrez/query.fcgi?cmd=Retrieve&db=PubMed &list_uids=10768694&dopt=Abstract

27 H.D. Critchley, E.M. Daly, E.T. Bullmore, S.C. Williams, T. Van Amelsvoort, D.M. Robertson, A. Rowe, M. Phillips, G. McAlonan, P. Howlin, and D.G. Murphy, "The Functional Neuroanatomy of Social Behaviour: Changes in Cerebral Blood Flow When People with Autistic Disorder Process Facial Expressions," *Brain* [Internet], November 2000, available from: http://www.ncbi.nlm.nih.gov/entrez/query.fcgi?cmd=Retrieve&db=PubMed&list_uids=11050021&dopt=Abstract

Chapter Five

What is the relationship between intelligence and learning disabilities?

I am the product of two generations of teachers (including a father who specialized in psychological measurement, a.k.a. testing), and have a bachelor's degree in developmental psychology with an emphasis in early childhood development. My own elementary education was at a university lab school that espoused the "developmental" theory of education: don't push an arbitrary schedule of learning (e.g., children must read in first grade), instead nurture self-esteem and love of learning by having children experience success, and when the child is developmentally ready, she or he will learn much easier.) For me, this was great; I could move along very rapidly. For my very bright but dyslexic sister, it was a recipe for disaster. She spent hours matching sounds to letters and words with no improvement. I should have paid greater attention to the lesson my parents learned with my sister: to overcome learning disabilities, intervene early and often. It would have saved my son much grief.

Deke was the first grandchild in our family. Although he began to speak somewhat late, he was always considered very verbal. I have always loved reading and I wanted to pass that on to Deke. He was constantly read to. In early school he didn't sit still much. His favorite subjects were recess, physical education, music, art, and math. But he was well behaved. Our school district is generally considered one of the best in the country. The school and its highly regarded academic principal were huge proponents of a developmental education. Because I had experienced it personally as a child, I was much more comfortable with the concepts and practices than my parental peers.

In second grade, Deke was reversing most of his letters and numbers. Reading math symbols was quite difficult for him, but somehow he knew how to arrive at the correct answer. Because of my sister, this raised a red flag with me, and I informed the teacher of my concerns. She said not to worry, Deke was a bright little boy and it would all work out in time. At the time, several articles theorized that much of children's dyslexia was temporary and that many, if not most, children were dyslexic at some time in their early development. Midyear, there was an "acting out" incident, an obvious plea for help. But after a "talking to" by the principal and the social worker, nothing was done. Several months later, Deke was still not reading. I thought that maybe he was bored with the curriculum as I had been reading him "The Lion, the Witch and the Wardrobe." In desperation, I worked with the local librarian to find joke books that were fun to read but still at his level.

Deke was always a whiz at math and this accomplishment seemed to distract teachers from the fact that he was reading well below his grade level. In fifth grade, he had a wonderful male teacher who inspired him and got him to read the "Redwall" series of books. My husband and I breathed a sigh of relief. Finally, Deke was really reading! He even got a poem published in a book of sixth-grade work. Still, he never really liked reading.

By eighth grade, the reading workload had increased and Deke was again struggling and getting C's in language arts. But he was an A-student in the district's accelerated math program. (In the sixth grade, he scored 660 on the math portion of the SAT.) He took high school algebra in seventh and geometry in eighth grade. His new advisor suggested testing. "Eureka!" I thought. Now we would discover why Deke was such a slow reader. Unfortunately, the test showed him on the "low end of normal." The school could do nothing, they said. He could receive no special help from the school district because he "passed" their evaluation.

Fast forward to the end of junior year in one of the country's best public high schools. Academics are at the college level. Deke scored 5's on college advanced placement (AP) tests in math and statistics in his junior year. He took four AP classes in his senior year. He received an 800 on the math SAT II. He excelled in music and sports as well. But the issue of Deke's low grades in English and Spanish and his ACT test scores caused concern during a meeting with his college counselor. Deke expressed the opinion that he just wasn't as smart as his friends. He admitted that he had not finished even one section of the ACT test, including math. The counselor suggested we have Deke tested for learning disabilities by an independent psychologist.

The private psychologist's report was both a relief and an eye opener. Deke performed exceptionally well in most areas, but his scores showed several very specific deficits in visual memory, alertness to details, processing speed, and cognitive fluency. These are highly correlated with dyslexia, exactly the same diagnosis that his aunt received 35 years ago. The psychologist judged his learning disabilities as being "severe." At this late point in life, we can only hope to help him cope. For optimal outcomes, intervention should have occurred by age eight.

Deke is relieved to know why he struggles to read and to complete tests on time. He knows that it's not because he's "dumb." I'm sad that my son will never enjoy reading as much as I do. As parents, we are frustrated and angry that our "superior" school system was unable and unwilling to help us discover our son's learning problems.

To anyone reading this account, I offer a summary of lessons learned:

1. There is no single "optimal" way that all children learn. If your school's method doesn't work for your child, find another.

2. Trust your instincts. You know your child better than anyone else. Even very good, wealthy school districts have limited resources. If necessary, have private testing done to get a diagnosis. Once you have a diagnosis, a range of options open.

3. Don't wait. There may be "windows of opportunity" for correcting certain learning problems. Just as we know that young children are more open to learning languages, so are they more open to adaptive learning strategies that can at least greatly ameliorate disabilities.

4. With learning disabilities, what is wrong and how to help are not always clear. You must be your child's advocate. Don't give up.

What is intelligence?

Generally speaking, intelligence is a trait involving learning, memory, comprehension, and problem solving. For example, *visual thinking* is analyzing spatial relationships, synthesizing them, and determining whether some action is possible. Many different theories of intelligence exist; no definition of intelligence is universally accepted. One theory hypothesizes that a general factor of intelligence, g, is measured by a composite IQ score because people tend to perform similarly in both the verbal and nonverbal components of the IQ test.

Evolutionary psychologists hypothesize that intelligence is a set of many specialized mental processes, reflected in the brain's modular organization and evident in the wide variety of human talents. The best-known in this group is multiple intelligence theory by Harvard's Howard Gardner. Originally conceived as seven multiple intelligences—linguistic, logical-mathematical, spatial, musical, bodily-kinesthetic, interpersonal, and intrapersonal—Gardner has added an eighth intelligence, naturalist, and proposes two more:

spiritual and existential. Each intelligence has a schedule of normal development and its own forms of perception, memory, thinking processes, coded symbol systems, and problem-solving or expression within a cultural context. Each intelligence also works independently or in concert with one another. Impairments in one system do not necessarily mean impairments to another system.

Another conceptual model states that intelligence cannot be measured until it materializes to modify a real-life situation. Individuals who capitalize on their strengths and compensate for their weaknesses demonstrate adaptiveness, itself an intelligent behavior.

Indeed, how the mind works remains an open question, making any intelligence theory difficult to prove. Speech-to-text and text-to-speech technologies have been cited as examples of artificial intelligence, which involves pattern recognition, automatic learning, and natural-language comprehension, among other capabilities.[1] Some researchers are considering experiments to test the idea that "the brain works by anticipating and completing patterns."[2] Such work could explain such phenomena like practice, experience, and intuition.

Intelligence or aptitude testing

About 100 years ago, Alfred Binet developed tests to identify French children who would have difficulties in primary school, with the purpose of helping these children. Soon thereafter in the United States, Lewis Terman and colleagues at Stanford University adapted Binet's tests for U.S. schools with new statistical measurements. In 1916, the Stanford-Binet test was introduced as a simple, inexpensive, 50-minute method to select students with the best potential for higher academic work. These IQ (or *intelligence quotient*) tests, based mostly on language and math abilities, have become controversial measures of intelligence. (Although different measurement scales exist, for general reference, an IQ below 70 is regarded as mentally retarded, around 100 is average, above 130 is gifted, and above 150 is genius.)

Intelligence testing has been contested on cultural, racial, gender, and economic grounds, and varies in each state. For such reasons, since 1979 in California, the courts have banned IQ testing of African American children even if parents have given permission for the evaluation. However, one African American mother has charged discrimination because the absence of intelligence testing prevented her son from receiving special education services; a similar case in

---

1   Ray Kurzweil, "Artificial Intelligence" [Internet], accessed 14 April 2002 from: http://www.kurzweilai.net/brain/frame.html

2   Pui-Wing Tam, "From Chips to Neurons: Palm's Inventor Sets His Sights on the Brain," *The Wall Street Journal*, 20 November 2001, p. B1.

Illinois in 1980 found that IQ testing did not discriminate against African American children.[3] David Wodrich, author of *Children's Psychological Testing*, suggests that appropriate use of IQ tests will resolve this controversy.[4] (Chapter 13 reviews the use of intelligence tests to establish a *discrepancy* when evaluating learning disabilities.) Perhaps it's a bit of a stretch to utilize Binet's predictive test of school performance as the basis for measuring intelligence in the first place. Binet himself cautioned against the misuse of and exclusive dependence on a simple numerical score for estimating a child's abilities.[5] In a 1968 study of high IQ participants in the longitudinal Terman Study of Gifted Children, "confidence, persistence and early parental encouragement" distinguished high from low achievers.[6]

In Western societies, the measurement of intelligence "is very dependent on verbal skill," leaving students with language disabilities at a disadvantage on IQ tests.[7] American teaching practices assume that the most important intelligence is characterized by language, memory, and analytical skills.[8] In truth, IQs may be really measuring how well one has learned to read and write,[9] both of which require the integration of many different subskills.

Be aware of what you hear and read. Some who can speak and write well may maintain that those with superior language abilities are most intelligent. Less is heard and read about the high intelligence of singers who have held entire audiences spellbound, or athletes who have rallied a team to victory in grueling worldwide competitions. Still, verbal skills are important for social communication, but what is being communicated? Wit is not the same as wisdom. Sophistry, like bad statistics, can cause trouble. Joseph Epstein, author, essayist, editor, and professor at Northwestern University has pondered the function and use of language:

> "To be well-spoken is a great advantage in life but scarcely an unfailing sign of high intelligence, let alone thoughtfulness. Demosthenes, the most famous orator of Athens, a city-state with the greatest

---

3   Wodrich, *Children's Psychological Testing*, p. 315.

4   Wodrich, p. 316.

5   Susan M. Baum, Steve V. Owen, and John Dixon, *To Be Gifted & Learning Disabled* (Mansfield Center, Connecticut: Creative Learning Press, 1991), p. 13.

6   Mitchell Leslie, "The Vexing Legacy of Lewis Terman," *Stanford Magazine*, July/August 2000, p. 51.

7   From Bender, William *Learning Disabilities*, 2/e © 1995. Published by Allyn and Bacon, Boston, MA. Copyright © 1995 by Pearson Education. Reprinted/adapted by permission of the publisher.

8   Cynthia Crossen, "Think You're Smart? Then Just Try to Sell a New Kind of IQ Test," *The Wall Street Journal*, 5 June 1997, p. A13.

9   Bruce Bower, "IQ's Evolutionary Breakdown," *Science News*, 8 April 1995, p. 221.

oratorical tradition in the history of civilization, was always brilliant but often wrong, and in his most important speeches decisively wrong. (Recommending war with Philip of Macedon was, to put it gently, a major historical error.) To be ungrammatical doesn't impugn a person's integrity; nor is a faulty metaphor a sign of bad character. To stammer while struggling to get at the truth is much to be preferred to seamlessly smooth lying."[10] [Reprinted by permission of *The Wall Street Journal*, Copyright © (2001) Dow Jones & Company, Inc. All Rights Reserved Worldwide. License number 712051294784.]

While IQ or aptitude tests can predict school performance, they "are only an indifferent predictor of performance in a profession after formal schooling."[11] Moreover, the people who perform well on ability tests are generally those who work easily with textbooks and excel on achievement tests because these items are produced by the same companies, observes Robert Sternberg, Director of the Center for the Psychology of Abilities, Competencies, and Expertise (PACE Center) at Yale.[12] According to Stephen Ceci, a Cornell University professor of developmental psychology, motivation and personality are more important for life success than intelligence.[13] Until the issues surrounding the meaning and measurement of intelligence are resolved, the more practical questions may be about the purposes of education. For example, a liberal arts-based education demands proficient language use; technological advancement requires state-of-the-art math and science instruction.

The SAT I has been used as part of the culling process for college admissions. As seen in other IQ tests, language difficulties can downgrade scores. The Scholastic Aptitude Test (SAT), familiar to baby-boomers, was renamed in the early 1990s as the Scholastic Assessment Test (SAT), then redesigned and renamed yet again in the mid 1990s as SAT, not an acronym for anything. The SAT I labels itself a *reasoning test*. (The SAT II refers to a variety of *subject tests* such as math, literature, writing, history, biology, and chemistry.) In contrast, the ACT (pronounced "A-C-T") Assessment more closely examines high school preparation, but with no consideration of the quality of a student's teacher, course content, textbooks, or state curriculum standards.

---

10 Joseph Epstein, "Going Without the Flow: Inarticulacy, uh, Reconsiderated," *The Wall Street Journal*, 26 January 2001, p. W13.

11 Howard Gardner and Joseph Walters citing Jencks' 1972 finding, "A Rounded Version," *Multiple Intelligences: The Theory in Practice* (New York: BasicBooks, 1993), p. 14.

12 Crossen, "Think You're Smart? Then Just Try to Sell a New Kind of IQ Test," p. A13.

13 Crossen, p. A13.

Perhaps reflected in the various name changes over the years, the validity of the SAT I's verbal section has been widely criticized for inherent socioeconomic biases. Richard Atkinson—a testing expert, psychology professor, and President of the University of California (UC)—proposed in 2001 that the SAT I be replaced by a better test in its undergraduate admission requirements. Having been appointed by the National Academy of Sciences in 1993 to investigate testing, Atkinson concluded that the SAT I was more of a size measurement of one's vocabulary[14] and less of an indicator of one's high school preparation for college.[15] (UC, with nine undergraduate campuses, is the largest user of the SAT I.)

In response, the College Board (www.collegeboard.com) announced a new SAT I format beginning in March 2005:

• The verbal section, worth 800 points, will be rechristened *critical reading*, replace verbal analogies with short reading passages, and retain current long reading passages.

• The math section, worth 800 points, will add higher-level algebra to the present basic algebra and geometry material.

• A new writing section, also worth 800 points, will include multiple-choice grammar questions and an essay requirement based on the SAT II Writing Test.

Thus, the SAT I will increase by 30 minutes to 3-1/2 hours, be worth a possible 2400 points instead of 1600 points, and perhaps create still more controversy over essay evaluations. (One suggestion is to emulate law and medical school applications processes, and send unscored essays to the prospective institution. Then the admissions office would not only be able to evaluate a student's writing ability, but also validate whether the student prepared the other essays in his or her application.) Atkinson expects UC to accept the revised SAT I.[16]

This controversy apparently affected the ACT (www.act.org) as well. (In contrast to the SAT, which was initially based on aptitude testing, the ACT is designed to measure high school achievement in English, mathematics, reading, and science reasoning.) An optional ACT Writing Test will be added to the ACT Assessment beginning in the 2004–2005 school year. Chapters 24 and 26 have more information about standardized testing.

---

14 Tanya Schevitz, "SAT Is to Achievement as ...," *San Francisco Chronicle*, 13 May 2001, p, C5.

15 Russell Schoch, "UC to SAT: RIP," *California Monthly*, April 2001, p. 18.

16 Tanya Schevitz, "SATs Gain an Essay, Lose the Analogies," *San Francisco Chronicle*, 28 June 2002, p. A3.

In any population, individuals differ by degrees of intelligence, however defined and measured. It's simplistic to classify someone as either *smart* or *not smart*.

Similarly, no bright lines distinguish those with learning disabilities from those without learning disabilities as shown below in Figure 5.1. For example, research has found no clear distinctions between readers with LD and either slow learners or normal readers; however, limited public resources force arbitrary cutoff points for determining service eligibility.[17] Those who *make the eligibility cut* can be identified as having a learning disability and can receive special help. In addition, some children may have more than one disability such as a reading disability *and* AD/HD.

Figure 5.1

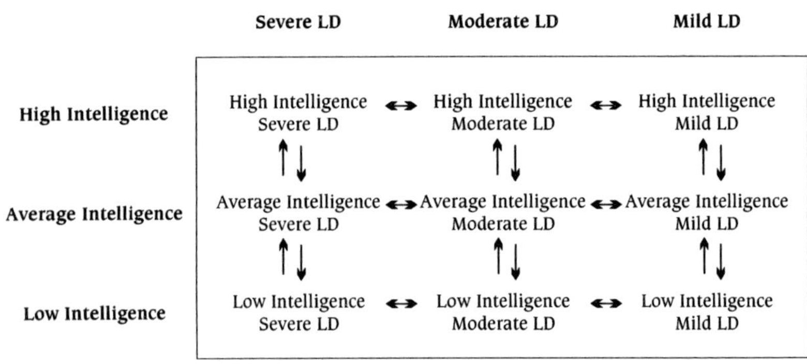

In summary, a range of abilities and disorders exist among individuals, disabilities being at the lower end of the spectrum. Children with IQs of 70 and below are identified early in life and so receive services from the school district; they may or may not have learning disabilities as well. By default, students placed in special education due to learning disabilities—usually of school age—will have average and above-average intelligence. Intelligence and learning disabilities are two different things.

---

17   G. Reid Lyon, "The State of Research," in *Learning Disabilities: Lifelong Issues*, ed. Shirley C. Cramer and William Ellis (Baltimore: Paul H. Brookes Publishing Co., 1996), pp. 25-26.

Learning disabilities and intelligence are separate issues although they affect one another. One-third of students identified as having learning disabilities also have gifted intelligence.[18] Gifted students with learning disabilities have been called *twice exceptional* and are often paradoxes to observers. These students *may*:

• Manipulate complex concepts like calculus but can't recall simple isolated facts like arithmetic.

• Have superior abilities in identifying underlying patterns and integrating them into global concepts and ideas,[19] but cannot organize their ideas into a linear presentation to others. Problems exist in sequencing specific thoughts to build the big picture, and in recalling isolated facts out of context.

• Have high creative potential but low academic success, resulting in more frustration, a poorer sense of competency, and a greater tendency toward misbehavior and vengeance for past insults than that observed in non-gifted students with learning disabilities.[20] Isaac Newton, for example, has been characterized by biographers as being reclusive and unforgiving. In school, bullies will zero in on students especially lacking in self-confidence and self-esteem.

• Have excellent oral abilities but poor reading, writing, and spelling skills.

Charles Schwab, founder of the first discount brokerage firm and a nonprofit parent information center, has a reading disability. In an interview, he explained how different kinds of thinking lead to different types of approaches to problems. "In my case, I knew I wasn't that smart, in English anyway. But I've always felt that I had very strong conceptual capabilities. I could imagine things much faster than some other people who were stuck thinking sequentially. That helped me in solving complicated business problems. I could visualize how things would look at the end of the tunnel."[21]

Identification issues. Psychological tests can reveal patterns of both gifted intelligence and learning disabilities. Additional information on student strengths is usually collected through records of achievements, observations, and interviews with the student and those who know the student well.

---

18   Baum, Owen, and Dixon, *To Be Gifted & Learning Disabled* p. 16.
19   Baum, Owen, and Dixon, p. 46.
20   Baum, Owen, and Dixon, p. 21.
21   Theresa Johnston, "Charles Schwab's Secret Struggle," STANFORD *Magazine*, published by Stanford Alumni Association, Stanford University, March/April, 1999, p. 73. Reprinted with permission of *Stanford Magazine*.

Twice exceptional students fall into three categories:[22]

• *Students identified as gifted but who also have subtle learning disabilities* have inconsistencies between *expected* and actual performance. For example, a mathematically talented student may receive a *C* in language arts, which for many teachers isn't a problem requiring psychoeducational testing. In elementary school, spelling, handwriting, memory, and organization problems may appear. In middle school, these students can have difficulties completing long-term writing and independent reading assignments. They become confused and depressed over their underachievement. (Parents should explore other causes of underachievement such as unrealistic expectations, boredom with an undemanding or irrelevant curriculum, social problems, poor motivation, or poor work habits.)

• *Unidentified students* have a high intellectual ability offset by their learning disability. Typically, they are seen as unexceptional students performing at grade level, and thus seldom referred for testing. Often, the gifted intelligence will emerge in a specific subject area, or in a non-traditional creative context like a design project or a school play.

• *Students with identified learning disabilities who are also gifted* are talented students at risk of failing school. Pessimistic outlooks and negative attitudes generate real feelings of inadequacy in sensitive students. Until the deficits are resolved, the giftedness is mostly ignored.

Education issues. Successful gifted students with learning disabilities perform exceptionally well in certain areas utilizing their identified strengths, commit to a particular interest or goal, devise compensating techniques when possible, and avoid specific areas requiring their identified weaknesses.[23] Many parents of gifted children with learning disabilities are frustrated with curriculums that cannot compensate weak areas and accelerate gifted areas simultaneously. Either the student is bored in a basic remedial curriculum, or the child faces unrealistic expectations in an honors program. For example, academic troubles can arise from accelerated studies that:[24]

• Heavily emphasize reading and writing, already an acknowledged weakness

• Presume the presence of organizational skills needed for independent study, and consequently provide inadequate structure and guidance to complete work

• Offer content not strongly connected to the student's specific interests or strengths

• Double the student's actual workload instead of substituting for a less-demanding course, for example, requiring a gifted student to fulfill

---

22 Baum, Owen, and Dixon, *To Be Gifted & Learning Disabled*, pp. 15-21.
23 Baum, Owen, and Dixon, p. 17.
24 Baum, Owen, and Dixon, p. 79.

elementary-level math curriculum requirements while concurrently enrolled in an accredited algebra course.

An ideal school solution simultaneously addresses academic giftedness and weaknesses, boredom and frustration in a positive peer environment. The arts and sports also offer discouraged students chances to shine. By being given opportunities to use a special talent in a highly visible way, a student will receive recognition from peers for a unique ability, and be further motivated to excel. A *Washington Post* article, "Students' Complicated Gifts" by Nurith Aizenman (published 22 June 2002) describes a model program in Maryland's Montgomery County public school system that places twice-exceptional students in regular gifted programs while simultaneously providing them special education services. Some other possible solutions:[25]

• A pull-out enrichment program provides opportunities to study a specific interest like computers; a variation of this is to embed high-level computer courses within special education classes in which students are at a high academic level. (*Pull-out* is described in Chapter 16.)

• Accelerated courses like an advanced placement course can coexist with less demanding or special education classes on a student's schedule.

• A schoolwide enrichment model offers students a wide variety of activity choices, rather than the student having to conform to a demanding but required activity; however, such choices may exist only in larger schools.

• Mentorships and internships provide individualized learning situations.

Parents unable to find the ideal school solution can cobble together a program by drawing on the resources of a larger community, perhaps even extending beyond the child's immediate locale through online learning. For example, Albert Einstein's intellectual development was nurtured by a mother who insisted on violin lessons, an uncle who taught him algebra, another uncle who provoked interest in the world beyond school, and a medical school acquaintance who recognized genius in the 13-year-old boy and brought him textbooks on physics, mathematics, and the philosophy of Immanuel Kant. Chapter 17 offers homeschooling information.

A science museum may suggest a bird-watching club; a telescope vendor may know of an astronomy study group; a college music department may have recommendations for private instruction. Behavioral issues like introversion, disorganization, and ill-timed comments or inquiries can be modified by encouraging positive group activities, planning, minimized clutter, and introspection. Many schools in

---

25 Baum, Owen, and Dixon, p. 81.

conjunction with local postsecondary institutions have established gifted programs. Many universities offer courses for precocious public, private, and homeschooled students, usually identified by unusually high performance on a standardized test, among them:

• Talent Identification Program (Duke University) 919/ 684-3847; www.tip.duke.edu

• Center for Talented Youth (The Johns Hopkins University) 410/ 516-0337; www.jhu.edu/~gifted

• Program for Talented Youth (Vanderbilt University) 615/ 322-8261; http://peabody.vanderbilt.edu/research_and_outreach/index.htm and click on *Vanderbilt Program for Talented Youth*.

• Midwest Talent Search (Northwestern University) 847/ 491-3782; www.ctd.northwestern.edu/programs/mts

• Rocky Mountain Talent Search (University of Denver) 303/ 871-2983; www.du.edu/education/ces/rmts.html

• Education Program for Gifted Youth (Stanford University) 650/ 329-9920 or 800/ 372-3749; www-epgy.stanford.edu

The Gifted Kids' Survival Guide: A Teen Handbook (Free Spirit Press, 1996) by Judy Galbraith and Jim Delisle lists additional resources and ideas for finding accelerated programs. ERIC Clearinghouse on Disabilities and Gifted Education (http://ericec.org or 800/ 328-0272 for voice and TTY) provides information on twice exceptional individuals.

Chapter Six

Will a learning disability prevent my child from succeeding in life?

"A good soldier is not made merely by making him think and work. There is something in every soldier that goes deeper than thinking or working—it's his 'guts.' It is something that he has built in there: it is a world of truth and power that is higher than himself."

—*George S. Patton*[1]

Learning disabilities are lifelong. Still, many people with LD have found their adult roles by gravitating toward careers and areas of study in which they could use their strongest talents and abilities. Difficult tasks were avoided through alternatives, delegated to someone else, or dispensed with altogether. Necessity is the mother of invention, and all these individuals found out-of-the-box alternatives to the more conventional pathways of success.

There are two sides to every coin. Individuals with learning disabilities can display characteristics with both negative and positive connotations. Examples are:

---

1   Carlo D'Este, *Patton: A Genius for War* (New York: HarperCollins Publishers, 1995), p. 686.

Negative trait	Positive trait
Noncompliant · · ·	Individualistic
Nonconforming · ·	Inventive
Stubborn · · · · ·	Persevering
Impulsive · · · · ·	Adventurous
Unfocused · · · · ·	Wide-ranging
Diverted · · · · · ·	Imaginative

A study of highly successful adults with learning disabilities identified a conscious decision to control their own destiny, defined goals, a will to succeed, adaptability, creativity, optimism, persistence, a supportive environment, and disciplined self-improvement.[2] A summary of a study by Marshall Raskind and Roberta Goldberg discusses the factors underlying life success in individuals with LD in "Positive Attitude Trumps IQ, Good Grades as Success Predictor for LD Adults" available at www.schwablearning.org/articles.asp?g=2&r=622.

Well-known people with learning disorders

Often, unusual accomplishments result from luck as well as ability —being at the right place at the right time. Many individuals with LD questioned conventional wisdom, recognized opportunities, and made extraordinary achievements. They knew their strengths, accepted their weaknesses, and moved on.

• **Richard Borcherds**, winner of the 1998 Fields Medal, the highest international honor in mathematics, has Asperger's syndrome.[3] He is a professor at the University of California at Berkeley. (The Fields Medal was first presented in 1936, and is awarded every four years by the International Mathematical Union to mathematicians not older than 40 "in recognition of work already done and as an encouragement for future achievements.")

• **Stephen Cannell**, Emmy Award winner, graduated from high school feeling "not very smart," and not realizing then that he had a reading disability. He recalls frustration from failing a history test despite long hours of study, while a friend barely glanced at the material and got an *A*. Cannell would register for extra college courses then selectively drop those with tough misspelling penalties. He worked relentlessly in his early writing career, if only to savor praise for his efforts. His ability to visualize, which "means nothing in school,"[4] has enabled him to create, write, and produce dozens of successful TV series, films,

---

2   Cecil D. Mercer citing study 1990 study by Gerber and Ginsberg, *Students with Learning Disabilities*, 4th Edition (New York: Macmillan Publishing Company, 1992), p. 401.

3   Ayala Ochert, "The Mathematical Mind," *California Monthly*, April 2002, p. 22.

4   Stephen J. Cannell, "A Writing Fool," *Newsweek*, 22 November 1999, p. 79.

and books. His biographies appear at www.cannell.com/biography/
bio_faq.htm.

• **John Chambers**, Chief Executive Officer of Cisco Systems, was
"laughed at for being a slow learner," which drove him to succeed. He
learned to compensate for reading difficulties by remembering nearly
all that he hears, and later received law and business degrees. At Cisco,
he expanded the business by emphasizing customer satisfaction; acquiring other companies; and integrating Internet technology, software
standards, and electronic message delivery into the first post-telephone
communication network. As CEO, he prefers one-page summaries or
short presentations.[5]

• **Fred Epstein** was dismissed by others as "dumb," found school
was absolute "torture," had chronic depression growing up, and was
rejected at every medical school he applied to. Still undaunted, he never
gave up his dream of becoming a physician, and through hard work and
"a lot of memorization" completed medical school. He became a pediatric neurosurgeon, pioneered techniques in spinal cord surgery and
brain stem tumors, and now runs the Institute for Neurology and Neu-
rosurgery in New York City as a mind as well as body healing center for
its young patients.[6]

• **Danny Glover**, producer, director, and star of theater, television,
and movie productions, among them *Lethal Weapon* and *Places in the
Heart*, also has trouble reading. He devotes much time to community
service, including Recording for the Blind & Dyslexic events, once re-
marking that he wishes that he had known about RFB&D when he was
a child.[7]

• **John (Jack) Horner** received many failing grades, and was told by
high school teachers that they wanted to flunk him except that they
didn't want to see him again.[8] Nevertheless, he was more curious about
science than concerned about passing classes. He later received a
MacArthur Foundation Award (informally known as *genius grants*) for
his discoveries in dinosaur paleontology. He is now a paleontologist at
the Museum of the Rockies at Montana State University. A summary of
his autobiography from *Succeeding with LD* by Jill Lauren is available
at www.west.net/~ger/JackHorner.html.

• **Paul Orfalea** had academic trouble through high school. His parents, however, never disparaged him, and only required that he converse intelligently. He majored in business; founded Kinko's Copies by

---

5   Andy Reinhardt, "Meet Mr. Internet," *Business Week*, 13 September 1999, pp. 134
    and 136.
6   Ted Koppel, "The Messenger," *Nightline*, ABC broadcast 4 January 2001, transcript
    prepared by Burrelle's Information Services, p. 2.
7   Recording for the Blind & Dyslexic, *Impact*, Spring/Summer 2000 newsletter, p. 1.
8   Jill Lauren, *Succeeding with LD: 20 True Stories About Real People with LD*
    (Minneapolis: Free Spirit Publishing, 1997), p. 20.

selling pens, pencils, notebooks, and copying services; and hired an employee to read to him.[9] Portions of his autobiography from *Succeeding with LD* by Jill Lauren are available at www.ldonline.org/first_person/orfalea.html.

• **Charles Schwab** remembers alphabet exercises as "demeaning,"[10] and used Classic Comic Books to help him through *Ivanhoe* and *A Tale of Two Cities*.[11] In college he focused on mathematics and economics, received a Stanford MBA, and later created the first discount brokerage. He and his wife launched the Schwab Foundation for Learning which supports information services on learning disorders, such as a website and medical research.

• **Larry Silver** was tied to his seat by his fifth-grade teacher, and had poor grades through junior high. Spelling was difficult, but he found word substitutions or wrote so tiny that the teacher could not find misspellings. However, he committed himself to academics during high school, and eventually became a professor of psychiatry at Georgetown Medical School, a former acting director of the National Institute of Mental Health, and author of numerous books, the writing of which has been eased with a word processor.[12]

Other sources with more examples

Dyslexia (1996) by Carol Sullivan Spafford and George S. Grosser refers to several individuals who were described as having social or learning problems during their lives. They include:[13]

• **Louisa May Alcott** was "awkward,"[14] impulsive, "strangely shy,"[15] and had a "stormy childhood"[16] "with moods of despondency,"[17] and "uncommon activity."[18] Her father's inability to handle money motivated Alcott, beginning at age 13, to become her family's chief means of support. Earning money for her stories also caused people to begin feeling "that 'topsy-turvy' Louisa would amount to something, after all."[19] She attended an unremarkable village school, but was tutored by Henry Thoreau and borrowed books from the library of Ralph Waldo Emerson.

---

9   Lauren, pp. 73-75.
10   Ann Marsh, "When the Alphabet is a Struggle," *Forbes*, 6 September 1999, p. 75.
11   Johnston, "Charles Schwab's Secret Struggle," p. 72.
12   Silver, *The Misunderstood Child*, pp. 377-378.
13   Spafford and Grosser, *Dyslexia*, pp. 26 and 70.
14   Marjorie Worthington, *Miss Alcott of Concord* (Garden City, New York: Doubleday & Company, 1958), p. 201.
15   Worthington, p. 121.
16   Worthington, p. 245.
17   Worthington, p. 220.
18   Worthington, p. 31.
19   Worthington, p. 73.

Although Alcott "never learned to spell very well" and "remained forever rather vague about figures"[20] her imagination and experiences fueled stories first for family and friends, then a Civil War audience, finally finding her niche with *Little Women* and other books for young readers. She sought serenity in order to write; an interruption would scatter her thoughts and she would have a hard time reassembling them.[21]

• **Ludwig von Beethoven** was unable to learn math beyond addition and, like his father, failed to make progress in school.[22] Cruelly bullied by his father during and outside of music lessons, the young boy became withdrawn but found expression in free fantasies on the clavier and violin. As school and friendships mattered little to Beethoven, music filled his time. In adolescence, music instructors and patrons drew him out from loneliness. As a 12-year-old, he began to work professionally, virtually becoming the head of the household, and later petitioned to be guardian of his father who had dissipated himself with drink. As an adult, Beethoven "was unquestionably depressed" with "suicidal thoughts" and "tempestuous mood swings."[23] Beethoven is remembered as one of history's greatest music composers, and created controversies by introducing deep flows of emotion into his work.

• **Michelangelo Buonarroti** had a brief grammar school education studying ancient Greece and Rome, but learned very little Latin and was truant.[24] Despite his misgivings, Michelangelo's father agreed that his son should train in design and painting. Though largely unschooled, Michelangelo became one of the greatest artists in history, creating heroic works of painting, sculpture, and architecture.

• **Winston Churchill** stuttered, did poorly in school, and had an unhappy boyhood. He entered the Royal Military College at Sandhurst after three attempts, but later graduated eighth out of a class of 150. He practiced writing with great effort as a young cavalry officer.[25] He became noted for his many abilities as a soldier, war reporter, author, speaker, social reformer, and painter. As one of the greatest statesmen in world history, Churchill foresaw the dangers of Nazi Germany, and heroically led Britain as Prime Minister with "blood, toil, tears, and sweat" during World War II.

• **Charles Darwin** wrote in his 1876 autobiography, "So poor in one sense is my memory, that I have never been able to remember for more

---

20 Worthington, p. 49.
21 Worthington, p. 231.
22 Maynard Solomon, *Beethoven* (New York: Schirmer Books, 1977), p. 20.
23 Marianne Szegedy-Mazak, citing interview with psychiatrist Richard Kogan, "The Sound of Unsound Minds," *U.S. News & World Report*, 13 January 2003, p. 46.
24 George Bull, *Michelangelo: A Biography* (New York: St. Martin's Press, 1995), pp. 10-11.
25 John Keegan, "His Finest Hour," *U.S. News & World Report*, 29 May 2000, p. 53.

than a few days a single date or a line of poetry."[26] Darwin believed his time in school studying the standard disciplines of his time as "wasted"[27] for "the first real training or education of my mind" was on his voyage of exploration aboard the *Beagle*.[28] Darwin reminisced that his "difficulty … in expressing [himself] clearly and concisely … had the compensating advantage of forcing [him] to think long and intently about every sentence" and to correct any errors of observation or reasoning.[29] Darwin's granddaughter noted how an example of his handwriting "shows how his thoughts jostled each other for priority, leading to additions and excisions."[30] He discovered that his most efficient writing method was not to think about how he would write a sentence before committing it to paper, but instead to "scribble in a vile hand whole pages"[31] quickly and then edit them afterward. He wrote many articles and books including the *Origin of Species* and *The Descent of Man*.

• **Thomas Edison** failed in school, was taught by his mother (a former teacher), and became a successful inventor, businessman, and philosopher. His exhaustive hands-on experimentation was impelled by his difficulties with rote learning. He received 1,093 U.S. patents and thousands more from other countries. His greatest invention though was the research laboratory itself.

• **Albert Einstein** was socially withdrawn as a child, began speaking at a late age, was not verbally fluent even at age nine, and even then responded "to questions only after consideration and reflection."[32] Einstein later in life acknowledged a weak memory especially for words, was bitter about his early schooling that emphasized rote learning, but knew that his self-study of math and physics had advanced him quite beyond his school's curriculum.[33] Nevertheless, school personnel told him they were pessimistic about his future,[34] and discouraged his father from selecting a profession for his son.[35] Einstein developed the theory of relativity and won the 1921 Nobel Prize in physics. When asked how this theory germinated, he replied that unlike normal adults who accept conventional notions of space and time, his childhood developmental differences led him "to wonder about space

---

26   Charles Darwin, *The Autobiography of Charles Darwin*, ed. Nora Barlow (New York: W.W. Norton & Company, 1958), p. 140.

27   Darwin, p. 58.

28   Darwin, p. 77.

29   Darwin, p. 136-137.

30   Nora Barlow, "Introduction," *The Autobiography of Charles Darwin* (New York: W.W. Norton & Company, 1958), ed. Nora Barlow, p. 14.

31   Darwin, p. 137.

32   Ronald W. Clark, *Einstein: The Life and Times* (New York: Avon Books, 1971), p. 27.

33   Banesh Hoffman, *Albert Einstein: Creator & Rebel* (New York: Plume, 1972), pp. 19-20.

34   Hoffman, p. 20.

35   Clark, *Einstein*, p. 27.

and time only when I had [already] grown up."[36] Perhaps the more difficult feat for Einstein was to explain his work in language accessible to others.[37]

• **Carl Jung** was timid, awkward, and bullied. He had psychosomatic fainting spells and behavioral problems, was predisposed to depression and imaginary friendships, and rather than compete with other boys for academic honors, he settled "into a comfortable niche in the middle of the class."[38] Although he felt "stupid" in his inability to grasp mathematical concepts,[39] he was linguistically apt and could navigate an education system that overwhelmingly emphasized classical studies. Jung was regarded as a troublemaker, however. A teacher considered a best-efforts essay as "morally worthless," and gave the 12-year-old a personal evaluation as being "glib cleverness and humbug"; the same teacher a few years later branded him "a liar" after disbelieving that Jung could have written a precociously brilliant composition on *Faust*.[40] As a medical school student and upon his father's death, he managed his family's household accounts after heeding an uncle's advice *to be a man*. He became a psychiatrist, founded analytical psychology, and influenced other fields of study including anthropology, philosophy, and theology.

• **Isaac Newton** was a premature infant, and did poorly in grade school, ranking second-to-last in a class of 80 students when education meant learning Greek and Latin. Yet he was considered quite clever. As a boy, he painstakingly made a mouse-driven miniature corn mill, water clocks, and accurate sundials on walls. After physically defeating a bully, Newton was determined to academically outperform the bully as well; Newton finished first in his class. Later at Cambridge, he did poorly in his college exams, which valued oral debate. His *Principia* (his three laws of motion and the theory of gravity) remained private musings for 20 years until a visiting colleague happened to find it and persuaded Newton, who was sensitive to criticism and disliked scientific debates, to let him publish it. Newton, considered one of history's greatest intellects, is also known for inventing calculus and discoveries in optics.

• **Louis Pasteur** was taciturn and shy, but also observant and drew with detailed precision. He remained an ordinary student in the French countryside until age 14, when he received tutoring from a scholarly family friend. Pasteur, "[a]n extraordinary mixture of self-doubt and

---

36 Thomas Hayden, "The Inner Einstein," *U.S. News & World Report*, 9 December 2002, p. 63.
37 Hayden quoting an observation by John Stachel, a physicist and founding editor of the Einstein Papers Project, p. 62.
38 Frank McLynn, *Carl Gustav Jung* (New York: St. Martin's Press, 1997), p. 31.
39 McLynn, p. 36.
40 McLynn, p. 32.

pride,"[41] decided to enter the prestigious École Normale Supérieure in Paris for teacher training but his Bachelor of Letters degree was insufficient. Though difficult academically and financially, he persevered through three extra years of study to pass the requirements for the Bachelor of Science degree and the entrance exams for the École itself. Pasteur struggled to visualize abstract mathematical concepts, and detested questions he thought irrelevant, immaterial, and semantic in nature.[42] Pasteur, however, discovered that hands-on experimentation thrilled him much more than transmitting acquired knowledge.[43] He put off a pedagogical career and found an appointment as a laboratory assistant. From this point, Pasteur began life as a research scientist, first in chemistry, then in bacteriology and medicine. He provided experimental foundations for microbiology and immunology, strengthened understanding of protective immunity, and pioneered the industrial practice of transferring scientific research to product development.

• **George Patton** was read classic literature at home as a child, though his family feared him to be "dim-witted."[44] Patton possessed a prodigious memory of military history and could quote the Bible and the *Iliad* at great length. Patton had reading, spelling, and punctuation troubles throughout life; felt lazy and stupid; and believed that through discipline of character he would overcome his weaknesses. A military historian observed that Patton "craved praise and recognition" and his "low self-esteem required constant bolstering."[45] He felt destined to continue his family's military traditions. While the high demands he placed on himself were essential to his leadership, they sometimes resulted in reprimands for overzealous command of others. His career was also compromised by impolitic public statements. He enjoyed physical activities, finished fifth in the modern pentathlon at the 1912 Olympics, and is mostly known for his hands-on leadership during World War I and World War II. Patton's strengths were his eye for terrain, tactical innovations, ability to train troops, and military writings.[46]

• **Auguste Rodin**, sculptor *extraordinaire*, was the worst student in his school[47] having reading, writing, spelling, and math troubles. His teachers labeled him *ineducable* and *an idiot*.[48]

---

41 Patrice Debré, *Louis Pasteur*, English translation by Elborg Forster (Baltimore: The Johns Hopkins University Press, 1998), p. 21.

42 Debré, pp. 19-20.

43 Debré, pp. 28-29.

44 D'Este, *Patton*, p. 39.

45 D'Este, p. 757.

46 D'Este, p. 811.

47 Barbara Z. Novick and Maureen M. Arnold, *Why Is My Child Having Trouble at School?: A Parent's Guide to Learning Disabilities* (New York: Villard Books, 1991), p. 8.

48 Silver, *The Misunderstood Child*, p. 376.

- **Leonardo da Vinci** excelled as a painter, sculptor, musician, architect, inventor, engineer, and scientist, but had little interest in history or literature. His difficult-to-read manuscripts contain *mirror writing*—backward script going from right to left, strange spellings, and peculiar abbreviations.[49] His writings provide evidence of perceptual difficulties.[50]

- **Woodrow Wilson** had reading troubles as a boy. His father homeschooled him until age nine (the Civil War had closed many schools), emphasizing field trips and exacting expression of ideas for clarity of thought. Wilson learned the alphabet at age eight and reading at age 11;[51] shorthand before entering Princeton; and debate in college. He became president of Princeton University, Governor of New Jersey, President of the United States, and winner of the 1920 Nobel Peace Prize.

"Successful People with LD and AD/HD" by Jodie Dawson lists many well-known individuals (available at www.schwablearning.org/articles.asp?g=3&r=258; or go to www.schwablearning.org, type "successful people" in the box labeled *Type in keyword* box, click on the arrow button next to it, then at the next screen, click on *Successful People with LD and AD/HD*). This website will link to several online profiles including those of:[52]

- **Terry Bradshaw**, football quarterback who led his team to four Superbowl victories, sports commentator, and author of *It's Only a Game* (Pocket Books, 2001) in which he mentions that he has AD/HD

- **Whoopi Goldberg**, comedienne, producer, humanitarian, and winner of one Grammy, two Golden Globe Awards, and the 1991 Oscar for Best Supporting Actress for her role in *Ghost*

- **Victor Villaseñor**, writer of acclaimed short stories and novels about his cultural heritage, and a native Californian who struggled to learn to read despite his disability and his first language being Spanish

- **Henry Winkler**, director and producer, but best known as "the Fonz" on the television show, *Happy Days* (his autobiography is also available at www.ldonline.org/first_person/winkler_henry.html).

---

49 Museum of Paleontology, University of California at Berkeley, "Leonardo da Vinci (1452–1519)" [Internet], p. 1, accessed 29 January 2003, available from: http://www.ucmp.berkeley.edu/history/vinci.html.

50 Silver, *The Misunderstood Child*, p. 376.

51 Silver, *The Misunderstood Child*, p. 376.

52 Jodie Dawson, "Successful People with LD and AD/HD" [Internet], created 22 January 2001 and updated 22 January 2003, available from: http://www.schwab learning.org/articles.asp?r=258

"Overcoming Dyslexia" by Betsy Morris is a May 13, 2002 *Fortune* magazine article (available at www.fortune.com/fortune/articles/0, 15114,373085,00.html or go to www.fortune.com, type in "overcoming dyslexia" in the *SEARCH FORTUNE* box, click on the *Go* button, then at the next screen click on *Overcoming Dyslexia* or *Dyslexic Achievers*) which interviews many business leaders on their tactics and strategies for success despite their learning disabilities. A chart, "Dyslexic Achievers," accompanies the article (available at www.fortune.com/fortune/articles/0,15114,373449,00.html or type in "dyslexic achievers" in the *SEARCH FORTUNE* box, click on the *Go* button, then at the next screen click on *Dyslexic Achievers*). Among the many individuals highlighted are:[53]

- **David Boies**, *magna cum laude* Yale law school graduate and trial attorney
- **Richard Branson**, billionaire founder and chairman of Virgin Group, itself the parent company of businesses that bear the Virgin name such as Virgin Atlantic Airways and Virgin Records
- **Craig McCaw**, billionaire and former CEO of McCaw Cellular
- **Diane Swonk**, Bank One Chief Economist and Senior Vice President, business school professor, the youngest president of the National Association for Business Economics, and a "Star Forecaster" according to *The Wall Street Journal*
- **William Butler Yeats** struggled in reading as a child, and learned geography and chemistry from his father's sketching tutorials; as an adult, Yeats confessed to grammar and spelling difficulties.[54] Yeats, a poet and playwright, is remembered today as reviving interest in traditional Irish literature, and as the winner of the 1923 Nobel Prize for Literature.

---

53   Betsy, Morris, "Overcoming Dyslexia," *Fortune*, 13 May 2002, p. 70.
54   R. F. Foster, *W. B. Yeats: A Life* (New York: Oxford University Press, 1997), p. 17.

Chapter Seven

What are some traits and emotions of students with learning disabilities?

It has been very hard for me and my parents to deal with my problem. I tried my hardest to blend in and erase the "learning disabled" label placed on me in the second grade. For me, these obstacles are my inabilities to stay focused, reading out loud, and working efficiently to organize my ideas while under pressure and time restraints. Through time management, hard work, and perseverance, I have proven to myself that I can do well in academics, sports, and be successful in life. It is not easy being a teenager with learning disabilities. Other students and teachers alike often do not understand what you endure. You can imagine my frustration in knowing I have a complete grasp of the concept but not enough time to put it down on paper. Rushing to finish a test compounds the scrambling of my thoughts causing even greater errors. My friends and fellow students, who are not aware of my problem, sometimes ridiculed me.

Attention and classroom behavior

Attention is "the ability to focus in a sustained manner" on a specific activity; otherwise, inattention may be observed in ready distractibility or troubled task execution.[1] In the classroom, *paying attention* translates into many behaviors such as visually focusing on the teacher while not comprehending, listening closely to the teacher's words while doodling, knowing the answer but being afraid to speak out in class, or

---

1   *Diagnostic and Statistical Manual of Mental Disorders*, p. 820.

responding in class without a prepared answer. Indeed, says Barkley, the definition of *attention* itself is controversial in the field of psychology, somehow involving internal and external responses to the environment.[2]

Attention assumes adequate instruction. Sometimes procedural instruction is unclear. For example,

$$\frac{4}{8} = \frac{1}{2}$$

may leave students clueless. An intermediate step would specify the required action:

$$\frac{4 \div 4}{8 \div 4} = \frac{1}{2}$$

In many cases, the required curriculum covers too many topics, thus sacrificing depth for breadth. Little time is provided for practice before moving on to the next topic. Control issues can emerge when overwhelmed students do not *get with the program*. Teacher expectations and disruptive students also affect classroom learning.

Of course, good instructors can engage students with a variety of methods. One algebra teacher keeps his students hanging on every word he says by promising no homework if they can catch five mistakes during a class presentation. Another idea suggested by Patricia Cross, an emeritus professor of higher education at the University of California at Berkeley, is the *one-minute paper*. Instead of students filling out course evaluations at the end of a semester, they can provide ongoing feedback to teachers by *anonymously* jotting down during the last couple of minutes of each class the main point and topics insufficiently explained. The papers are dropped into a box by the door and teacher needs only five minutes to review what students understood, misunderstood, and how to begin the next class session.[3] Surmises Harold Koplewicz, a New York University pediatrician and psychiatrist and Director of the Child Study Center, "The number-one cause of inattention, in my view, is a boring teacher."[4]

The lack of a consensus definition of attention aside, many researchers have nevertheless attempted to measure the concept of attention. *Time-on-task* is the actual time that a student spends on an assignment. *Distractibility* measures a student's off-task behavior. The

<hr>

2   Russell A. Barkley, "Critical Issues in Research on Attention," in *Attention, Memory, and Executive Function*, ed. G. Reid Lyon and Norman A. Krasnegor (Baltimore: Paul H. Brookes Publishing, 1996), p. 48.

3   Richard J. Light, *Making the Most of College: Students Speak Their Minds* (Cambridge, Massachusetts: Harvard University Press, 2001), pp. 66-67.

4   Dianne Hales, "Is Your Child At Risk?" *Ladies Home Journal*, November 1999, p. 106.

research on attention in children with learning disorders has produced conflicting results.

One problem is that a study may include children with different types of problems. A child with a perceptual disorder may welcome any distractions because class lectures or assignments are incomprehensible, much like watching a foreign film without the subtitles. A child with AD/HD is inherently distractible and will have trouble staying on track. Bullied children may be fearfully anticipating recess and cannot shift gears to focus on the task at hand. Then there are students having more than one disorder. Teachers, however, generally perceive these students as behavior problems. In general classroom—but not in small group—activities, 63% of teacher-initiated interactions with students having LD were interventions over inattention or rule violations, and partially explain classroom "grouping practices for students with LD."[5]

The three-year Carolina Longitudinal Learning Disabilities Project identified seven different behavior patterns in 44 children with learning problems based on variables from the Classroom Behavior Inventory. (These behaviors were stable over the three years of the study.) Teachers rated students on various measures of academic competence (dependence, independence, task orientation, distractibility, but not verbal intelligence in this study); personal adjustment (introversion and extroversion); and social competence (considerateness and hostility). These factors have been statistically linked to achievement in school.[6] The patterns found and their relative percentages in the studied population are:[7]

Children		Description of Behavior
No.	%	
13	30	Normal social behavior with attention-deficit problems
10	22	Normal behavior with considerate and introverted tendencies
8	18	Conduct problems: distractible and hostile
3	7	Withdrawn behavior: dependent and significantly introverted
5	11	Normal behavior but hostile, distractible, and dependent tendencies
3	7	Weak positive behaviors especially in task-orientation
2	5	Global behavior problems

---

5   James D. McKinney, "Longitudinal Research on the Behavioral Characteristics of Children with Learning Disabilities," in *Cognitive and Behavioral Characteristics of Children with Learning Disabilities*, ed. Joseph K. Torgesen (Austin, Texas: PRO-ED, 1990), p. 120.

6   McKinney, p. 118.

7   McKinney, pp. 124-135. The Carolina Learning Disabilities Project was begun in 1978–1979 school year and funded by the National Institute of Child Health and Human Development and the Department of Education.

Over three years, the students in the Carolina project without significant behavioral problems or who were withdrawn progressed linearly in school as did normal students but at a lesser rate; students with behavior problems progressed at a declining rate over time compared to all other students. By selecting children who would be identified for special education by age seven, the relative number and types of patterns found in this study may have been skewed by students with AD/HD: students with perceptual disorders are usually not identified for special education until the third grade and up. Regardless of any experimental bias though, what is important to understand is that because no typical student with learning disorders exists, no stereotypical LD behavior exists either.

Additional articles of interest are:

• "Problem Behaviors in the Classroom: What They Mean and How to Help" by Amy Bobrow, available at www.aboutourkids.org/letter/novdec02.pdf, presents a method to objectively analyze problem classroom behaviors—a *Functional Behavioral Assessment*—and suggestions for interventions—for either an individual child or an entire class.

• *E-ssential Guides* series on "Problem Behavior" and "Behavior Basics," by various contributors, available at www.schwablearning.org/articles.asp?g=4&r=698.

Learning preferences

Learning style describes an individual's responses to the environment, but is not the same as multiple intelligence.[8] An intelligence uses perceptual skills, a base of knowledge, and certain ways of thinking to solve problems. Beethoven, for example, could compose music even though he was deaf; he knew how notes and dynamic markings on a page would translate into sound. In contrast, a learning style uses preferred perceptual skills in order to acquire knowledge. Linguistic thinkers order thoughts through verbal concepts and sequential language pathways. Visual thinkers scan recognized patterns and study unfamiliar detail. Kinesthetic thinkers learn through experience and rehearsal, a valuable skill for on-the-job training. However, the best learning is typically multi-dimensional because understanding new information usually requires some combination of these styles. For example, learning is enhanced when one can read print as well as hear the subtle nuances of speech; visualize demonstrations as well as listen to descriptions; or see and hear explanations as well as practice techniques.

A *field-dependent* child interprets a visual perception in the context of its background, and is capable of learning social information.

---

8   Gardner, "Multiple Intelligences, p. 44.

A lonely field-dependent child is more likely to join a crowd in a destructive activity than a field-independent child.

An impulsive child is unlikely to reflect on various alternatives before responding on a test. Students with learning disabilities tend to be more impulsive than normal students.

Confidence and feelings of control

Self-confidence, *self-esteem*, *locus of control*, and *self-efficacy* have all been used to describe personal feelings about being able to succeed in an activity, including the capabilities to override difficulties and influence the surrounding environment or situation. These feelings also determine a person's resiliency and motivation.[9] Students with learning disorders know that they cannot rely on their neurological functions as can most other people. Unless properly educated about their disorder, these students may think of themselves as crazy, immoral, or intellectually deficient. This section will primarily discuss these personal feelings as a locus of control, the other terms being self-explanatory.

Locus of control is grounded in objective reality but it is also perception of that reality. An *internal locus of control* is a personal belief that one can effectively control his environment. Perceived effectiveness leads to optimism, hope, eager participation, and persistent effort. An *external locus of control* is a personal belief that factors outside the person's control determine success; perceived ineffectiveness leads to pessimism, resignation, anxiety, avoidance, and *learned helplessness*. Having LD is a condition of not being in control as one would wish.

Teachers, being credible sources, also signify progress and an implied ability with their patterns of feedback. Unfortunately, these professionals may stereotype students with LD and have lower expectations for them even when actual academic performance is adequate.[10] Students can sense this and so diminish their own abilities.

Teachers also create a learning environment and influence impressionable students. Geometry teachers, for example, should not announce at the beginning of the course that students who did well in algebra may not do well in geometry. While this may be true for some students and the teacher meant well, such dim prospects discouraged my son—who did well in algebra—from even trying to do well in geometry. It would have been better not to have said anything at all.

---

9   Robert Brooks, "Islands of Competence," *LD Matters*, a Schwab Learning Publication, Winter 1997, p. 1.

10   Dale H. Schunk, in "Self-Efficacy and Cognitive Achievement: Implications for Students with Learning Problems," in *Cognitive and Behavioral Characteristics of Children with Learning Disabilities*, ed. Joseph K. Torgesen (Austin, Texas: PRO-ED, 1990), p. 140.

Figure 7.1[11] illustrates the dynamics between self-confidence and performance, and the internal characteristics a student brings to the task and the external characteristics of the task to be done:

Figure 7.1

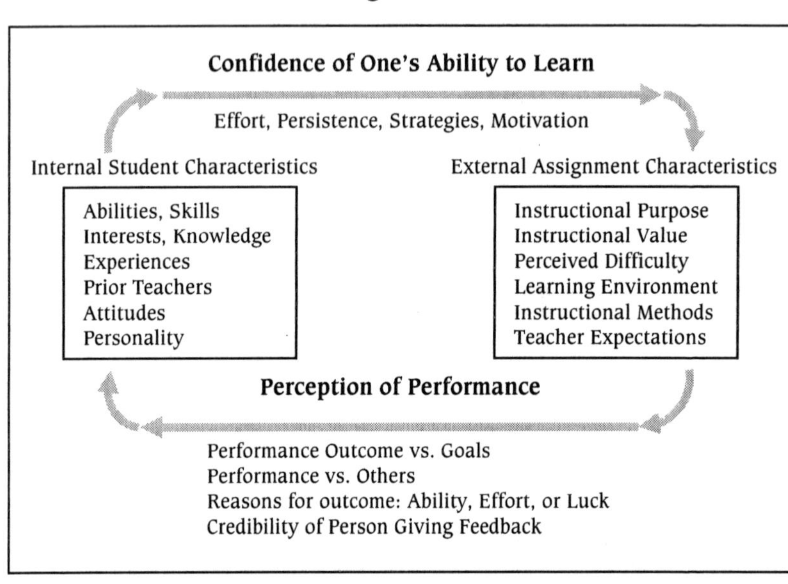

Students with an internal locus of control, who believe that their internal student characteristics strongly influence outcomes, perform better under less structured conditions. These are the confident individuals who generally manage well on their own and may have their own procedures for accomplishing tasks. In contrast, students with an external locus of control, who believe that external factors control results, perform better when assignments are structured into explicit steps to guide completion of the work.[12] (See *rubrics* in Chapter 18.) For many reasons, this latter group of students should learn *strategies* for better inner direction, or learning how to learn.

Better performance leads to higher self-confidence which, in turn, creates satisfaction and a greater willingness to initiate more activity.[13] Parents and teachers can channel student energy into a cycle of learning behavior. For example, students with higher self-confidence will answer more questions correctly and will review more problems that

---

11 Diagram is author's graphic interpretation of text by Schunk, pp. 142-150.

12 Bender citing a 1980 study by Bendell, Tollefson, and Fine, *Learning Disabilities*, p. 146.

13 Bruce Bower citing 2003 Baumeister study, "Findings Puncture Self-Esteem Claims," *Science News*, 7 June 2003, p. 365.

were missed, no matter the level of ability.[14] (Motivation is presented in Chapter 20.) One mother hung the following quotation by Charles Swindoll in her son's room:

Attitude

The longer I live, the more I realize the impact of attitude on life. Attitude, to me, is more important than facts. It is more important than the past, than education, than money, than circumstances, than failures, than successes, than what other people think or say or do. It is more important than appearance, giftedness, or skill. It will make or break a company...a church...a home. The remarkable thing is we have a choice every day regarding the attitude we will embrace for that day. We cannot change our past...we cannot change the fact that people will act in a certain way. We cannot change the inevitable. The only thing we can do is play on the one thing we have, and that is our attitude...I am convinced that life is 10% what happens to me and 90% how I react to it. And so it is with you...we are in charge of our Attitudes.

Focusing on the *disability* instead of the abilities of a student can cause self-loathing because he or she feels less than perfect. But no one really is perfect, and, in truth, disability is a relative condition. A man with one arm may regard another without legs as being really disabled. And learning disabilities in themselves are not fatal. With a humane approach, students with learning disabilities can become optimistic despite their difficulties.

Stress and anxiety

"That's the effect of living backwards," the Queen said kindly: "it always makes one a little giddy at first—"

"Living backwards!" Alice repeated in great astonishment. "I never heard of such a thing!"

"—but there's one great advantage in it, that one's memory works both ways."

"I'm sure mine only works one way," Alice remarked. "I ca'n't remember things before they happen."

"It's a poor sort of memory that only works backwards," the Queen remarked.

—Through the Looking-Glass

---

14 Schunk, "Self-Efficacy and Cognitive Achievement," p. 141.

Many teachers believe that if a student works hard, then he or she will perform well in class. Hard work, however, may not be apparent if a student has trouble comprehending the questions and then putting together words to answer them—more related to input-output problems than with thinking and knowing. This is difficult for many people to understand because they only see minimal output. It doesn't take long for a child with learning disabilities to learn that hard work and good grades have a capricious relationship. Government statistics for 1999–2000 show that the rate of serious emotional disturbance nearly doubles as students become teenagers, from 5.7% in 6- to 11-year-olds, to 10.9% and 9.3% respectively in 12- to 17-year-olds and 18- to 21-year-olds.[15] (The 18- to 21-year-old figure is not entirely representative of this age group because most students in this age group are no longer tracked after leaving high school.)

For children who haven't given up and still care about school, the result is additional stress to an ongoing competitive situation of grades and test scores. There can also be real fears of dealing with people at school who ostracize, bully, humiliate, or scold. In the fourth grade, my son threatened to run away from home because *we* were forcing him to go to school. Anxiety results from fears of not meeting expectations, or from the student's relentless efforts at compensating for deficits. Depression is the sadness you can see in the child's face, of feeling incompetent, of not being able to please others by doing well in school. For some children, treatment of the learning problem will resolve the anxiety; otherwise, if anxiety co-exists with the learning problem, then treatment for anxiety should be explored.[16]

Priscilla Vail, an author and expert on learning and emotion urges adults to monitor a student's emotions. Flight and fight impulses are incompatible with learning language, math, and social skills. "Anger, fear, rejection, frustration, and prospects of failure or humiliation .... cut ... access to memory, the ability to reason, the ability to make novel connections, [and] the ability to organize thought."[17] One study has demonstrated this fear effect on learning. By disrupting working memory, math anxiety causes reduced performance.[18]

Many people have made psychological adjustments to their condition but have gone to great lengths to maintain their privacy, particularly as the diagnosis carries a stigma with it. Then there are children with a learning disorder that is physically invisible (except to

---

15   U.S. Department of Education, "Twenty-third Annual Report to Congress," p. II-26.

16   Nadeau, Littman, and Quinn, *Understanding Girls with AD/HD*, pp. 158-159.

17   Priscilla L. Vail, *Words Fail Me: How Language Works and What Happens When It Doesn't* (Rosemont, New Jersey: Modern Learning Press, 1996), p. 37. Copyright © 1996 by Priscilla L. Vail. Reprinted with permission of Modern Learning Press.

18   Bruce Bower citing 2001 Ashcroft and Kirk study, "Math Fears Subtract from Memory, Learning," *Science News*, 30 June 2001, p. 405.

medical research), and he or she may find it hard to accept its existence. The presence of a chronic illness is associated with a greater risk for psychological problems, probably resulting from difficulties and experiences posed by the illness.[19] Children may cope with their fears in several ways:[20]

- **Internalizing the stress**: The student avoids school, avoids schoolwork, avoids being alone, withdraws from potentially frustrating or upsetting situations, or becomes enveloped by a generalized anxiety disorder or depression.

- **Externalizing the stress**: The student projects blame for any problems onto others, and by not accepting any responsibility, has eliminated his or her anxiety. This child may become defiant, and often fights with other children. These types of behaviors can become oppositional and conduct disorders. Adolescent resistance to school and adult authority may lead to truancy, delinquency, dropping out of school, promiscuity, running away from home, or substance abuse.

- **Somatizing the stress**: The student experiences real discomfort like headaches or stomachaches usually on school days. Staying at home or going to the school clinic reduces stress and thereby relieves physical symptoms. More information can be found in the January/February 2002 issue of the *Child Study Center Letter* entitled "Psychosomatic Illness in Children and Adolescents," by Melvin Oatis, available at www.aboutourkids.org/letter/janfeb02.pdf.

- **Controlling the situation**: Other coping mechanisms include being the class clown to hide feelings of worthlessness; passive-aggressiveness; learned helplessness; and overly mature and controlling behavior especially when not accepted by peers.

Understand the unusual stress that your child faces. Don't expect your child to meet goals that are unsustainable, unrealistic, and even inappropriate. Put yourself in your child's shoes. Examine the cause of your child's stress. There may be many. The stress can be objective like being bullied or the threat of being humiliated in class, or subjective like being afraid of taking a test. Offer real solutions, not platitudes. Squarely managing the problem—coping with it emotionally, solving it objectively, or both—is better than blame or avoidance.[21] Take the time to talk to your child. Build your relationship into a trusting and long-lasting friendship. Some references for further guidance:

- The March/April 2001 issue of the *Child Study Center Letter* entitled "Children with a Chronic Illness: The Interface of Medicine and Mental

---

19 Robin F. Goodman, "Children with a Chronic Illness: The Interface of Medicine and Mental Health," *Child Study Center Letter* [Internet], March/April 2001, p. 2, available from: http://www.aboutourkids.org/letter/marapr01.pdf
20 Silver, *The Misunderstood Child*, pp. 121-130.
21 Goodman citing 1997 Kliewer finding, "Children with a Chronic Illness," p. 3.

Health," by Robin Goodman, discusses psychological risk factors and management. It is available at www.aboutourkids.org/letter/marapr01. pdf. Alternatively, bring up the home page at www.aboutourkids.org, then click on *CSC LETTER*, which brings up an index with many choices of articles.

• "Dr. Hallowell Talks to Teens: Do You Feel Worried or Sad?" by Edward Hallowell; available at www.schwablearning.org/articles.asp? g=2&r=514, offers advice from one who found life happiness despite having both dyslexia and AD/HD. This site links to his other publications.

• Once a teenager with little self-confidence can get past the title, *The Complete Idiot's Guide to Dealing with Stress for Teens* by Sara Jane Sluke and Vanessa Torres (2002) offers help, because it acknowledges feelings, offers solutions, addresses a variety of specific situations, is easy to understand, and can be conveniently reread at any time.

• Adolescents who are not treated for their overwhelming anxiety, feelings of worthlessness, or depression are at greater risk of injuring themselves. Symptoms and treatment can be found in the November/ December 2001 issue of the *Child Study Center Letter*, "Self-Injurious Behavior," by Lisa Ferentz, available at www.aboutourkids.org/ letter/novdec01.pdf.

Mood states: Loneliness, depression, and suicide

Compared to students without learning disabilities, students with LD tend to be lonely, depressed, and suicidal; one 1985 study has suggested that 50% of adolescent suicides involved students with learning disabilities.[22] Depression is seen in sadness, apathy, and hopelessness. This is a hard subject. Risk factors and intervention can be found in the May/June 2001 issue of the *Child Study Center Letter*, "Youth Suicide," by Carmen Alonso and Anita Gurian, available at www.aboutourkids. org/letter/mayjun01.pdf.

Harold Koplewicz, a professor of pediatrics and psychiatry at the New York University School of Medicine, stated that denial of these feelings in young people is the biggest problem, "Fewer than 20 percent of these kids get the treatment they need."[23] Once rare, suicide is now the third leading cause of death in the U.S. for individuals 15–24 years of age.[24] Koplewicz's advice on recognizing at-risk behaviors, demographics, and treatment issues appears in Appendix 2.

---

22 Bender citing 1985 Peck study, *Learning Disabilities*, p. 149.
23 Hales, "Is Your Child At Risk?" p. 102.
24 Connie Alonso and Anita Gurian, "Youth Suicide," *Child Study Center Letter* [Internet], May/June 2001, p. 1, available from: http://www.aboutourkids.org/letter/ mayjun01.pdf

Chapter Eight

How will having a learning disability affect my child socially?

The schoolyard bullying began in the third grade—at a time when violent video games were becoming popular—and grew into a frenzy by the sixth grade. 'Looking out for Number One' seemed to dominate recess interactions. When I brought up an incident with another mother after witnessing her son, unprovoked, hitting and ripping Jason's jacket, she coolly replied that my son deserved it. (I considered the source: She and her son were later asked to leave the school.)

Bullying incidents were both overt and covert. A classmate egged on by others (and later diagnosed with AD/HD) picked my boy up and threw him to the ground. In response, the school counselor ran two group sessions to tell the boys not to bully each other and pulled Jason out of class for 'devictimization' counseling. This was useless. He missed class time and the bullying never stopped. A classmate, an altar boy, seated in front of Jason, pushed my son's books off his desk during lectures, once tripped him so that his new uniform pants were ripped, and tried to claim Jason's jacket as his even though my son's name was sewn on the jacket. Another boy, known to many other parents as a troublemaker, gave Jason Nazi salutes— once in front of the church—and called him 'son of Hitler.' Such name-calling was clearly ridiculous, but it indicated the degree of malice in this boy and the lengths he could go to hurt another person. One afternoon, Jason fell apart after I dropped him off at a professional tutoring session; he was almost inconsolable for an hour. My son heard probably all variations of remarks from the majority of his classmates having to do with intelligence, homophobia, and ethnicity. Jason resorted to spitting on his favorite lunchtime food, pizza, in order to discourage bullies from taking it from him. He's had years of martial arts—the training recommended by a preschool teacher—but using it would only get him into trouble. Once after using the school's bathroom, he was attacked by the troublemaker lying in wait for him, but because it was after dismissal, the administration would do nothing about it. This bully also "accidentally" pushed another child at my younger son which resulted in some bleeding when the orthodontic braces dug into his lip. Again, the school did nothing.

Bullying incidents had to be witnessed by school personnel before any punishments could occur, which was seldom. My reports were regarded as those of an overanxious difficult mother until one day, the counselor happened to witness a bullying incident. He was shaken in seeing the hatred that was directed at my son. The crackdown that began in the eighth grade in the K-8 program was too little and way too late. Patterns were set. Bullying found more victims, and although my son was more protected than before, he still wasn't immune. The bullies also picked on the female custodian, who prided herself on keeping the school neat and clean.

Ongoing peer rejections led to Jason's talking to himself in nonsense syllables. It was his way of saying that if he was to be socially ostracized, then he was going to give them a reason for rejecting him. He had no friends, but he was—and still is—close to his younger siblings. He was socially awkward, and while children naturally establish playground pecking orders, the unusual cruelty of his classmates drove me to put him into extracurricular activities outside of school. Not only did these efforts provide respite, they also provided wonderful experiences I did not realize even existed. Now it seemed that the worst place I could put my son was in school.

Jason and I wanted to transfer him to another school but my husband—who instituted some financial management practices at the school, coached the soccer and baseball teams, and was president of the school board—was against this, afraid that the boy would drop through the cracks in a new unfamiliar system. It seemed that I spent as much time bucking Jason up as tutoring him. Upon my request, the principal mandated that two particularly troublesome boys be physically kept away from my son. Nevertheless, the harassment problems seemed beyond the control of the junior high school teachers, school counselor, and school staff: suspensions of the offenders seemed to make no difference. The atmosphere was so negative that the boys turned on each other as well, once prompting the police and FBI to investigate E-mail death threats. Two boys were expelled—one for downloading bomb-making instructions off the Internet, the other for one incident of addressing a minority instructor with a racial slur—but these were not the boys bullying my child. The administration seemed to have the attitude of 'boys will be boys' and was just waiting for graduation to eliminate all problems.

It was no surprise when an evaluation around Christmas time reported that Jason "has been traumatized by being teased and bullied by his peers." Looking back, I wonder how he finished elementary school at all given his general level of anxiety and time out of the classroom for special education classes and counseling.

It took the first two years of high school with special efforts from the teachers and me to help him develop even a modicum of self-confidence. Many of the teaching practices were quite innovative. Though the student body was under a thousand, a wide variety of extracurricular activities were available. His special-ed teacher was welcoming and made one feel hope for the future. Jason finally gained some peer approval through a demanding school extracurricular activity.

But my vigilance was still important. Once, Jason alarmed many teachers when classmates reported him saying that life didn't seem to be worth all the trouble he was going through. It turned out later that a younger boy, another honors student (Jason also made the honor roll several times), was picking on him calling him a "retard," gave him the "evil eye" during lunchtime, had searched his bookbag for money, tried to shine a laser light in his eyes, and had boasted of other physical assaults on my son. Teachers would reprimand the bully for an incident, but then another would occur.

All this came out when my son was having trouble doing homework with me one evening. A few teachers and I knew he had been extremely anxious, but couldn't figure out why. Now I had the full picture. Jason and I talked and then he knew what to do. Although he had tried to stop the bully by himself and reported incidents to teachers, it was his complaint to a school administrator that finally made some headway. When the bullying ceased, Jason was happier and better able to focus on his schoolwork. But the bully hadn't given up. About a couple of weeks later and in retaliation, he launched a covert harassment campaign against another of my sons, and then against Jason again. A few of my sons' classmates decided that they had had enough as well and isolated the bully. A couple of them even made sharp comments to him. According to my son, the bully had to dominate someone in order to feel good about himself. At this point, I talked to the school about the bullying and my general concerns about school safety. I have been through this too many times already. This time the bullying really stopped.

One of the school counselors recommended a private psychologist for Jason, but he didn't want to use whatever free time he had available because hours of counseling never did stop the bullying back in *elementary school. Jason found a book that gave him perspective on bullies; this understanding seems to give him more self-confidence. Through all this, he is learning to advocate for himself. He's been at the bottom of the pile and knows that enough is enough. But he's smiling a lot more these days. A school administrator told me that she has never seen him happier. Still in the back of my mind I worry because nothing in life is predictable. And Jason remains suspicious that the bully is lying low for now.*

The special education administrator at my son's high school said that kids with LD are traumatized much more commonly than people want to admit. One mother that I happened to meet at community functions told me that two of her sons, who have learning differences, had been similarly traumatized at school. Another mother believes that her son suffered more from bullying problems than from academic issues. Having LD shouldn't mean being treated worse than a dog.

Many adults minimize the child's experience with "it's only school," or he or she "will outgrow these problems." To illustrate the pressures on the child, *When Your Child Has LD* recasts the student's experience into an adult experience:

> "Imagine being at a job for eight hours a day, five days a week, where nearly everything you do is hard for you. Your supervisor constantly corrects your mistakes and tells you that if you don't improve, you'll be terminated. Your coworkers make fun of you, and when you return home from work, your spouse complains about your job performance. You have difficulty sleeping at night, you start making excuses for missing work, and you may abuse alcohol or other drugs to dull the pain you feel."[1]

Adults forget that children can't just opt out of school like adults can change jobs.

Learning disabilities and social problems

Not all learning disabilities result in social isolation. Children with excellent speaking but poor reading skills may be very popular on the playground. Conversely, poor verbal skills, weak behavioral control, anxiety, and poor social receptiveness can cause a child to be

---

1   Excerpted from *When Your Child Has LD (Learning Differences): A Survival Guide for Parents*, by Gary Fisher, Ph.D., and Rhoda Cummings, Ed.D. © 1995. Used with permission from Free Spirit Publishing, Inc., Minneapolis, MN: 1-800-735-7323; *www.freespirit.com*. All rights reserved.

ostracized. Two groups of children in which learning disabilities can lead to *social inability* are:[2]

• Those who offend others with disruptive and aggressive behaviors. These children are actively rejected by peers.

• Those who make little social contact. These children are disregarded.

In general, compared to normal peers, students with learning disabilities may be:[3]

• Less skilled in conversing, negotiating, resolving conflicts, complimenting, accepting criticism, and resisting adolescent peer pressure (Hazel, Schumaker, Sherman, and Sheldon, 1982)

• Less accurate in understanding nonverbal communication (Bryan and Bryan, 1981)

• Less able to fulfill the social demands of a regular classroom (Bryan 1974; Bruininks, 1978; Garret and Crump, 1980; LaGreca and Mesibov, 1981)

• Less likely to attend structured social activities like school sports events (Deshler, Schumaker, Alley, Warner, and Clark, 1982)

• Less likely to go out and less likely to invite others out (Deshler and Schumaker, 1983)

• More likely to be ignored by teachers and peers when making verbal statements (Bryan, 1978)

• Inclined to verbalize negative statements (Bryan, Wheeler, Felcan, and Henek, 1976; Bryan 1974)

• More likely to sense teacher disapproval (Skrtic, 1980)

• Expected by teachers to be disruptive and disobedient in class (Keogh, Tchir, and Windeguth-Behn, 1974)

• More likely to have unsatisfactory relationships with family and parents (Warner, Schumaker, Alley, and Deshler, 1980)

• More likely to be rejected by peers, teachers, and parents (Bryan and Bryan, 1981).

Social rejection from a school activity, unrelated to an actual ability of performance such as playing ball, can cause any student general unhappiness, and low self-concept.[4] Some children become desperate for companionship, but an inability to interpret the intentions of others may cause students with learning disabilities to be persuaded into inappropriate behavior. Primate research has shown that being at the bottom of a social hierarchy makes monkeys more susceptible to

---

2   Mel Levine, *Educational Care: A System for Understanding and Helping Children with Learning Problems at Home and at School* (Cambridge, Massachusetts: Educators Publishing Service, 1994), pp. 226-227.

3   Catherine Trapani, *Transition Goals for Adolescents with Learning Disabilities* (Boston: College-Hill Press, 1990), pp. 42, 46, 50, and 52.

4   Bender, *Learning Disabilities*, p. 151.

substance abuse than those at the top.[5] In high school, non-academic problems often outweigh the academic ones. A teenager's poor self-concept, poor social skills and social relationships, lack of motivation, and poor attitudes toward school can lead to loneliness, depression, retaliation, and suicide.

All individuals need to be treated with dignity and respect if they are to thrive. Society suffers an economic cost with underachievement. Too often, schools only reinforce the brutal social pecking order of the playground. Joseph Epstein recently wrote, "… all snobbery is, in some sense, ill bred—in the sense that everything is ill bred that does not seem to have behind it kindness, generosity, and a good heart."[6] Many communities have programs that can explicitly instruct social skills to children with learning disorders. Chapter 18 presents some classroom concerns under the subheading of *Social integration: Classroom strategies*. More information is available at:

- "Social Cognition and Children with Learning Disabilities" at www.ldonline.org/ld_indepth/social_skills/rejectedneglectedkids.html
- "Social Skills and Learning Disabilities" by Jean Schumaker and Donald Deshler at www.ldonline.org/ld_indepth/social_skills/socialskills_and_ld.html
- "Do's & Don'ts for Fostering Social Competence" by Richard Lavoie at www.ldonline.org/ld_indepth/social_skills/lavoie_dos.html
- "Helping Kids with Learning Differences Understand the Language of Friendship" by Janet Giler at www.schwablearning.org/articles.asp?g=2&r=575
- "About Discipline—Helping Children Develop Self-Control" by Robin Goodman and Anita Gurian at www.aboutourkids.org/articles/discipline.html
- "Child Abuse and Neglect: Definitions, Consequences, and Treatment," by Elissa Brown and Shamir Khan at www.aboutourkids.org/letter/marapr03.pdf.

Bullying: Who's in charge at school?

Defining *bullying*. When the victim fears more humiliation or harm if he tries to stop the aggressor, adults must seriously consider the existence of a bullying situation.[7] An NIH study more precisely defined bullying:

---

5   Bruce Bower citing 2002 Nader study, "Biology of Rank," *Science News*, 26 January 2002, p. 53.

6   Joseph Epstein, *Snobbery: The American Version* (New York: Houghton Mifflin, 2002), p. 18.

7   Robin F. Goodman, "Bullies: More Than Sticks, Stones, and Name Calling" [Internet], p. 1, posted 1 March 2000 and updated 28 December 2000, available from: http://www.aboutourkids.org/articles/bullies.html

> "Bullying is a specific type of aggression in which
> (1) the behavior is intended to harm or disturb, (2) the
> behavior occurs repeatedly over time, and (3) there is
> an imbalance of power, with a more powerful person
> or group attacking a less powerful one. This asymme-
> try of power may be physical or psychological, and the
> aggressive behavior may be verbal (e.g., name-calling,
> threats), physical (e.g., hitting), or psychological (e.g.,
> rumors, shunning/exclusion)."[8]

In many schools, not fighting back is a sign of weakness and an invitation for more bullying. One of my children physically fought off a bully, spent time in detention after school, but was left alone after that. Carl Jung, a large boy, was prohibited from fighting back by his clergyman father and was bullied often. One day, enraged after being beset by seven smaller boys, he swung one around, mowed the others down, but was never attacked again. Jung, however, was punished and branded as a *troublemaker* by the school headmaster.[9] Indeed, boys may be between a rock and a hard place, having to defend themselves then getting into trouble for doing so. Schools may also be under the illusion that if no physical violence is occurring, no bullying exists as well.

Many people associate large physical size with bullying. Instead, bullying is more often a mind game and less overt. A child with an expressive language disability is a sitting duck for verbal abuse. Female bullying involves manipulation and indirect aggression. *Odd Girl Out: The Hidden Culture of Aggression in Girls* (2002) by Rachel Simmons provides many illustrations. Robert Goodman, Clinical Associate Professor of Psychiatry at the New York University School of Medicine emphasizes that the point of bullying is to leave the victim feeling powerless through an ongoing pattern of relentless intimidation. Furthermore, bullying does not necessarily occur through one-on-one confrontations of physical size or strength, but usually through "… an assistant and an organization of helpers … who may carry out the acts. The bully may be in charge but may not be the one caught."[10]

A determined bully knows no limits, especially if adults try to intervene. (The November 20, 2002 issue of *The Wall Street Journal* profiled the life of one bully in a front-page article, "Violent, Unhappy And Brief—the Life Of a School Bully" by Jonathan Eig.) Norwegian

---

8   Tonja R. Nansel, Mary Overpeck, Ramani S. Pilla, W. June Ruan, Bruce Simons-Morton, and Peter Scheidt, "Bullying Behaviors Among US Youth," *JAMA*, 25 April 2001, Vol. 285, pp. 2094-2100.

9   McLynn, *Carl Gustav Jung*, p. 32.

10 Goodman, "Bullies: More Than Sticks, Stones, and Name Calling," pp. 1-2.

Dan Olweus of the University of Bergen, has found that for boys in first through ninth grades in the U.S. and Scandinavia:[11]

• Bullies are aggressive and impulsive even towards parents and teachers, and have little empathy as they dominate their victims.

• Victims are generally anxious, insecure, and physically weak compared to the bullies.

• The long-term effects of regular school bullying are depression and low self-esteem, even in former victims at age 23.

A survey by the National Institute of Child Health and Human Development concurs with the Olweus findings, stating that bullies are social deviants, 60% of them having at least one criminal conviction, while victims are "socially isolated and lack social skills"; students both bullying and being bullied are particularly at risk.[12] Furthermore, its survey of over 15,000 public and private students throughout the U.S., in grades six through 10 revealed that:[13]

• 29.9% reported moderate ("sometimes") or frequent (at least weekly) bullying events, 10.6% of them were bullied, 13.0% bullied others, and 6.3% were both victim and bully.

• Bullying was greater among boys than girls, and highest during the sixth, seventh, and eighth grades.

• Boys were more likely to be hit, slapped, or pushed; girls were more likely to be the targets of rumors or sexual comments.

• Belittlement about speech or looks occurred at least twice as frequently as belittlement about race or religion.

Thus, the most likely victims are middle-school boys, who may have some unusual physical feature or communication difficulties.

The effects of bullying. Bullying at any age is debilitating. Adults can easily dismiss childhood bullying but yet can be overwhelmed by a bully (a *difficult* colleague or a boss) in their own work environment. In particular, *tough boys*, who may not be well-liked by a majority of their classmates, enhance their social status through physical threats, manipulation, and classroom disruptions, and so model behavior for unpopular aggressive students to follow.[14] Unchecked, a hostile environment develops.

Goodman warns that bullying eventually affects not only the victim but the entire group, because those not victimized are intimidated and will avoid empathizing with the victim so as not to appear on the bully's radar screen. "Children [unlike adults] should not be expected to

---

11 Bruce Bower, "Growing Up in Harm's Way," *Science News*, 25 May 1996, p. 333.
12 Nansel, Overpeck, Pilla, Ruan, Simons-Morton, and Scheidt, "Bullying Behaviors Among US Youth," pp. 2098-2099.
13 Nansel, Overpeck, Pilla, Ruan, Simons-Morton, and Scheidt, pp. 2096-2097.
14 Bruce Bower citing 2000 Rodkin study, "Popular Boys Show Their Tough Side," *Science News*, 22 January 2000, p. 52.

handle bullies on their own. Kids need to be taught that bullying is unacceptable."[15] Levine agrees, "Schools need to intervene" when popularity means malice towards another child, especially one with weak social abilities.[16]

Bullying defeats the purpose of a child being in school—to learn. Notes Bruce Perry, a Baylor College of Medicine professor of child psychiatry, "If a child is anxious, uncomfortable, or fearful, he will not learn. When a child becomes unwilling to explore or is anxious with anything new, he begins to self-limit his potential. ... the tired, confused, or fearful child does not care about new things—all she wants are familiar, comforting, and safe things."[17] Moreover, chronic mistreatment can cause long-term changes. One longitudinal research project has shown that boys with a certain biochemical predisposition, if neglected or abused through childhood, were almost twice as likely to engage in antisocial and criminal behaviors than the others in the study.[18]

Bullying victims with learning disabilities. A parent can expect some bump and grind between kids in school. However, poor academic performance often elicits taunting, which leads to discouragement, anxiety, stress, and continued poor performance, which again leads to more taunting, rejection, and even scapegoating. The child develops a sense of failure, not a *growth experience*. In a regular school environment, 33% of special education students are bullied compared to 8% of their normal peers.[19] Students with emotional or physical handicaps, depression, or low self-esteem may be "less able to effectively cope with teasing behavior."[20] Many parents of students with LD have found school bullying more distressful than academic problems. "Understanding Bullying and Its Impact on Kids with Learning Differences" by Marlene Snyder offers more information at www.schwablearning.org/articles.asp?r=692.

Being called a *retard* is as much of a form of discrimination as any racial epithet. In my experience, however, a school is more likely to intervene if the victim is female, and bullying involves race or religion—that is, a well-established *protected class*. A school that does not

---

15 Goodman, "Bullies: More Than Sticks, Stones, and Name Calling," p. 3.
16 Mel Levine, *Educational Care: A System for Understanding and Helping Children with Learning Problems at Home and at School* (Cambridge, Massachusetts: Educators Publishing Service), p. 227. Copyright © 1994 by Melvin D. Levine, M.D. Reprinted with permission of Educators Publishing Service, Inc.
17 Bruce D. Perry, "First Experiences," *Scholastic Parent & Child*, September 2000, pp. 58 and 60. Reprinted with permission of *Scholastic Parent & Child*.
18 Sharon Begley, "Genes May Determine Which Abused Kids Will 'Grow Up Bad,' " *The Wall Street Journal*, 20 September 2002, p. B1.
19 Goodman, "Bullies: More Than Sticks, Stones, and Name Calling," p. 2.
20 Goodman, p. 1.

control bullying and, like many schools, requires victims to become *snitches* and *tattle* on bullies, essentially sets up victims for more bullying by disarming them and making them targets for bully retaliation. Students with communication difficulties may also have trouble articulating bullying problems to school authorities.

In a 2000 letter to school principals, superintendents, and college and university presidents, the Department of Education stated its findings and reasons for making *disability harassment* an important issue:

> "Through a variety of sources, both OCR and OSERS have become aware of concerns about disability harassment in elementary and secondary schools and colleges and universities. ... [W]e heard about the often devastating effects on students of disability harassment that ranged from abusive jokes, crude name-calling, threats, and bullying, to sexual and physical assault by teachers and other students.

> "We take these concerns very seriously. Disability harassment can have a profound impact on students, raise safety concerns, and erode efforts to ensure that students with disabilities have equal access to the myriad benefits that an education offers. Indeed, harassment can seriously interfere with the ability of students with disabilities to receive the education critical to their advancement. We are committed to doing all that we can to help prevent and respond to disability harassment and lessen the harm of any harassing conduct that has occurred."[21]

Conventional wisdom holds that parental involvement in schools leads to happier students. That may be so, but greater parental involvement at school is associated with bullied children, the involvement perhaps reflecting the parents' recognition of their child's victimization.[22] One father volunteered much time and energy in developing a computerized accounting system and addressing ERISA issues for a school; nevertheless, his son "got it the worst" according to a classmate. If a school chooses not to effectively deal with the bullying (and it is a choice)—especially given your involvement—enroll elsewhere.

Bullying solutions. Teachers may be unaware of bullying problems, especially if the incidents take place on the playground or in an

---

21 Norma V. Cantu and Judith E. Heumann, "Dear Colleague" Letter to educators that harassment based on disability is wrong and illegal [Internet], 26 July 2000, available from: http://www.ed.gov/offices/OCR/docs/disabharassltr.html

22 Nansel, Overpeck, Pilla, Ruan, Simons-Morton, and Scheidt, "Bullying Behaviors Among US Youth," p. 2098.

after-school program where the teacher cannot see them. Adults might also choose to ignore the problem thinking that, without attention, the behavior will stop. One teacher was surprised when a student reported on a self-assessment test that he had no friends in his class, though she had been informed many times of ill-treatment by his classmates. In contrast, a vice-principal at another school told me that she aggressively nips incidents in the bud before a pack-animal mentality mushrooms into being. John Stossel's report, "The 'In' Crowd and Social Cruelty," at http://abcnews.go.com/onair/2020/stossel_020215_popularity.html is an article on playground cruelty. (An alternative method to reach this website is to go to http://abcnews.go.com and click on *2020*; at the next screen click on the photo of John Stossel; at the next screen scroll down to *The 'In' Crowd* and then click on it.)

Many schools have increased their efforts to reduce bullying. Vermont's school safety program, BEST, assumed that less than 1% of a school's population were the worst troublemakers. Instead, 5–10% of students were found to be persistent miscreants. Today, Vermont's school safety program anticipates problem behavior, employs a broad disciplinary code covering verbal and physical transgressions, trains teachers and administrators to talk with disruptive students, and removes unruly students from classrooms thus freeing teachers to instruct the remaining students.[23] Some schools include learning disabilities as part of their diversity educational program. "Early Warning, Timely Response: A Guide to Safe Schools" (www.ed.gov/offices/OSERS/OSEP/Products/earlywrn.html) identifies warning signs of school aggression, along with intervention and prevention measures.

A child who cannot trust school personnel and classmates may only be able to trust his or her parents. Do not blame your child or trivialize his or her feelings. Your child may be the victim of someone with a *conduct disorder*. Robin Goodman and Anita Gurian discuss this problem in "About Conduct Disorder" available at www.aboutourkids.org/articles/about_conduct.html. Silver's *The Misunderstood Child* (1998) lists the *DSM* diagnostic criteria for a conduct disorder on pages 126 and 127.

Parents of bullied students with LD may need to help their child articulate the event's who, what, where, when, how, and why in order to identify any transgressions; the child may be unable or ashamed to describe any incident. (When questioning my own child for details, I generally run three separate interrogation sessions, to see if the story is unvarying.) Take down names of possible witnesses or gather other details that could confirm his story with school officials. Document and notify school officials of bullying.

---

23   Tom Lauricella, "Your Kid Your Choice," *Offspring*, September/October 2000, p. 101.

A psychologist and co-author of *Raising Cain* (2000), Michael Thompson, offers suggestions on the website, "Popularity Wars," available at www.abcnews.go.com/sections/community/DailyNews/chat_thompson021902.html. Rachel Simmons in *Odd Girl Out* and LD Online in "Bullying: Peer Abuse in School" (available at www.ldonline.org/ld_indepth/social_skills/preventing_bullying.html) recommends many actions for students, parents, teachers, and school administrators. Parents must remind their children to not take on the characteristics of their tormenters. Above all, parents must see to it that school officials regain control of the situation and end the bullying.

Bear in mind that behavioral problems which may be beyond your child's control, may potentially result in school expulsion. In 2003, The House of Representatives amended IDEA such that schools could expel any student with a disability for violating the school's conduct code, regardless if the behavior was a result of the disability or in reaction to being harassed or bullied. (For more details, refer to "IDEA, HR 1350 and Section 504 Discipline," available at www.ldonline.org/ld_indepth/legal_legislative/section_504_discipline.html.) At the time of this writing the Senate has yet to review this House legislation.

If the school does not stop the bullying, parents do have options:

• Remind the school's principal that bullying is a serious issue with a copy of the "Dear Colleague" letter reprinted in Appendix 3, and available at www.ed.gov/offices/OCR/docs/disabharassltr.html. This document refers to Section 504 and Title II of the ADA, applicable to public schools. For private schools, you should also include a copy of Section 301, Title III of the ADA (www.usdoj.gov/crt/ada/statute.html) which defines "a nursery, elementary, secondary, undergraduate, or post-graduate private school, or other place of education" as places of public accommodations and therefore subject to this antidiscrimination law. If the situation does not improve, and in fairness let the school make a good-faith effort, you may file a complaint with the OCR. Bear in mind that once a complaint is filed, the OCR is legally obligated to conduct an investigation; there is no going back.

• File a police report, and have an attorney inform the school and the parents of the bully of potential damages. Be sure of the facts. Collect any evidence like notes or hate literature. Take photographs of any bodily harm or property damage. Contact a parent information center for details. Unlike IDEA and Section 504, the ADA provides for civil suits and penalties (*28 CFR §§ 35.172, 36.501, and 36.504*), and public entities are not immune under the Eleventh Amendment (*28 CFR § 35.178*).

• Change schools to end the bullying especially if you are paying tuition to attend the school. If the bullying does not stop, you must assume that the school is not really interested in your child's learning and development. Actions speak louder than words: a school's stated support for diversity is an inadequate substitute for an ongoing passivity to bullying. While many schools feel it is outside their academic mission to control bullying, they must also understand that students are not given the option of leaving school and thereby avoiding degradation. And school is where the bullying is occurring: it would be unusual for parents to knowingly invite a bully into the home to torment their children. Changing schools may be appealing if you do not wish to appear as a troublemaker initiating legal action. However, the same social difficulties for a child with LD may appear at the new school. I have heard of one parent who finally gave up altogether on schools because of bullying and homeschooled her child.

• The Office for Civil Rights (OCR) enforces federal laws prohibiting discrimination in education programs and activities receiving federal financial assistance, on the basis of disability—as well as race, color, national origin, sex and age—for complaints filed within 60 days of the "extraordinary circumstance." The Department of Education has centralized its information on harassment at its website, "Know Your Rights" at www.ed.gov/offices/OCR/know.html. More information, including that of state and regional offices, is available at http://bcol01. ed.gov/CFAPPS/OCR/contactus.cfm, or go to www.ed.gov/offices/OCR and click on *Contact Us*. You may also reach the OCR in other ways:

U.S. Department of Education   Phone: 800/ 421-3481
Office for Civil Rights   TDD: 877/ 521-2172
Customer Service Team   Email: OCR@ed.gov
Mary E. Switzer Building   Fax: 202/ 205-9862
330 C Street, SW
Washington, D.C. 20202

• The U.S. Commission on Civil Rights (www.usccr.gov or 800/ 552-6843 or hearing impaired 800/ 877-8339) has no enforcement powers but investigates complaints of discrimination and has a complaint referral service. Its web page, "Getting Uncle Sam to Protect Your Civil Rights: When and Where to File a Complaint—Education," reviews situations constituting discrimination, the time period allowed for filing a complaint, and the agency that should receive the complaint for nonprofit private schools, for-profit private schools, and any school receiving federal financial assistance. This web page can be found by going to www.usccr.gov and then clicking on the following keywords as they appear on successive screens: *Filing a Complaint*; *Getting Uncle Sam to Enforce Your Civil Rights*; *When and Where to File a Complaint*; and finally *Education*.

Learning problems can easily become disciplinary problems. At least 36% of youths in the juvenile court system have severe learning disabilities.[24] Unfortunately court officers and judges are often unaware of disability issues and IDEA's provisions, and so "most youthful offenders emerge from correctional programs without basic literacy, vocational, or adaptive behavior skills."[25] (*34 CFR* § *300.311* specifically applies to students with disabilities in adult prisons.)

Learning disabilities, however, are different in each person. The issue, then, is not a generalized linkage between learning disabilities and juvenile delinquency, but identifying the types of learning disabilities that can make an individual more likely to become a juvenile delinquent. General impulsiveness and poor judgment of social situations have been found to be more predictive of persistent juvenile delinquency in youths with learning disabilities than school failure or acting-out behaviors.[26] Indeed, impulsiveness and poor judgment may be two aspects of the same characteristic because individuals acting without circumspection for immediate rewards lack strategies to overcome distractions and frustrations. For information, consider:

• "Addressing the Needs of Youth with Disabilities in the Juvenile Justice System: The Current Status of Evidence-based Research," by the National Council on Disability, available at www.ncd.gov/newsroom/publications/juvenile.html

• "Addressing Invisible Barriers: Improving Outcomes for Youth with Disabilities In the Juvenile Justice System" by David Osher, Gerald Rouse, John Firman, Mary Magee Quinn, Kimberly Kendziora, and Darren Woodruff, available at www.ldonline.org/ld_indepth/legal_legislative/invisible_barriers.pdf

• "Juvenile Justice" by the Pacer Center available at www.pacer.org/jj

• A search of LD Online's resources; go to www.ldonline.org, enter "juvenile justice" in the white box and click on *SEARCH LD ONLINE*.

For parents raising children with AD/HD, Barkley urges that consequences be positioned as closely as possible to the behavior that is to be managed. Specifically, children not held to account "will be in the most serious trouble they've ever been in, because ... it [isn't] the

---

24 Marc Lewkowicz, "Helping Children Through Juvenile Court: The Youngster with Learning Disabilities," *The GRAM*, September 1995, p. 5.

25 U.S. Department of Education, "Twenty-third Annual Report to Congress on the Implementation of the Individuals with Disabilities Education Act" [Internet], 2001, Washington, D.C., pp. IV-25 and IV-26, available from: http://www.ed.gov/offices/OSERS/OSEP/Products/OSEP2001AnlRpt/Section_IV.pdf

26 Karen Waldie and Otfried Spreen, "The Relationship Between Learning Disabilities and Persisting Delinquency," *Journal of Learning Disabilities*, June/July 1993, pp. 421-422.

consequences that are the problem; it's the delay to the consequences that kill them."[27] Thus, the way to help is not by having an attorney claim diminished capacity, but by holding the child responsible for his actions so that he or she can act appropriately in general society.

One study hints on the importance of good parenting in developing judgment and control of impulsive behavior. A 20-year longitudinal study found that premature babies—who often develop more academic troubles than full-term babies—do not necessarily have more risk-taking behaviors as adults, and in fact, may be less likely to have substance and delinquency problems than their normal peers.[28] An accompanying editorial in *The New England Journal of Medicine* attributes this better-than-expected finding to the resilience of these young people and their families in facing substantial challenges.[29]

Moral development

In the 1950s, Harvard professor Lawrence Kohlberg hypothesized six stages of moral judgment, still used to measure a person's development of reasoning. These stages, with examples, are shown in Figure 8.1:

Figure 8.1

LEVEL 1: SELF-INTEREST	
• Stage 1: Deference to power	I will behave so I don't get punished.
• Stage 2: Pragmatic reciprocal rewards	I'll scratch your back and you'll scratch mine.
LEVEL 2: SOCIAL CUSTOM	
• Stage 3: Social conformity	I won't make waves so that people will like me.
• Stage 4: Law and order	Thou shall not steal.
LEVEL 3: ABSTRACT IDEALS	
• Stage 5: Social contract on individual rights	No state shall ... deny to any person ... equal protection of the laws.
• Stage 6: Universal principles	Do unto others as you would have them do unto you.

---

27 Barkley, "ADHD: Theory, Diagnosis, and Treatment," p. 72.

28 Maureen Hack, Daniel J. Flannery, Mark Schluchter, Lydia Cartar, Elaine Borawski, and Nancy Klein, "Outcomes in Young Adulthood for Very-Low-Birth-Weight Infants," *The New England Journal of Medicine*, 17 January 2002, p. 153. The study also discussed results with respect to male versus female behaviors, socioeconomic factors, learning disabilities, and attention deficit disorders.

29 Marie C. McCormick and Douglas K. Richardson, "Premature Infants Grow Up," *The New England Journal of Medicine*, 17 January 2002, p. 197.

Intended to explain normal development, this scheme outlines how many people can misinterpret LD as a moral problem. Learning disabilities hinder people from following instructions (stage 1) or positively interacting with peers (stage 2). As they grow older, they may have trouble conforming to social conventions (stage 3). If boundaries are crossed (stage 4), society intervenes: incarceration is a real alternative to those without functional job skills.

Kohlberg's theory may also help you understand the inner workings of the many people in your child's life. While a young person with LD may need help negotiating even stages 1 or 2, you may come across noncompliant child professionals whose apparent development seems no better. You may also encounter many compassionate professionals who have dealt with learning disabilities in their own personal lives (stages 5 and 6). For more information, references, and criticisms of this theory, refer to "Stages of Moral Development" by Lawrence Kohlberg (1971) available at www.xenodochy.org/ex/lists/moraldev.html.

Chapter Nine

How will my child's learning disability affect our family?

Caring for someone with a chronic problem is quite stressful. It helps to have some philosophy or diverting activity to provide some perspective to a discouraging situation. Family and friends may feel uncomfortable talking about learning disabilities, but with so many media reports these days, at least fewer people express total skepticism over the existence of LDs. Some family members may show their concern and offer you generic self-help books on child-rearing without knowing that conventional practices can result in adolescent self-destructive behaviors in this at-risk population. Formal or informal parent LD support groups are better forums for talking over common feelings, frustrations, or obtaining new information.

Learning disabilities don't go away. One leading clinician has noted that dealing with a learning disability is a series of grief reactions, one after each successive crisis, often with no final resolution.[1] With the right approach, parents can develop an emotional acceptance of their child's problems, find successful methods of coping, and implement appropriate strategies to deal with the difficulties. It also helps to be flexible as the individual course of treatment will have its own twists and turns. In *The Misunderstood Child*, Silver reviews the normal psychological and psychosocial growth of a child, specific problems related to a child with LD, family reactions to these problems, and social disapproval. Another source of information is "The Expert Answers: Dr. Betty Osman on LD & Family Dynamics" available at www.schwablearning.org/pdfs/expert_osman.pdf.

---

1   Russell Barkley, "ADHD: Theory, Diagnosis, and Treatment," p. 80.

Parents should understand their own and their child's personal limits. While I am open to suggestions and recommendations, I find myself drawing lines in the sand. For example, I was able to decline a class weekend retreat on behalf of my son because I felt that the adults, who were not familiar with the individuals in the group, would not be able to provide the level of supervision that I felt necessary. (My feelings were predicated on a similar trip the year before and then with adults who did know the students better.) After the retreat, another mother said that my action was a "good call" because her daughter had trouble with peers on the trip. You can't change the big things, in this case, the presence of a learning disability, but you can change the little things and secure some peace of mind. A couple of years later, my son was happy to participate in another opportunity of a school-sponsored excursion away from home.

Siblings will have their own developmental issues. Keeping the family together as a cohesive unit can be challenging if each child's issues are widely divergent. I have found that if I demand an equal amount of effort from each of my children *at an individual level*, then the message is clear that everyone must work hard, no matter how talented or gifted. It will still be tough for the child with a disability to see that he will have to try harder for average accomplishments, but this realization would have to happen at some point anyway. Such is life.

When younger siblings are gifted, the deficits felt by an older child with learning disabilities are greatly magnified. Rivalries can build easily, one child resenting the ease of learning the others have, the other children resenting the preponderance of parental time being spent on treating learning disorders. Thus in my household, while one child receives tutoring and special classes, the others receive equally tough instruction. For this latter parental assignment, finding programs geared toward children with teachers who do not underestimate a child's abilities can be tricky. This is special education at the other end of the learning spectrum. Precocious *at-promise* children may fulfill the adage, *early to ripe early to rot*, unless they are disabused of the notion that life is easy before they meet their first real academic challenges in college. For example at the time of this writing, my 11-year-old did quite well in a university-affiliated honors algebra course, and my 13-year-old learned Debussy's *Clair de Lune* at a local music conservatory. The goal is to give each child equivalent individual attention by challenging each at his or her level of ability. There is method to what may seem like madness to others.

Family life of children with learning disabilities

Most family investigations involve children with severe disabilities. In situations involving LD, both child *and parent* may have the same neurological difficulty, complicating family communication and child development. Bender has summarized some studies indicating that family interactions can worsen the disorders:[2]

• Parents have lower academic and behavioral expectations for a child with a disability (Bryan and Bryan, 1983) and less support for the child's efforts.

• Parents are more controlling of a child with a disability (Bryan and Bryan, 1983).

• In some families, communication is disjointed, and behavioral expectations are vague (Green, 1990; Margalit and Almough, 1991); often a parent as well as the child will have LD.

Research on families have identified many common reactions to the presence of a disability in a child:

The Family Unit

• Many parents experience a social reaction, a stigma, for not producing a *perfect* child. They feel shamed, defensive, isolated, and inconsequential.[3] A child with a disability is more likely to be socially excluded rather than the family as a whole being avoided.[4]

• The stigma puts many family members on the defensive, and may explain reduced community relationships. Parents correct misconceptions, explain behaviors, ignore insensitivity, stifle anger, endure embarrassment, feign indifference, or develop a mordant sense of humor.[5] Parents may also project an image of the child as being competent and compliant or restrict information altogether.[6]

• Parents of a child with behavioral disorders are less likely than parents of other children to visit relatives, neighbors, friends, or co-workers; or join social groups.[7]

• The family's diminished community interactions may be offset by supportive relationships between parents.[8] In particular, a two-parent household is linked to effective coping with the disorder and to emotional support of the family as a whole.[9]

• Conflicts over a child's academic achievement may increase the risk of alcoholism and marital discord. Conversely, parental harmony

---

2   Bender, *Learning Disabilities*, pp. 156-157.

3   Thomas M. Shea and Anne M. Bauer citing 1979 Darling study, *Parents and Teachers of Children with Exceptionalities: A Handbook for Collaboration*, 2nd Edition (Needham Heights, Massachusetts: Allyn and Bacon, 1991), p. 39.

4   Shea and Bauer citing 1981 Suelzle and Keenan study, p. 40.

5   Shea and Bauer citing 1977 Marcus study, p. 40.

6   Shea and Bauer citing 1972 Voysey study, pp. 39-40.

7   Shea and Bauer citing 1973 McAllister, Butler, and Lei study, p. 35.

8   Shea and Bauer citing 1968 Lowenthal and Haven study, p. 33.

9   Shea and Bauer citing 1982 Germain and Maisto study, p. 30.

will affect an adolescent's achievement and self-concept.[10]

• Families with more personal, social, and financial resources are better able to manage disabilities than families with limited means.[11]

Mothers

• Mothers are more likely than fathers to wait a year before becoming concerned that a learning disorder exists.[12]

• Mothers do most of the caregiving for their children, even when fathers are at home.[13]

• Mothers are more critical of a child with AD/HD than fathers.[14]

• Mothers are the primary decision-makers of their children's educational needs.[15]

• The quality of the mother-child relationship depends on the child's compliance, age, intelligence, degree of disability, and the number of other children without disabilities in the household.[16]

• Mothers lacking social support, family cohesion, and financial independence suffer high stress levels.[17] Compared to fathers, mothers feel more time limitations, poorer physical and emotional health, greater sensitivity to family interactions, and deeper concerns over the child's social adjustments into family and society.[18]

Fathers

• Fathers report less stress, higher self-esteem, and a greater sense of control over the situation—but also less support—than mothers.[19] Peter Fraenkel discusses many views on fatherhood in "All About Fathers" available at www.aboutourkids.org/letter/novdec99.pdf.

• Fathers of children with a disability did not undertake more child care duties than fathers of normal children. If children are severely developmentally delayed, fathers assume fewer tasks than mothers.[20]

---

10 Trapani citing 1981 Faerstein, and 1978 Kaslow and Cooper studies, *Transition Goals for Students with Learning Disabilities*, p. 83.

11 Shea and Bauer citing 1977 Abrams and Kaslow study, *Parents and Teachers*, p. 35.

12 Roper Starch Worldwide, *Measuring Progress in Public & Parental Understanding of Learning Disabilities*, p. 19.

13 Shea and Bauer citing 1986 Levy-Shiff study, *Parents and Teachers*, p. 31.

14 Nadeau, Littman, and Quinn citing 1990 Barkley, et al. study, *Understanding Girls with AD/HD*, p. 85.

15 Schwab Learning. "Navigating the LD Journey: A Study on the Experiences and Needs of Mothers of Children with Learning Differences" [Internet], January 2002, p. 18, available from: http://www.schwablearning.org/articles.asp?g=4&r=452

16 Shea and Bauer citing 1984 Harper study, *Parents and Teachers*, pp. 30-31.

17 Shea and Bauer citing 1975 Holroyd, Brown, Wikler, and Simmons, study, p. 35.

18 Shea and Bauer citing 1974 Holroyd study, p. 26.

19 Shea and Bauer citing 1986 Goldberg, Marcovitch, MacGregor, and Lojkasek study, p. 26.

20 Shea and Bauer citing 1989 Erickson and Upshur study, p. 26.

- Fathers—more than mothers—are likely to help their children without teacher assistance, to attribute laziness as being the cause of learning problems, and to resist an evaluation which would potentially stigmatize the child with LD.[21]
- Fathers may manage offspring with AD/HD better than mothers.[22]

Siblings
- Children with disabilities may receive up to twice as much time from mothers than normal siblings.[23]
- Siblings may assume guilt for not having a disability as well; embarrassed if teased at school; angry if parents have double standards for behavior or spend little time or money on them; or revenge-seeking by setting up the child with disabilities for parental disapproval.[24]
- Siblings may be stigmatized with the same difficulty as the child who actually has the disorder.[25]
- Siblings reacting to family stress may have behavioral changes or feelings of isolation, vulnerability, or incompetence.[26]
- Siblings may want an evaluation themselves, either misunderstanding that LD is contagious or wanting more attention from the parents.[27]
- Siblings may imitate the child with LD to attract attention.[28]
- Some siblings can successfully instruct and improve socially by assisting the sibling with a disability.[29]
- Children with LD may envy siblings' superior abilities, be angry about performance difficulties, feel guilty about family sacrifices, be embarrassed by failures, or worry about day-to-day existence in school and about the future.[30]

Demographic issues

Cultural, ethnic, and racial perceptions may affect how parents are engaged in their children's education. The Special Education

---

21 Roper Starch Worldwide, *Measuring Progress in Public & Parental Understanding of Learning Disabilities*, pp. 22-24.

22 Nadeau, Littman, and Quinn, *Understanding Girls with AD/HD*, p. 85.

23 Shea and Bauer citing 1979 Cantwell, Baker, and Rutter study, *Parents and Teachers*, p. 31.

24 Silver, *The Misunderstood Child*, pp. 162-164.

25 Shea and Bauer citing 1980 Featherstone study, *Parents and Teachers*, p. 31.

26 Shea and Bauer citing 1988 Milstead study, p. 253.

27 Novick and Arnold, *Why Is My Child Having Trouble at School?*, p. 117.

28 Novick and Arnold, p. 117.

29 Shea and Bauer citing Schreibman, O'Neill, and Koegel study, *Parents and Teachers*, p. 253.

30 Novick and Arnold, *Why Is My Child Having Trouble at School?*, p. 117.

Elementary Longitudinal Study (SEELS) showed some wide differences between groups in 2000 as follows, though income may be a factor:[31]

Family Involvement, by Student Ethnicity*

Percentage Reporting	WH	AF	HS	AS	NT
Attended school meetings	81.7	65.4	65.4	47.8	91.5
Attended school/class events	53.6	34.5	35.3	32.6	32.2
Parents volunteered at school	87.8	84.1	79.2	72.6	85.5
Read to student $\geq$ 3×/week	65.6	68.2	65.0	47.9	81.2
Talked regularly about school	94.5	84.5	80.3	79.9	99.2
Helped with homework $\geq$ 3×/week	82.3	85.9	78.6	73.8	84.7
Had rules on acceptable grades	37.7	64.2	50.8	76.1	60.3
Had a home computer	77.1	43.1	38.3	65.1	65.5
Student does household chores	90.8	91.5	85.2	57.5	93.3
IEP involvement about right	73.3	48.8	56.3	39.5	69.0
Want more IEP involvement	26.4	49.7	42.0	60.5	30.4

* Ethnicity key is as follows: WH = White, AF = African American, HS = Hispanic, AS = Asian/Pacific Islander, NT = Native American

Some other demographic research exists, but should not be used to stereotype behavior:
- Minority children are disproportionately placed in special education.[32]
- African-Americans may perceive teachers as having low expectations for their children.[33]
- Hispanic-Americans may have language barriers to full parental participation in their children's educational programming.[34]
- Asian-Americans feel shame from disabilities affecting academic achievement.[35] Traditional respect for teachers and the need to *save face* can inhibit open and direct communication.[36]
- Low-income parents may be unaware of the variety of special education services, and unfamiliar with concepts such as *due process* and *least restrictive environment*.[37]

---

31 U.S. Department of Education, "Twenty-third Annual Report to Congress on the Implementation of the Individuals with Disabilities Education Act" [Internet], 2001, p. III-27-29, available from: http://www.ed.gov/offices/OSERS/OSEP/Products/OSEP 2001AnlRpt/Section_III.pdf

32 Thomas Hehir, "An Opportunity to Improve Educational Results for Students with Disabilities," in *Rethinking Federal Education Programs for Children with Disabilities* [Internet], January 2002, p. 6, available from: http://www.ctredpol.org/ specialeducation/timelyidea2002.pdf

33 Shea and Bauer citing 1978 Lightfoot study, *Parents and Teachers*, pp. 249-250.

34 Shea and Bauer citing 1987 Lynch and Stein study, p. 250.

35 Shea and Bauer citing 1986 Chan study, p. 251.

36 Shea and Bauer citing 1987 Morrow study, p. 251.

37 Shea and Bauer citing 1987 Brantlinger study, p. 252.

Chapter Ten

What should I do if I or a teacher suspects that my child has a learning disability?

The private-school third-grade teacher suggested that Max be tested at one of several local clinics. I wasn't confident about the purpose of the testing. Tests after ear-tube surgery when he was three deemed his hearing to be normal. A psychologist's screening during a kindergarten admissions process diagnosed him as mentally retarded. A speech therapist during his kindergarten year identified mispronunciations which were easily corrected. Another specialist recommended during first grade found his performance to be within the normal range for his age.

The reading specialist at the private school mentioned that the public school could test him but said something about him not "qualifying." I thought she was referring to services for low-income students. No one in the private school specifically mentioned that the public school offered free testing services for every student residing in the district, both private and public, until I happened to discuss the problem with a public elementary school's vice-principal at a social gathering a couple of years later. Again, it didn't make sense to me that a child who could identify all alphanumeric symbols by age two and a great number of fish species would be considered for special education. In the meantime, my son's self-esteem was plummeting along with his schoolwork.

Before the beginning of the fourth grade, Max received a comprehensive battery of tests from a private child development center. (Such testing is not covered by insurance, because many parents rely on the same tests to determine whether their child is genius material.) The center, located at a reputable hospital, recommended their services. After working with my son for many months, the educational therapist told me that the school district was paying for the same services received by other children that I was paying thousands for—without any insurance reimbursement—and that she believed he was qualified to receive them. This knowledge, corroborated by my social acquaintance—the vice-principal—made me receptive to the fifth-grade teacher's suggestion that he be tested by the public school district. Later, after testing, Max was considered eligible to receive special education services and speech therapy for free.

Prepare yourself for a wide range of emotions

Dealing with learning problems is quite trying. Understanding the manifestations, causes, and effects of an invisible disability leads parents through many emotional states. Initially, there is some awareness of a problem with some denial, as the parents both learn about learning disabilities and try to reduce the seriousness of the situation. As academics become more demanding, parents become angry and can blame teachers, the child, or each other. Bargaining, or a search for solutions can begin at any time during this process. Depression can occur when parents feel helpless regarding the child's academic frustrations, others' belief that their parenting skills are inadequate, and the child's very real social difficulties.

Courses of action

If you suspect your child may have an LD, begin your own investigation. Observe your child on class field trips, at recess and lunchtime, and during class time. Talk to your child, the teacher, school guidance counselor, your pediatrician. Many websites and publications suggested in this book will give you much of the information you need. Sometimes discrete discussions with other parents in the school may uncover other insights or information about the general classroom situation affecting your child. It's advisable to have different opinions from different professional fields.

Reporting observations and suspicions of problems to teachers and other professionals isn't whining. The question is finding someone who is knowledgeable, sympathetic, and can appropriately help your child. Use the wisdom of hindsight to your advantage. Relatives and acquaintances may not be so understanding, feel uncomfortable in discussing your child's difficulties with you, or may give you panaceas, platitudes, or blame for not controlling the situation better.

Many parents will opt to have their child privately tested to avoid an official acknowledgment of a learning disability in their child's school records. For other families, an assessment through the public school system opens the door to free special education services and accommodations. Additional issues exist. Whether to do a private or public evaluation is discussed in "Assessment—Public or Private?" by Jan Baumel, available at www.schwablearning.org/articles.asp?g=1& r=326. Bear in mind that a diagnosis can result in feelings ranging from despair over their child's future to relief in an objective problem identification.

Whichever route is chosen, parents must commit themselves to effectively remedy the difficulties. More than one LD specialist has urged early appropriate intervention, because "most children can be expected to adjust to and compensate for learning deficits."[1] Life, like art, demands character, not nonchalance, in order to realize potential. As one music teacher once told me, "Either you do, or don't do."

Types of service providers

Three major professional groups will be involved in assessing whether your child indeed has any difficulties undermining school performance. *Medical personnel* diagnose and treat physical problems that can interfere with a child's development. Your child may require hearing and vision examinations as part of the school district's evaluation.

Psychologists examine the strengths and weaknesses of a child's innate abilities, personality, motivation, and social traits. Psychologists test behavior in various ways in order to determine perceptual, processing, or expressive problems causing the difficulties in school.

Teachers help a child acquire skills. Class performances and achievement tests are methods of measuring a child's skill levels. Based on experience alone, a teacher can be fairly accurate in predicting which students will have learning problems.[2]

IDEA demands that professionals treating children with learning disabilities meet "the highest requirements" for state licensing, including academic degrees and certification requirements (*34 CFR § 300.136*). Many professionals are not only competent but also quite able to ease your fears. Occasionally, you will encounter a professional who will provide an extra measure of emotional support. Others, perhaps through burnout, may appear indifferent to your concerns, and will cause you to question whether your child's learning needs are

---

1   Pasquale Accardo, "Learning Disabilities Just Don't Add Up," *The Journal of Pediatrics*, September 1998, p. 320.
2   Mercer, *Students with Learning Disabilities*, p. 321.

being fully addressed. You will probably gravitate toward professionals who demonstrate understanding and experience, and who treat your concerns with empathy. However, beware of those trying to sell you a dream. Be skeptical of unusual claims. Effective help and bedside manner can be two different things. (Chapter 25 reviews controversial therapies.)

States have jurisdiction over professional licensing. Professionals providing diagnostic and treatment services for children are usually subject to state licensing requirements, and should be prepared to disclose them to parents. Ensure that the person is currently licensed (if required by the state), experienced, and recommended by someone reputable or someone you know and trust. Some professionals undergo a Diplomate exam, which is a peer review of an individual's competency in a given professional field. The professional should also be current with new advances pertaining to the area of expertise and have experience with children. Your state licensing board, a professional organization, or the Internet can provide information about an individual's credentials and areas in which that person is qualified to practice. Many parent information groups may also reveal the individual's commitment and organizational affiliations not necessarily captured in a brief factual report.

Medical doctors are licensed by states to provide medication for illnesses; they must have an M.D. (Doctor of Medicine), adhere to various state requirements, and keep up-to-date in their specialty. The Federation of State Medical Boards of the United States provides information about state licensing boards at www.fsmb.org/members.htm.

• *Child psychiatrist* specializes in the diagnosis and treatment of emotional and behavioral disturbances of infants, children, and adolescents.

• *Neurologist* specializes in the diagnosis and treatment of brain and nervous system disorders. However, the techniques used in a neurological exam cannot conclusively diagnose the presence of a learning disability, especially in a child with a maturing nervous system.[3]

• *Ophthalmologist* specializes in the diagnosis and treatment of all eye diseases, including medication and surgery.

• *Otologist* specializes in diseases of the ear. An *otolaryngologist* diagnoses and treats ear, nose, and throat (ENT) diseases.

• *Pediatrician* is a primary care physician specializing in childhood illnesses, from infancy through adolescence. As the child's first physician, a pediatrician would provide early identification of unusual growth and development. If you suspect a learning disorder, set up an appointment to discuss your concerns and send in copies of your child's

---

3   Mercer, p. 84.

current report card and standardized test battery beforehand. Usually, pediatricians refer patients to specialists for complex diagnoses. Some pediatricians, however, are trained to evaluate children for learning, developmental, and attention deficit disorders.

Other treatment specialists are subject to varying state licensing requirements.

• *Audiologist* assesses any hearing loss over certain ranges by testing responses to sounds and vibrations. An audiologist evaluates the effects of any hearing problems on school performance, fits hearing aids, and can teach lip reading. A Certificate of Clinical Competence from the American Speech-Language-Hearing Association (ASHA) is required. Bachelor's, master's, and doctorate degrees in audiology exist. Some states do not regulate audiologists. ASHA provides information about state licensing boards at www.professional.asha.org/resources/states/index.cfm#state.

• *Occupational therapist (OT)* evaluates and provides therapy for improving muscular strength, and motor or sensory coordination and functioning. An OT treats mental and physical disabilities with everyday basic skills such as dressing, bathing, eating with utensils, and playing with toys. A clinical professional must have either a bachelor's or master's degree in occupational therapy. Teaching, research, and administrative positions require either a master's or a doctorate degree. The National Board for Certification in Occupational Therapy links to information about state licensing boards from its homepage at www.nbcot.org.

• *Optometrist* diagnoses a person's abilities to see clearly at various distances, prescribes corrective lenses, and in about two-thirds of the states may treat some eye diseases with medication; otherwise diseases *in* the eye are referred to an ophthalmologist. Training is four years and confers an O.D. degree (Doctor of Optometry). The Association of Regulatory Boards of Optometry links to information about state licensing boards from its homepage at www.arbo.org.

• *Physical therapist (PT)* uses equipment, exercises, and self-help devices to increase muscle tone, strength, and endurance; and to improve balance, coordination, body function, and posture. Training programs in physical therapy offer a bachelor's degree, or a master's degree or a certificate to those already holding a bachelor's degree in an unrelated field. The Federation of State Boards of Physical Therapy provides information about state licensing boards at www.fsbpt.org/directory.cfm.

• *Speech and language therapist or pathologist (SLP)* assesses and treats speech and language disorders. A child may also require medical and psychological treatment. Although a bachelor's degree is available, a master's or doctorate degree and a Certificate of Clinical Competence from the American Speech-Language-Hearing Association (ASHA) is required. Some states do not regulate SLPs. ASHA provides information about state licensing boards at www.professional.asha.org/resources/states/index.cfm#state.

Psychologists with doctoral degrees can be licensed to practice independently in most states. Depending on their subspecialty, individuals with master's degrees are usually supervised by a licensed or certified psychologist in about half of the states; in other states, those with master's degrees may practice independently. The Association of State and Provincial Psychology Boards links to information about state licensing boards (click on *Links*) and general consumer advice (click on *Consumer Information*) at www.asppb.org. The American Association of State Counseling Boards links to information about state licensing boards from www.aascb.org/state.htm.

• *Clinical psychologist* specializes in behavioral problems, emotional disturbances, and personality disorders; is trained in developmental and abnormal psychology; and can provide in-depth non-medical diagnosis, counseling, and therapy for individuals or groups. A doctorate degree is required.

• *Neuropsychologist* conducts psychoeducational assessments and other psychological tests to evaluate learning and specific areas of brain functioning. A doctorate degree is required.

• *School psychologist* examines intellectual, social, adaptive, and emotional development of students. These psychologists specialize in identifying learning problems and appropriate educational programs. They can provide information about a child's development, educational needs, and management of the disability. They are trained in classroom management techniques and learning styles. School psychologists must have at least a master's degree. Some states require school psychologists to practice only in school settings, while others allow a broader practice if supervised by psychologists licensed for independent practice. Other states require doctorate-level psychologists to administer diagnostic tests or supervise the person making the educational evaluation. About half the states have established credential standards in conjunction with the National Association of School Psychologists (http://nasp online.org or 301/ 657-0270).

• *School counselor* provides therapy and counseling on school sites for students age 4–18. They work with teachers and school administrators. They are advocates for children and, as such, are obligated to report problems like abuse to authorities. A master's degree is required.

• *Family counselor* assists family members to understand the nature of the learning disability involved, how their behaviors affect each other, and offer assistance in improving relationships. A master's degree is required.

• *Social worker* can offer family and individual counseling and therapy. Social workers follow the child's history, and can recommend community resources to assist in education, finances, neighborhood problems, vocational training, and job opportunities. The Association of Social Work Boards links to information about state requirements and licensing boards from its homepage at www.aswb.org.

Teachers, besides parents, are the primary therapists of any child with learning problems because treatment must be at the actual point of performance,[4] the classroom. The federal *No Child Left Behind Act* (www.ed.gov) requires that a "highly qualified" teacher be found in every classroom by the end of the 2005–2006 school year. Each state determines its own requirements to fulfill this law. National teacher certification programs have also emerged. At the time of this writing, the National Board for Professional Teaching Standards (www.nbpts.org) offers one certificate program; the philosophically different National Council on Teacher Quality (www.nctq.org) is developing another program. The National Association of State Boards of Education links to information about state education agencies at www.nasbe.org. A general discussion on teacher certification as a standard of competence is presented in "What's Wrong with Teacher Certification?" by Arthur Wise (*Education Week on the Web*, 9 April 2003), available at www.edweek.org/ew/ewstory.cfm?slug=30wise.h22.

• *Teacher* adheres to the curriculum standards set by each state. Colleges and universities offer most teacher-training programs, which include course work in the subject to be taught, child development, teaching methods, and teaching practice in a real classroom. Every state requires its public school teachers to be certified at the elementary through high school levels. Most states issue separate certificates for teaching at either the elementary or secondary school level; teachers at the secondary (and sometimes at the elementary) school level must also fulfill requirements for teaching a certain subject. Some states also require certificates for private schools, nursery schools, and junior colleges. Some states relax these requirements with fast-track programs to alleviate a projected shortage of two million teachers over the next 10 years.[5] Professional development keeps teachers current with new concepts and practices in education. *In-service* training after school hours, workshops, reading materials, and conferences are some examples that serve this purpose. No consensus exists on the specific characteristics of an effective teacher. "Teacher Quality" by Melissa McCabe (*Education Week on the Web*, 19 March 2003), reviews some studies at www.edweek.org/context/topics/issuespage.cfm?id=50.

---

4   Russell Barkley, "ADHD: Theory, Diagnosis, and Treatment," p. 73.
5   Christine Foster, "Why Teach?" *Stanford Magazine*, September/October 2001, p. 52.

- *Learning specialist or special educator* assesses academic achievements and works to improve the academics of a child with learning disabilities. The special education teacher also assists other teachers in the school to better address learning problems in the regular classroom, and meets with other involved individuals such as parents, therapists, and psychologists. Each state has its own licensing requirements, beginning with a bachelor's or master's degree. A special education teacher can advance to become a program administrator. The National Information Center for Children and Youth with Disabilities links to much more information from its homepage at www.nichcy.org. (Once at this address, click on *Our Publications*, enter "Who's Teaching Our Children with Disabilities?" in the white box and click on the *Search* button. This will bring up an index of titles in alphabetical order. Scroll down until you reach the title you entered in the previous screen, and click on it. You will be offered a choice of text or pdf formats.) A list of the 10 most recommended graduate programs in special education are published annually by *U.S. News & World Report* in its annual edition of *America's Best Graduate Schools*.

- *Educational therapist (ET)* develops and executes remediation and learning strategies for school-related behavior and learning problems, which may involve some familiarity with the child's interests and background. An educational therapist can formally or informally make educational assessments, and works with the school, parents, and other involved professionals. Requirements vary. Federal positions require a bachelor's degree in education, or a bachelor's degree in psychology or occupational therapy with additional course work in education. Some universities offer a certificate in educational therapy for master-degree candidates in special education, or as a subspecialty for practicing professionals, such as classroom teachers, speech and language specialists, counselors, social workers, psychoeducational consultants, and occupational therapists. The certificate program is operated under the auspices of the Association of Education Therapists (www.aetonline. org or 800/ 286-4267). At the time of this writing, AET is working with states to develop licensing programs.

- *Tutor* provides instructional support in academic areas such as remediation, skill building, enrichment, and strategies for attaining better grades. No specific training is required.

Attorneys and advocates may participate in the process of securing special education services and accommodations for your child. Hieros Gamos provides information about state bar associations at www.hg.org/northam-bar.html.

- *Attorney* provides legal assistance to parents about issues pertaining to federal and state special education laws and regulations. Experience with IDEA, Section 504, and the Americans with Disabilities Act is

not an area of practice common to most attorneys. The attorney must be in good standing with the state bar and be licensed to practice in your state.
• *Advocate* represents parents in legal issues related to special education, but may not act as an attorney.

Determining what services you need and who will provide them

Parents should ask hard questions of themselves and professionals before engaging their services. Unless you do your own investigations, you may not realize that you have alternatives better than what you've already heard. Some parent information centers can help direct your search. An information search is not the same as a professional assessment however, but it will prepare you to understand information that you receive and optimize your child's treatment. "How to Choose a Professional" suggests general questions, available at www.ldonline.org/ld_indepth/assessment/how_to_choose_a_professional.html. Schwab Learning offers "A Guide to Finding Local Resources When Your Child Has Learning Disabilities or AD/HD" at www.schwablearning.org/articles.asp?r=688. Schwab Learning also lists questions to ask professionals when you are thinking about engaging services in these areas:
• "Questions to Ask Professionals Who Assess for LD," available at www.schwablearning.org/articles.asp?g=1&r=84
• "Questions to Ask Professionals Who Assess or Treat AD/HD," available at www.schwablearning.org/articles.asp?g=1&r=85
• "Questions to Ask Speech and Language Specialists," available at www.schwablearning.org/articles.asp?g=1&r=79
• "Questions to Ask Counselors," available at www.schwablearning.org/articles.asp?g=1&r=83
• "Questions to Ask Tutors," available at www.schwablearning.org/articles.asp?g=1&r=80
• "Questions to Ask Attorneys or Advocates," by Linda Broatch, available at www.schwablearning.org/articles.asp?g=2&r=82

The New York University Child Study Center offers "Choosing a Mental Health Professional for Your Child: Who, What, When, Where, Why, How," by Robin Goodman at www.aboutourkids.org/articles/choosingmh.html. Included are suggestions for prospective questions about treatment.

"Questions to Ask the Professionals" is provided at www.ldonline.org/ld_indepth/assessment/questions.html for any inquiries of:

- audiologists
- educational consultants
- learning specialists
- neurologists
- neuropsychologists
- occupational therapists
- psychiatrists
- psychologists
- reading specialists
- social workers
- speech pathologists
- tutors

LD Online also offers "How to Find and Use Professionals for Your Case," by Roger Meyer, available at www.ldonline.org/ld_indepth/legal_legislative/find_attorney.html.

The beginning of Chapter 25 suggests other issues to consider when an alternative treatment is contemplated.

$$\text{Chapter Eleven}$$

What is an evaluation and what does it involve?

The fifth-grade teacher initiated the paperwork for a public school evaluation of my son. The school district had a long waiting list and so I was told any evaluation would be six months away.

With respect to learning disabilities, an *assessment* is an appraisal of a student's prospective capabilities based on a diagnosis. A *diagnosis* is a conclusion formed from an analytical investigation of symptoms, tests, observations, and interviews. Different types of assessments probe different levels of problems. Parents and teachers continuously screen children for serious problems. A school counselor may conduct some testing, make some observations, and discuss findings with parents and teachers. Some deeper problems require more expertise from a psychologist, a developmental pediatrician, or a speech-and-language pathologist. The most difficult, chronic, and puzzling problems will require a multidisciplinary team of specialists to diagnose and treat the problems. In short, assessments are used to:
- Screen for significant problems
- Evaluate current overall intellectual performance
- Identify academic strengths and weaknesses
- Examine behavioral strengths and weaknesses
- Observe problem-solving strategies used by the child
- Determine the effectiveness of ongoing instructional programs, services, and current school placement
- Determine eligibility for the school district's special education program

- Establish near-term goals and strategies for a student's unique educational plan
- Direct long-term planning to maximize academic social, and vocational development.

An *evaluation* is a complex legal requirement for determining the presence of a disability, is contained within the language of IDEA, and is further explained in Chapter 13. Thus, a diagnosis will determine the presence of a disorder, an assessment or evaluation will render an opinion on whether some action is required, but only an evaluation conducted under IDEA or Section 504 will determine the presence of a disability and access to IDEA services or school accommodations. Otherwise, outside the world of special education, *assessment*, *diagnosis*, and *evaluation* are roughly synonymous terms.

Appendix 4 provides a brief overview of the special education evaluation process. *Negotiating the Special Education Maze* provides action steps for you to manage this high-stakes evaluation process, rather than you being managed by the process. The book examines whether to give permission for the evaluation, preparing for the evaluation, monitoring the testing process, and preparing for the conference in which the eligibility decision will be made. The book is available in both English and Spanish. Another source on the intricacies of special education law is *The Complete IEP Guide: How to Advocate for Your Special Ed Child*, by Lawrence M. Siegel. *The Misunderstood Child: Understanding and Coping with Your Child's Learning Disabilities* by Larry Silver provides guidance on the diagnostic process itself.

Child Find identifies suspected disabilities

At the time I was selecting an elementary school, I didn't know that the public school district had a federal mandate under IDEA to identify, locate, and evaluate children in all private, parochial, and public schools with potential learning problems for possible early intervention.

Child Find is a federally mandated screening requirement of public schools. (In this book, Child Find is capitalized to denote it as a unique program; IDEA does not capitalize this term. This service has various local school-district names such as *Student Success Team* or *Child Study Team*.) States must locate and identify *all* children, from birth through age 21, *suspected* of having disabilities, not just count up those actually referred for evaluation. This provision under IDEA applies to all students in different situations as well—public, private, and parochial schools; migrant and homeless children; and even those "advancing from grade to grade" but deemed to be having trouble. These children may then be referred for evaluation for special needs:

> "[The State must ensure that] All children with disabilities residing in the State, including children with disabilities attending private schools, regardless of the severity of their disability, and who are in need of special education and related services, are identified, located, and evaluated ...."
>
> —*34 CFR § 300.125*

Child Find is reiterated under 34 CFR § 300.451. This provision specifically requires school districts to "locate, identify, and evaluate" all children placed in private schools *by their parents*, including religious schools. Child Find activities are separate from special education and related services.

The effectiveness of Child Find varies across the U.S. Some states have weak referral and identification systems, while other states have "very effective awareness and outreach systems."[1] Don't wait to find out how well Child Find works in your area. You can initiate the evaluation process yourself.

A referral begins the evaluation process

A teacher-recommended speech therapy program diagnosed specific pronunciation problems but wait-listed my son; in the meantime, I had him practice tongue-twisters and successfully cleared up his speech. (Health insurance would not pay for speech therapy.) In the first grade, he was receiving extra help in reading from a teacher's aide.

All school children—public, private, and parochial—are entitled to free public school assessments. There are three ways of getting a referral for an evaluation (*34 CFR § 300.527*):

* If Child Find has already identified a child as possibly having disabilities, the local school system and the state division of special education have rules and regulations specifying procedures for referring the child for an evaluation.
* The classroom teacher or school personnel makes the referral following district guidelines. The teacher is the most valid single informational source on a child's development.[2] The educational professional may have you complete a form and add examples of the child's work. Figure 11.1 is an example of a teacher's referral for special education.

---

1   U.S. Department of Education, "Twenty-third Annual Report to Congress," p. IV-8.
2   Levine, *Educational Care*, p. 243.

Figure 11.1[3]

Special Education Referral Form	
Student:	
Referring Teacher:	
Class:	**Date:**
Describe your concern regarding this student's performance in your class.	
Evaluate the student's test performance: (Can he complete tests within the allotted time? How does he or she perform on different types of tests? Do you notice signs of test anxiety?)	
Evaluate the student's homework performance: (Does he or she complete assignments on time? What is the quality of work?)	
Evaluate the student's class work performance including behavior: (Is (s)he prepared with necessary materials? Does (s)he focus on his or her learning tasks? Is (s)he easily distracted? Is his or her classroom behavior appropriate? Is (s)he organized?)	
What interventions have you attempted with the student? Complete the attached intervention forms. (Have you spoken with his or her parents? Have you involved his or her counselor? Has the student sought extra help?)	

---

3 Adapted from Martin Procaccio, *Special Education Referral Form*, unpublished, 2001. Reprinted with permission of Martin Procaccio.

Documentation of Previous Classroom Modifications
(to be completed and attached to Referral Form)

Student name:_________________________ Teacher:_____________________________Date_________
Please date all modifications that have been attempted. (Example: Feb. 3–20 repeat directions)

Modifying the teaching mode:
_____repeat directions
_____provide written directions
_____provide taped directions
_____use peer-partner (study buddy)
______for note-taking
______to check assignment book
______to help correct work
______as established contact if needed
_____for clarification from home
_____specific instruction in study skills
_____increase active participation
______provide think time before calling
_____on student
______warn student (s)he may be called on
______use pairs to increase
_____interdependence
______have student paraphrase information,
_____directions, other students' responses
_____teacher circulates around room
_____provide visual prompts (at board/desk)
_____provide immediate feedback (student
_____corrects own work)
_____frequent review of key concepts
_____speak more slowly or clearly
_____use individual contract
_____use cross-age or peer tutoring
_____small group instruction
_____individualized instruction
______teacher
______aide
______parent volunteer
______before / during / after school
_____(circle any that apply)
_____Other___________________________

Modifying the teaching setting:
_____Preferential seating
______front of room
______away from certain other students
______away from distractions (door,
_____pencil sharpener, computers)
______near buddy for support
_____modify schedule
______non participation / participation
_____for no grade in ___________

Modifying assignments:
_____reduced homework load based on
______time (i.e. no more than 20 minutes for math)
______physical need (i.e. stop reading when fatigued)
_____simpler curriculum
__________________________________specifically?
_____use aids: calculator, word processor, other?
_____encourage color-coding of materials
_____use books on tape
_____use graphic organizers (mind maps, charts, webs, etc.)
______encourage use of paper stickies when studying
______encourage use of pictures/symbols in note-taking
_____and making study guides

Modifying student's behavior:
_____have student repeat directions
______to teacher
______to class
______to partner
_____clearly defined, written expectations
_____frequent reminder of rules
_____use mild, consistent consequences
_____ignore minor infractions
_____opportunity to help teacher
_____opportunity to help other students
_____peers
_____younger students
_____private discussion regarding rules
_____secret signal between teacher and student
_____emphasis on student's special talents

Modifying assessments:
_____offer extended time (with aide/after school)
_____modify weight of examinations
_____oral tests
_____opportunity for oral responses after taking written test
_____taped tests
_____modified format
_____administer orally
_____credit for projects
_____alternate modes for demonstrating mastery of material

Please keep a record of all modifications attempted. If the student is referred for assessment, please document which modifications were attempted, duration of time they were attempted, and their degree of success. Thank you!

• Parents can initiate the referral process in two ways: 1) by expressing "concern in writing (or orally if the parent does not know how to write or has a disability that prevents a written statement) … that the child is in need of special education and related services" to the principal of their neighborhood public school, or 2) by requesting an evaluation of the child. Basically, any parent can ask the principal at the local public school (commensurate with student's grade level) for an evaluation for any reason.

After receiving the referral, the principal convenes a screening committee (different names exist like *Education Management Team*, *Child Study Team*, or *Student Study Team*) often composed of the principal, the person making the referral, and the teacher or professional most familiar with the child's problems; parents are not required to attend this meeting. This committee determines whether the problems are serious enough to warrant an evaluation. That is, while the committee is legally obligated to consider the request, it does not have to agree to an evaluation. If the committee recommends a full evaluation in writing, the principal gathers special education diagnostic professionals to test your child. If no evaluation is recommended, you may either engage a private practitioner to test your child or/and appeal the decision through a due process hearing.

A successful referral for psychological testing is based on specific hypothesized reasons for the occurrence of unusual observed behaviors. (Classroom success also depends on your child's motivation and unique learning situation such as instructional quality, but neither of these are part of a typical assessment.[4]) For example, a helpful referral may direct an investigation into a possible visual perceptual problem based on a child's incomplete and poorly executed written work.[5]

In contrast, some referrals may be too specific, presuming an explanation, and in essence, telling the specialist which tests to conduct. In the inadequate referral profiled at the beginning of this section, a teacher noted pronunciation problems in a kindergartner and recommended speech therapy (instead of a full evaluation). The speech therapists then identified specific articulation deficits, but did not diagnose an underlying phonological processing problem. Although pronunciation improved, school problems continued. *An observation is not a diagnosis.*

Some referral questions may be too vague requiring the psychologist to investigate the reasons underlying the referral in the first place.[6] Other referral questions may be inappropriate such as those requesting testing to determine the ultimate cause of the problem (etiology), predict the future course of the problem (prognosis), or shift the child's problem to someone else.[7] Psychological testing describes a current condition but does not treat the problem.

You can help the referral process by recognizing the critical features of your child's problems. Particularly helpful is a systematic approach presented in *Educational Care* by Levine, summarized in the

---

4   Wodrich, *Children's Psychological Testing*, p. 156.
5   Wodrich, p. 28.
6   Wodrich, p. 27.
7   Wodrich, *Children's Psychological Testing*, p. 29.

list below.[8] Many of the behavioral patterns described in his book are too subtle to be identified in assessment tests, but are those little things that parents and teachers notice as perhaps affecting performance. Levine purposely avoids diagnostic labels because problems manifest themselves differently in each individual:

WEAK EXECUTIVE FUNCTION
- Weak mental energy control
- Weak processing control
- Weak production control

REDUCED REMEMBERING
- Inadequate memory encoding
- Insufficient active working memory
- Incomplete consolidation in long-term memory
- Reduced access to long-term memory

CHRONIC MISUNDERSTANDING
- Weak language processing
- Incomplete concept formation
- Weak visual processing
- Slow data processing
- Small cache size
- Excessive top-down processing
- Excessive bottom-up processing

DEFICIENT OUTPUT
- Weak language production
- Disappointing motor performance
- Persistent organizational failure
- Inefficient problem solving and strategy use

DELAYED SKILL ACQUISITION
- Slow reading development
- Inaccurate spelling patterns
- Impeded written output
- Underdeveloped mathematical ability

POOR ADAPTATION
- School-related anxiety
- Somatic stress
- Noncompliant behaviors
- Social inability
- Lost motivation

Unfortunately for most children, consistent school failure is the usual prerequisite for a referral. The students who are struggling academically but least likely to get referrals are:[9]

• Compliant, quiet, shy, and withdrawn students whose unhappiness and frustration build into attendance, crying, and conduct troubles;

• Gifted students whose learning disabilities undermine their true potential;

• Hard-working students whose parents essentially homeschool them for hours in what should have been learned in class. These students may also have private tutors.

---

8 Mel Levine, *Educational Care: A System for Understanding and Helping Children with Learning Problems at Home and at School* (Cambridge, Massachusetts: Educators Publishing Service), p. 8. Copyright © 1994 by Melvin D. Levine, M.D.. Reprinted and adapted from Table 1.1 with permission of Educators Publishing Service, Inc.

9 Silver, *The Misunderstood Child*, p. 366.

School systems have different methods of initiating an evaluation. Some parents are very much aware that their child has been referred for evaluation, and some are not at all aware of any ongoing process concerning their child. In all cases, however, school districts are required to notify parents of their rights, and provide descriptions of considered alternatives, relevant rules and procedures, and in a way that they can understand the material. The school district must obtain *informed* parental consent before it:
• Initiates, changes, or refuses a request about a child's identification, evaluation, placement, or provision of services (*34 CFR § 300.503*)
• Initially evaluates or reevaluates, or initially provides special education and related services (*34 CFR § 300.505 (a)*)
• Discloses personal information to anyone other than relevant education officials (*34 CFR § 300.571*).

Evaluations conducted under IDEA's procedures are required in order to receive special education and related services. Second opinions are possible as provided by this law. In some cases, parents may refuse to allow the state to evaluate their child. IDEA also addresses this issue:

> "If the parents of a child with a disability refuse consent for initial evaluation or a reevaluation, the agency may continue to pursue those evaluations by using the due process procedures ... or the mediation procedures ... except to the extent inconsistent with State law relating to parental consent."
>
> —*34 CFR § 300.505 (b)*

Beginning the evaluation

A complete diagnostic assessment of your child's academic strengths and weaknesses is a time-consuming process, gathering information about the child's background and progress in school, such as:
• Parents' education and economic status
• Child's primary language, home environment, and developmental and medical history, including any recent hearing and vision tests
• Parent and teacher reports
• Work samples, standardized test scores, and school report cards
• Previous test results and reports from other specialists.

Under IDEA, the school district's evaluation procedures must observe the following requirements (*34 CFR § 300.532*):

- The evaluation cannot be based on a single test but must include a *variety* of technically sound methods to accurately assess functioning and achievement levels.
- Tests must not merely "provide a single general intelligence quotient" but assess specific areas of educational need.
- The assessment must cover all areas related to the suspected disability, including cognitive, academic, communicative, behavioral, emotional, social, developmental, and physical factors.
- Tests must be selected and administered on a nondiscriminatory basis, either racially or culturally, and in the child's native language or other communication mode.
- If the child has limited English proficiency, then tests must measure the presence of a disability, not a child's English language skills.
- Tests must be validated for the specific purpose being used.
- Tests are administered by trained personnel according to the producer's instructions.
- Nonstandard conditions must be noted, such as breaks taken during testing.

You are entitled to *request* a free evaluation through the school district. Unfortunately, because of limited public resources, assessments may become eligibility screenings for publicly funded services rather than in-depth studies of students' abilities, as they should be. In *A Guide to 85 Tests for Special Education*, Carolyn Compton warns that school districts reduce evaluation costs by:

> "… administering only those tests necessary to establish eligibility for special education services. These tests may or may not be good tools for diagnosing a student's disabilities. The same tests are sometimes repeated the following year to measure progress; and there may be little awareness of whether the instruments were even designed to measure progress. The lengthy battery of diagnostic tests designed to tease out the details of a student's learning difficulties is becoming increasingly rare in public school special education programs. Such testing is more likely to occur in research projects or in private or hospital clinics, with private practi[ti]oners."[10]

Should you have trouble getting an evaluation, contact a parent information center for more information. A child's inexplicable difficulties in school warrant investigation.

---

10   From *A Guide to 85 Tests for Special Education* by Carolyn Compton © 1990 by Globe Fearon, an imprint of Pearson Learning Group, a division of Pearson Education, Inc. Used by permission.

Chapter Twelve

What is psychoeducational testing?

Psychology is the study of mental processes and behavior. *Psychoeducational testing* refers to the psychological tests used to analyze the mental processes underlying your child's educational performance. As part of the assessment, your child will undergo psychoeducational testing. This chapter describes this process.

In *When Your Child Needs Testing*, the authors sympathize with parents' normal uneasiness to suggestions that their child undergo a psychological evaluation. Many of these reactions may "reflect erroneous assumptions about the nature of psychological testing": These tests are not about discovering character flaws in the child, excluding parents from decision-making, nor revealing parental inadequacies.[1]

Numerous tests exist. Some are better than others. Because these tests will be used to determine the nature and severity of any underlying disorders, *you* should try to understand what these tests mean.

Preparing your child for testing

Preparing your child for psychoeducational testing can reduce anxiety and encourage cooperation through the upcoming battery of tests. One practice is to introduce the discussion by the number of days as the child is old; if the child is eight years old, discuss the evaluation at least

---

1   Milton F. Shore, Patrick J. Brice, and Barbara G. Love, *When Your Child Needs Testing: What Parents, Teachers, and Other Helpers Need To Know About Psychological Testing* (New York: The Crossroad Publishing, 1992), p. 50.

eight days in advance of the testing.[2] Reassure your child that the reason for testing is to understand why school is a struggle despite hard work and attempts to do well. Explain that the tests will contain a variety of questions, puzzles, drawings, stories, and games; and that the tests are neither painful nor about whether the child is crazy. Most importantly, offer the child hope in that the evaluation should show adults how best to help. Be open and honest as much as possible.

The psychologist doing the testing should have been trained in managing children with a history of academic failure. Test administrators try to make children comfortable. Do not expect your child to be aware of his or her actual test performance; correct answers are not supposed to be given out in order to maintain the professional integrity of the test. What really matters is whether the child is putting his or her best effort into each test administered. Some tips:
• Schedule the test sessions (there will be many) during the time of day when your child usually functions best. Identify any classes or activities that the child would not like to miss. Ensure that the child is well rested and not hungry. Take something along to do while you wait; stay in the area during the testing. My son felt better knowing that someone familiar was nearby whenever he was being tested even if he was familiar with the proceedings.
• Your child will want to know about what will happen. Students should understand the roles of the professionals conducting the testing and the reason(s) for the assessment. If possible, visit the test site with your child before the first day of testing. When scheduling the assessment, you should be able to find out about the expected types of questions, testing methods, and the length of each session. The test administrator should explain all that the child needs to know in order to do the test. Your role is to get the child to the test site on time and in a condition to do the best work possible.
• For many tests, observations of the student's behaviors are important. Tests of skills, for example, present increasingly difficult problems or tasks until the child fails three or more times. The test administrator will note the situations causing fatigue, inattention, frustration, or delayed responses. This is all part of the diagnostic process. Tell the child to do his or her best and not to be discouraged. The child should remain calm and collected during testing. The test administrator should permit breaks as needed.

Since the test results will affect the child's future, a child should be able to ask about the results and the impact of these results. The assessment period will be an anxious time for you as well.

---

2   Shore, Brice, and Love, p. 78.

Learning patterns, which can explain observed behaviors, appear within a battery of tests. For example, a seemingly inattentive child who has problems following directions may also score low on tests of oral comprehension. In *Educational Care*, Levine has presented tables of evaluation components:[3]

Evaluation Component	**General Description of Subcomponents**	
Educational	• Psycho-educational testing—observations of academic performance on standardized testing with documentation of "breakdown points"	
	Reading	- Decoding accuracy and speed - Comprehension - Recall - Summarization proficiency - Overall speed and proficiency
	Spelling	- Accuracy - Error types - Spelling in context (during writing activities)
	Writing	- Pencil grip - Graphomotor fluency, rhythm, ease of output - Legibility (manuscript and cursive) - Mechanics (actual use of punctuation, capitalization; recognition of errors) - Language usage (compared to oral language) - Ideation (topic selection and development) - Organization
	Mathematics	- Factual recall and degree of proficiency

---

3   Mel Levine, *Educational Care: A System for Understanding and Helping Children with Learning Problems at Home and at School* (Cambridge, Massachusetts: Educators Publishing Service), pp. 248 and 250. Copyright © 1994 by Melvin D. Levine, M.D. Adapted from Tables 8.2 and 8.3 and reprinted with permission of Educators Publishing Service, Inc.

Mathematics (continued)	- Procedural recall and degree of proficiency - Understanding of concepts - Word problem-solving skill - Visualization/geometric ability
General Observations	- Patterns of attention during academic work - Use of strategies to facilitate work - Level of performance anxiety - Understanding of learning (metacognition) - Enthusiasm, degree of interest - Creativity - Specific content affinities

• Direct classroom observations[4] and error analyses by teachers

• Interpretations of historical data from parents and possible interview with the student

Behavioral and Affective	• Direct observations, projective tests, and interviewing of the child to assess affect, seek other psychological conditions, determine child's feelings about school problem(s) • Use of parent, teacher, and (when possible) student questionnaires to elicit patterns of behavior and behavioral concerns
Cognitive and Developmental	• Direct intelligence, neuropsychological, and/or neurodevelopmental testing to detect relevant neurodevelopmental strengths and weaknesses • Use of questionnaires to document past and present neurodevelopmental function, affinities, and styles
Environmental	• Interview with parents to elicit relevant factors in the current and past home environment of the child • Consideration of cultural, peer-related, and community-based issues related to the student's performance

---

4   Classroom observations are to be made by at least one evaluation team member other than the child's regular teacher, according to *34 CFR* § *300.542*.

Medical

    • Review of child's medical history to uncover current or previous factors affecting school performance

    • Complete physical examination to rule out any definable medical disorder associated with the child's learning difficulty

    • Complete neurological examination to detect any possible central nervous system disorder

Psychological test caveats

A full assessment is a differential diagnosis about the abilities and traits of a child. Interpretations of numerical scores can lead to conclusions about a child's ability to perceive, process, and express information. Appendix 5 lists specific tests reviewed in books available to the public. Only *some* of these tests will be used to assess your child. Before you enter any discussions about test results with school personnel, you should find out from the test administrators which tests will be used and obtain independent information and reputable opinions about those tests. Libraries and parent information centers are good places to begin your search.

A psychological test is just one measurement. No single definitive test exists to diagnose a learning disability with 100% accuracy. A diagnosis results from the convergence of many tests. Often, observations of a child's adaptive behavior and social skills assist the identification process. Some children, however, have multiple problems that confound the diagnostic process.

These psychological assessments are not perfect and can be influenced by the testing environment and the psychologist's experience and training. There are many issues affecting psychological testing:

• The test may have been developed with a purpose and a population very different from those of your child.

• The overall condition and attitude of the child can affect test results. Testing over many days can lessen the impact of unusually good or unusually bad test sessions.

• The test may not be a true measure of what it is supposed to be measuring. Statistical adequacy of the tests, also known as *psychometric properties*—such as *standardization*, *reliability*, or *validity*—determine a test's assessment value.

• Test scores can be misinterpreted and thus lead to a misdiagnosis of your child's problems. The test administrator should be adequately trained to avoid scoring errors, to disregard statistically insignificant differences (such as a one-point IQ gain), or to overgeneralize a diagnosis based on one test alone.

- Many psychological tests include standards for determining typical categories of learning patterns, but not every possible combination if multiple problems are involved. Thus a child who does not fit conveniently into one of the typical cognitive profiles may receive an incorrect differential diagnosis to explain his or her inability to learn.
- Repeating the same test later may be an invalid measure of the child's progress.

Since tests today are used to determine things important in people's lives such as program admissions and educational placements, it is crucial that they be understood. The Department of Education has reviewed many test issues in a report, "The Use of Tests as Part of High-Stakes Decision-Making for Students: A Resource Guide for Educators and Policy Makers," available online at www.ed.gov/offices/OCR/testing/TestingResource.doc.

Statistics

Most psychological tests are formal statistical measures of behavioral responses to test items that, over time and professional experience, have been accepted as appropriate measures of abilities and achievements. The basic issue of psychological testing is whether the test truly fulfills its claims. In order to understand psychological testing, some underlying statistical concepts must be reviewed.

Representative norm group. Like a control group in any scientific experiment, a representative *norm* group establishes the range of normal performance on a test. The individuals must be chosen at random from a larger population, and be truly representative of individuals with certain characteristics of age, intelligence, and so on. For example, if the representative norm only consisted of male students, then the test results comparing a female student's performance against this norm may be inaccurate. The accuracy of the performance range is also dependent on the size of the representative sample: The larger the norm group, the more accurately defined is the normal range.

With respect to psychological tests, revised tests anticipate IQ gains of the general American population each generation (an example of the *Flynn effect*). Thus, a child could score lower on a restandardized test than on the version just retired.

At the statistical scoring extremes of a population, a few points of change can greatly affect school placement decisions, whereas a few points of change around the population average can be dismissed as random error.

Test reliability is about scoring accuracy. A reliable test reproduces the same results upon a second test administration, assuming no prior learning or actions that would alter the trait being tested.

A reliable test is also longer rather than shorter; a large number of test items can reduce test problems such as a child's confusion or attentional lapse with a particular question.

Standard error is another indicator of reliability. Test measurements of ability, achievement, and so on, are not single numerical scores but are really a range of possible outcomes as indicated by that test's standard error of measurement. For example, a test score of 100 with a standard error of 5, suggests that the real score lies in the range of 95–105. A less reliable test could have a standard error of 10, meaning that the real score lies between 90–110.

Test validity is about effectively measuring the trait. According to David Wodrich, Clinical Director of Child Psychology at The Phoenix Children's Hospital in Arizona, a test title is frequently a "poor guide" on what that test or subtest measures.[5] **Content validity** indicates whether the test contains items that truly measure a certain trait. For example, an *intelligence test* limited only to math items would really be a test of quantitative ability. Special attention should be given to standardized national achievement tests, which rarely match local curricula exactly. **Construct validity** denotes how well a test captures characteristics of a trait, as predicted by a particular theory. **Predictive validity** is a measurement of a test's usefulness to predict outcomes. For example, IQ tests began as an effort to identify people who would do well in college. **Concurrent validity** means that a test correlates well with other similar measures of the same trait.

Test uniformity and objectivity is the main difference between a formal standardized test and an informal test, such as asking a child the color of his shirt that day. Uniformity refers to one test being administered to a great number of people, and the test results can be used for later statistical analysis. Objectivity refers to unbiased scoring of test answers, a quality desirable, for example, in a baseball umpire calling balls and strikes.

Quantifiable scores support interpretation of the test results. Most psychological tests provide numerical scores, which allow statistical comparisons. Examples of tests without numerical scores are the Rorschach inkblot, projective drawings, and incomplete sentence tests.

Age and grade equivalent scores indicate the level of performance of the child. Thus, "10–3" represents the typical performance of a child of age 10 years and 3 months. Similarly, a fourth-grade, third-month performance level would be represented by "4–3." These are rough guides, however, because actual skills depend on the actual material presented in the classroom. A more reliable interpretation of a test result is the statistical difference of the individual's score from the norm population's average performance.

---

5   Wodrich, *Children's Psychological Testing*, p. 20.

Percentile ranks indicates the percentage of students in the representative norm or sample group who scored below your child's score. A 60th percentile indicates that the child scored better than 60% of the population norm. Percentile ranks are a numerical ordering of test scores, from 1 to 99. This ranking method, however, does not provide information on the intervals between percentile values. For example, a few points difference in the score around the middle could dramatically alter a child's percentile ranking. Conversely, a few points difference at the very low or very high end may not result in any change in the child's percentile rankings at all.

Mean (often symbolized by μ; known in the dictionary as *mu*, the twelfth letter of the Greek alphabet; and is pronounced as "myoo" or "moo") is the average of the test scores of the norm, calculated by adding the values of the test scores and then dividing this sum by the number of tests taken. In Figure 12.1, the standardized test has a mean of 100; an IQ test is an example. The best psychological tests should have been developed using a large number of individuals that would be truly representative of a certain target population. For example, in a general ability or achievement test, an *average* result really would be

Figure 12.1

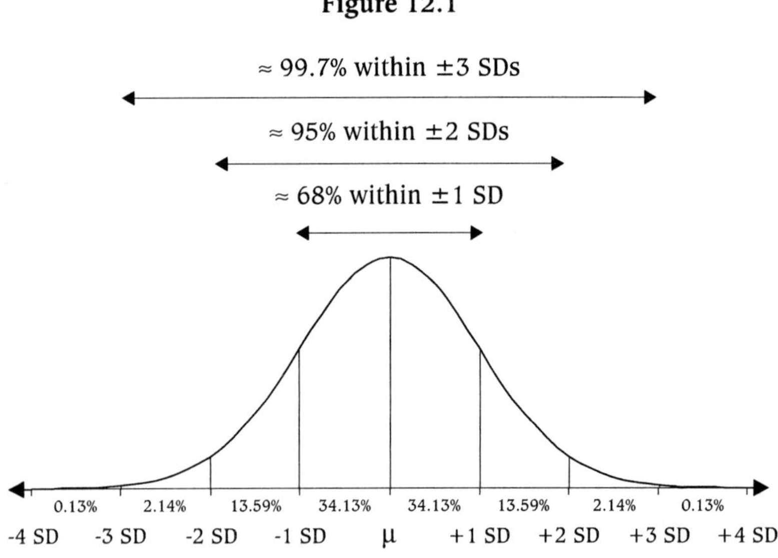

Standard scores typically have $\mu = 100$, and $\sigma = 15$
T-scores report $\mu = 50$, and $\sigma = 10$
Z-score report $\mu = 0$, and $\sigma = 1$

the average score of the general population having the same characteristics as the test-taker.

If the test scores of the large population sample were lined up in
numerical order, most of the scores would be near the mean. Some
scores would lie quite far from the mean. This **normal distribution** of
scores is pictured in the area under the curve in Figure 12.1. **Standard
deviation** or **SD** (often symbolized by σ; known in the dictionary as
sigma, the eighteenth letter of the Greek alphabet; and is pronounced
as "sig'muh") is the rough equivalent of the average distance of the test
scores from the mean. (A basic statistics text should provide information on the exacting calculation of standard deviation.) When the
scores have a normal distribution, about 68% of all the test scores lie
within one standard deviation from the mean (either below or above).
About 95% of all the test scores lie within two standard deviations from
the mean. About 99.7% of all the test scores lie within three standard
deviations.

Significant or meaningful differences are two standard deviations
away from the mean. For example, if one standard deviation is a span
of 15 points away from the mean on a particular test, then two standard deviations equals 30 points away from the mean. On IQ tests with
SD = 15 and mean = 100, an IQ at or below 70 is *mentally retarded*,
and an IQ at or above 130 is *gifted*.

A test can also be divided into nine levels of performance or
stanines (Figure 12.2). The middle stanine is the fifth one; it contains
the middle 20% of the scores. Each stanine interval, except the first and
last ones, spans half of a standard deviation. Figure 12.2 shows the
percent of the group which lies in each stanine. What is measured is the
distribution of the performance of a population, not the percentage of
test questions right or wrong. This statistical method of reporting
results resembles the normal population distribution as seen in Figure 12.1. Therefore, the stanine to which a score is assigned would

Figure 12.2

Stanine scores	1	2	3	4	5	6	7	8	9
Percent in Stanine	4%	7%	12%	17%	20%	17%	12%	7%	4%

depend on an individual's performance relative to the norm population, not on the raw test score, such as 17 correct responses on a 27-question test. For example, the fifth stanine could conceivably include a score of 23, if the mean score of the group is 23. A score of 17 out of 27 could be the second stanine if it is at the far lower end of how the group did.

Tests and assessments have limits. A quick test is unlikely to accurately diagnose *the* cause of a multi- dimensional learning disability for example. Be forewarned that some test administrators "ignore measurement limitations, are unfamiliar with research literature, or lack training and experience with children."[6]

Putting it all together: Making the diagnosis

The *DSM-IV-TR* provides diagnostic guidelines for determining the presence of a learning disorder, but each state has its own set of rules for establishing the presence of a learning disability based on IDEA. Many definitions use the concept of *discrepancy*, an underachievement difference between actual performance and expected performance in a child, given her or his intelligence, home environment, and school attendance, among other factors. A discrepancy of two or more standard deviations (of actual language or math performance below that expected for a given intelligence level) is considered significant, and is one way to qualify a student for special education. If the discrepancy is between one and two standard deviations, then other factors may be considered such as cognitive problems affecting intelligence testing, an emotional disorder like depression, a general medical problem, or cultural background. Conversely, if a sensory deficit exists, then the discrepancy must be greater than normally found in people with that same deficit.[7] Discrepancy is discussed in greater detail in Chapter 13.

The significance of "statistically significant"

Laws have differentiated *disability* from *disorder* (see the beginning of Chapter 3). IDEA does not state which evaluation measures are to be used in the identification process, nor any threshold levels for determining the presence of a disorder or a disability. Over the past century, medical diagnostic tests have proven inadequate, and so psychological tests, however flawed in inferring neurological problems, have been the best set of tools available to assess learning performance.

---

6   Wodrich, *Children's Psychological Testing*, p. 336.
7   *Diagnostic and Statistical Manual of Mental Disorders*, pp. 49-50.

Nevertheless, psychological tests are statistical instruments, and using statistical concepts has become accepted practice in fulfilling the law. According to Section 504, a learning disorder becomes a disability when learning performance is "substantially" limited. It is easy to understand, then, how *substantially limited* has become equivalent to *statistically significant*. Thus, *disability*—and therefore *eligibility*—have been defined as pertaining to those performing 2 standard deviations away from the mean, or the bottom 2-1/2%. Some definitions set the disability threshold at the bottom 5% of a norm-reference population, the same total figure of those who would lie either significantly below *or above* the mean. Thus, numbers have come to define *disability*.

Be wary of population figures that say that about 2%–5% of the school population has a certain type of learning disability, because disability may have been defined as being the bottom 2%–5% in the first place. This is the reason for the dissatisfaction in the identification process. Indeed, Shaywitz has found the incidence of reading disorders approaching 20% in a longitudinal study, and Shalev acknowledged that her 5% cutoff underestimates the incidence of dyscalculia especially given that children initially scoring in the bottom 20% continued to perform poorly.[8] (You can wonder what would happen if only the worst 5% of cancer victims were treated, and in which pessimistic professionals offered little help or hope because no one ever recovered.) Children whose everyday school performance is *not failing enough* to flag a referral for an evaluation, for whatever reason—nightly tutoring by well-educated or sacrificing parents, extraordinary effort on the part of the child, environmental deprivations precluding any possibility of an unexpected discrepancy, or extreme giftedness compensating for the disorder—will probably not be regarded as falling below a 5% threshold.

We live in a marvelous age of scientific inquiry. One current frontier of investigation is the human brain. Over the past decade, medical researchers have been trying to discover reliable physical tests that characterize these invisible performance problems. A promising line of medical research uses non-invasive imaging technology such as functional magnetic resonance imaging (fMRI), positronic emission tomography (PET), and more recently, magnetoencephalography (MEG) scans to identify differences in brain processing. This type of research identifies patterns of brain functioning during certain activities such as object recognition and reading. Performance differences have been documented between normal brains and those with disorders.

---

8   Shalev, Manor, Auerbach, and Gross-Tsur, "Persistence of Developmental Dyscalculia," pp. 359-361.

The ability to more directly image performance problems promises more accurate diagnoses of learning disabilities than current methods that infer underachievement. A combination of medical and psychological assessments could go a long way in confirming the presence of LD in an individual, and in determining the extent and severity of any problems. Environment, personal resources, and intelligence then become side issues. Indeed, many researchers foresee functional imaging studies as providing definitions of disorders and disabilities in the near future.

Chapter Thirteen

What happens if a learning problem is identified?

Making the eligibility cut

Since neurological problems underlie learning difficulties, many parents assume that a treatment model for a diagnosed learning disorder would resemble a medical model:

Diagnosis $\Rightarrow$ Disorder $\Rightarrow$ Treatment

In reality, special education becomes available upon the legal finding of a *disability,* not the presence of a disorder:

Evaluation $\Rightarrow$ **Disability** $\Rightarrow$ Eligibility for IDEA services and/or
Section 504 accommodations

If the condition is not severe enough to be a disability, then the remaining alternative is:

Evaluation $\Rightarrow$ **Disorder** $\Rightarrow$ Private Treatments

You might be surprised at how severe the condition must be in order to be defined as a disability. For example, the *Egg Drop* essay in Appendix 6 was painstakingly written by a fifth-grader, heavily tutored and above-average in intelligence, whose problems were considered only borderline. For comparison's sake, an essay by a fourth-grader from the same family appears next to it. A third essay shows a possible academic outcome, as the student who wrote *Egg Drop* received appropriate help. Quite often though, students with similar problems eventually drop out of school.

Diagnosis is a determination of the cause(s) of a disorder. *Evaluation*, with respect to special education, is an appraisal of the significance of the problems. Note that IDEA uses the terms *evaluation* and *eligibility*, not *diagnosis* and *treatment*.

Sources for the *DSM* diagnostic criteria for AD/HD and Asperger's syndrome are provided in Chapter 4. IDEA defines the basic criteria for identifying a student with a specific learning disability (SLD):

> "(a) ... a child has a specific learning disability if—
> (1) The child does not achieve commensurate with his or her age and ability levels in one or more of the areas listed in paragraph (a) (2) of this section, if provided with learning experiences appropriate for the child's age and ability levels; and
> (2) The team finds that a child has a severe discrepancy between achievement and intellectual ability in one or more of the following areas:
> (i) Oral expression.
> (ii) Listening comprehension.
> (iii) Written expression.
> (iv) Basic reading skill.
> (v) Reading comprehension.
> (vi) Mathematics calculation.
> (vii) Mathematics reasoning.
> (b) The team may not identify a child as having a specific learning disability if the severe discrepancy between ability and achievement is primarily the result of—
> (1) A visual, hearing, or motor impairment;
> (2) Mental retardation;
> (3) Emotional disturbance; or
> (4) Environmental, cultural or economic disadvantage."

—34 CFR § 300.541

As new discoveries about learning disabilities occur, new proposals to modify these criteria for determining LD appear. The decisions in determining the above definition's components have not changed much since passage of the 1969 Specific Learning Disabilities Act, and were "made without the benefit of research data, for none existed."[1]

In 2003, an amendment to IDEA which would have required medical evidence of an SLD was defeated as being an overly restrictive eligibility criterion. The concern here was that too many students are

---

1   *Students with Learning Disabilities* 4/E by Mercer, © 1992 by Macmillan Publishing Company. Reprinted by permission of Pearson Education, Inc., Upper Saddle River, NJ.

identified as having SLD and therefore needing expensive special education services. However, *if* medical evidence were required—most likely to be fulfilled by brain scans—not only could identification costs increase but perhaps also the population of students with SLD as more subtle cases would be diagnosed. At some point in the near future, such imaging tests could be part of a standard evaluation procedure. But before then, a more wide-ranging debate (see *Myth 6* in Chapter 14) should occur than a fast-track amendment focused on minimizing costs. Be careful of what you wish for.

Problems often mentioned with the federal definition (which has been adopted by most states) include:

• Learning disabilities are lifelong, and should not be defined as existing only in children.

• The presence of blindness; deafness; motor impairments; emotional, cultural, or economic problems; or mental retardation are defined as reasons for not recognizing the presence of a learning disability. Two groups of students are involved here. The first group with mental retardation, blindness, deafness, motor impairments, and emotional problems are most likely already receiving special education services. The second group, however, with cultural or economic problems may have LD as well. This latter group is caught in a nature vs. nurture argument, with a hidden assumption that visible or other tangible circumstances caused their poor school performance. While many studies have shown that children from disadvantaged backgrounds often do poorly in school, the presence of learning disorders in the parents may have led to family disadvantages in the first place. (Beware of studies that confuse correlation with causation.) Thus, underachievement can result from many co-existing factors, such as an individual having poor economic circumstances—which can diminish intellectual development—and a co-existing learning disability.

• Learning disabilities are neurological problems, which until recently, lacked physical evidence of their existence. Current law has not established uniform methods for determining their presence.

• Many standardized tests used to measure intelligence and achievement are controversial and statistically inadequate. For this reason, work samples and observations become part of the determination of eligibility, which is more art than science.

• Discrepancy criteria, requires 1) significant academic underachievement compared to what would be expected given an individual's intelligence, and 2) the underachievement cannot be explained by other factors such as poor instruction or environment. This discrepancy concept arose in 1964,[2] but today the intelligence-achievement gap nei-

---

2   Mercer, p. 45.

ther really defines what a learning disorder is nor explains how it occurs. For example, intelligence is unrelated to remediation improvements.[3] Thus, discrepancy criteria ignores the fact that one does not have to be a genius in order to read, but directs help towards the geniuses who can't read well. Moreover, states with budget limitations can manipulate the degree of discrepancy required in a learning disability definition of eligibility, so that the cases with the widest disparity of high-intelligence/low-performance or chronological-age/actual-performance receive assistance. The discrepancy criteria, therefore, has led to late identification of learning problems because failure in school—whether two standard deviations apart or two grades behind—is required.

• Learning disorders are not all-or-nothing phenomena, like whether one walks on two legs or not at all. Learning disabilities exist in a continuum from mild to severe, and appear in different combinations of problems. Costs, however, are controlled by the school district determining the degree of disability at which students will receive services. For a state like California which educates one out of eight of the nation's children,[4] costs are a major concern. Thus, only severe cases are eligible for services. Since special education is known for accepting only the poorest performers, many regular teachers have come to expect minimal achievements from special education students, and students assigned to special education are stigmatized. As a result, many struggling students don't receive the help they need either because they have not failed enough, or because they don't want to be stigmatized as a special education student.

What is "eligibility?"

The evaluation team determines eligibility. You as a team member should attend the eligibility conference. Do not assume that children who need services will get them. For example, one public school principal was only able to secure Section 504 accommodations for her child when memory problems occurred after brain surgery.

There are 13 categories of eligibility defined under IDEA by which a child may receive special education. Each school district has a program for identifying and providing services, preferred evaluation methods, and prescribed interventions, based on federal and state laws. The 13 categories and their respective numbers and percentages of students,

---

3   Linda S. Siegel, "The Discrepancy Formula: Its Use and Abuse," in *Specific Reading Disability: A View of the Spectrum*, ed. Bruce K. Shapiro, Pasquale J. Accardo, and Arnold J. Capute, (Timonium, Maryland: York Press, 1998), p. 130.

4   Almanac of Policy Issues, "U.S. Education Spending: 1999-2000" [Internet], p. 1, accessed 16 January 2003 from: http://www.policyalmanac.org/education/archive/doe_education_spending.shtml

ages 6–21, receiving special education services during the 1999–2000 school year are (*34 CFR* § *300.7*):[5]

Category of Disability	Number of Students	Percentage of Students in Each Category
1. autism	65,396	1.2
2. deafness *and* blindness	1,840	-
3. deafness	71,539[6]	1.3
4. hearing impaired		
5. mental retardation	613,207	10.8
6. multiple disabilities	112,345	2.0
7. severe orthopedic impairment	71,264	1.3
8. general health impairment	253,795	4.5
9. serious emotional disturbance	469,407	8.3
10. specific learning disability	2,861,333	50.5
11. speech or language impairment	1,086,849	19.2
12. traumatic brain injury	13,843	0.2
13. visual impairment	26,540	0.5
developmental delay[7]	19,057	0.3
All disabilities	5,666,415	100.1[8]

General population growth, improved methods of identification, heightened public awareness of the issues, and better informational sources for parents of struggling students have probably contributed to an expanding population of students in special education. In 1969, 120,000 children were identified as having learning disabilities.[9] In 1999–2000, The Department of Education reported 2,861,333 students with specific learning disabilities or 51% of all children identified with disabilities. This latter figure does not include students with learning disabilities existing in other categories such as serious emotional disturbance or other health impairments. Figures 13.1 and 13.2 show these increases over the past decade.[10]

---

5 U.S. Department of Education, "Twenty-third Annual Report to Congress on the Implementation of the Individuals with Disabilities Education Act" [Internet], pp. A-2, A-3, and A-4, 2001, available from: http://www.ed.gov/offices/OSERS/OSEP/Products/OSEP2001AnlRpt/Appendix_A_Pt1.pdf

6 Government statistics combined categories of deafness and hearing impairments.

7 This group of children is defined as being delayed in physical, cognitive, communication, social, emotional, or adaptive development, and are not coded as belonging to the other categories. IDEA specifies these categories and allows *developmental delay* as a naming alternative. Indeed, many categories contain quite heterogeneous disabilities.

8 Figure reflects rounding error.

9 Mercer, *Students with Learning Disabilities*, p.18.

10 Statistics were gathered from U.S. Department of Education, "Twenty-second Annual Report to Congress on the Implementation of the Individuals with Disabilities Education Act" [Internet], p. A-92, 2000, available from: http://www.ed.gov/offices/OSERS/OSEP/Products/OSEP2000AnlRpt/PDF/Appendix-A.pdf; and U.S. Department of Education, "Twenty-third Annual Report to Congress," p. A-2, 2001.

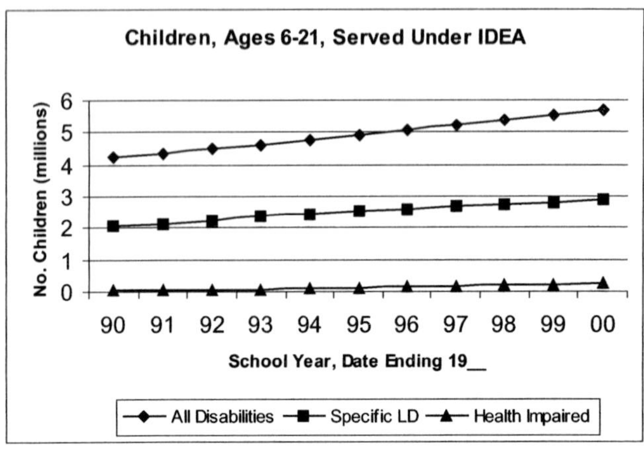

Figure 13.1

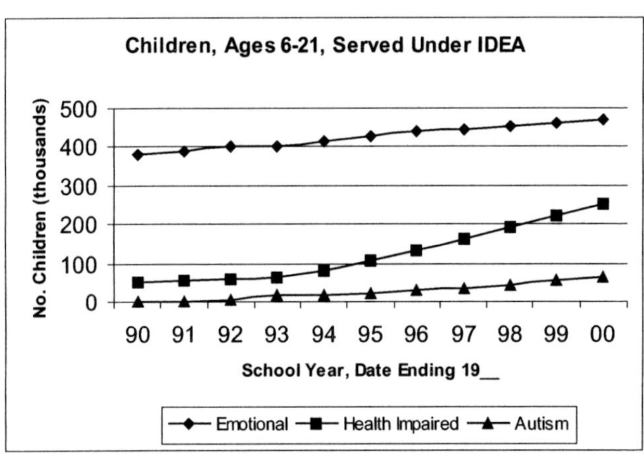

Figure 13.2

In its *Twenty-third Annual Report to Congress*, the Department of Education noted:

• That a 351% increase in the category of *other health impairments* during the school years 1990–91 to 1999–2000 was related to the addition of students with ADD and AD/HD, perhaps because a 1991 memorandum from the Office of Special Education and Rehabilitative Services provided IDEA eligibility for these students.[11]

---

11 U.S. Department of Education, "Twenty-third Annual Report to Congress," pp. II-23 and II-24.

• A 21% increase in the category of autism from 1998–99 to 1999–2000;[12] in 1994, the DSM-IV first provided the diagnostic criteria for Asperger's syndrome in the United States.

For specific learning disabilities, each school system has its own methods for determining eligibility. Different cutoffs are used, and there are many examples: one standard deviation, two standard deviations, bottom 5%, one year behind, or two years behind. Thus, where you live can determine whether your child gets help. Appendix 7 shows different percentages of students identified with LD in each state for 1999–2000. However, as almost all states permit professionals to use clinical judgment, eligibility may be more of an "attitudinal" issue within district boundaries,[13] involving school budgets, skepticism about learning disabilities, and parents not knowledgeable, confident, nor dedicated enough to deal with school officials. Surmised Catherine Trapani, Director of Education at the Marcus Institute and Clinical Associate Professor of Pediatrics at Emory University:

> "… [T]he extent and quality of service provided reflects the socioeconomic level and culture of the community served by the school and the degree of influence of the advocates for special education on district officials."[14]

Matthew Cohen provides some specific concerns on the autism, emotional disturbance, specific learning disability, and other health impairment categories in "The Scarlet Labels: An Overview of the 13 IDEA Eligibility Categories," available at www.ldonline.org/legal/cohen_paper_label_2.html.

Evaluations cost money. Services cost even more money. With tight budgets and competing priorities, school officials could be motivated to manage eligibility quotas. Pasquale Accardo, Professor of Pediatrics at the Medical College of Virginia, reports that most field clinicians have found that "schools generally underdiagnose and underserve" children with learning disabilities; he regards such treatment as tantamount to child abuse:

> "Emotional abuse, in terms of repeated assault on a child's self-image, probably has a more damaging long-term impact on adult outcomes than the actual

---

12 U.S. Department of Education, p. II 23.

13 Pasquale J. Accardo, "A Developmental Pediatric Perspective on Neurologically Based Specific Learning Disabilities," in *Learning Disabilities: Lifelong Issues*, ed. Shirley C. Cramer and William Ellis (Baltimore: Paul H. Brookes Publishing, 1996), p. 103.

14 Excerpt from *Transition Goals for Students with Learning Disabilities* by Catherine Trapani, p. xi. Copyright © 1990 by Catherine Trapani, Ph.D., and published by College-Hill Press. All rights reserved. Reprinted with permission of Catherine Trapani.

failure to provide appropriate classroom interventions. ... [B]ehavioral diagnoses as 'oppositional
defiant disorder' and 'conduct disorder' .... most often
simply reflects a typical response on the part of the
child to the school's inappropriate handling of the
child's educational needs."[15]

Once a student is determined to be eligible for special education, an
individualized education plan (IEP) will be developed. The IEP is
described in Chapter 15. A student who is not eligible for services may
be eligible for accommodations under Section 504 or the ADA.

A student does not retain eligibility for services through age 21
(or longer if provided by state laws) if the disorder is no longer disabling; this is determined through an evaluation. Parental consent is
required—or the student's consent if 18 years old—for any changes of
services. That is, your child cannot just be dropped from receiving services. At graduation, most students exit special education because
IDEA does not provide for any successor institution to public secondary
schools. Thus while a high school can graduate students who have
received both FAPE and adequate services preparing them for
postsecondary life, school districts may not graduate students—and
simply end services—if students have not met normal graduation
requirements.[16] (Chapter 24 reviews the controversy over high school
exit exams.)

Assessment completed: The eligibility conference

Preparing for the conference. Many people are bewildered by the tor-
rent of technical jargon that is used to discuss the child's learning
problems. The eligibility conference will gather many experienced professionals, and it is incumbent for you to do your homework
beforehand. Learn how they think. You may find that even a two-hour
meeting will not be enough time for you to grasp unfamiliar terms and
concepts and their consequences even though you are entitled to explanations from these professionals. Help yourself help your child.

Each specialist who tests your child generates a report. Parents
have the right to obtain a copy of each specialist's report prior to the
conference.

---

15 Accardo, P.J. (Copyright © 1996). "A Developmental Pediatric Perspective on
    Neurologically Based Specific Learning Disabilities." In Editors Cramer, S.C. and
    Ellis, W. *Learning Disabilities: Lifelong Issues*, (pp. 106-107). Baltimore: Paul H.
    Brooks Publishing Co. Reprinted with permission of Paul H. Brooks Publishing Co.
    and Shirley C. Cramer.
16 Osborne, *Legal Issues in Special Education*, p. 19.

Read the results of the tests and learn about the tests utilized. Make an effort to understand the terms and concepts explaining the findings. Ask yourself whether you agree with the findings. In particular, analyze reports for their accuracy, completeness, consistency, relevancy to the child's current functioning, assumptions, and personal bias.[17] Be persistent in getting clarity if you do not fully understand the material presented in the report. The authors of *Negotiating the Special Education Maze* state "that school personnel are themselves sometimes uncertain as to the exact meaning of the definitions."[18] If you wish to seek expert help for reviewing the reports or local eligibility criteria call a reputable parent information center, which can either answer your questions directly or refer you to a more appropriate resource. Don't assume that any one expert will know everything there is to know, especially if you are trying to obtain special education services for your child. Get a second opinion if you're not satisfied with the first one. Talk to other parents whose situations are similar to yours, and learn from their experiences.

Make an executive summary listing findings and those of other evaluations, if any. Use the summary as a handout at the meeting, build your case, and help bring focus to what you see as critical issues.

Both parents should attend the conference, if possible, and can bring professional assistance such as a consultant or a lawyer. Listen carefully to the other evaluation team members. Ask for any clarifications of unfamiliar terms, methods, and examples of blanket characterizations. Let the team know that you need to understand their findings and recommendations in order to help your child better. For specific LD, IDEA states:

> "... [D]ocumentation ... of eligibility ... must include a statement of—
> (1) Whether the child has a specific learning disability;
> (2) The basis for making the determination;
> (3) The relevant behavior noted during the observation of the child;
> (4) The relationship of that behavior to the child's academic functioning;
> (5) The educationally relevant medical findings, if any;
> (6) Whether there is a severe discrepancy between achievement and ability that is not correctable without special education and related services; and

---

17   Anderson, Chitwood, and Hayden, *Negotiating the Special Education Maze*, p. 59.
18   Anderson, Chitwood, and Hayden, p. 68.

(7) The determination of the team concerning the effects of environmental, cultural, or economic disadvantage."

—34 CFR § 300.543 (a)

Generally parents passively participate in eligibility and IEP conferences; they ask few questions, infrequently comment or respond, and usually acquiesce to the decision.[19] The Department of Education has noted that some states do not ensure that parents are involved in the eligibility decision.[20] Some researchers have urged more parent education and more active parent participation in meetings to secure appropriate services for their children. In contrast, a very small minority of parents (3% in 1971) actively seek more information about the diagnosis and may be perceived as shopping around for another diagnosis; part of the problem may be that some professionals encourage this behavior by underestimating the severity of the disability or suppressing information.[21]

Essential questions. The evaluation (*34 CFR § 300.534*) addresses the child's eligibility for special education. During the conference, some hard questions will be answered:

Evaluation Team Questions

• Is this discrepancy primarily due to environmental factors such as cultural differences, economic disadvantage, limited school experience or poor attendance?

• Is the discrepancy the result of a behavior disorder or social maladjustment?

• Is this discrepancy related to a processing disorder?

Parent Questions

• Do you have evidence suggesting that my child has a serious learning, emotional, social, or other neurological problem?

• What is my child's current ability and achievement levels?

• What are the strengths and weaknesses in my child's learning pattern?

• How well is my child progressing in school considering his or her abilities?

---

19   Mercer citing 1990 Turnbull and Turnbull study; and 1988 Vaughn, Bos, Harrell, and Lasky study, *Students with Learning Disabilities*, p. 124.
20   U.S. Department of Education, "Twenty-third Annual Report to Congress," pp. IV-12.
21   Shea and Bauer citing 1971 Kiern and 1984 Donnellan and Mirenda studies, *Parents and Teachers of Children with Exceptionalities*, p. 34.

• If the discrepancy does not exist, but evaluations do indicate that the student may benefit from special education, would the Team certify this student for special education?

• Can this pupil's needs be met through modifications of the general education program?

• What recommendations do you have to improve my child's current performance?

• Who will coordinate these recommendations?

• How is my child's progress to be measured? When specifically should progress be reviewed, which may require future action?

Bear in mind that this situation has a potential for conflicts of interest, in that the school district, who will be providing services, weighs in heavily on whether your child can receive services.

Accepting the decision. Several outcomes are possible. Your child may be found eligible or not eligible. A child whose learning problems are determined not to be serious enough to require special education services may be eligible for accommodations and related services under Section 504. (For more details about 504 eligibility, see "Section 504: What Teachers Need to Know" by Tom Smith, available at www.ldonline.org/ld_indepth/legal_legislative/section_504_for_teachers.html.) Or the evaluation team may agree on a diagnosis and treatment with which you may disagree. If you do not agree with the findings and can successfully demonstrate that the school district's evaluation was inappropriate, you can receive a free independent educational evaluation (*34 CFR § 300.502*). At this point, you will most likely be dealing with the school district's attorneys. A booklet jointly produced by CADRE and the Technical Assistance Alliance for Parent Centers, "Special Education Mediation: A Guide for Parents," is available at www.directionservice.org/cadre/parentbooklet.cfm and provides an overview of the mediation process and additional resources.

If the evaluation team finds your child eligible for special educational services, then a diagnostic label and treatment course has been established. Sometimes two problems are found, one primary, the other secondary. Sometimes problems co-exist. Bear in mind that different types of services exist for different types of problems. Services cannot begin without parental consent, and you are part of the team making this determination. More information on matching diagnosis and treatment is found in "IDEA Eligibility Categories: What Difference Does the Label Make?" by Matthew Cohen, available at www.ldonline.org/legal/cohen_paper_label.html.

You on behalf of your child can appeal the eligibility decision, or any other decisions such as placement (reviewed in Chapter 16).

Remedies are limited to compensatory, not punitive measures. Before you do so, and if you haven't done so already, consult an information center or an attorney. Obtain a copy of the test results, minutes of the eligibility meeting (Siegel's *The Complete IEP Guide* offers suggestions on this), and explanations of any items in the written report that were not part of the eligibility conference. Be well-acquainted with applicable laws. Information sources are listed at the back of the book.

If a child satisfies eligibility requirements, the evaluation team becomes the IEP team and may *immediately* move into the IEP meeting because everyone connected with the case is already present. You, however, may not be prepared for determining the best program, services, and treatment options for your child. You may ask for another meeting (which must be held within 30 calendar days) to prepare for this next meeting (*34 CFR § 300.343 (c)*).

If you are satisfied with the diagnosis, discuss with your child the findings of the eligibility conference. If a learning disability was identified, explain that these problems just happen to people, and that he or she is neither crazy nor lazy. While it seems unfair, the child's job is to somehow deal with the disability as well as come to terms the same problems that other people face. Your child's acceptance of the invisible but disabling condition is important, otherwise getting the student to use and self-advocate for services and accommodations may be difficult. A six-page article, "Talking with Kids about Anxiety, ADHD and Learning Disorders" by Robin Goodman is available online in the March/April 2000 issue of the Child Study Letter at www.aboutourkids. org/letter/marapr00.pdf. Two books written for children, both by Levine, may also be helpful. *All Kinds of Minds* is for elementary school children. *Keeping A Head in School* is for children 11 years and older. Both books are also available as audio cassettes. Free Spirit Press also publishes books for young people on understanding their learning disabilities. "A Children's Guide to Asperger Syndrome" is available at www.asperger-syndrome.com.

<hr>

Chapter Fourteen

<hr>

What shall I tell others?

"When I use a word," Humpty Dumpty said, in rather a scornful tone, "it means just what I choose it to mean—neither more nor less."

"The question is," said Alice, "whether you can make words mean so many different things."

"The question is," said Humpty Dumpty, "which is to be master—that's all."

Alice was too much puzzled to say anything, so after a minute Humpty Dumpty began again. "They've a temper, some of them—particularly verbs: they're the proudest—adjectives you can do anything with, but not verbs—however, I can manage the whole lot of them! Impenetrability! That's what I say!"

—Through the Looking-Glass

Controlling information

Basically, you don't need to tell anyone anything. Still, you may want to talk about your child's problems on a need-to-know basis, such as with teachers, if it will help your child in school. Discussing learning disabilities with acquaintances may be akin to discussing religion and politics. Many people don't believe that learning disabilities exist, or have formed opinions based on bad or outdated information.

Dealing with rude comments and unsolicited advice is as old as parenthood. Some remarks may be helpful and some will be useless. You can, of course, thank those concerned and decline to discuss intrusive questions. Other people may assume that you are receiving help from the schools and can't fathom the problems you face. A few parents may even resent your child's presence in *their* child's classroom. Problem behaviors and academic performance are often judged as indicators of poor parenting, bad attitudes, or emotional troubles. In particular, mothers—unlike fathers—are held responsible for the results of abuse by others "beyond all logic, beyond any possibility that they could stop it. We live in a culture where we want mothers to do everything, and where whenever something goes wrong it's the mother's fault," says Mary Becker of DePaul University, a professor of family and domestic violence law.[1] All these adult attitudes trickle down to your child's classmates, who won't hesitate to tell your child how they feel about him or her. Many parents of children with learning disabilities often feel isolated, defensive about whether they are obtaining the best treatment(s) for their child, and unsure of whether their child can achieve full independence.

It is probably best to follow your child's lead in discussing learning disabilities with acquaintances. Many children prefer to conform to their normal peers, and so do not wish to disclose their disability, which, after all, is invisible to most people. Legally, educators are to maintain the confidentiality of school records; however, in small classroom environments, word gets around who requires special education services, accommodations, or medications. Nevertheless, respect your child's wish for privacy. The most comfortable forums for sharing ideas and experiences about learning disabilities is with other parents in similar situations, such as at your child's school or through a parent's support group. (Chapter 1 briefly discusses social stigmas.)

There are genuinely curious folk whom you may not wish to quickly dismiss. As you become more knowledgeable about learning disabilities, you will be able to help others understand not only the difficulties, but also the possibilities of your child. Here are six common myths that you may encounter:

Myth 1: Learning disabilities are the same as mental retardation. A 2000 Roper Starch Worldwide poll found that 65% of the American public believe this myth.[2] (This is an improvement from the 85% figure when a similar poll was taken in 1995.) Because learning disabilities are not outwardly apparent, unexpected delays in performance cause uninformed observers to jump to conclusions about mental ability. Learning disabilities and intelligence are two different

---

1   Adam Liptak, "Judging a Mother for a Crime by Someone Else" [Internet], pp. 1-2, accessed 29 November 2002 from: http://www.nytimes.com/2002/11/27/national/27MURD.html

2   Roper Starch Worldwide, "Measuring Progress in Public & Parental Understanding of Learning Disabilities," p. 1.

things (see Chapters 5 and 6). To understand learning disabilities, try doing any of the following simulations:[3]

• Take notes from a recording of an important lecture played back at least one and one-half times normal speed (an auditory processing problem).

• Give a two-minute speech using *only* three-syllable words (an expressive language problem).

• Read the passage mimicking visual perception difficulties presented in Figure 3.1.

These simulations demonstrate the time-consuming difficulties posed by learning disabilities. Using a computer analogy, many learning disabilities reduce modem speed.

Placement of a child in special education does not necessarily mean mental retardation either. IDEA specifically mentions many circumstances that could also undermine educational performance, including asthma and sickle cell anemia. Special education only means that a child receives specialized assistance in his or her educational program.

Myth 2: Learning disabilities are just excuses for being lazy. The 2000 Roper Poll showed that 48% of adults agreed and 48% disagreed with this statement.[4] Poor academics may have many causes, none simple to solve. What may seem like underutilization to others may be processing difficulties or discouragement because the work is too difficult. For example, brain scans have shown individuals fully engaged in word recognition and pronunciation tasks, but their accuracy is less than normal.[5] Indeed, the brains of people with learning disorders may actually be working harder than normal. Neuroimaging studies demonstrate larger areas of brain activation than would be typically observed, reflecting greater difficulty in task execution.[6] Similarly, Swanson has found individuals with learning disabilities to be *multidirectional* thinkers rather than *inactive learners* (see Chapter 3 under *Memory*).

The simulations listed under Myth 1 give an idea of how an individual must try harder or develop strategies to accomplish the same work as a person without learning disabilities. To finish the same academic tasks as their normal peers, day in and day out, students not only put in more homework time, but also are committed to long hours of evaluations, tutoring, therapy, and counseling. To work so hard for average gains would be quite discouraging for anyone.

3　Ernest Rose, "Changing Attitudes and Enhancing Knowledge About Learning Disabilities," pp. 135-136.

4　Roper Starch Worldwide, "Measuring Progress," p. 22.

5　Rumsey and Eden, "Functional Neuroimaging of Developmental Dyslexia," p. 50.

6　Rumsey and Eden, p. 51.

The belief that a child is not trying hard enough is rooted in skepticism over or denial of the existence of learning disabilities in the first place. To illustrate the point that achievement may be unrelated to effort, Accardo presents the following profile to his medical students:

"Before he started school, Billy seemed just the smartest little boy to his proud mother, who anticipated absolutely no problems. His kindergarten teacher noted what appeared to be some signs of immaturity, but he nevertheless seemed to have mastered enough to go on to first grade —and he was so enthusiastic about school. In first grade, he struggled with the alphabet, phonics, and counting; he brought home unfinished papers to work on while the rest of the class had no homework. He was passed into second grade with some reservations. He would spend several hours a night on homework that took the other children less than 15 minutes, and he would lose recess because of incomplete class work. His attitude toward school was definitely changing for the worse, and the social reward of being with his peers was being undercut by his miserable academic performance. There were one or two subjects in which he would at least occasionally do well enough to document to the significant adults in his life that he was intelligent and could learn. Outside of school, he seemed like a normal child, able to associate with his peers, and quite happy during summer vacations that were free from the pressures of schoolwork. In third grade, despite no recess, detention after school, 3-4 hours of homework a night, which was driving his mother crazy, and several hours of tutoring a week, his grades were consistently failing. Stomachaches and headaches reflected his psychosomatic response to the stress of schoolwork. At this point, when his parents or his teacher were questioned as to what they saw as the fundamental cause of his academic difficulties, the almost universal answer was that he was not trying hard enough! No recess, hours of homework each night, private tutoring, parents driven to distraction—and he was not trying hard enough!"[7]

Higher academic standards, more penalties for the student, and shaming parents for *spoiling* their child will not improve this child's schoolwork.

It would be an injustice to assign hard-working students with learning disabilities to a generalized group of underperforming students. The message would be clear: Effort is not going to make any difference. The child will question whether she or he should continue

---

7   Accardo, P.J. (Copyright © 1996). "A Developmental Pediatric Perspective on Neurologically Based Specific Learning Disabilities." In Editors Cramer, S.C. and Ellis, W. *Learning Disabilities: Lifelong Issues*, (p. 104). Baltimore: Paul H. Brooks Publishing Co. Reprinted with permission of Paul H. Brooks Publishing Co. and Shirley C. Cramer.

working or even try at all. You must prevent your child from being categorized as an uncaring student by an instructor indifferent to effort.

Myth 3: People eventually grow out of learning disabilities. People do not *grow out* of learning disabilities because they are neurological in nature, and therefore lifelong. That is, the disorder seldom improves on its own with maturity. Many individuals have learned to compensate for deficiencies however. In others, difficulties are alleviated with strategies and tactics to get around the disability. A possible exception is Shaywitz's finding that a second language center develops in females during adolescence and may alleviate existing difficulties (see Chapter 3), but does not *cure* the original disorder.

Some parents may be overwhelmed and so hope that dealing with the inevitable can be postponed; unfortunately, *inevitable* often becomes *intractable*. The 2000 Roper Poll found that a majority of parents would wait at least a few months to a couple of years before considering the presence of a serious learning problem in their child.[8]

Some recent evidence of neuroplasticity is emerging in studies of violinists, Braille readers, stroke victims, and dyslexics. Fast ForWord, a phoneme training program (reviewed in Chapter 22), has been found to improve a brain region typically impaired in those with auditory processing problems.[9] Research has shown that early specialized reading instruction can improve skills (presented in Chapter 23). But these activities represent interventions, without which the natural developmental course would be discouraging. Beware of quack cures, however, that may exploit this concept of neuroplasticity, a current area of scientific investigation.

Myth 4: Learning disabilities affect only schoolwork. The problems causing learning disabilities exist 24 hours a day, 7 days a week. While these problems may be most evident to others during classroom hours, they can also cause difficulties in other aspects of everyday life such as doubling a recipe or correctly dialing telephone numbers. For example, Johnny may have an auditory perception disorder, which would affect his ability to read signs, follow directions, and understand conversations. Indeed, the term *learning disability* too narrowly defines the scope of the problems involved.

Myth 5: Poor home environments cause learning disabilities. The 2000 Roper Poll found that 56% of those surveyed believe this statement.[10] Moreover, a child struggling in school can be legally excluded from receiving services for a learning disability if the child's performance is perceived as having been compromised by

---

8   Roper Starch Worldwide, "Measuring Progress," p. 16.
9   Sharon Begley citing 2000 Gabrieli study, "Survival of the Busiest," *The Wall Street Journal*, 11 October 2002, p. B4.
10   Roper Starch Worldwide, "Measuring Progress," p. 25.

environmental, cultural, or economic disadvantages (*34 CFR* §
300.541). Except for the possibility of prenatal insults or traumatic
injuries, this is the equivalent of maintaining that a disadvantaged
home environment causes the types of neurological disorders associated with LD. If anything, the opposite may be true: Learning
disabilities can lead to poor home environments as shown in Chapter 9.

Myth 5 is a nature-versus-nurture issue. The struggling students
more likely to receive help are those with enriched environments—an
inference that if nurture is not somehow a cause of poor school performance, then nature, in this case LD, probably exists. The students less
likely to receive help are those with both nurture and nature difficulties: Besides the child not being able to perform successfully in school,
a parent with perhaps the same problems may not be able to work in the
economic mainstream of society. (This nurture-versus-nature causation issue is rooted in the concept of nurture interacting with nature:
That is, a poor home environment diminishes intellectual development.) Many teachers, however, refer low-income students for special
education despite IDEA's exclusionary criteria.

Myth 6: Too many students are in special education. Many critics of special education decry the three million students with LD
receiving IDEA services, particularly since the disability is not easily
seen. But if three million is too many, then what should the number be?

Given the 2000 U.S. Census K-12 enrollment estimate of 53 million
students, a 5% LD prevalence rate translates into 2.6 million students
with LD (53 million × 0.05 = 2.6 million). However, Shaywitz found a
prevalence rate approaching 20% in the Connecticut Longitudinal Study.
Schwab Learning cites an estimate of 10,000,000 students who have
significant reading problems.[11] The 2000 Roper Poll found that 27% of
all parents are deeply concerned with their child's academic performance.[12] Public Agenda found that 69% of parents of children with
disabilities believe that many students would not require special education had they received sufficient help earlier on in school.[13] These
numbers mean that there is a service-rationing process occurring that
emphasizes emergency care over developmental *wellness*. Thus, a major
failure of special education is not that too many students are placed in
special education, or that too many students don't seem to improve so they
can exit special education. Rather the failure is that too many students who
could be helped are not receiving help or are receiving it too late.

---

11 Schwab Learning, "Educator's Guide to Learning Differences [Internet], 2002, p. 20,
    available from: http://www.schwablearning.org/articles.asp?r=433&g=4
12 Roper Starch Worldwide, *Measuring Progress*, p. 17.
13 Jean Johnson, Ann Duffett, Steve Farkas, and Leslie Wilson, *When It's Your Own
    Child: A Report on Special Education from the Families Who Use It*, (New York:
    Public Agenda, 2002), p. 26.

Many critics of special education focus on costs, which during the 2001–2002 school year for 6.1 million students was $44.5 billion, or $7,300 per student.[14] (In contrast, average spending for an average pupil was $6,911 during the 1999–2000 school year.[15] Public schools are reimbursed for each student attending the school and an additional amount for each student requiring special education.) Federal funds supplement state funds for special education, and are disbursed to the state educational agency. IDEA allows a federal contribution of *up to* 40% of the total cost of services:

> "The maximum amount … a State may receive … is … [t]he number of children with disabilities in the State who are receiving special education and relevant services … multiplied by … [f]orty (40) percent of the average per-pupil expenditure in public elementary and secondary schools in the United States."

> *—34 CFR § 300.701*

The actual federal contribution, however, is 17%,[16] the amount being part of the annual Congressional appropriations process. (For all school funding during the school year 1999–2000, states contributed 50%, local sources add 43%, and the federal government provides 7%.[17]) Thus IDEA is somewhat of an unfunded federal mandate, so states and local school districts carry most of the financial burden for delivering services. (In 2003, the House of Representatives amended IDEA by instituting a cap on federal special education funding to 13.5% of a state's total student population. This funding limitation would have thus affected six states as shown in Appendix 7 during the school year 1999-2000. For more information, refer to "Spec. Ed. Growth Spurs Cap Plan in Pending IDEA," by Lisa Goldstein, available at www.ldonline. org/news/pending_idea.html. At the time of this writing, the Senate has yet to review the House legislation.)

If federal funding were increased to the 40% maximum contribution allowed by IDEA, about $18 billion would be required.[18] Funding this amount is controversial because the educational needs are little understood. Parents, at least, don't receive information on how funds are actually used. The solution, however, may lie in being more proactive than "the current practice of late intervention, typically in the

---

14 U.S. Commission on Civil Rights, "U.S. Commission on Civil Rights Recommendations for the Reauthorization of the Individuals with Disabilities Act" [Internet], May 2002, p. 4, available from: http://www.usccr.gov/pubs/idea/recs.htm
15 Almanac of Policy Issues, "U.S. Education Spending," p. 2.
16 U.S. Commission on Civil Rights, p. 4.
17 Almanac of Policy Issues, "U.S. Education Spending," p. 1.
18 U.S. Commission on Civil Rights, "Recommendations," p. 4.

fourth or fifth grade, for students with learning or behavioral disabilities ...."[19] Early intervention programs have been shown to be effective, and fewer students would require academic intensive care, namely, special education. A proactive approach is worth trying, especially given that 70.1% have either language or learning disabilities (using the percentage figures in Chapter 13's table of disability categories).

A solution to ameliorate the high-cost, high-failure special education system is outlined by Thomas Hehir, a former Director of the Office of Special Education Programs and currently a Lecturer on Education at Harvard University. He suggested that Congress should subsidize school districts outright for the estimated 20% of students who receive IDEA services (or 2% of the total student population) for blindness, deafness, and moderate-to-severe mental retardation—which tend to be low-incidence, high-cost, and medically based—and separately fund early intervention efforts for learning or behavioral difficulties. He emphasized that these research-based efforts "should be regular education interventions" and could also reduce inappropriate referrals to special education.[20]

As a parent of an at-risk child, don't let the focus on special education costs distract you from the potential problems you may be facing as the result of your child receiving an inappropriate education such as underachievement, substance abuse, imprisonment, and emotional disorders—as if they are inconsequential. That's tantamount to saying, *It's not my job*. Such thinking like this misses IDEA's educational purpose of guiding youngsters to become functioning citizens. Not enabling children with LD to realize their potential portends an enormous social as well as a personal cost. National problems are macrocosms of local problems. Certainly, schools can't do it all but no one is saying that they should. Parents are quite willing to help if only they knew how. Much can be done to help problematic students, but it's not getting to them routinely unless a proactive parent intervenes. Per-person annual costs are $9,500 for an average out-of-state public college,[21] or $20,000 for prison.[22] Ye reap what ye sow.

---

19 Thomas Hehir, "An Opportunity to Improve Educational Results for Students with Disabilities," p. 9.

20 Hehir, p. 9.

21 Justin Ewers, "No Room at State U.? Here Are Some Things You Can Do," *U.S. News & World Report*, 23 September 2002, p. 66. This is the average cost for out-of-state tuition at a public institution.

22 Wisconsin Legislative Audit Bureau, "97-18 Correction Costs, Department of Correction [Internet], 1997, p. 1, available from: http://www.legis.state.wi.us/lab/ Reports/97-18summary.htm. Figure was derived by multiplying Wisconsin's slightly higher-than-national-average 1997 daily inmate cost of $53.51 by 365 = $19,531, then rounding up to $20,000 because costs would have increased by 2002. Costs vary enormously between the states.

Eligibility was attained in the spring. The special ed classes were full at the neighborhood school so Max had to travel to another school for services. There, the special education teacher was 'reluctant' to teach my child for the two remaining months of the school year. He offered excuses for not scheduling classes—including that my son really didn't need help and that the personnel at my neighborhood school were incompetent in their evaluation of him—probably the reason why he had available slots if this is what he did to others. Services were finally provided after complaints from my neighborhood school and me to the school district. Still, he refused to work with my son's classroom teacher despite her requests for a meeting. Upon my request, he did provide me with some suggestions for the summer—the reason I wanted services during the two months—but was quite aloof. I didn't know if his problems were due to burnout, but I couldn't feel sorry for him. When the school year was finally over, there was no love lost.

For the following year, I was able to find a middle school that used a 'pull-out' model instead of an 'inclusion' model for providing services; it would still be my responsibility to schedule these services and drive Max daily from the private school to the public school to receive services. Unlike the elementary special-ed teacher, the ones I met in middle school were very understanding. My son liked these classes and learned to interact positively with most of the other students. He had two different speech therapists over two years and both were very nice people. The difference between the two schools was like night and day.

A complex law. IDEA is "… an exceedingly complicated law, with recent educationally oriented requirements layered on top of civil rights and procedural requirements."[23] As a result, according to Lawrence Gloeckler, State Director of Special Education and State Director of Vocational Rehabilitation of New York:[24]

•   Families with resources are better able to secure IDEA's benefits than those without resources.

•   Attention to technical rules may be irrelevant to the child's educational needs: Compliance based on *process* (meetings, forms, etc.) is easier to observe than compliance based on *substance* (appropriate instruction, placement, etc.).

---

23   Lawrence C. Gloeckler, "It's Time to Simplify and Focus on Performance," in *Rethinking Federal Education Programs for Children with Disabilities* [Internet], January 2002, p. 23, available from: http://www.ctredpol.org/specialeducation/timelyidea2002.pdf

24   Gloeckler, p. 18.

- IDEA's emphasis on legal processes has created a small army of legal consultants to assist parental challenges or school district defenses of decisions.

Tight budgets intensify what should be a disinterested inquiry of disability into an adversarial relationship. Parents must emotionally and legally deal with finding support for a child having academic—and often behavioral—difficulties. Bureaucrats are quite aware of the costs of evaluations and services. The Department of Education has noted that many states neither identify noncompliant school districts nor correct noncompliance where it is found. The major areas of noncompliance are 1) involving parents in special-education decision processes, 2) compromising the development and execution of IEPs, and 3) inadequately coordinating high school or work transition activities that could lead to career or college success.[25]

Federal law holds state education agencies responsible for disseminating information about policies, procedures, and any changes affecting children with disabilities to the general public, including public hearings and opportunities for comment (*34 CFR § 300.280–300.284*). While you will receive notices from your public school on policies and procedures, you can also obtain news about any federal government activities (such as scheduled hearings) in your local area at the Department of Education's website at www.ed.gov.

The role of parents. Federal law recognizes the rights of parents to advocate for their children with disabilities. Parents are the most likely people to make personal expenditures of time, resources, and energy to improve the child's well-being. Schools are required "to ensure that ... parents ... are afforded the opportunity to participate" (*34 CFR § 300.345*). Moreover, parents may include "other individuals who have knowledge or special expertise regarding the child ...." (*34 CFR § 300.344 (a) (6)*). To be an effective advocate, however, parents must become informed consumers, a difficult task considering the complex and individual nature of the problems. Advocacy helped bring these laws into existence:

- PL 91–230 in 1969 defined specific learning disabilities.
- PL 94–142 in 1975 qualified learning disabilities as a condition for special education.
- PL 98–199 in 1983 strengthened the administrative aspects of the special education system.
- PL 99–457 in 1986 extended IDEA to infants and preschoolers.
- PL 101–476 in 1990 expanded services to children with autism and traumatic brain injury.

---

25   U.S. Department of Education, "Twenty-third Annual Report to Congress," p. IV-15.

- PL 105–17 in 1997 added AD/HD as a condition eligible under the category of *other health impaired.*

As in most aspects of life, it's true that *the squeaky wheel gets the grease.* If you know the law and can speak on behalf of your child's developmental interests, you will be better able to obtain real help for your child. Ideally, some satisfactory situation can be arranged. Too often though, the system seems designed for frustration: you will either give up or you will become a tenacious advocate.

As a parent, you will have to experiment a bit in order to help your child. You may find yourself plowing new ground and seeking permission from school authorities to try a new activity or technology in order to improve your child's academic performance. If so, ensure that your child's teacher is aware that the IEP or accommodation plan permits the use of a word processor in the classroom, for example, or that your child has permission to be dismissed early from class to receive a new effective therapy. Make it easier for school officials to act on your request by providing information and some flexibility in your proposal. Too many educators, who may indeed be overwhelmed, may misperceive your requests as a control issue. This is unfortunate. (Chapter 19 discusses parent-teacher communications.)

If school officials will not accommodate your request, carefully follow their reasoning. Sometimes a detail may be misunderstood. Sometimes some creative compromise can be reached. Don't enter into disagreements with maximum force; overreacting is as bad as underreacting. Your child will not receive much help if the neurological issues get pushed aside in a politicized *us vs. them* argument.

If nothing can be negotiated, though, seek second and third opinions from reputable and knowledgeable professionals or parent information centers. You should not hesitate to seek an independent opinion in matters of importance. Libraries and reputable Internet sites offer some guidance. The website, "Legal Briefs from Matt Cohen Esq." at www.ldonline.org (click on *LEGAL BRIEFS FROM MATT COHEN*), reviews special education law and answers questions of general interest. Document interactions with schools, governmental agencies, and other relevant parties. One mother successfully ran for president of the parent board of her child's school and, with the help of many sympathetic parents, was able to institute some significant reforms.

Many parents shy away from advocacy for many reasons such as believing that schools know all the answers, not wanting to create a disturbance, or perhaps having a language disorder themselves. However, the LD Online website mentioned above receives inquiries from specialists as well as parents, indicating that even people professionally involved with special education don't always understand everything about current laws and practices. Advocacy involves:

- Maintaining your child's records and monitoring progress.
- Negotiating arrangements with your child's teachers and other service providers and documenting activities and interactions with personnel.
- Joining or forming a parent support group to share personal experiences and information.
- Developing a base of special education information resources and local providers.
- Learning about effective programs and practices that can help your child.
- Understanding your and your child's legal rights under IDEA, and other relevant federal and state laws.
- Mediating through due process and litigating if necessary.
- Advocating to the public in general and legislators in particular on behalf of your child and others so as to ease their entry as adult contributing members of society. An "Advocacy Tutorial" is available at www.schwablearning.org/articles.asp?g=2&r=559. One mother's metamorphosis from a business executive into a public advocate is portrayed in "Mom-Turned-Advocate Still Honors Her Roots," by Linda Broatch, available at www.schwablearning.org/articles.asp?g=3&r=712. (Ideally, public advocacy leads to logical rational policies. Kenneth Kavale and Steven Forness examine how some efforts may confuse instead of enlighten in "The Politics of Learning Disabilities," available at www.ldonline.org/ld_indepth/legal_legislative/politics. html.)

Self-advocacy. In high school, your child must learn to assume responsibility for this advocacy role. Not only should students understand their goals after high school and how their disabilities affects their education, but they should also understand laws applicable to their disabilities, situations in which disclosure would be helpful, and when and where to go for help. High schools may not wish to teach self-advocacy though, especially in environments in which only minimal services are provided.

You can teach your child self-advocacy skills yourself, providing your child accepts the disability as a problem to be addressed. Begin by coaching your student to make simple requests. By doing so, your child will not only be learning self-sufficiency, but you can concentrate more on bigger issues. Be prepared to follow up should your child's efforts prove unsuccessful. Additional tips for self-advocacy are found by going to www.ldonline.org (enter "self-advocacy" into the white box and click the *SEARCH LD ONLINE* button), and at "Self-Advocacy: A Valuable Skill for Your Teenager," by Jodie Dawson, available at www.schwablearning.org/articles.asp?r=522.

If parents cannot provide this instruction, a third party is needed to teach self-advocacy skills. Silver's 1997 *The Misunderstood Child* provides an example on page 151. Two books which may be useful are *College Students with Learning Disabilities: A Handbook* by Susan A. Vogel and *College and Career Success for Students with Learning Disabilities* by Rosyln Dolber.

School records

Negotiating the Special Education Maze devotes a chapter on getting access to your child's school records, interpreting them, and obtaining access to records after your child turns age 18. *The Complete IEP Guide* also tells you how to obtain copies of your child's records as well as letter samples to help you draft your written requests. Both workbooks advise that information in your child's school records may be crucial in determining the seriousness of your child's learning difficulties and the types of services that your child may require. Also covered are procedures for amending materials you find inappropriate, biased, incomplete, or inaccurate. A thick file is a warning flag to a new teacher; you may want to extract unnecessary material from the file. Many parents have regretted not reviewing their child's records at least annually.

Under IDEA:
- Your child's special education records can be amended (*34 CFR § 300.567*).
- A hearing can be convened to review inaccurate or misleading records, or any violations of privacy (*34 CFR § 300.568*).
- Your child's records can be destroyed, such as after graduation (*34 CFR § 300.573*). Such destruction will protect against unauthorized disclosure but will also wipe out information which may be required for other purposes like social security benefits.

The Family Education Rights and Privacy Act (FERPA) of 1974 (*34 CFR § 99*) is available at www.ed.gov/offices/OII/fpco/ferpa/ferpa regs.html. IDEA states that FERPA provides the rights of parents and their children in gaining access to school records (*34 CFR § 300.561.*) Under FERPA, also known as the Buckley Amendment:
- Schools must notify parents annually of their rights with respect to their child's records.
- Schools must consider a parent's request to amend inaccurate or misleading information in their child's school records.
- A school has a maximum of 45 calendar days to comply with a parent's request (or the request of a student over 18 years) to access, seek to amend, or consent to disclosures of these records.
- Before any records are given to a third party, permission is required by the parents (or student over 18).

The Family Policy Compliance Office enforces FERPA. More information is available at www.ed.gov/offices/OII/fpco/ferpa/parents.html. Complaints about a school must be submitted in writing within 180 days of the time you discovered the alleged violation to:

Family Policy Compliance Office
U.S. Department of Education
400 Maryland Avenue, SW
Washington, D.C. 20202–4605

Take care of yourself

The stresses on care givers are well-known to medical professionals. The issues surrounding treatment can be demanding, especially if you are simultaneously dealing with several frustrations:
- The learning disability itself
- Continuing disappointments with school performance
- The child's increasingly poor attitude toward school and motivation for academics
- Family disharmony
- Negative attitudes toward the child from peers, other parents, and often teachers themselves
- Little recognition of your efforts, if any, for helping your child.

Whatever you do, don't beat up on yourself if you learn later that something should have been done differently. Hindsight is better than foresight. Realize that you are probably making decisions under conditions of imperfect information and chronic stress. Bear in mind that depression has been linked to poor health.[26] Also beware of sacrificing yourself to your child's learning disability: These problems should not become the purpose of *your* life. A codependency will neither lead to independent adult functioning of your child nor any balance in your life.

You can't change the past, but you can change the future. Pace yourself. Prioritize. Don't try to solve all the problems all at once and don't isolate yourself. Find a support group, find a diversion or a hobby. Visit information centers and find unbiased information. Help is available. Some additional suggestions are found in an article, "Preventing Parent Burn Out: Model for Teaching Effective Coping Strategies to Parents of Children with Learning Disabilities" by Sherry Latson, available at www.ldonline.org/ld_indepth/parenting/preventburnout.html.

---

26 Marianne Szegedy-Maszek, "The Melancholy Body," *U.S. News & World Report,* 16 December 2002, pp. 48-49.

PART II:
GETTING HELP

Chapter Fifteen

What is an individual education plan (IEP)?

Adjusting behavior, assignments, and the learning environment

A learning disorder forces changes in behavior, assignments, or environment in order to focus on subject comprehension and providing evidence of it. *Remediation*, *compensation*, *modification* and *accommodation* are methods to improve execution. Often a student employs more than one of these methods to overcome difficulties.

Remediation is teaching proficiency[1] in a skill that is required for progress in school. Examples of remedial skills taught are reading and arithmetic. Various forms of remedial instruction exist, but usually have a drill-and-practice approach. Students, for example, can work with a teacher or an educational computer software program. Intensive rehearsal, however, may not significantly improve word decoding or math facts memorization. And while remediation may improve proficiency, a neurological weakness may not necessarily improve into an accomplished strength.

Somewhat related to remediation is *strategies instruction*. Students with learning disabilities may require explicit strategies to help them

---

1   H. Lee Swanson has cautioned use of the term *automaticity* because theoretical models differ. Automaticity in one model means rapid proficiency through practice, experience, and learning. Automaticity in another model means processing unalterable with learning. You may read that students with learning disabilities have *poor automaticity*; unclear would be the author's implication on whether these students can benefit from instruction. (From Swanson, "Information Processing," pp. 145-146.

compensate for their disability. An individual can offset a processing deficiency with an alternative behavior, perhaps with an equivalent result. For example, someone with a poor auditory memory can use a map to get to a destination. In other words, the student would use *compensating strategies* to effectively accomplish a task. Research has shown that these students can be taught to recognize the problem and follow through with steps to execute the task.

Modifications and *accommodations* are adjustments to the task environment. (No legal distinction in federal law exists between these two terms according to a federal district court in *Juleus Chapman et al., v. California Department of Education et al.* See Chapter 24.) Basically, function takes precedence over form in order to accomplish the goal. These methods provide access to information and communication channels so that individuals with LD can reflect on, control, or manipulate the material in a meaningful way. Using audiotapes instead of reading, word processors instead of pencils and paper, or calculators instead of memorized math facts is not weakening the curriculum for students with processing or memory disabilities. If 12 years of schooling mean the *acts* of calculating numbers (arithmetic), generating script (writing), decoding symbols into sounds (reading), coding sounds into symbols (spelling), and reciting memorized facts (rote learning), then machines are eligible for high school diplomas. For some observers, modifications and accommodations may seem like using a rocket ship to go to the grocery store, but if it works, then so be it. What is more important is *critical thinking*.

Courses of treatment: Be sure you know what you want

Understanding your child's learning disorder will help you understand what measures must be taken. Most often, one single approach will be inadequate. The many experts contributing to your child's IEP may be unaware of new research findings relevant to treatment. Alternatively, if your child was not found eligible for services or accommodations, you will have to coordinate services yourself.

When selecting appropriate activities, reflect on the best means to an adult end result. Only then do the real issues become apparent. Some problems can't be remedied with available therapies. For example, instead of asking why Johnny can't add even after days of remediating practice, maybe the question should be about Johnny using a calculator. Other problems need to be dealt with some perspective of the child's overall needs. One mother refused to relinquish an art class, an activity her child enjoyed and in which he demonstrated some talent, in order to carve out more time to remediate academic skills. A freshman's literature grade dropped when he joined the swim team, but he lettered, received an award for *most improved*, and broke a school junior varsity record. During the next year, the hard work devoted to swimming transferred to academics, and he was recommended for AP classes. Focus on the whole person.

An initial remediation scheme in the early school years may rapidly evolve into a complex program involving remediation, compensation, classroom modifications and work accommodations. Every now and then, you will need to pause, reflect a bit, and take a compass reading to find the directions for the next part of the journey. Each child has a unique set of problems and circumstances.

The rest of this chapter will discuss what you can expect in the IEP development process. School issues are covered in Chapters 16 and 17. Accommodations are discussed in Chapter 18.

The individualized education plan (IEP)

An IEP is a legal document specifying public school service commitments to a child deemed eligible to receive them. The IEP is developed, written, and revised by the public school district for children receiving services in public schools, or through the public school for children placed by the public school in a private school or facility. Charter schools—which may be part of the school district or function as school districts themselves—are subject to IDEA regulations. Members of the IEP team include, at a minimum, parents, regular and special education teachers, and a school representative who can ensure provision of curricular or other resources. Within 30 calendar days of determining that a child is eligible for services, the evaluation team must meet again to develop an IEP. The IEP team must consider other special factors such as behavioral interventions and assistive technology. A sample IEP form, which has many parts, is found at a California Department of Education's web site, www.cde.ca.gov/spbranch/sed/iepsmpl/ iepsmpl.htm, or in Siegel's *The Complete IEP Guide*.

A public or charter school must provide services to its students eligible to receive them. A private school does not have to provide services unless the child has been placed in the private school by the school district, and thus is being paid by the public school to provide those services. An IEP will give you information for determining service options for your child.

> "The [content of the IEP] ... must include—
> (1) A statement of the child's present levels of educational performance ...

(2) A statement of measurable annual goals, including benchmarks or short-term objectives ...

(3) A statement of the special education and related services ... and a statement of the program modifications or supports for school personnel that will be provided for the child ...

(4) An explanation of the extent, if any, to which the child will not participate with nondisabled children in the regular class ...

(5) ... A statement of any individual modifications in the administration of State or district-wide assessments of student achievement ...

(6) The projected date for the beginning of the services and modifications ... and the anticipated frequency, location, and duration of those services and modifications ...

(7) A statement of ... [h]ow the child's progress toward the annual goals ... will be measured; and ... [h]ow the child's parents will be regularly informed ...."

—34 CFR § 300.347

In many ways, the IEP is similar to a job performance review, in which current skills are appraised, and further skills development is planned. In this case, your child's performance is being appraised and future is being planned. And similar to the performance reviews in many organizations, effectiveness depends on how the IEP is used. Bear in mind that your child's individual needs override those of the school district.[2] That is, if the school district has no existing program that addresses your child's needs, then the district must still provide the requisite services. Any substantial deviations from the IEP, especially those that affect the services to be provided or portions not implemented, would violate IDEA.

Schools must implement IEPs "as soon as possible" (*34 CFR § 300.342 (b)*). Note that team members may *suggest* treatment options, but unless a service is *recommended*, it has not been identified as being required and so the school district will not pay for it.[3] The IEP, as the centerpiece of special education, is explained at length on many websites including www.ldonline.org and www.schwablearning.org. The better supported websites should provide you with more complete and accurate information. Also consider reading the law itself and informational workbooks, such as *Negotiating the Special Education Maze* and *The Complete IEP Guide*.

---

2   Osborne, *Legal Issues in Special Education*, p. 96.
3   Silver, *The Misunderstood Child*, p. 370.

You should be monitoring the school's special education situation throughout the year. Given the heavy caseloads of special education professionals, you might want to begin inquiring about scheduling the next round of IEP evaluations and conference at about six months from the last IEP, and certainly a few months before the end of the school year. IDEA states that an IEP should be in effect at the beginning of each school year (*34 CFR § 300.342*), and be reviewed at least once a year (*34 CFR § 300.343 (c)*). The child's instructor(s) should be involved. This year's personnel may not be next year's personnel. Springtime is an ideal time for a review so that a new plan will be in place at the beginning of the new school year, and before any decisions on summer school programs and a new schedule of classes for the following year. The IEP team can revise the program during the year as necessary to address a lack of progress, new findings from a reevaluation, or any other relevant matters.

At the time of this writing, Congress is considering legislation that would allow parents the *option* of reviewing the IEP—a legal document—once every three years instead of every year. While school administrators approve of paper reduction, children's advocates warn that learning needs will be neglected. (Few parents would be pleased if parent-teacher conferences—with different teachers and escalating grade requirements—were held once every three years because schools complained about scheduling and assembling work samples.)

A psychoeducational reevaluation is also required at least every third year:

> "Each [school district] shall ensure … That a reevaluation of each child … is conducted if conditions warrant a reevaluation, or if the child's parent or teacher requests a reevaluation, but at least once every three years."
>
> *—34 CFR § 300.536*

If a child no longer requires services, this must be demonstrated in an evaluation. Any alterations in services must have written permission from the parents (*34 CFR § 300.503*).

Periodically reexamine your child's IEP and evaluate whether you see progress toward your child's long-term goals and short-term objectives. Because you are managing your child's educational program, you should not only be considering your child's performance, but also the performance of everyone involved—teachers, therapists, counselors, school officials, and yourself as well. Investigate possible improvements in:

* *Reasonable provision of services.* Did the child receive the special services required in order to perform at the required level of

proficiency? Were services scheduled at the same time that the regular teacher taught academic material? Was there adequate individual instructional time? Silver advises that any school shortages of personnel "is the school's problem" and that your job is to ensure "that your child gets what she is supposed to get."[4]

• *Realistic goals.* Were the goals a wish list? Looking back, were they realistic? Is your child receiving appropriate treatment? One mother of a high school student once wondered aloud to me whether all the years spent remediating basic skills was really worth it. Perhaps other modifications and accommodations would be more appropriate.

• *Measurement of achievements.* What measurements were used during the year? Were they appropriate given the child's development or the actual curriculum taught? Was there a trend in performance?

• *Environment.* Was the environment conducive for learning? Does the child know material but cannot demonstrate this knowledge on a test? Were any bullying problems successfully addressed?

• *Rate of progress.* Did these achievements occur as expected? Why or why not? Is there a better therapy or treatment available? What should be appropriate summer activities?

• *Communication.* Does a productive school-home collaboration exist? If not, why not?

This list is only a beginning. You will have additional issues relating to your particular situation. Time may heal all wounds, but, for now, you're working against the ever increasing curriculum demands, year by year. IDEA services effectively end upon high school graduation. More suggestions for transforming the IEP from a *pro forma* process to an effective work plan are found in *Better IEPs: How to Develop Legally Correct and Educationally Useful Programs* (Sopris West, 1998), by Barbara D. Bateman and Mary Anne Linden.

Implementation: IEPs for public schools, individual service plans (ISPs) for private schools

For many parents, enrolling their child full-time in an undesirable neighborhood school or a school with hundreds if not thousands of students is an unacceptable situation, especially if their child is most likely to be grouped[5] with other classmates performing poorly for any number of reasons. Until recently, many parents solved this problem by enrolling their child in a private or parochial school and then

---

4   Silver, *The Misunderstood Child*, p. 234.

5   Tracking was held to be a discriminatory practice in 1967 because ability assessments could be inaccurate, and, once a student was placed in a certain track, he or she rarely moved out of that track; from Osborne, *Legal Issues in Special Education*, p. 5.

transporting the child to a public school offering services in a pull-out model.[5] (Public schools delivering services through an inclusion model cannot provide services to private and parochial students because these services are integrated into the entire curriculum and do not exist independently as stand-alone, separately scheduled special education classes or therapy sessions. Thus, to receive services from a public school using an inclusion model your child must be enrolled full-time.)

Today, however, if you enroll your child in a private or a parochial school and this enrollment was not recommended by the IEP team, you risk carrying the financial costs of properly educating your child.

> "No private school child with a disability has an individual right to receive some or all of the special education and related services that the child would receive if enrolled in a public school."
>
> *—34 CFR § 300.454 (a)*

Many parents were caught by surprise when this and related regulations were issued in 1999. Many students, defined in IDEA as *private school children with disabilities (34 CFR § 300.450)*, were left without special education services in the *middle* of the 1999–2000 school year. The 1999 regulations (following the 1997 amendments to IDEA) do not require public school districts to fund services for all students with disabilities *unilaterally* placed in private schools by their parents. Before these regulations, services followed the individual student who had an IEP. Now, school districts may opt out of providing services to *individual* private and parochial school children eligible to receive them.

Private school children with disabilities are funded as a *class* by the school district. Each public school district has the discretion to offer different types or levels of services for certain groups of students residing in its jurisdiction but enrolled by their parents in private, parochial, or religious schools:

> "Each [public school district] shall consult, in a timely and meaningful way, with appropriate representatives of private school children with disabilities ... the number of private school children with disabilities, the needs of private school children with disabilities, and their location to decide—
> (i) Which children will receive services ...
> (ii) What services will be provided ....
>
> *—34 CFR § 300.454 (b)*

Thus, private-school children with leaning disabilities may be excluded from services even though their parents pay taxes that

---

5   Special education models are explained in the next chapter.

support these services. Margaret McLaughlin, the Associate Director of the Institute for the Study of Exceptional Children and Youth at the University of Maryland, noted that any future "adjustments to the finance formula must be placement-neutral and not provide incentives for moving students with disabilities out of public school classrooms and environments."[6] One possible solution at the individual level is *double enrollment*, in which a private or parochial student may simultaneously enroll at a public school for services required in the IEP. The public school providing these services would then receive reimbursement from the state based on the student's attendance. In 2003, the House of Representatives legislated changes to IDEA for private school students, as reported in "Private Schools Pushing for IDEA Changes," by Mary Ann Zehr, available at www.edweek.org/ew/ewstory.cfm?slug =36idea.h22.

Students unilaterally placed in a private school by their parents and *eligible* for special education services but not receiving them can have *individual service plans* (ISPs) prepared by the school district (*34 CFR § 300.452*). ISPs are required to follow the same provisions governing IEP content (*34 CFR § 300.455*), except for portions related to district-wide assessments (not required of private schools) and transition to adulthood if the school does not handle adolescents. Some private schools prepare their own service plans in-house. Private schools may use private professional evaluations. Alternatively, states are obligated to continue evaluating at least every three years all private students eligible to receive special education services. You can request the annual individual service plan or the triennial psychoeducational evaluation (*34 CFR § 300.536*) from the school district. If the private school's program does not have service plans, then the program is not a special education program but is instead a *learning assistance program*. The regulations pertaining to "Children With Disabilities Enrolled by Their Parents in Private Schools" are 34 CFR sections 300.450 to 300.462.

In the short-term, school districts may have "saved" money by cutting services to students mainstreaming in non-public schools. In the long-term, populations of students with LD may become more concentrated in the public schools because private schools have few dedicated resources to help these children. The impact of the No Child Left Behind Act—through which children who have not made adequate progress may opt out of failing schools—remains untested.

---

6   Margaret J. McLaughlin, "Issues for Consideration in the Reauthorization of Part B of the Individuals with Disabilities Education Act," in *Rethinking Federal Education Programs for Children with Disabilities* [Internet], January 2002, p. 38, available from: http://www.ctredpol.org/specialeducation/timelyidea2002.pdf

Chapter Sixteen

How could my child receive special education services?

"It may be of interest to future generals to realize that one makes plans to fit circumstances and does not try to create circumstances to fit plans. That way danger lies."[1]

—George S. Patton

What is "placement?"

The most important decisions concern the actual educational treatment of your child, or *placement*. Placement decisions ideally balance the student's specialized educational needs with the general educational purpose of integrating the child into society. Some placement decisions may be too optimistic and overemphasize integration at the expense of special needs, sending a *sink-or-swim* message to the student with learning disabilities. Other placement decisions may be too pessimistic and cautious, thereby discouraging and restricting a child's access to higher education. For example, a school principal recommended vocational school instead of college prep classes for Dr. Larry Silver.[2] In both overly optimistic and pessimistic situations, the child loses.

The IEP team determines placement, generally based on the student's needs as identified in the IEP and a location reasonably close to the student's home. You do not have to enroll your child in the public school system, but if you do not you may forfeit access to free services. Each school district determines whether it will offer services to nonpublic school students.

---

1   D'Este, *Patton: A Genius for War*, p. 706.
2   Silver, *The Misunderstood Child*, p. 377.

You are unlikely to be successful in requesting that your public school district place your child in a private school and pay the private-school tuition, but you can request a change in placement based on the services required in the IEP. (Some tips are offered in "Winning Services, Placements and Reimbursements for Students with Dyslexia and Other Learning Disabilities" by Barbara Bateman, available at www.ldonline.org/ld_indepth/special_education/ida_bateman.html.) Many parents are choosing public alternative, magnet, and charter schools—which have public support for special education services. Because private schools differ enormously, this chapter will mostly concern itself with public schools. Bear in mind that you may be predetermining the types of services available to your child wherever you decide to enroll.

Placement must "be based on the child's unique needs" and include programs available to nondisabled children such as "art, music, industrial arts, consumer and homemaking education, and vocational education" (*34 CFR* § *300.305*). Placement must also enable the equal opportunity participation of children with disabilities in nonacademic and extracurricular activities including meals, recess periods, counseling services, athletics, transportation, health services, recreational activities, disability information agencies, clubs, and employment (*34 CFR* § *300.306* and *34 CFR* § *300.553*). Public school districts must offer a continuum of instructional services and delivery systems, seven of which are listed in IDEA (*34 CFR* § *300.551*):

- Regular classrooms
- Itinerant instruction
- Resource room
- Special classes
- Special schools
- Home instruction
- Instruction in hospitals and institutions.

IDEA has a *status quo* or *stay put* provision (*34 CFR* § *300.514*) in cases of contested placements. The child "must remain in his or her current educational placement" during the administrative or judicial proceedings with some exceptions such as an initial application to public school. Sometimes resolution may take years, and most courts hold that a final administrative decision is required before any change in placement can occur.[3] The status quo provision can even prohibit a school district from graduating a student undergoing an appeal.[4] The courts consider graduation to be a change of placement because it ends all special education services.[5]

---

3   Osborne, *Legal Issues in Special Education*, p. 54.
4   Osborne, p. 49.
5   Osborne, p. 50.

The next section will cover some terminology, which is not merely more vocabulary, but has real effects in determining your child's education. These words have subtle implications for placement through which parents must negotiate in order to receive special education services. The problems result from the funding limitations and the costs of special education, and where there are costs, there are politics.

Placement terminology: FAPE and LRE

Placement is subject to many conditions, including:
* a *free appropriate public education* (FAPE):

> " ...*free appropriate public education* or *FAPE* means special education and related services that ... Are provided at public expense ... Include preschool, elementary school, or secondary school education ... and ... Are provided in conformity with an individualized education program ...."
>
> *—34 CFR § 300.13*

* and a *least restrictive environment* (LRE):

> "... to the maximum extent appropriate, children with disabilities, including children in public or private institutions or other care facilities, are educated with children who are nondisabled; and ... That special classes, separate schooling or other removal of children with disabilities from the regular educational environment occurs only if the nature or severity of the disability is such that education in regular classes with the use of supplementary aids and services cannot be achieved satisfactorily."
>
> *—34 CFR § 300.550*

***Appropriate education:* Reasonable, not optimal.** A special education program must facilitate *reasonable*—not minimal, not full-potential—academic achievement and be uniquely suited to address your child's situation.[3] A student, deemed ineligible to receive services by the school district, can be awarded compensatory educational services if the courts find that FAPE has been denied.[4] The courts have determined that an education should provide students with disabilities a measurable *meaningful* benefit, not a trivial one, delineated in the following examples of appropriate and inappropriate education:[5]

---

3   Anderson, Chitwood and Hayden, *Negotiating the Special Education Maze*, pp. 88-89.
4   Osborne, *Legal Issues in Special Education*, p. 63.
5   Osborne, pp. 98-101.

APPROPRIATE EDUCATION
• Significantly benefiting from a program in which a student had passing grades and an improved ability to focus on tasks
• Demonstrating an *adequate* educational benefit in a public school, regardless of a *greater* educational benefit at a private school
• Completing graduation requirements with exceptional performance in regular classes
• Lacking progress due to poor attendance and motivation, not necessarily due to an unavailable appropriate education.

INAPPROPRIATE EDUCATION
• Progressing only four months during an academic year
• Placing a 15-year-old student with a first-grade reading level in regular high school classes
• Continuing in a program not demonstrating educational benefit
• Regressing educationally after terminating a program or service
• Using only *one* of the following indicators of student progress, which alone do not prove an appropriate education: promotion to the next grade, passing grades, *or* graduation with a high school diploma.

If a state standard is higher than the federal standard, the state standard determines *appropriate education*.[6] Under IDEA, a state must have performance indicators to measure the progress of children with disabilities as meeting the goals of IDEA (*34 CFR § 300.1*), including test performances, drop-out rates, and graduation rates (*34 CFR § 300.137*). States are to report progress on these indicators to the U.S. Department of Education, which then compiles these reports for the public. The most recent report at the time of this writing, the *Twenty-third Annual Report to Congress on the Implementation of the Individuals with Disabilities Act*, is available at www.ed.gov/offices/OSERS/OSEP/Products/comppubs.html, or call the Office of Special Education at 202/ 205-5507.

Least restrictive environment: **Primary or secondary objective?** The concept of *least restrictive environment* was developed at a time when students with disabilities were shunted away in specialized facilities with few academic opportunities. One purpose of education law was to broaden the educational and career possibilities of children with learning disabilities, allowing regular classes along with specialized classes. The pendulum, however, may have swung too far the other way toward *full-inclusion* (see an explanation of this under "Placement options"). Parents often disagree with school officials on the true meaning of *least restrictive* placement as being an *appropriate* placement under FAPE.

---

6   Osborne, p. 100.

Some courts view an appropriate education as a primary goal and LRE as a secondary integration objective. Other courts have held LRE as a mandatory requirement—almost tantamount to a prohibition on segregated situations—"no matter how appropriate that setting might be."[7] Your job in all this is to see the classroom as your child sees it. Says Louisa Cook Moats, a researcher, psychologist, educator, and a clinical associate professor of pediatrics at the University of Texas:

> "... [S]tudents with LD receive little or no special instruction in large general education classes. Those who learn differently often are not taught differently. Classroom teachers are often unable to instruct children with LD effectively, even though they are willing, because they do not have the time, resources, collaborative working conditions, expertise, or energy to be all things to all students."[8]

In other words, a one-size-fits-all approach in the classroom could be a set-up for educational failure, especially for students whose abilities have been measured as being two standard deviations from the norm. Moreover, an environment with low expectations that is not warm and responsive, however enriched, is less likely to improve social, intellectual, and communication skills.[9] Placing a child with LD in the general education classroom does not mean that she or he will receive effective instruction or be socially integrated with same-age peers. Instead, academic progress depends on whether instructional methods meet "the individual's needs for pacing, concept representation, corrective feedback, and reinforcement .... [S]ocial well-being arises not from inclusion but from genuine social acceptance and academic success."[10]

Mainstreaming: **Who really benefits?** Most people erroneously assume that *mainstreaming*, a term not defined in special education law, means *least restricted environment.* Indeed LRE, as commonly practiced, places every child with a disability into regular classrooms, unless it is clear that a special class or other special accommodations would be better (*34 CFR § 300.552 (c)*). Bear in mind, though, that students are not required to receive special education services on the general premises of a public school:

---

7   Osborne, p. 110.

8   Moats, L.C. (Copyright © 1996). "Implementing Effective Instruction." In Editors Cramer, S.C. and Ellis, W. *Learning Disabilities: Lifelong Issues* (p. 89). Baltimore: Paul H. Brookes Publishing Co. Reprinted with permission of Paul H. Brookes Publishing Co. and Shirley C. Cramer.

9   Bruce Bower, "Disabilities Develop as Family Affair," *Science News*, 3 November 2001, p. 276.

10 Louisa Cook Moats, "Implementing Effective Instruction," in *Learning Disabilities: Lifelong Issues*, ed. Shirley C. Cramer and William Ellis (Baltimore: Paul H. Brookes Publishing Co., 1996), p. 89.

> "... [A] child with a disability who is placed in or referred to a private school or facility by a public agency ... [must be] provided special education and related services ... In conformance with an IEP ... At no cost to the parents ...."
>
> *—34 CFR § 300.401*

There is a subtle distinction between *mainstreaming*, or placing a child with disabilities in the regular classroom, and *least restrictive environment*, which seeks to increase the opportunities of a child with learning disabilities depending upon the individual's ability to function in a broader society. Mainstreaming emphasizes a method for delivering curriculum instruction; it means children with disabilities will attend regular classes but will receive special education services either inside or outside those regular classes. LRE emphasizes an environment as normal as possible so long as the child benefits; it means a child should be placed in an environment, ranging from an institution to the neighborhood school, so that he or she will academically benefit. In practice, the problem arises when a child with LD is overwhelmed or intimidated in the mainstream environment. If a mainstream school has tried its best but failed to educate a student with disabilities, the courts will require a more restrictive placement.[11] An example of the distinction between *LRE* and *mainstreaming* is presented in "Least Restrictive Environment: How Do We Prepare Both Our Special Educators and Our General Educators to Comply with the Provision?" by Carolyn Cannon Kuehne, available at www.ldonline.org/ld_indepth/legal_legislative/complying_with_provision.html.

Typically, adolescents with learning disabilities are likely to be placed in lower-level classes.[12] Says William Bender, author and professor of special education at the University of Georgia, "Most mainstream teachers modify their classes very little and only when essential. These teachers have not been trained to conduct the instructional strategies that would facilitate successful mainstreaming."[13] A chaotic classroom situation is seen in Appendix 8. To reduce this problem, some states now require general teacher training to include experience with different types of students, including those in special education.[14]

Students with learning disabilities have also been mainstreamed on the assumption that peer role models in the regular school environment would provide social role models.[15] As a group, though, children

---

11   Osborne, *Legal Issues in Special Education*, p. 113.

12   Bender, *Learning Disabilities*, p. 182.

13   Bender, p. 333.

14   David L. Marcus, "One Class, and 20 Learning Styles," *U.S. News & World Report*, 9 April 2001, p. 94.

15   Bender citing 1993 assumption by Madden and Slavin, *Learning Disabilities*, p. 151.

with LD are less able to converse, socialize, and develop friendships. Thus, many students may be overwhelmed academically and socially.

For many school administrators, LRE is a less convenient concept to implement than regular school attendance. Indeed, one state school superintendent has remarked that "it is easier to determine whether a child has been mainstreamed than whether the educational program provided is appropriate."[16] LRE does not equal mainstreaming, but results from a continuum of alternative placements, one of which would be most appropriate for your child. Mainstreaming may just happen to be an appropriate least restrictive learning environment for many students, but not all.

A 1989 study found that mainstreamed students with learning disabilities had higher failure and dropout rates than similar students not mainstreamed.[17] Sweden uses another concept, *normalization*, which focuses on developing a fully functional adult instead of a method of delivering instruction.[18] In the end, you must decide which school options offer the best program for your child. Many public schools have a wide variety of resources. Many private schools with specialized programs offer tuition assistance.

One fundamental problem underlying the differences between FAPE, LRE, and mainstreaming, is that little agreement exists on the goals of education itself. A decade ago, Trapani asked some questions which have yet to be answered:

> "American society has chosen to provide [appropriate] education without defining what [appropriate] means. Does [appropriate] mean the right to sit in a mainstreamed class during one's youth, but be separated from high-achieving peers in adulthood? Is it the freedom to learn to the best of one's ability, receiving effective instruction in skills that will foster employment opportunities and quality in lifestyle?"[19]

In most instances, school budgets really determine the availability of remedies. The population of students with diagnosed learning disabilities has increased from over 100,000 in 1969 to almost

---

16 Glenn A. Vergason and M. L. Anderegg, "Preserving the Least Restrictive Environment," in *Controversial Issues Confronting Special Education: Divergent Perspectives*, ed. William C. Stainback and Susan Bray Stainback (Needham Heights, Massachusetts: Allyn and Bacon, 1992), p. 52.

17 Vergason and Anderegg citing 1989 Wagner study, p. 52.

18 Vergason and Anderegg, p. 47.

19 Excerpt from *Transition Goals for Students with Learning Disabilities* by Catherine Trapani, p. 108. Copyright © 1990 by Catherine Trapani, Ph.D., and published by College-Hill Press. All rights reserved. Reprinted with permission of Catherine Trapani with her 14 January 2003 text revisions noted in brackets.

three million by 2000 (see Chapter 13). While an increasing number of children are being identified as having learning disabilities, school districts generally prioritize services toward those with more severe disabilities.[20] Each child in special education, however, brings two types of public funding to the school for: 1) attending just like any other student on the campus and 2) special education services. (There are also other types of funding, such as Title I for low-income students.) You may wish to learn from the principal whether the special education funding attached to your child goes toward the school's special education operations or is commingled with the school's general operating budget. Then ask yourself whether your child is receiving the help he or she needs.

Placement options

Aside from state laws, teacher contracts may also specify student-to-teacher ratios for various categories of special education students and maximum case loads for special education professionals, such as resource specialists, speech clinicians or psychologists. Union contracts may be posted on the Internet.

Students with moderate and severe learning disabilities: Specialized classes. Self-contained classrooms and special day and residential schools offer low student-to-teaching staff ratios such as 8 to 1. Classes may be self-contained, in which one teacher may instruct the entire academic curriculum, with nonacademic activities such as physical education, art, or music taught by other instructors. Other schools may provide teachers specializing in certain curriculum areas who rotate through all classes according to a daily schedule. Depending on individual need, students with moderate or severe learning disabilities may attend special classes part-time or full-time.

If the school district places a student in a private learning environment, parents incur no costs. Otherwise, many of these schools can adjust tuition. Some educators deem self-contained placements as no more effective than regular school placements with appropriate modifications, while others suggest that some needs are better addressed in more controlled settings.

Extended school year (ESY) services. The IEP may recommend services over the summer months (*34 CFR § 300.309*) as part of FAPE. Each school district has criteria for ESY eligibility such as the likelihood of a *substantial* regression or irretrievable loss of critical skills, or delayed progress toward an IEP objective.[21] Courts have required consideration of current skill level, degree of disability, rate of

---

20 Bender, *Learning Disabilities*, p. 335.
21 Silver, *The Misunderstood Child*, p. 235.

improvement, likelihood of regression, expected recovery time of lost skills, and alternative available resources.[22] ESY not only includes academic classes, but also enrichment and recreational programs for addressing the emotional and physical needs of the child.[23]

Students with mild and moderate learning disabilities: Regular classes. As with more restrictive environments, there are advantages and disadvantages with each model for providing instruction to your child. The program factors which enable students to successfully integrate into regular classes include:[24]

• Scheduling classes that stretch the student's abilities yet provide a reasonable level of success, which, in turn, improve motivation, attitude, academic progress, and classroom behavior
• Pacing task requirements in areas of difficulty, so as not to overwhelm the student during the school day or during the school year
• Monitoring student progress and providing continuous performance feedback
• Involving students in choosing their educational options
• Employing a wide variety of techniques and materials
• Encouraging students to help each other
• Teaching students self-management skills
• Teacher collaboration on instructional tasks.

States have different teacher certification standards, some states providing a credential in specific categories and others providing a credential for all categories. While one senses that different instructional approaches should be used with different categories of disabilities, research has not shown any type of resource program or teacher training to be more effective than another.[25] Indeed, the larger issue appears to be a shortage of special education teachers. At the beginning of the 1999–2000 school year, 12,241 positions were vacant or filled by substitute teachers.[26] (State statistics on teacher shortages in special education are presented in Appendix 9.)

Several delivery models of special education instruction exist:

Itinerant Teaching Model. A special education teacher who travels between different regular classrooms during the day giving individualized instruction to many students or to a single student is an *itinerant teacher.* This method of providing specialized instruction may exist as one of many placement possibilities within a single school, or as part of an inclusion model (discussed later in the Chapter).

---

22   Osborne, *Legal Issues in Special Education*, p. 126.
23   Osborne, p. 126.
24   Mercer citing 1985-1986 findings of Wang and Baker; and 1985 study by Waxman, Wang, Anderson, and Walberg, *Students with Learning Disabilities*, p. 189.
25   Bender, *Learning Disabilities*, p. 339.
26   U.S. Department of Education, "Twenty-third Annual Report to Congress," p. III-36.

Pull-out Model. For part of the day, students with learning disabilities are placed in a modified classroom environment and receive specialized instruction. This allows an individualized mix-and-match approach with both generalized and specialized classes. This pull-out schedule can actually be quite flexible, and class time can be spent on a mixture of academics, basic skills, and weekly speech therapy sessions. An elementary school student would leave (be *pulled-out of*) the regular classroom and go to the special education classroom according to a predetermined schedule. A high school student could schedule honors and regular classes with a special education class. In some states, according to a 1984 study, over 90% of the total student population having disabilities were served by resource rooms.[27] Since then, many schools have migrated to an inclusion model.

A pull-out program may also be called a *resource specialist program (RSP)*. A *program administrator* is responsible for ensuring compliance with special education regulations. A special education teacher is called a *resource specialist*. This person assesses and instructs students with learning disabilities, assists the mainstream teachers, and meets with other relevant individuals such as parents, therapists, and psychologists. In middle schools and high schools, parents may direct their concerns to the resource specialist, instead of all the child's teachers.

Special education classrooms are called *resource rooms*. There, students receive part-time specialized assistance in math, reading, writing, spelling, and other fundamental academic skills. They may also be a place where students are given extra time to complete classroom tests. Often, social skills instruction supplement academic instruction. The resource room is often scheduled for an hour a day or one class period per day, five days per week. Unless each student in the class requires the same instruction, group instruction is inappropriate. Special education law requires individualized instruction. For this reason, most states permit up to 25 students per resource room over the course of a day.[28] Be aware of how the time for a pull-out session is used. Silver cautions that too many students in a pull-out class may not receive individualized instruction, too much time may be lost in getting to and settling into class, the resource specialist or therapist may not effectively communicate with regular teachers on the child's particular problems, or the child may miss academic instructional time while attending a pull-out session.[29] In elementary school, many students feel embarrassed to leave the regular classroom to go to the resource room. For this last reason, many schools adopted the inclusion model. Some students, however, may prefer the safety of resource rooms.

---

27 Bender citing Friend and McNutt study, *Learning Disabilities*, p. 325.
28 Bender, p. 327.
29 Silver, *The Misunderstood Child*, pp. 233-234.

A combination of regular classes and resource room instruction has been shown to increase academic achievement for all types of students.[30] Different types of resource rooms exist:[31]

• *Categorical resource rooms* specialize in one of the various 13 defined categories of disabilities (explained in Chapter 13).

• *Cross-categorical resource rooms* combine students across different disability categories but with similar levels of achievement.

• *Noncategorical resource rooms* serves all students with disabilities. Once a substitute teacher, U.S. Education Secretary of Education Rod Paige remembers the difficulty in teaching—much less learning—in the classroom "equivalent of a tossed salad—kids with short attention spans and those who were mildly mentally retarded."[32]

• *Specific-skills resource rooms* specialize in one or more skill areas regardless of the student's identified disability:

Instructional Emphasis	Benefits	Drawbacks
Basic skills remediation	- Instruction targets reading, writing, math skills compromised by the disability - Students of similar ability can develop camaraderie	- Remediation may not improve basic skills proficiency - Prolonged remediation delays classroom modifications and accommodations usage
Subject matter tutorials	- Assists learning of academic content (e.g., history, science) in addition to basic-skills areas	- Special educators may be uncertified to teach secondary subjects
Learning strategies	- Provides students with methods for managing tasks better, regardless of the subject matter	- Regular teacher may not reinforce strategy use
Functional skills and vocational programs	- Stresses life-survival skills such as money management and job skills	- Discouraging assessment of potential capabilities

• *Itinerant resource programs* are common service centers shared by several schools which may be small, rural or remotely located.

Consultation Model. In a consultation model, a learning consultant with specialized knowledge of learning disabilities works with the regular teachers to improve student performance. The consultant makes classroom observations and then recommends changes in curriculum, teaching style, and classroom discipline. From an organizational point of view, the regular teacher would be responsible for both subject content as determined by school officials, and special education achievement as provided by the consultant's recommendations. In one version of this model, the learning consultant only works with the classroom teachers. In another version, the consultant works both with the teacher and the student with learning disabilities.

---

30 Bender, *Learning Disabilities*, p. 329.
31 Bender, p. 325.
32 Ruben Navarrette Jr., "In Special Ed, Accountability Is Left Behind," *Los Angeles Times*, 17 April 2002, p. B13.

Many states require consultants to have some experience in regular and special education instruction. The model assumes that students with disabilities can progress in a regular learning environment with indirect specialized instruction. This model also assumes that regular teachers can adapt their classes according to the consultant's recommendations. If your child's school uses this model, ask whether your child is receiving services from appropriately trained personnel.

Compared to the pull-out model, the consulting model is less effective but also less expensive on a per-pupil basis; for this latter reason, the consultation model is preferred by many school administrators.[33] This model may also be used for students not requiring daily services but needing more help than that provided by a 504 Plan.

Inclusion Model. An *inclusion model* is not mainstreaming per se, but refers to only one method of mainstreaming a child with disabilities. In an inclusion model, *all* special education services are delivered within the regular classroom to all children with different types of disabilities. In contrast, mainstreaming means children with disabilities will attend regular classes but will receive services either inside regular classes or outside in specialized classes.

In the late 1980s, The Regular Education Initiative (REI), developed by the federal Office of Special Education and Rehabilitative Services, recommended that *all* special education students receive services in the regular classroom, and that resource rooms as well as the continuum of special education services be eliminated. Students would not be stigmatized or embarrassed in having to go to *special ed*, and more children—not eligible for special education—could receive extra help. Assumed in this delivery model of special education services is that the regular classroom could be adapted to facilitate improved academic achievement with better teaching methods.[34]

The inclusion model combines students with and without disabilities with a special education teacher and the curriculum instructor in the same classroom. The instructor provides curriculum content, and the special education teacher works with the students with disabilities—as well as other students without disabilities—during class time. IDEA allows "services provided in a regular class … even if one or more nondisabled children benefit from these services" (*34 CFR § 300.235*). Ideally, students with disabilities are better integrated in the regular classroom, and the regular teacher and the special education teacher can coordinate their activities. Many parents of regular students like this model because they regard the special education teacher as a teacher's aide in their child's classroom.

---

33   Bender, *Learning Disabilities*, p. 332.
34   Mercer, *Students with Learning Disabilities*, p. 187.

At the time this inclusion model was implemented in the early 1990s, no "solid evidence" supported the inclusion concept.[35] Moreover, with ongoing teacher shortages especially in special education, employing a good number of special education instructors to cover many classrooms simultaneously may be more difficult to realize and prove more expensive than a dedicated resource center.

Educators today are divided over methods of delivering special education services, that is, whether it is more effective to have a continuum of different specialized service sites or to locate all services in one classroom. Accardo suggests that underlying this debate are assumptions of whether students with disabilities have more specialized needs than students without disabilities:

> "...inclusion represents a ... philosophy that children with LD do not really have any problems that could not be handled by their trying harder. The publicly stated promise of providing whatever special services might be needed for success in the general education classroom is belied by the private statements of these same [school] administrators who see inclusion as a money-saving device when even the simplest arithmetic demonstrates that it might very well be more costly."[36]

Ask how much actual individual instruction your child would be or is receiving in an inclusion model. Your child should not have to compete for individualized help within the classroom though a "normal" classmate may indeed require specialized instruction. Parents of children with disabilities in private schools should also not be the only ones paying for a special education instructor if that person helps other students in the regular classroom.

Which model is best? General considerations. Aside from the aforementioned pros and cons of each model, how well a special education program works in a particular school also depends on how students are taught. For example, elementary schools—which teach basic input-output skills such as decoding, handwriting, and arithmetic in one classroom—may prefer an inclusion model. Middle schools and high schools, however, may find that complex text comprehension and writing skills are better addressed in a pull-out model because a special education class can be scheduled just like any other class on the student's schedule. In particular, an inclusion model in the higher grade

---

35 Bender, *Learning Disabilities*, p. 335.

36 Accardo, P.J. (Copyright © 1996). "A Developmental Pediatric Perspective on Neurologically Based Specific Learning Disabilities." In Editors Cramer, S.C. and Ellis, W. *Learning Disabilities: Lifelong Issues* (p. 106). Baltimore: Paul H. Brooks Publishing Co. Reprinted with permission of Paul H. Brooks Publishing Co. and Shirley C. Cramer.

levels does not specify how students will receive help with assignments to be completed *outside* of class. Moreover, a special education teacher in an inclusion classroom at the higher grade levels may be redundant if either the regular teacher employs techniques to teach a classroom of diverse learners or students preview the material before it is presented to the entire class. Thus, any discussion surrounding which model is *best* should consider the school's general instruction delivery model. Still, the most important factors of any special education program are the quality of your child's special educator and the school's support.

The relative merits of these service delivery models are also reviewed in:

• "Pull-Out or Pull-In? What Works Best?" by Kathleen Ross-Kidder, available at www.ldonline.org/ld_indepth/special_education/inclusion_pullin.html

• "Thinking about Inclusion and Learning Disabilities: A Teachers Guide," by Katherine Garnett, available at www.ldonline.org/ld_indepth/teaching_techniques/dld_ecologies.html

• "The Social Face of Inclusive Education: Are Students with Learning Disabilities Really Included in the Classroom?" by Shireen Pavri and Richard Luftig, available at www.ldonline.org/ld_indepth/teaching_techniques/the_social_face.html

• "Inclusion & Learning Disabilities: Frequently Asked Questions," by Jerome Schultz, available at www.ldonline.org/ld_indepth/special_education/schultz_inclusion.html.

Summer vacation: What to do? ESY is not considered a placement option for students with "less severe" disabilities. You have alternatives, but you must investigate a program's suitability for your child. Some private organizations offer summer tutoring or other improvement opportunities for students with learning and behavioral problems. Many resources offer information about selecting an appropriate summer camp or other ideas for the summer:

• "Summer Places for Children with Attention Deficit Disorders," by Steven Kurtz, available at www.aboutourkids.org/articles/summer_adhd.html

• "Summer Camps for Kids with Learning Differences," by Nancy Firchow, which also links to different websites about specific camps, available at www.schwablearning.org/articles.asp?r=285

• www.ldonline.org, type in "summer" in the white box then click on the *SEARCH LD ONLINE* button.

You can be your own camp director and take advantage of the summer activities in your community. Summertime is also a good time to schedule hands-on experiences, explore new places, practice academic skills, and preview upcoming courses. Nevertheless, provide a real break from the stresses of the academic year just completed.

Chapter Seventeen

What types of schools might work for my child?

While my son needed to work harder than the average middle-school student, time-pressured projects and homework every weekend seemed over the line. Math brain teasers stumped me as well as him. Essays assigned to the entire class as punishment for the inappropriate conduct of a few students raised peer pressure and reduced camaraderie. A handful of the same students would star in the school's few high-profile activities year-after-year. Parents grumbled among themselves, but no one wanted to rock the boat and risk jeopardizing their child's recommendations to high schools. A neighborhood couple belatedly discovered that their son's private K-8 program did not recommend him to any school to which he applied, perhaps for a second-grade incident; he did find a high school finally and is now at a major university.

Since the local public high schools struggled with academic standards or overcrowding, private options seemed better. Conventional wisdom held that being admitted to a private high school would be easier if a student graduated from a private K-8 school. Eric wanted out and I can't say I could blame him.

That parents often end up teaching their kids to do the assignments, if not do them themselves, seems to occur at many private K-8 schools that pride themselves on academics. A Boston couple joked about passing sixth grade again. Another mother who is a teacher herself complained about having to help her child construct a model of an historical structure in a week's time—in addition to other homework. One seventh-grader at a tony all-girls school stays up until midnight to complete her homework and an hour of piano at which she excels.

I don't understand the point of these school assignments that require so much commitment at such a young age.

Eric is now an honors student in a college prep high school, taking regular classes and getting the support he needs. He likes his teachers, and is more confident and independent in school. My son can hardly wait to get to class each morning. He still struggles but is motivated to do his best. Essays are exercises of heartfelt expression, not forced confessions of 500 words. Looking back at the last school, I realize that many of the assignments were so unnecessary.

Factors involved in choosing a school

Look hard at the school environment. Are they really trying to help *your* child? Do they encourage the best in *all* their students, not just a chosen few? Is your child happy there? What's the level of school politics, even in an elementary school? How does the school teach individuals who think and learn differently, such as those profiled in Chapter 6? Has the school settled on a suboptimal educational trajectory for your child?

One of the most important jobs you have is making sure your child is receiving help in an emotionally supportive situation. Some schools allow parents to observe class activities. The Marcus Institute in Atlanta uses an *open school* model, which permits parents and teachers to study classroom practices unnoticed from a separate room. Usually though, many parents volunteer time to help in the classroom in order to observe their children.

At least annually, evaluate the child's current school. The most intensive evaluations should occur at natural transition points when all children will be new to a school in the following year, for example, the sixth grade in middle school or the ninth grade in high school. You will not be alone in wondering whether you have made the right decisions.

A reputable school may have an unstructured environment suitable for self-confident, highly motivated students with proven academic track records. Often, these students teach themselves. In contrast, a vocational high school may have instructors prepared to work intensively with its students in a highly structured program. A smaller school may be less complex to navigate but lack a wide variety of peers, activities, or classes that your child may prefer. High schools trying to reduce their dropout rates may find their average test scores declining. You must determine where your child can best learn. Before committing to a program or school, examine:
- Specific offerings of support and services
- Physical plant and equipment that your child will use
- Integration of regular academic and special education instruction
- School's philosophy and support of school's administration (beyond boilerplate remarks) toward students with learning disabilities

- Observations of playground bullying or children wandering alone friendless
- Training, classroom approaches, and credentials of teachers, especially those in special education
- Whether students with learning disabilities make the honor roll
- Current extracurricular participation—for example, how students assume sports, theater, or leadership roles
- Past outcomes of students with LD at the school and beyond.

Statistics. Many websites offer statistics. See, for example, www.schoolmatch.com and www.bestplaces.net/html/schools.html. Schools can be screened for LD programs at www.greatschools.net. Still, information on private schools is not as available as for public schools and perhaps not directly comparable. Lists of school statistics are often incomplete, flawed and may even be misleading: teachers' degrees may be unrelated to what they teach, uncredentialed teachers may be included in a teacher-pupil ratio, administrative and building costs may be added to the per-pupil spending figure, a sizable portion of students may not have participated in a standardized test, and test scores may not reflect the actual curriculum. More revealing facts about a school must be obtained from various sources:

- The school district, diocese, or charter/private school principal: budget items such as types of available special education services at a specific school site, special education and academic class sizes, number of credentialed teachers, and instructional spending on teacher salaries and classroom materials
- The school itself: types of continuing education opportunities for teachers; supplementary instructional funding by parents; teacher turnover; and test-score patterns revealing the school's instructional value by comparing the periodic progress *of* a group not *between* groups—for example, this year's fifth grade versus last year's fourth grade, not this year's fourth grade versus last year's fourth grade
- Classroom observations: time spent on standardized test preparation, types and publication dates of textbooks, displays of work demonstrating originality or conformity
- Discussions with parents of students: effectiveness of the special education program, school safety issues especially during adolescence, flexibility of teachers, available tutoring, homework and long-term projects, parent assemblies and newsletters, parent-teacher meetings, and parent input requirements for academics and school support.

Socioeconomic demographics. In contrast to an earlier study suggesting that private schools had a freer hand in managing school-site issues than public schools, a recent study linked school quality to the school population's affluence. That is, public and private schools serving low-income populations had more in common with each other than all public schools together or all private schools together,[1] as shown schematically in Figure 17.1:

Figure 17.1

Public low-income schools	Public affluent schools
Private low-income schools	Private affluent schools

That many parents pay a premium to live in a neighborhood with excellent public schools corroborates this study. The study also found:
- Low-income private and public schools rarely fire teachers, due to problems in finding replacements and potential lawsuits.
- Teachers in low-income public and private schools complained that parents are not involved in their children's education.
- Teachers in affluent public and private schools complained of too much parent involvement.

Some other findings revealed the degree of open parent-school communications:
- Rather than fire teachers, private schools often ask families to withdraw when parents are perceived as too demanding.
- Compared to parents at affluent public schools, parents at affluent private schools are more reticent because they understand that their children can be replaced by candidates on the waiting list.
- Archdioceses highly regulate Catholic schools.

Thus, not only do schools differ in quality, but also in consequences for speaking candidly.

School safety. Many recent studies have demonstrated that the degree of *school connectedness*—a feeling by students that they are important contributors to their school community and that they are cared for—is tied to the risk of violent behavior, substance abuse, and promiscuity. Using data from the National Longitudinal Study of Adolescent Health, a 2002 study by the Center for Adolescent Health and Development of the University of Minnesota found that harsh discipline, such as zero-tolerance policies, results in students feeling less safe than those in schools with more moderate measures.[2] Moreover, teachers promoting a welcoming environment and strong relationships with students—irrespective of experience and academic degrees— encourage positive attitudes toward school.[3]

---

1   Debra Viadero, citing research by Benveniste, Carnoy, and Rothstein, "Public or Private, Study finds Schools Similar" [Internet], 22 January 2003, pp. 2-3, available at http://www.edweek.org/ew/ewstory.cfm?slug=19private.h22

2   Michael A. Fletcher, "Connectedness Called Key to Student Behavior" [Internet], p. 3, accessed 12 April 2002 from: http://www.washingtonpost.com/ac2/wp-dyn?page name=article&node=&contentId=A34686-2002April11

3   Fletcher, p. 3.

Parents should thoroughly investigate the school's disciplinary philosophies, actual methods used, and whether problems really get resolved; printed statements of policies may not guide actual practice. Parents might also investigate the class management techniques of prospective teachers, and whether recess, especially at the middle-school grade levels, is more of an ordeal than an academic respite for students like your child. Some schools try to keep a lid on academic and social stress. Others, however, foster a competitive sink-or-swim attitude with no safety net for students who can't survive this tough-love philosophy. The personality of each class will also create its own internal dynamics.

Good sources of information might be several parents similar to yourself whose children are average or unsuccessful students, of the same gender as your child, and older thereby possessing the wisdom of hindsight. Understanding what can happen when things go wrong will be much more instructive than hearing only the success stories.

Extracurricular activities and school size. Not only should you review the types of extracurricular activities offered at the school, but whether your child may be able to participate. For example, large schools have a wide variety of activities but also lots of competitors for available slots. Small schools may be nurturing, but have fewer activities. Also, a bully in a small school can be a constant reminder that the victim has nowhere to hide. As a rule of thumb, students in schools with under 1200 students felt less isolated from each other than students at larger schools.[4] At-risk behavior increases when individuals feel less integrated with the social life of school.

Class size and teacher quality. A 1990 study found that small classes, defined as 22 or less children per teacher, are most beneficial to students *at-risk*, especially during kindergarten through third grade.[5] This and other studies were the foundation for class-size reductions in California's public schools—which produced no clear benefits.[6] However, class-size reductions came at the expense of losing credentialed experienced teachers in urban, predominantly minority schools to more affluent suburban communities, as well as extracurricular programs. Untrained and inexperienced teachers are less likely to recognize learning problems. Meanwhile, two other statistically robust studies showed significant academic improvements with class sizes of 12 to 17 students;[7] optimum solutions are not possible for most schools however.

---

4   Fletcher, p. 1.
5   Mercer citing Robinson study, *Students with Learning Disabilities*, p. 227.
6   Nanette Asimov, "Effect of Smaller Elementary Classes Unclear, Study Says," *San Francisco Chronicle*, 28 June 2002, p. A19.
7   Ronald G. Ehrenberg, Dominic J. Brewer, Adam Gamoran and J. Douglas Willms, "Does Class Size Matter?" *Scientific American*, November 2001, p. 83.

While small classes can make a difference in academic performance, the best results may occur where teachers encourage more group discussions, assign hands-on projects, provide more feedback on written work, and develop personal relationships with the students.[8] Teacher quality seems more important than class size; the percentage of fully certified teachers in a school is one of the strongest predictors of student achievement.[9] A 1996 Tennessee study found that three years of effective teaching improved fifth graders' math scores by 83%, compared to a 29% improvement with three years of ineffective teaching;[10] the presence of teachers aides made little difference.[11] Additional factors determining teacher quality are the teacher's verbal ability, and background in a subject area, particularly at the secondary level.[12]

School staff. Special education teachers, like math teachers, are in especially short supply. Moreover, special education instruction is a burnout profession because of the large population of students with widely diverse academic and emotional problems. At the beginning of the 1999–2000 school year, 12,241 special education positions were vacant or filled by substitute teachers.[13] A 2002 *USA Today* survey suggested that, nationally, up to 40% of practicing special education teachers plan to quit their positions within five years.[14] (In response to the article's report that excessive paperwork caused teacher dissatisfaction, a legal organization, DREDF, argued that the real issue is not paperwork but compliance. See "Law is Not the Problem," by Diane Lipton, available at www.usatoday.com/news/opinion/2002/06/19/ncoppf.htm.) In comparison, approximately 30 percent of new regular classroom teachers quit within five years.[15]

Other issues can affect your child's learning environment. Some teachers better appreciate the consequences of school demands after raising their own offspring. Another problem is frequent teacher absenteeism, which can result in inadequate instruction because substitute teachers may not realize that your child has learning issues. Be concerned if many of the teachers *that you like* leave the school, not necessarily all at once. Be sensitive to situations in which a teacher—resentful over having to provide *special rights* for something not physically visible—is supported by the school administration. Too often, the

---

8   Ehrenberg, Brewer, Gamoran, and Willms, "Does Class Size Matter?" pp. 81-82.

9   Tom Lauricella, "Your Kid Your Choice," p. 97.

10   William C. Symonds, "How to Fix America's Schools," *Business Week*, 19 March 2001, p. 69.

11   Ehrenberg, Brewer, Gamoran, and Willms, "Does Class Size Matter?" p. 83.

12   Ehrenberg, Brewer, Gamoran, and Willms, p. 85.

13   U.S. Department of Education, "Twenty-third Annual Report to Congress," p. III-36.

14   USA Today Editorial/Opinion, "Paperwork Pushes Patience of Special-ed Teachers" [Internet], 19 June 2002, p. 1, accessed 25 June 2002 from: http://www.usatoday.com/news/comment/2002/06/19/nceditf.htm

15   Christine Foster, "Why Teach?" p. 52.

parents are blamed for the problems, the child receives little real help, and the school moves on to other concerns. *You* are on your own.

Structure. A curriculum requires specific concrete performance. For students with learning and motivational issues, a program appropriately structured can be the ticket to getting through school. For example, a highly motivated, verbal child may tackle a research paper with little assistance. A child not particularly motivated because of past failures in school will need someone to map out each step and bring focus to what must be done: choice of a topic, research, integration of the material, conclusion, written drafts, and final paper.

Many parents are marginalized when their children cannot conform to a school's curriculum demands; the assumption is that more parental input would lead to better academic performance. However, I have found that such a school may be capable of only teaching one way, and children performing either below or above must conform to its system. To illustrate, one of my children—concurrently enrolled in an honors advanced algebra course at a major university—was not only required to sit through the school's eighth-grade regular beginning algebra course but was also penalized on exams because he arrived at correct solutions to simple problems without exactly following the teacher's "time-consuming" arithmetic methods. (He had chosen to remain with his class through graduation though. All the prospective high schools saw no problem in crediting him for his accelerated math courses.) The moral is not to feel apologetic if your child's ability and achievement are at odds with the school's regular program. Rather, the school is doing your child a disservice by not working out a plan that is educationally beneficial.

Pace of instruction. A traditional teacher-centered approach imposes an instructional schedule for learning material. At its worst, this approach is inflexible, a *my-way-or-the-highway* scripted routine. A child-centered approach addresses students' individual situations by adapting curricula, allowing choices for demonstrating knowledge, and reviewing material as needed.

Instructional methods. In a study of high school Advanced Placement classes, the National Research Council found that teachers who emphasized memorization over "active problem solving and discussion" were often poorly prepared instructors.[16] Memorization is not the equivalent of comprehension. For this reason, Harvard University no longer accepts AP scores of less than *5*.

At the middle school and high school levels, teachers generally rely on lectures and textbooks to instruct students unlike elementary school teachers. Visual demonstrations and hands-on learning benefit students

---

16 Justin Ewers, Ulrich Boser, and Rachel Hartigan Shea, "Getting In: What's New, What's True," *U.S. News & World Report*, 23 September 2003, p. 72.

with poor language and reading skills. Sadly, higher academics often means that *visual learners or kinesthetic learners need not apply.*

Daily class schedules. The traditional routine of physically moving between six or seven classes a day can create logistical obstacles to learning. Students must learn to organize their schedules, assignments, books, and materials, and get to each class on time. In the course of teaching maybe 150 students a day, teachers will be less informed about each student's learning difficulties.

Some regular high schools have tinkered with the traditional schedule of 50-minute classes. A *block schedule* provides longer class periods of 80 minutes or more, thus allowing more class discussion and hands-on learning. Class time lost in settling down, taking attendance, and preparing to leave is reduced. Many schools have developed various methods of scheduling these blocks of time. One school may alternate six classes year round, such as three classes on Tuesdays and Thursdays, the other three classes on Wednesdays and Fridays, and all six classes on Mondays. Another schedule may consist of four classes that meet daily each semester, thus resulting in eight classes per student per year. A hybrid schedule can have two classes alternating every other day year round, and three daily classes during each semester. Many other schedule variations exist, some quite complex. The advantages are stronger teacher-pupil relationships, more instructional time, and fewer problems from not having to manage 6–8 classes every day.

Consequences for student underachievement. Although schools are under pressure to raise students' levels of academic competence and end *social promotion*, research is proving that grade retention without specialized help is not the right answer. Students who fail the first time will often fail the same curriculum the second time, and are twice as likely to become school dropouts by age 16 if they have had one or more grade retentions.[17] Linda Darling-Hammond, an education professor at Stanford University, wrote in the November 1998 *Educational Digest* that grade retention assumes that poor school performance is the fault of the child; instead, a reexamination of classroom or school practices should occur before the child experiences the same ineffective instruction. She adds that "Children [held back] give up on themselves as learners. Even small children perceive that being held back is a stigma."[18] Many of these issues are explored in:

• "Promote or Retain? Questions about Tougher School Standards," by Susan Schwartz, available at www.aboutourkids.org/articles/promoteretain.html

---

17   Susan Schwartz, "Promote or Retain? Questions about Tougher School Standards" [Internet], p. 2, posted 1 October 1999 and updated 5 December 2000, available from: http://www.aboutourkids.org/articles/promoteretain.html
18   Schwartz, p. 2.

- "Grade Retention: The Pros and Cons," by Colleen Shea Stump, available at www.schwablearning.org/articles.asp?r=315.

In middle school and high school, teachers of specialized subjects do not feel responsible for basic-skills instruction. Some schools have responded to the achievement gap with mandatory after-school and summer programs (*Education Week on the Web* reported mixed results in "Chicago Summer Progress Found Short-Lived," by Catherine Gowertz, available at www.edweek.org/ew/ewstory.cfm?slug= 27summer.h22) or by adding an additional year after eighth grade.

Sibling birth order. If your older children were stellar students at school, you are more likely to find teachers willing to work with you on a younger child's learning problems. In contrast, you may want to consider transferring normal younger siblings from the school if you have had significant differences with school personnel on an older child's troubles. Faculty rooms buzz with stories about *difficult parents*, and teachers are more likely to ignore the needs of your younger children or assume that some behavior is due to an unrecognized learning disability. Teachers will have lower expectations of younger siblings, and there even may be subtle retaliation against these innocent bystanders. Each child needs a clean slate.

School selection. Applying to schools in some cities can be more difficult than applying to college, because most parents geographically limit the choices close to home or work. (In San Francisco, for example, one even applies for the opportunity of enrolling in the neighborhood *public* school.) It is quite easy to get caught up in the application frenzy in such a situation. While parents need affirmation of their difficult task in raising a child with learning difficulties, getting such students into a demanding program may be better for the parents' egos than for the child's developmental needs. It could be stressful for your child to be a small fish in a big pond. This doesn't mean that a demanding program is impossible or inadvisable. Still, step back a bit and realistically identify programs suitable in both content and support. School should also be fun.

Realism does not mean relinquishing a dream or lowering expectations. Knowing the student's range of interests and whether the school will work with your child must be part of any flexible long-term strategy. Disappointment early on can bring intensive retrenching efforts for success later on. Be patient. One boy, overwhelmed at a highly competitive academic program, transferred to a less demanding program then dropped out altogether. Meanwhile, another boy attended a less regarded high school, struggled successfully, then moved on to college. In adult life, few people ask which preschool, elementary school, middle school, or high school one attended. Many U.S. presidents graduated from non-Ivy or obscure colleges. More important are the actual skills and approach to life one has acquired.

Public schools

Public schools are usually best equipped to serve the needs of kids with learning disabilities, because they have a governmental mandate to provide free services to children with learning disabilities. IDEA fully applies to public charter schools, and some may themselves be responsible for ensuring that the regulations governing special education be met (*34 CFR* § *300.312*). A charter school that has a child-centered approach to instruction may be one of the best learning environments for your child. For example, Gateway High School of San Francisco (of which Mel Levine is an Advisory Board member), emphasizes individual attention to students in a college preparatory program, of which 25% of the student body have LD. Despite dyslexia, one teenager graduated with a 3.5 G.P.A., was captain of the varsity basketball team and senior class president, and went on to Mount Holyoke.

In *Choosing the Right School for Your Child*, authors Brandi Roth and Fay Van Der Kar-Levinson advise parents to investigate specific school placement with public school officials, because not all services are offered at every local school. Most students with learning disabilities are placed in a regular classroom environment with some support.

There are some caveats in attending public schools however. The Department of Education has noted that personnel shortages have compromised the development and execution of IEPs.[19] Your child may need more help than the school offers: public schools are required to provide only a *reasonable*, not *optimal* education. Finally, public-school students may be required to pass state proficiency exams in order to receive a high school diploma.

Independent of either a public or private school situation, you can hire additional services to provide the individualized help your child needs (see Chapter 23). For many parents, the stark choices are 1) *free* and *reasonable* instruction in a public school with the possibility of not graduating, or 2) *appropriate* or even *optimal* instruction in a private program with a diploma—because you will pay to make it happen.

Private schools

In the private kindergarten, social competition began, as if the children were finding a pecking order for their wants and needs. Kindergarten

---

19   U.S. Department of Education, "Twenty-third Annual Report to Congress," pp. IV-13.

If you decide to go the private school route, find a school with an appropriate program. Private school alternatives are fine if classes are smaller, and the curriculum and teaching methods are more flexible than public school. Some public school districts have not only provided LD services to private and parochial school students, but have also delivered services on the premises of these schools (*34 CFR § 300.456*). In contrast, other school districts have eliminated special education services for mainstream private and parochial students (see Chapter 15).

Many parochial schools are inclusive (aiming to serve all children in their parish), but have a teacher-centered traditional approach that may not work for a child who requires nontraditional approaches. Beware of schools in which *parent participation* in class projects becomes a proxy social competition or a tacit expectation for home instruction even for regular students. In general, if your child's academic performance is quite disparate from that demanded of their standard curriculum, seriously examine other schools.

Private schools are often a bit squeamish about the issues surrounding students with learning disabilities. Many private schools are very hesitant to specifically admit that they take youngsters with learning disabilities for fear of being labeled as a school specifically for such children. One aspect of this concern is the school's reputation: If the population of children with disabilities grew to even a large minority, the school could lose its mainstream identity.

Yet you will also find some private schools with a child-centered curriculum, a program that teaches at the child's individual level: maybe more remediation here, maybe more acceleration there. A mother found that her son's school troubles largely disappeared in this type of a school—she already had tried three other more traditional programs. This school, which has small class sizes, also accommodated her on tuition costs.

One common question is whether to tell the private school to which you are applying that your child has a learning disability. The answer is yes, because when the school discovers that the truth was not revealed on the application (applications often ask this) or in the interview, the school will feel deceived, and accommodations may be made only grudgingly. In the long run, it's best to deal with the issue up front. If the school is unwilling to work with your child, then that school would not have been a good place for your child anyway. Remember that with private schools, you can always be asked (directly or indirectly) to leave. It is much different from the public system where you have a right to attend, in addition to other legal protections.

Some private schools have resources for children with learning disabilities but prefer to devote them to children already admitted to their schools. (Most private elementary schools accept most applicants at age 4–5, when learning disabilities may not yet be apparent.) A private school without resources may still be willing to work with your child, but you will probably have to arrange special education services yourself. Sometimes the school will refer you to independent specialists already working with other students on campus. Experience—your child's or that of someone else—will indicate whether these professionals can effectively improve performance. In all circumstances, you must ensure that the teachers and specialists coordinate their efforts.

In June 2001, the U.S. Supreme Court decided in *Zelman v. Simmons-Harris* that Cleveland's voucher program was constitutional. A concern not specifically addressed in this case was that private schools—even those in voucher programs—are reluctant to accept students with special needs, as shown in "For Students with Disabilities, Vouchers Fail the Test," by Jim Ward (*San Francisco Chronicle*, 19 June 2002, p. A19, available at www.sfgate.com/cgi-bin/article.cgi?file=/chronicle/archive/2002/06/19/ED176816.DTL). Many private schools do not participate in voucher programs.

In summary, each private school is unique. Your child may not flourish every year at that school. Some private K-8 programs may have divergent educational missions, for example, offering both a developmental kindergarten (a blend of more play than a standard kindergarten and more academics than a standard preschool) and a rigorous middle school (to facilitate acceptance to prestigious high schools). Approach with caution any school with personnel who believe that learning disabilities reflect deficient moral upbringing. Mary Cathryn Haller in *Learning Disabilities 101* offers other insights, among them:[20]

- Military schools demand an ability to follow directions.
- Independent religious schools may receive insufficient church funding for qualified teachers or good curriculum material.
- Admission to preprofessional precollegiate schools in the arts is highly competitive and may not address the disability; any program claims require investigation. (See Chapter 26, "Vocational Training.")
- Specialized boarding schools can provide treatment for learning disabilities around the clock.

Some ideas on questions to ask yourself and private schools appear on the website, "Questions to Ask Private Schools," by Linda Broatch, available at www.schwablearning.org/articles.asp?r=81. Worksheets accompany this article to help you organize the application process.

---

20 Mary Cathryn Haller, *Learning Disabilities 101: A Primer for Parents* (Highland City, Florida: Rainbow Books, 1999), pp. 170-175.

Supplemental programs. Supplemental programs, such as remedial tutoring, might not be included as part of the basic private tuition. Some schools have a resource specialist program (RSP) available through a tuition surcharge to families utilizing special education services. One mother, a child psychiatrist whose son had auditory processing problems, acknowledged that many families at expensive private schools staff up a small army of specialized service providers at personal expense. Other schools may not permit privately arranged therapy on school premises.

Some learning assistance programs only *monitor* student performance, but do not *intervene* with explicit support or services. Teachers may neither be appropriately trained nor credentialed in special education. For these reasons, you should examine what exactly a school means when it characterizes itself as *meeting the needs of students with learning disabilities*. These institutions may offer one of three general levels of service:

• *Minimal support:* Few if any specialized services, student progress monitoring, and 504 accommodations; the student must self-advocate and understand his own learning needs.

• *Moderate support:* A centralized office for information, a program administrator to work with other faculty members and coordinate services, monitoring student progress, and 504 accommodations; the student usually self-advocates.

• *Comprehensive support:* A specialized structured program for information, counseling, and advocacy, credentialed special education instructors, tutoring and remedial services, monitoring student progress, and 504 accommodations.

A school may not offer a certain level of support for all grade levels. For example, a college preparatory program may provide a moderate level of support during the freshman and sophomore years, then require its students to become more self-reliant by providing only a minimal level of support during the junior and senior years. Of course, students with learning disabilities have access to the counseling and tutoring services available to all other members of the student body. You should investigate the quality of these generalized services as well.

Boarding schools

A boarding school with specialized programs may be necessary if you cannot find a local school that can provide an appropriate education for your child. A boarding school placement can be recommended and funded by the local school district; otherwise, the boarding school option is quite expensive. One mother hired an educational consultant who found a Colorado program for her son who had both a learning disability and behavioral problems. Another mother found a boarding school that not only offered support for his LD but also preprofessional theater training.

Some college-prep boarding schools work exclusively with students having learning disabilities. The Gow School in South Wales, New York and Landmark School in Prides Crossing, Massachusetts are briefly mentioned in a *U.S. News & World Report* issue on boarding schools.[21] In *Learning Disabilities 101*, Haller discusses boarding schools, an option she chose for her son. Information about individual boarding schools is available from the special educator of your local school, library directories, information services listed at the end of this book, and the following sources:

• The Association of Boarding Schools (TABS): 202/ 966-8705 or www.schools.com for information on its 300 member schools; 800/ 541-5908 for a printed directory of boarding schools

• Independent Educational Consultants Association: 703/ 591-4850 or www.educationalconsulting.org for a free directory of consultants.

Consultants will assist you in selecting a school program for a fee. Although largely aimed at parents of college applicants, "On the College Track," by Kristin Davis (*Kiplinger's*, January 2003) reviews the educational consulting industry, including services offered, costs, and precautions to take before engaging one.

Homeschooling

Parents often choose this option to avoid putting their children in dangerous or poorly performing schools, to permit year-round education, to better tailor a curriculum based on their child's unique abilities and interests, or because of religious beliefs (to avoid secular education or to ensure that the child's education is consistent with their own religious beliefs). Top colleges report admitting increasing numbers of students who have been homeschooled. Homeschooled children have also participated in professional theater productions and national spelling bees. For children with learning disabilities, homeschool offers increased flexibility, especially if the child is especially gifted in areas outside traditional academics. Traditional learning from textbooks, quite difficult for children with learning disabilities, can be compensated with activities—such as field trips, hands-on experiences, and videos—using the other senses.

Many parents may feel that their tutoring is tantamount to homeschooling already—without the chronic problems of bullying and

---

21 Rachel K. Sobel, "Hope for the Learning Disabled," *U.S. News & World Report*, 14 May 2001, p. 62.

teacher misunderstandings. Local libraries and the Internet offer vital information. A few private high schools allow students who are homeschooled to enroll in a limited curriculum including extracurricular activities and sports for which groups are required. This way teens who are homeschooled don't lose out on important social and peer experiences. Some references on homeschooling children with LD are available on the website, www.ldonline.org (enter "homeschool" in the white box and click on *SEARCH LD ONLINE*).

Factors affecting homeschooling are available parental time, parental educational level, and whether parents regard school as a welcome break from 24-hour daily care. One book (not meant to insult anyone's intelligence), *The Complete Idiot's Guide to Homeschooling* (2001, Alpha) by Marsha Ransom, is one of the better self-help books on this subject. It assumes that the reader has no previous knowledge about homeschooling.

Remote learning is gaining popularity among those with Internet access. For example, A.Word.A.Day (www.wordsmith.org) examines a new vocabulary word every day, including an audioclip of the word's pronunciation, etymology, and meaning. Some model programs are emerging, though not specifically addressing the problems of learning disabilities. Cyber schools can provide educational content for homeschoolers; homeschool information centers can provide recommendations. Your involvement is key here because your child may not yet have developed the organizational skills and tenacity to stick with a demanding course. For students wanting advanced material but unable to conveniently obtain the instruction or keep pace with a school's honors curriculum, working out a self-paced course of study may be an ideal solution. Education Program for Gifted Youth (www-epgy. stanford.edu) offers math, science, and writing courses on CD-ROMs, supplemented by whiteboard classes, Internet communications, and tutors on toll-free numbers. (Other gifted programs are listed at the end of Chapter 5.)

Each state has its own laws on homeschooling, some regulating student identification, proof of an existing curriculum, course outlines and periodic evaluations. Many websites offer state-specific information on regulations and resources; use a search engine to find these sites. Home School Legal Defense Association (www.hslda.org or 540/ 338-5600) "will assist home school families seeking related services that have been denied because of home schooling," but "will not assist home school students to obtain access to special education in the public school."[22] The website also provides information on

---

22 Home School Legal Defense Association, "Answers to Frequently Asked Questions about HSLDA" [Internet], p. 2, accessed 17 March 2003, available from http://www.hslda.org/docs/faqs/default.asp

homeschooling children with LD. Several other websites dedicated to help you with homeschooling are:

- Homefires (www.homefires.com)

- Home Education Magazine (www.home-ed-magazine.com)

- Homeschool.com (www.homeschool.com)

- National Association of Catholic Home Educators (www.nache.org)

- Homeschool World (www.home-school.com)

- Cafi Cohen's Homeschool Teens & College (www.homeschoolteens college.net)

An ideal school

The universal school movement began a century ago to standardize curriculums and educate the American populace *en masse*. Today most schools still use a single approach to teaching, attempting to squeeze different kinds of minds into standard schedules of learning. But some effective changes are taking root. "Collaboratively Speaking," available at www.schwablearning.org/articles.asp?r=693&g=4, identifies some successful public school models.

In "Lighting the Path to Excellence," by Joan Ryan (*San Francisco Chronicle*, 15 April 2001, available at www.sfgate.com/cgi-bin/article.cgi?file=/chronicle/archive/2001/04/15/SC78380.DTL), Levine offered his model of an ideal school, which would educate everyone according to his or her strengths. Levine's model school presents specific ways for implementing a *differentiated curriculum*, or multiple intelligence theory (see Chapter 5) in education:[23]
- Classroom practices should facilitate learning for everyone.
- The curriculum planning must fulfill the learning needs of all.
- School programs should address the growth of the whole person: mentally, physically, and emotionally.

A more general discussion, "Differentiation of Instruction in the Elementary Grades," by Carol Tomlinson is available at www.ldonline.org/ld_indepth/teaching_techniques/differentiation.html.

---

23 Starr Cline and Diane Schwartz, *Diverse Populations of Gifted Children: Meeting Their Needs in the Regular Classroom and Beyond* (Upper Saddle River, New Jersey: Prentice-Hall, 1999), p. 15.

Chapter Eighteen

What can regular teachers do to address learning disabilities?

"If the child does not learn the way you teach, then you must teach the way he learns."[1]

Classroom modifications

A new school year usually means working with a new teacher. Some teachers provide accommodations only grudgingly, while others have gone beyond the mandated accommodations and experiment with additional classroom strategies. Some teachers teach only using the methods that have helped *them* learn, while others are open to learning alternative methods from their students. Some teachers are quite sensitive to parents' struggles with learning issues while others are indifferent at best. Consider the following teacher responses when asked about their help provided to a student:

> "Todd needs to express himself more fully and answer directly the question or essay topic. His oral performances have been outstanding—serious, well thought-out, and obviously well prepared. He is receiving extra help on basic grammar and vocabulary, and should practice written skills daily. Parents are advised of reading assignments ahead of time in

---

1   Attributed to Harry Chasty in *Mathematics for Dyslexics: A Teaching Handbook* by Stephen J. Chinn and J. Richard Ashcroft (London: Whurr Publishers, 1993), p. 4. Reprinted by permission of Whurr Publishers, Ltd.

order to secure audiotapes of the books. Preferential seating and modified expectations in written work provide better classroom support." (Class grade: C)

"Todd is not required to answer the essay questions that are too abstract for his skills. He does fine on the rest of the work. He needs to continue to have help with concept formation and higher level thinking skills." (Class grade: B)

"Not really needed. He needs to study for tests and take responsibility for his learning." (Class grade: D+)

Try to work with your child's teachers. Learning is more than the 3 R's of reading, remembering, and regurgitating. Accommodating students with LD is too often interpreted as compromised educational standards instead of universal access and multiple intelligences. Call the special educator (if available), school administrators, or outside experts if you need help working with an instructor. You might ask yourself whether a certain teacher is more of a *consumer*—judging performance as a reflection of effort and interest—or a *facilitator*—guiding the processes for better learning and execution. You may find it tougher to negotiate expectations with the former than to discuss successful methods of approach with the latter.

All schools are required to provide accommodations mandated by Section 504 of the Rehabilitation Act of 1973 (Section 504) and by the 1990 Americans with Disabilities Act (ADA). That public schools must provide accommodations is well understood by most people. Section 504 and Title II of the ADA cover government-funded facilities and services. Many people, however, do not realize that these requirements also apply to private schools.

Title III of the ADA applies to private facilities and services not receiving government support. (A copy of the ADA statute is available online at www.usdoj.gov/crt/ada/statute.html and is referred to in this discussion. Information on obtaining copies of relevant federal regulations are in the Resources section of this book. Regulations are the actual legal codes for implementing laws.) Section 301 of the ADA has defined places of education—"a nursery, elementary, secondary, undergraduate or postgraduate private school"—as public accommodations *(42 USC 12181)*. Section 302 requires that these accommodations must observe the general rule prohibiting discrimination "on the basis of disability in the full and equal enjoyment of the goods, services, facilities, privileges, advantages, or accommodations" unless demonstrated to be not "readily achievable" *(42 USC 12182)*. In 1997, Boston University was found in violation of both Section 504 (almost all colleges and universities receive some form of federal funding) and the ADA by denying accommodations to students with learning disabilities. The *Boston Globe* published an article by Patricia Nelson on August 16, 1997 that reviews this lawsuit; it is available at www.nifl.gov/nifl-ld/1997/0254.html.

In general, students with learning disabilities do not require architectural modifications to a building. (Cost issues are discussed in "Update on Section 504: How Much Will Schools Pay for Compliance," by Charles Russo and Timothy Morse, available at www.ldonline.org/ld_indepth/legal_legislative/update_504.html.) Establishing a space to offer specialized services may be a dilemma for some schools but is usually resolvable; one private elementary school, for example, set up a cubicle in the faculty lounge for remediation services. Instead, problems of accommodations lie elsewhere. In 2001, the Department of Education identified classroom methods and materials that bar access to general curricular activities:[2]

• Outdated practices that neglect the diverse instructional needs in the classroom, including those of students with LD
• Inadequate provision of supplementary aids and services to improve performance
• Textbooks, instructional materials, and assessments unavailable in more appropriate formats and media.

Thus, if your child can learn better through an alternative means than that normally provided by the school, you must see that appropriate adjustments occur. This is true of private as well as public schools under Title III of the ADA—if not requiring an *undue hardship* or "significant difficulty or expense" (*28 CFR § 36.104*) of the school. The ball is in your court. Some general questions to ask:

• Have the child's IEP and/or accommodations been implemented?
• Are school materials confusing, erroneous, or overwhelming?
• How are homework assignments helpful or counterproductive?
• Is the material adequately presented, practiced, discussed, and reviewed *before* an assessment is made on how well the student has learned the material?
• Would assistive technology such as word processors, calculators, or audio or video recordings help? (Given the many excellent TV documentaries available with companion textbooks, it's too bad that this dual-media format is not applied to educational settings. Indeed, some publishers offer books with CD-ROMs tucked in the back cover.)
• Would behavioral changes, such as study breaks or not rushing through a test, enhance performance?
• Are the current approaches appropriate?
• Is the school environment positive and supportive?

---

2 U.S. Department of Education, "Twenty-third Annual Report to Congress," [Internet], p. IV-23.

- Are course substitutions or waivers for certain academic requirements possible?

Many private schools truly cannot afford to provide specialized services and materials. Teachers, however, are capable of adjusting their lesson plans to accommodate various learning needs. "LD Support for Teachers Worldwide," by Fawco.org has assembled classroom suggestions, available at www.ldonline.org/ld_indepth/teaching_techniques/fawco_strategies.html. Martin Procaccio, who has developed model special education programs within private schools, maintains that "Teachers are facilitators" and with simple actions can turn failure into success. For students with auditory disorders, teachers should write material on the blackboard then turn around and speak facing the class, instead of writing and speaking facing the blackboard. For students with visual impairments, 12-point type instead of 9-point should be used on tests.[3] Given that universal schooling is required by law, communicating material in different ways improves education for all students. Procaccio, now Director of Academic Services at Marin Catholic High School in Kentfield, California, developed the following list[4] of possible classroom modifications, many applicable in other grade levels:

MODIFYING THE PRESENTATION OF MATERIAL
- Break assignment into segments of shorter tasks.
- Use concrete examples of concepts before teaching the abstract.
- Relate information to the student's experiential base.
- Reduce the number of concepts presented at one time.
- Provide an overview of the lesson before the beginning.
- Monitor the student's comprehension of language during class instruction.
- Schedule frequent, short conferences with the student to check for comprehension.
- Provide a consistent review of any lesson before introducing new information.
- Allow the student to obtain and report information utilizing audio recorders, dictation, wordprocessors, interviews, and calculators.
- Highlight important concepts to be learned in the textbook.
- Monitor the rate at which material is presented.
- Give additional presentations through repetition, simpler explanations, more examples, and modeling.
- Require verbal responses to indicate comprehension.
- Give frequent reminders of homework assignments.

---

3   Sharon Abercrombie, "Going Extra Mile: Riordan Program Reaches Out to Kids with Special Needs," *Catholic San Francisco*, 26 January 2001, p. 7.
4   Martin Procaccio, *Making Modifications in the Classroom: A Collection of Checklists*, unpublished, 2001. Reprinted with permission of Martin Procaccio.

- Provide clear concise directions and concrete examples for home-work assignments.
- Assign tasks at an appropriate reading level.
- Allow for the oral administration of tests.
- Check the assignment sheet for accuracy.

MODIFYING THE ENVIRONMENT
- Use study carrels.
- Seat the student in an area free of distractions.
- Use preferential seating.
- Allow the student to select his/her seating.
- Help keep the student's work area free of unnecessary materials.
- Use checklists to help the student get organized.
- Frequently check the organization of the student's notebook.
- Monitor the student's use of his/her assignment sheet.
- Check the assignment sheet for accuracy.
- Provide opportunities for movement.

MODIFYING TIME DEMANDS
- Increase the time allowed for completion of tests or assignments.
- Reduce the amount of work or length of tests.
- Prioritize assignments and/or steps to assignment completion for the student.
- Space short work periods with breaks or changes of tasks.
- Consistently follow a specific routine.
- Alternate quiet and active tasks.
- Set time limits for specific task completion.

MODIFYING THE MATERIALS: Visual Motor Integration and Written Expression Problems
- Allow for spelling errors.
- Allow the student to use either cursive or manuscript.
- Set realistic and mutually agreed upon expectations for neatness.
- Let the student type, record, or orally give answers instead of in writing.
- Avoid pressures of speed and accuracy.
- Provide copies of notes.
- Reduce the amount of copying from text and board.
- Accept key word responses instead of complete sentences.

MODIFYING THE MATERIALS: Visual Processing Problems
- Highlight information to be learned.
- Keep written assignments and work space free from extraneous and/or irrelevant distracters.
- Avoid purple dittos.
- Provide clear and well-defined work sheets.

- Review the visual task with student to ensure that the student clearly understands all parts of the assignment from the beginning.
- Avoid having the student copy from the board.
- Have the student verbalize instruction before beginning task.
- Avoid crowded, cluttered worksheets by utilizing techniques such as *blocking* (blocking assignments into smaller segments), *cutting* (cut worksheets into sections, *folding* (fold worksheets into sections) and *highlighting*, *color coding*, or *underlining*.

MODIFYING THE MATERIALS: Language Processing Problems
- Give written directions to supplement verbal directions.
- Slow the rate of presentations.
- Paraphrase information.
- Keep statements short and to the point.
- Avoid abstract language such as metaphors, idioms, and puns.
- Keep sentence structures simple.
- Encourage feedback from the student to check for understanding.
- Familiarize the student with any new vocabulary before beginning the lesson.
- Reduce the amount of extraneous noise such as conversation, radio, TV, outside noises, etc.
- Alert the student's attention before expressing key points.
- Ensure that the readability levels of the textbooks are commensurate with the student's language level.
- Utilize visual aids such as charts and graphs.
- Utilize manipulative, hands-on activities whenever possible.
- Always demonstrate how new material relates to previously learned information.
- Cue the student by calling his/her name before asking questions.

MODIFYING THE MATERIALS: Organizational Problems
- Provide an established daily routine.
- Provide clear rules and consistently enforce them.
- Contract with the student and reward for contract completion.
- Check the student's notebook to insure the use of dividers, assignment sheet, and calendar.
- Provide due date on written assignments.
- Provide a specific place for turning in completed assignments.

USE OF GROUPS AND PEERS
- Utilize cooperative learning strategies when appropriate.
- Assign a peer helper to check understanding of directions.
- Assign a peer helper to read important directions and essential information.
- Assign a peer tutor to record material dictated by the student.

HELPING FOCUS ATTENTION

- Establish relevancy and purpose for learning by relating to previous experiences.
- Shape approximations of desired behavior by providing direct reinforcement such as praise or immediate feedback or correct answers.
- Seat the student close to the teacher.
- Make positive, personal comment every time the student shows any evidence of interest.
- Make frequent checks for assignment progress/completion.
- Give advance warning of when a transition is going to occur.
- Use physical proximity to help student refocus.

ASSISTING THE RELUCTANT STARTER

- Give a personal cue to begin work.
- Give work in smaller units.
- Provide immediate reinforcements and feedback.
- Make sure the appropriate books and materials are open to the correct pages.
- Introduce the assignment in sequential steps.
- Check for student understanding of instructions.
- Check on progress often in the first few minutes of work.
- Provide time suggestions for each task.
- Provide a checklist for long, detailed tasks.

DEALING WITH INAPPROPRIATE BEHAVIOR

- Provide clear and concise classroom expectations and consequences.
- Consistently enforce rules.
- Avoid the use of confrontational techniques.
- Provide the student with alternatives.
- Designate a *cooling off* location within the classroom.
- Assign activities which require some movement.
- Use praise generously.
- Avoid power struggles.
- Ignore attention getting behavior for a short time.
- Avoid criticizing the student.
- Communicate frequently with parents.
- Monitor levels of tolerance and be mindful of signs of frustration.
- Speak privately, without the audience of peers, to student about inappropriate behavior.

A teacher should employ discretion when handling a child's learning disability, at least to avoid overwhelming or humiliating a child. A child may be embarrassed to read aloud, especially when classmates are unwilling to overlook mistakes. Moreover, downgrading a student with a reading disability for poor oral reading is disability discrimination; other grade components such as tests, reports, and class participation may be used instead.[5] Figure 18.1 is an example of a test in which—along with some oral clarification—the student received full credit for demonstrating comprehension without losing points for writing ability. Penalizing an entire class with 500-word essays for the few who talked in class is not only an onerous task for a student with language disorders, but also sends a message that writing is punishment (besides being unjust to those who didn't talk and creating animosity towards those that did). A paper returned covered with red corrections and topped with a *D* or an *F* is quite discouraging; a numerical score is probably enough to communicate performance. Misspellings can be underlined a bit to call attention to the error; misspellings need not be

Figure 18.1

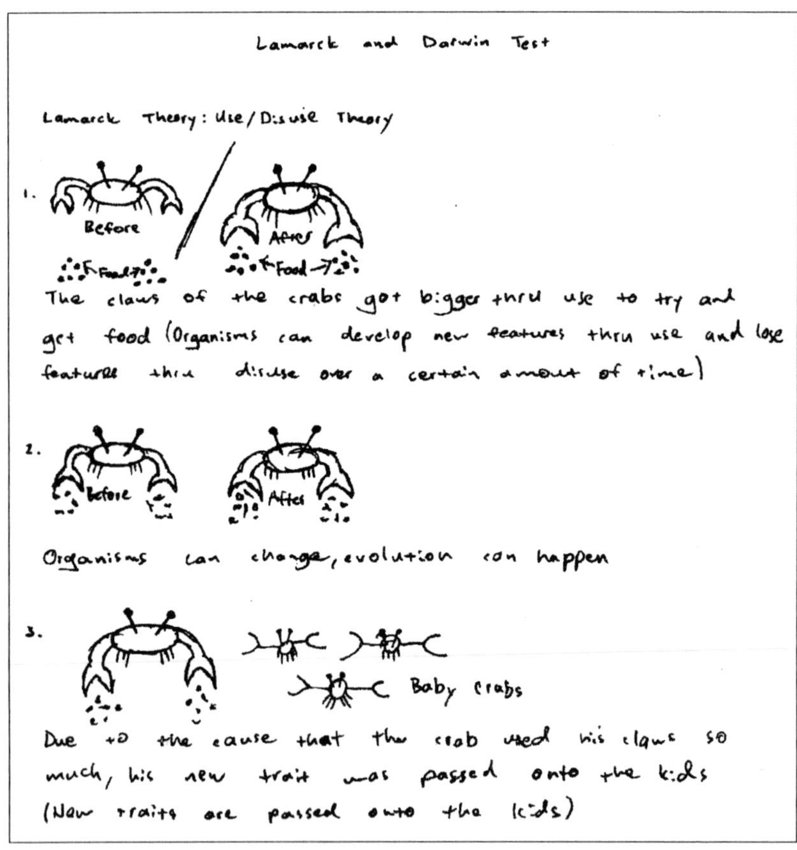

---

5   Silver, *The Misunderstood Child*, p. 152.

Darwin Theory: Natural Selection

1. 

There was a variation in the population ~~sur~~ for the crabs over food (Variation in population)

2. 

Due to cause that there was too much competition food, the long-clawed crabs struggle to survive over food (struggle for existence)

3. 

The long-clawed crabs were the fittest to survive for food (Survival of the fittest)

4. 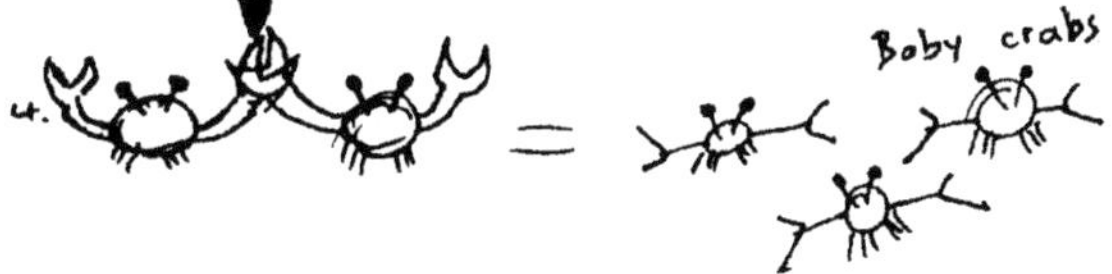

Because the two long clawed-crabs survived, they reproduced and had little long-clawed crabs (Reproduction of the fittest)

Ever since then, the long-clawed trait became more common over the next generations (Good adaptations become more common over generations)

deducted in scoring exams in content subjects like science or history. (Other spelling suggestions for teachers are presented in "The Underlining Option: Using the Personal Spelling & Usage Sheet," by C. Wilson Anderson, Jr. available at www.ldonline.org/ld_indepth/teaching_ techniques/anderson_underlining. html.) Handwritten worksheets and exams may be indecipherable for children with visual acuity problems.

Materials and experiences require careful planning. Many teachers provide hands-on demonstrations, simulations, or dramatizations of subject material. Instructions for assignments should be written, and should carry information that will help parents or tutors assist with the assignment's purpose, organization, and any other expectations. Written directions sometimes require further explanation such as examples of solutions. Advance notice of curriculum tasks allows students to obtain an audio recording for an upcoming literature assignment (which may take weeks and is further detailed in Chapter 22), or for the family to arrange a field trip relevant to the topic.

Methods to improve recall of reading material include previewing the text (oral may be better than silent reading), retelling the story, and using pictures to organize the information. Mnemonic devices like the sentence, *Please Excuse My Dear Aunt Sally* can help a student remember the order of math operations: 1) **p**arenthetic expressions, 2) **e**xponents, 3) **m**ultiplication, 4) **d**ivision, 5) **a**ddition, and 6) **s**ubtraction. Vocabularies can be enlarged by using the *cloze procedure* in which the student supplies an appropriate word to a reading passage in which about every fifth word is missing.

Direct instruction can generally refer to an individualized teaching approach, with demonstrations, guided practices, frequent assessments, and immediate feedback to the student. (Alternatively, *Direct Instruction* is a commercially available reading remediation strategy of scripted instructional exercises to improve higher-level reading skills; it is presented in Chapter 23.) *Reciprocal teaching*, in which the role of discussion leader rotates among group members, allows a student with learning disabilities to ask questions without embarrassment. Group discussion should include concept clarifications, story summarization, plot predictions, and identification of likely test questions.

Accommodations do not necessarily mean *watering down* the curriculum but can entail a different way of instruction. "Watering Up the Curriculum for Adolescents with Learning Disabilities," by Edwin Ellis, offers teaching methods in which classroom success is less dependent on reduced expectations and memorization, and more focused on approaches to information processing and depth of understanding. His procedures appear at www.ldonline.org/ld_indepth/teaching_techniques/ watering_up1.html. A general approach for adapting the curriculum is presented in "Three Steps for Gaining Access to the General Education

Curriculum for Learners with Disabilities," by Margaret King-Sears, available at www.ldonline.org/ld_indepth/general_info/three_steps.html.

Many courses progress in a sequential fashion, building on the previous material. Some students with LD, however, learn better if first given an overall structure onto which details can be later integrated. Advance outlines of class lectures can provide an idea of what's important and space for note taking; the teacher should occasionally indicate which item on the outline is being discussed. Susan A. Vogel (not the publisher of this book) originated a college program for students with learning disabilities at Barat College in Lake Forest, Illinois in 1980. Among her numerous suggestions, she recommends that teachers:[6]

• Provide a course syllabus when students are deciding which courses to take and to be available for questions.

• Select a textbook with a study guide, if possible; offer review and quiz sessions.

• Encourage students to find study partners and organize study groups.

• Prepare practice exams having similar format and content as the real exam.

• Avoid syntactic confusion that can result from double negatives, unnecessarily complex sentence structure, and questions-within-questions in exams.

• Give partial credit for the solution process as well as the final solution itself, for example, in solving math, chemistry, or physics problems.

• Encourage students to share with faculty the nature of their learning disability, how to facilitate their learning, and/or to clarify concepts or assignments.

Behavioral approaches to teaching: Using external rewards

Most people are familiar with the model of behavioral modification, such as rewarding children with candy for appropriate actions:

$$\text{Stimulus} \Rightarrow \text{Behavior} \Rightarrow \text{Consequences}$$

In the behavioral education model, teachers present information to students who practice and memorize it. Learning is linear and reactive.

---

6   From *Success for College Students with Learning Disabilities*, ed. Susan A. Vogel and Pamela B. Adelman, "A Retrospective and Prospective View of Postsecondary Education for Adults with Learning Disabilities," by Susan A. Vogel, pp. 13-14. Copyright © 1993 by Springer-Verlag New York, Inc. All rights reserved. Reprinted with permission of Springer-Verlag GmbH & Co.KG and Susan A. Vogel.

Behavioral approaches for manipulating behavior presuppose that the teacher can objectively define the problem, accurately measure a student's classroom behavior, determine an appropriate and attainable goal, select appropriate materials and a timetable for achieving the desired result, and consistently enforce positive or negative consequences. The teacher should also know when an approach isn't working and whether to try something else.

Some positive reinforcement techniques exist in many mainstream classrooms. A *behavioral contract* is a written agreement between a child and teacher identifying the desired behavioral change and the reward for the change, the time period for the change to occur, and the conditions, activities, and methods for measuring the change. A *token economy* is a payment system that rewards desirable behavior with tokens, items, or privileges. *Precision teaching* daily assesses a child's progress, as opposed to periodic determinations of whether a child learned the material at the next chapter test.

Time-out procedures are negative classroom penalties to reduce undesirable behavior. A discreet prearranged signal from a teacher, like a dropped paper clip, will remind a student to behave appropriately. An *activity time-out* removes a desirable activity or item, akin to *grounding*. A *teacher time-out* is when the teacher shuns the misbehaving child. A *contingent observation* allows the child to observe but not participate in the group activity. An *exclusion time-out* places the child into another area of the classroom like a time-out corner. *Over-correction* assigns one or more worksheets to be done during a time-out in the classroom. A *seclusion time-out* is the removal of a very disruptive child from the classroom, to a predesignated room or area, not necessarily the principal's office.

Cognitive approaches to teaching: Internalizing learning-to-learn behavior

In the cognitive education model, teachers explicitly guide students' thinking in reasoning and problem-solving. They teach them to identify the circumstances for applying certain procedures on selected information. Learning is proactive and multi-dimensional with task procedures and side tracks of self-monitoring (please refer to the executive function graphic Figure 3.3). *Executive function* enables the student to *recognize* progress in order to complete all phases of a task. That is, *self-monitoring* is crucial for knowing when all aspects of an assignment have been sufficiently addressed. *Cognitive learning strategies* emphasize inner language, the *little voice* of executive function, to coach oneself through an activity.

Many students with learning disabilities have inefficient execution methods due to a deficiency of executive function. This can be seen when they don't know *when they don't know*, resulting in befuddlement from the unforseen ramifications of incomplete task analysis. Thus explicit instruction is not only required to understand, recall, manipulate, and express knowledge in a class discussion, essay, or exam, but also to acquire strategies or algorithms to better prioritize, integrate, and coordinate all components of a task.[7]

This learning model has been recast as acronyms that specify action steps. Learning strategies can improve performance. Training students to use these strategies can take at least 30 instructional periods of 45 minutes each. Bender offers some examples:[8]

Skill to be Improved	Acronym	Action Steps
reading comprehension	RIDER	R = Read sentence I = Imagine a picture from the reading D = Describe the picture E = Evaluate whether the picture captures the meaning of all the words in the sentence R = Repeat steps with next sentence
note taking	SLANT	S = Sit up L = Lean forward A = Activate thinking N = Name important information T = Track the speaker
paragraph writing	PLEASE	P = Pick topic L = List ideas about the topic E = Evaluate list A = Activate writing with a topic sentence S = Supply supporting sentences E = End with a concluding sentence and Evaluate the work
multiple-choice tests	SCORER	S = Set a work pace C = Clue word use O = Omit difficult questions R = Read carefully E = Evaluate choices R = Review answers

In content classes, learning can be made more efficient if instruction emphasizes the integration of associated knowledge rather than the accumulation of disparate facts. For example, various biological facts fall into place if one understands how all the parts work together. That is, a student is taught how to think in terms of biological systems

---

7 Swanson, "Information Processing," pp. 140-141.
8 Bender, *Learning Disabilities*, pp. 275-278.

instead of memorizing isolated anatomical names. Indeed, says Light, the professors that students remember most are those who go beyond a scattershot approach of dispersing facts, and integrate material into thought processes relevant to solving a problem.[9] Moreover, pulling the pieces together also makes the subject much more interesting.

Social integration: Classroom strategies

Many teachers mistakenly assume that bad behavior at school begins in the home, when in fact, the opposite may be true: Bad behavior is learned at school and brought home. Placing a child with learning disabilities and neurological behavioral disorders among students known for malevolent behavior—as often occurs with mainstreaming—works against parents' efforts to keep the at-risk child away from trouble. Periodically monitor seat assignments by asking your child who sits around him or her. Sadly, a lonely child may find companionship only by joining in malicious acts and may even become the designated fall guy. Contrast the comments of two teachers about a student with LD:

> "Scott interacts only sporadically with his classmates in class—sometimes in a friendly positive way but other times he is teasing and laughing *at* others, unprovoked."

> "Scott misjudges social cues and will sometimes join others in distracting, if not immature, behavior in class."

Some classroom interventions exist for encouraging peer acceptance of students with disabilities. *Cooperative instruction* is team building in mainstream classes, often guided by a special education teacher in a full-inclusion program. This is not the same as one or two individuals completing the work of the entire group, as often occurs in group projects. Variations of team building depend on the method of forming the group, assigning specialized roles for contributing to the group, and in comparing the success of one group against that of another group in raising the skill levels of all its members. Although many schools employ programs to improve relations between all students, a teacher's philosophy of acceptance is often the most important factor. The understanding and creativity of your child's teacher will lead to many informal ways of integrating a student into classroom activities. One teacher posted the intricately illustrated science laboratory reports of a student with a language disability. The work was apparently enough to impress his peers and he came to be regarded as one of the top students in the class.

---

9   Light, *Making the Most of College*, p. 117.

Not enough can be said about the classroom atmosphere established by the attitudes of the teacher. Betty Osman, an author and psychologist specializing in learning disabilities, states that teachers do more than instruct subject matter, they also convey attitudes and model behavior for their pupils to follow:

> "Teachers play a crucial role in influencing a child's social status. In fact, their feelings toward a child with special needs often determine how that youngster is viewed by his peers. A teacher can embarrass a child or compliment him, support or denigrate him, enhance his self-image or destroy it."[10]

Humiliating a child in front of peers, even unintentionally, does more damage than many teachers realize. Recess can become a very cruel ordeal as immature peers will emulate what they interpret as an exercise of absolute power. And for every action, there is a reaction. A shamed child may become defiant. An elementary school girl relocated from Chicago, was called *Yankee* by her new teacher in Atlanta. The playground taunts of *Yankee* soon ensued and the girl was crying after school every day. Unfortunately, the teacher begrudged the girl's objections to being called *Yankee* during class, and the mother's demands that the teacher stop the name-calling that she had unwittingly begun.

A teacher who resents your child's presence in the classroom can cause incidents that some parents may call at best *clueless*. At least a couple of examples were presented in the Introduction. Another teacher made her class wait while a female student completed her exam on extended time as provided on her IEP. In one more example, a teacher questioned a student during class as to why his parents were not sending in scrip orders (a major school fundraising source today). This not only reflected a judgment implying that the family did not support the school, but also an inappropriate inquiry of a young student over money matters and his parents' behavior. It never occurred to this teacher that because the student was routinely pulled out for afternoon disability services (and therefore would not be present to receive scrip delivered before dismissal), that the family's scrip orders had been funneled through the classroom of a younger sibling. When this teacher discovered that the family had been ordering scrip all along, she never offered a public apology to the student she had singled out for humiliation.

---

10   Excerpted from *No One to Play With: Social Problems of LD and ADD Children*, by Betty B. Osman and Henriette L. Blinder, p. 97. Copyright © 1982, 1995 by Betty B. Osman and Henriette L. Blinder. Reprinted with permission from Academic Therapy Publications, Novato, California. All rights reserved.

If a particular teacher is generally known to be difficult and could be your child's instructor, you should investigate the situation. I have heard of emigrations of many families from schools just to avoid a certain instructor. (Correlational studies linking poor academic progress and multiple school placements are only part of the story.) A tough teacher can inspire or discourage learning—but you'll have to decide what is best for your child. Often very bad feelings about a teacher are widespread and quite visceral, as signaled by a couple who volunteered extensively for many school activities—except for any having to do with a particular instructor. Disability harassment may be involved (see Appendix 3). From my experience, teachers who won't work with students with learning disabilities don't work well with other students either. In the Introduction to this book, one teacher did not meet the needs of a boy with LD *and* a girl with gifted abilities. These types of teachers don't make information accessible to diverse learners; instead, children are expected to learn the way and at the pace the adults teach.

Parents with access to a special educator in either public schools or in some private schools can work through this professional in handling everyday issues. Otherwise, changing schools is a common solution when a student fails to thrive in the classroom, particularly when complaints to the principal are disregarded.

Modifying special projects

For students who test poorly, special projects are opportunities to raise grades. A special project is an excellent opportunity for teachers to teach students how to apply study skills, reading, writing, and thinking skills. Special projects have their own typical milestones: selection of an appropriate topic, research, outline, rough draft, editing, and final paper. Students should have a clear idea of what is expected of them and how to approach the project. Teachers should lead young students through project milestones, and not rely on the guidance of parents who may have little time, subject knowledge, or skills to help execute the project. An assignment with too little teacher instruction can set up an unhappy situation in which a parent is unable to effectively assist the child, and then ends up blaming the child for receiving a poor grade.

Ideally, parental support should be minimal; students can develop a sense of competency and pride if given an appropriate project. Realistically though, a parent often becomes the project manager if teacher requirements are overly ambitious and execution guidelines consist only of a style sheet on footnotes. While it's easy to get pulled into expediting the work your child must do, you must consider the appropriateness and educational value of the project before addressing any of your concerns to the teacher.

• Special projects may be assigned *after* the class has completed study of the related unit and moved on. Instead, the teacher can assign the project *at the beginning* of the relevant unit. Not only can students gain a better understanding of the unit being studied, but they also may be able to use some of the information on exams.

• Projects may have tight deadlines. Research is not a straight-line process, but meanders through side issues and new discoveries. Planning and executing the finished product will also take time. Sometimes a creative project will require a student to halt an ongoing unsuccessful effort and begin anew. Reducing the time allowed for completion of a project will not reduce the amount of work. Indeed, even talented Ivy-league college students spend 40 percent more time writing four five-page papers (about 12 hours per week) than writing one 20-page paper (less than nine hours per week).[11] Tight deadlines only create needless stress, frustration, burnout, and almost beg the student to copy someone else's work.

• Teachers can design creative assignments that can also draw upon a student's integrative thinking. Students could have term-paper alternatives, such as a storyboard, dramatization, or a multimedia presentation. In contrast, a written report with one or two illustrations is still basically a written report.

• For many children with learning disabilities, each stage of the project must be broken down further into discrete steps. You may also write into your child's IEP that time for special projects be significantly lengthened to accommodate your child's learning disability, or that your child be given extra assistance on managing complex projects. Alternatively, you should approach the teacher at the beginning of the school year, if not before summer vacation, to give your child the extra time to read, absorb, and ponder the material. Indeed, a trip to a site pertaining to the project, can make the topic more interesting.

• Middle and high school teachers should observe when activities or projects in the other classes are due. For example, the presentation of a major science experiment does not have to coincide with the due date of a major social studies research project. Weekends should also allow children to relax and spend time with their families.

I didn't really understand this last point until one of my children without a learning disability was assigned a research project on a Friday due the following Monday—no time to contact the teacher on postponing the due date. This assignment was due the same day that another major paper was due (two weeks allowed for this project!), and in addition to other weekend homework. Of course, that weekend had already been scheduled with out-of-town relatives, a school fundraiser, a family birthday, and a brunch honoring student volunteers in the

---

11   Light, *Making the Most of College*, pp. 56-57.

community. I had come to expect that one child may need tutoring help; I was not happy when a child who should have needed no extraordinary help almost passed out from exhaustion. This was not a matter of multiprocessing or better scheduling on our part. In this instance, schoolwork became anti-family and anti-community. Learning should not be an ordeal, but structured to inspire curiosity.

Be alert to such distressful time conflicts and false choices. Realize that many teachers often respond to mandates for higher educational standards by working students harder, not smarter. For example a middle-school spelling book with exercise sets for 20 words each week doesn't have to be supplemented with a vocabulary book with another 20 words for each week. The people in charge of curriculum matters should pick the better book and concentrate on teaching it well. (At some point you begin to wonder whether school is for children or for adults.) Chapter 23 presents some research on the appropriate length of homework assignments.

If your child is clearly overwhelmed, send a note to the teacher explaining the situation and offer to discuss ways to better manage the project. Alert your child's special education teacher to any difficulties as well. Work with other parents who share your homework concerns; there may be strength in numbers. Try to avoid being your child's indispensable research and administrative assistant. This may be inevitable though if your child's teacher provides little or no project guidance.

Accommodations for foreign language course requirements

Studying a foreign language in high school or earlier (many educators suggest before adolescence) can make foreign language study in college easier. A year in high school is the equivalent of a semester in college. One European dyslexic better understood the language structure of his native English after he learned French and German. Students with substantial language disorders, however, may not be capable of handling a foreign language until even the eleventh grade.[12] Levine suggests that for students who are really unable to learn a foreign language, schools could require instead advanced cultural studies such as world literature, geography, history, or political science.

Diagnostic language tests can identify the presence of a general language learning disability. The Modern Language Aptitude Test (MLAT) or the Language Aptitude Battery (LAB) specifically test foreign language aptitude. Other indicators of language ability could be the auditory memory or phonological ability subtests of more commonly

---

12   Levine, *Developmental Variation and Learning Disorders*, p. 382.

used psychological tests. Levine recommends five or six private lessons with a foreign language instructor who could then assess ability. [13]

Teachers can recommend audio recordings (available at booksellers and computer software vendors) for additional practice. Difficulties with foreign languages can be addressed with course waivers, substitutions like an advanced language immersion program at an overseas campus, or classroom accommodations such as: [14]

- Reading instead of listening or speaking the language for students with auditory problems
- Simultaneous audiovisual presentations
- Tutoring with special education support either for facilitating success or for documenting the existence of language difficulties
- Slower learning pace; short drills of few repeated words instead of long drills of many words.

Colleges and college preparatory programs recommend or require a diagnosis of a learning disability or documentation of foreign-language learning problems in petitions for waivers and course substitutions. Often, such documentation comes at the time and expense of failing a language course despite hard study. Not completing two years of a foreign language during high school creates obstacles in the college admissions process. It is better to proactively find an acceptable substitute than to limit your college options. Strategically selecting certain languages can avoid some known obstacles.

- *Chinese* uses a logographic writing system in which each character symbolizes a word or part of a word and meaning depends on the context. There are no verb tenses and no phonetic decoding of an alphabet. Reading a newspaper requires knowledge of about 4,000 characters. *Tones* or spoken pitches differentiate similar sounds into different meanings; for example, *ma* can mean *mother*, *horse*, or *scold* depending on how it's said. In a sense, Chinese is whole-word reading. One student with phonetic processing problems found Chinese easier to learn than his native English.
- *Latin* emphasizes reading rather than oral communication. Because many English words have Latin origins, learning Latin can improve one's vocabulary and spelling skills. Latin's precise expression may lead to more precise thinking, according to some educators. Word roots, suffixes, and prefixes may pose problems for some students. Students with phonological processing deficits can successfully complete a modified university-level Latin class. [15]

---

13 Levine, p. 380.

14 Ganschow and Sparks, "'Foreign' Language Learning Disabilities," pp. 298-301.

15 D.M. Downey, L.E. Snyder, and B. Hill, "College Students with Dyslexia: Persistent Linguistic Deficits and Foreign Language Learning," *Dyslexia* [Internet], July-September 2000, available from: http://www.ncbi.nlm.nih.gov/entrez/query. fcgi?cmd=Retrieve&db=PubMed&list_uids=10840510&dopt=Abstract

• *Spanish* uses a uniform pronunciation and writing system. Many words will be familiar to English speakers. Remembering the gender of nouns or tenses of verbs can be troublesome even for students without learning disabilities.

• *American Sign Language* fulfills the language requirement at many colleges and universities. Gestures express ideas and concepts, not specific words. For particular words and names, the American Manual Alphabet can *fingerspell* each letter of the alphabet. Studies have documented activity in language areas of the brain, thus reflecting linguistic processing and not merely spatial analysis of gestures.[16]

Secondary schools and colleges will have their own foreign language requirements. Students' choice of a foreign language may be based on their motivation for learning a specific language, or knowing that a specific teacher has demonstrated patience, flexibility, and subject expertise with similar students. Students should explore an institution's support systems, alternatives, and petition policies and procedures. My high school son took American Sign Language through *concurrent enrollment* at a community college over a summer. He was thus able to fulfill part of his high school *and* college language requirement simultaneously. Another student's parent liked the community college instructor so much that, through her recommendation, he was later hired to teach sign language at the high school.

Grading benchmarks

Much of the current educational reform movement is being driven by *standards-based assessments*. These reforms are being felt from the classroom level to the statewide level. (It is far beyond this book to review educational reform. Chapter 24, however, offers some rethinking on the teaching of reading, writing, and math as ways of connecting ideas rather than as an end in themselves. It will also discuss testing.) How these reforms are implemented can help or hinder your child.

Benchmarks vs. A–F grading. The U.S. Department of Education stated in 1998, "Performance standards clearly define what student work should look like at different stages of academic progress and for diverse learners. They describe how good is good enough in reading the content standards."[17] One response from educators is a new classroom evaluation practice—grading specific skills based on *benchmarks*.

---

16 Bruce Bower citing 1996 Corina study, "Language Mastery Goes Native in the Brain," *Science News*, 23 November 1996, p. 326.

17 U.S. Department of Education, "Goals 2000: Implementing Standards-Based Reform," *Goals 2000: Reforming Education to Improve Student Achievement* [Internet], p. 2, 30 April 1998, available from: http://www.ed.gov/pubs/G2K Reforming/g2ch3.html

Benchmarks provide more performance detail than the traditional A-through-F system. Thus, instead of a snapshot of a child's progress over time (such as a quarter or a semester), a parent will receive a series of measurements indicating one of four levels of mastery of required lesson topics, from minimal competence to advanced understanding. More emphasis is also placed on what a student has achieved in absolute terms than on how well a student performs when compared to other students (known as *grading on a curve*).

Conversely, weaknesses in a student's performance can be pinpointed more easily, analyzed, and adjustments and modifications made more quickly. To see how benchmarks could actually work, the table entitled *Physical Science Moon Lab Grades* (Figure 18.2 has been abbreviated for illustration purposes. The original list contained 33 scoring items, including more data sets, graphs, diagrams, hypotheses, and appendix items.) It looks like a tedious evaluation system, but it actually functions as a detailed work plan.

Moon Lab was a four-month ninth-grade science project, and all students were provided with this list of specific concrete evaluation standards. The points assigned at each level of achievement in each category cumulate toward a summary project grade. It may seem like punching tickets, but it worked quite well for one teenager with LD, giving him independence to successfully complete the project with minimal parental oversight. In fact, his project was among those in the entire freshman class receiving the highest number of points.

For a student with learning problems and an external locus of control (see Chapter 7), breaking a large project into discrete constituent pieces clarifies teacher expectations on performance and organizes student efforts for efficiency. The parent's nagging role is concomitantly reduced. This idea of incorporating procedures into a mix-and-match evaluation system evens up the playing field. Students who are *self-starters*, have had better training in doing such projects, or have access to knowledgeable tutors, receive the same set of technical instructions as do students who have none of these advantages. Parents and tutors can more easily help students distribute effort throughout the project and avoid overkill in one area, neglect in another. Such concrete standards also reduces grading differences between course instructors, although gray areas always require good judgment.

The rubric, *Physical Science Moon Lab Grades* was a collaborative effort of several instructors off-and-on over many years. In other words, establishing clear performance standards for students takes much thought and preparation on the part of teachers. Once accomplished, however time-consuming, these standards become one more instructional tool—easily reproducible—to lead a student to success.

Figure 18.2[18]
Moon Lab Grades

Physical Science — Moon Lab Grades — 132 total points possible

	Missing 0 points	Beginner 1 point	Intermediate 2 points	Proficient 3 points	Expert 4 points
Cover Page	Incomplete	Complete with name, title, teacher's name and date	Complete with name, title, teacher's name, date, and student-attempted picture	Complete and the picture describes lab content and is well executed
Table of Contents	Incorrect, incomplete, and messy	Incorrect and incomplete or messy	Correct, but incomplete or messy	Correct, complete, and neat
What is the purpose of the lab?	The answer is general and incomplete	The answer is general, complete with 3-4 answers	The answer is a paragraph, specific, and complete with 3-4 items	The answer is a well-written paragraph, specific and complete with 5+ items
Definitions of key terms	Definitions are missing; Key terms: *orbit, axis, satellite, rotation, eclipse, revolution*	All definitions are present, minus examples or some are inappropriate	All definitions are present, appropriate, and some include examples	All definitions are present, appropriate, and include examples
What is your hypothesis? (Student changed hypothesis, project=0)	The answers are incomplete and 2 of the hypotheses are not explained	The answers are incomplete and/or one of the hypotheses is not explained	The student has answered all of the hypothesis questions and one of the hypotheses is not explained	The student has answered all of the hypotheses. All answers are complete and well-explained
Moon Date: Weeks 3-4	Missing most altitudes, times, directions, or clear pictures	3 Complete data points per week or they are missing a major part throughout the data	4 Complete data points per week with altitudes, times, directions, and clear pictures	5 Complete data points per week with altitudes, times, directions, and clear pictures
Graph 1: The pattern of rising and setting times for the moon for a month	Graph grade of 6/10; based on handout "Basic Rules of Graphing"	Graph grade of 7/10; based on handout "Basic Rules of Graphing"	Graph grade of 8/10 or 9/10; based on handout "Basic Rules of Graphing"	Graph grade of 10/10; based on handout "Basic Rules of Graphing"
Graph paragraph 1	Does not describe the graph and the trend of the line	Does not describe the graph and the trend of the line	Generally describes the graph and the trend of the line	Specifically describes the graph and the trend of the line, calculating the slope

---

18 Adapted from *Physical Science Moon Lab Grades* by the Science Faculty of Archbishop Riordan High School, San Francisco, 2001, unpublished. Reprinted with permission of Archbishop Riordan High School.

Figure 18.2
(continued)

Physical Science   Moon Lab Grades   132 total points possible

Missing 0 points	Beginner 1 point	Intermediate 2 points	Proficient 3 points	Expert 4 points
Diagram 1 Showing the various phases of the moon	Diagram is not labeled, messy, and does not show the motion of the moon and earth in relation to the sun	Diagram is not labeled, messy or does not show the direction of motion of the moon, earth, and the sun	Diagram is labeled, messy or does not show the direction of motion of the moon and earth in relation to the sun	Diagram is labeled, neat and shows the direction of motion of the moon and earth in relation to the sun
Diagram paragraph 1	Does not describe the diagram *and* the motion of the objects	Does not describe the diagram *or* the motion of the objects	Generally describes the diagram and the motion of the objects	Specifically describes the diagram and the motion of the objects
Discussion 1: Why do we have eclipses?	The answer is incorrect and does not refer to data or diagrams	The answer is incorrect *or* not explained using the data, graphs and diagrams	The answer is correct, but does not use the data, graphs, or diagrams to explain the answer	The answer is correct and the student explains how the data, graphs and diagrams support the conclusion
Discussion 6: Questions and answers you have collected along the way	3-4 Original questions are listed and one is answered correctly	3-4 Original questions are listed and answered correctly	3-4 Original questions are listed and answered correctly	5+ Original questions are listed and answered correctly
Discussion 7: Sources of Error	2 General sources of error are listed	3 General sources of error are listed	3-4 Specific sources of error are listed	5 Specific sources of error are listed
Discussion 8: Suggested Improvement	One general suggested improvement is listed	2-3 General suggested improvements are listed	3-4 General suggested improvements are listed	4 Specific suggested improvements are listed
Bibliography	Some sources missing and cited incorrectly	Some sources missing or cited incorrectly	All sources identified, but some cited incorrectly	All sources identified and cited correctly
Appendix 1 Lecture notes Moon phases rising times Moon map NASA article Moon facts summary	Missing 3 items or they are all incomplete	Missing 2 items, but the rest is complete, neat and well done *or* all work is present and incomplete	Missing one item, but the rest is complete, neat and well done *or* all work is present and complete, but not well done	All work is present, complete neat, and well done

Properly executed, benchmarks can significantly help a student "take responsibility for his own learning," a frequent teacher criticism. From a student's point of view, maybe teachers needs to provide better road maps to help navigate the ever-increasing expectations at each grade level. With practice, a student can generalize these procedures when working on various types of assignments in the future.

Benchmarks can also evaluate and reward each accomplishment directly. Without specific corrective feedback, a student may not understand how to improve performance and so just gives up. Using the Figure 18.2 as an example, a student may want to improve his information sources, and thus the accuracy of his reported facts.

Writing Assessment (Figure 18.3)—based on a real class handout—is a table of evaluation elements in the form of four-column benchmarks, but reflects the thinking of an all-in-one traditional A–F grading system. For example, content, organization, and writing skills are intertwined in one level of achievement. It is not clear what would happen if the student's work had substantive material but insipid writing, or terrific writing but unreliable information. Diverse learners can have these problems, a reason for the collaborations between many of society's luminaries, ghost writers, and production people in the commercial world.

Figure 18.3 also is a checklist of qualities recommended in a writing assignment, but offers few details on how to execute the writing. It's the difference between knowing what you like to eat and having the recipes to prepare them. This particular table could be improved by providing separate guidance on style versus substance. (One way to separate the medium from the message is to imagine how the report could be done in another format, such as a video instead of a paper.) In short, the student must still somehow break down this lump of an assignment into a work plan and may require much help to complete the final product.

In contrast, *Persuasive Essay Rubric* (Figure 18.4) is a better tool, recommending depth of material and sequences of statements. This paint-by-numbers approach might be scripted writing, but this rubric addresses content and compositional elements. Light discovered that college students believe that they best learned to write *"when instruction is organized around a substantive discipline."*[19] In other words, when people have something to say, they will work hard to say it right. Style comes with experience but there has to be a first step. In professional fields such as medicine, writing style is done away with altogether as scripted writing focuses more of the effort on analytical content and production efficiency. More suggestions on writing are presented in Chapter 24.

---

19   Light, *Making the Most of College*, p. 59. Italics are from Light's text.

Figure 18.3[20]

Writing Assessment
(Total points possible shown)

	Distressed: 70	Tolerable: 80	Useful: 90	Exemplary: 100
Appearance	Recommended format not used. Messy. Not double-spaced. Not 12-pt. type. Poor print quality. 5-6 spacing & indentation errors.	Recommended format partly used. Neat. Double-spaced. Not 12-pt. type. Passable print quality. 3-4 spacing & indentation errors.	Recommended format used. Neat. Double-spaced. 12-pt. type. Good print quality. 1-2 spacing & indentation errors.	Recommended format used. Neat. Double-spaced. 12-pt. type. Good print quality. Proper spacing & indentation.
Composition Skills	Missing or unresolved purpose for writing. No organization of main ideas. No logical flow.	Poor organization. Weak paragraphs for introduction and conclusion. Topic sentences often unclear, undeveloped body paragraphs. Lacks transitions between sentences and paragraphs.	Organization evident. Functional paragraphs for introduction and conclusion. Most topic sentences clear. Body paragraphs developed but lack focus at times. Adequate transitions.	Clear organization. Engaging paragraphs for introduction and conclusion. Clear topic sentences. Body paragraphs developed. Smooth transitions.
Content	Thesis unaddressed. No logic or serious thought. No examples or illustrations.	Thesis addressed but unanswered. Logic gaps. Vague ideas. Weak examples or illustrations.	Thesis generally but not specifically answered. Logical, functional thought. Some examples and illustrations.	Thesis fully answered. Logical, creative, interesting ideas. Many examples and illustrations used.
Vocabulary	Insufficient to be able to discuss thesis.	Too colloquial for formal writing. Little descriptive or figurative language.	Intelligible, adequate, not verbose. Some descriptive and figurative language.	Articulate, clear, direct. Effective descriptions. Good figurative language.
Writing Mechanics	Poor sentence construction. 6+ word errors. Tense, capitalization, and punctuation errors.	Most sentences complete, but awkward in parts. 4-5 word errors. Punctuation and capitalization mostly correct	Sentences & verb tenses mostly correct. 2-3 word errors. Punctuation and capitalization correct.	Sentences complete. 0-1 word errors. Tenses, punctuation, and capitalization correct.
Spelling	5+ errors.	3-4 errors.	1-2 errors.	No errors.
Due Date	More than 2 days late.	Two days late.	One day late.	On time.

---

20 Anonymous. Based on an actual class handout.

Figure 18.4[21]

Persuasive Essay Rubric
48 Total Points Possible

	Beginner: 3 points	Intermediate: 4 points	Proficient: 5 points	Expert: 6 points
Introduction	Little to no background information is provided for the thesis.	Irrelevant information or loosely connected information leads up to the thesis.	Well chosen background information leads up to the thesis. Sentence structure is choppy.	Well chosen background information leads up to the thesis. The sentence structure flows.
Thesis	The thesis statement is unclear.	The thesis statement vaguely pertains to the topic.	The thesis statement is good.	The introduction closes with an insightful and well articulated thesis.
Topic Sentences	All topic sentences fail to identify the purpose of the paragraph.	One or more topic sentences identify the purpose of the paragraph but fail to establish a connection to the thesis.	The topic sentences identify the purpose of the paragraph and connect back to the thesis.	The topic sentences both identify the purpose of the paragraph and are clearly connected back to the thesis statement.
Supporting Evidence	Little or no background research supports the topic sentence.	Weak research supports the topic sentence. Most statements are supported with research.	Good research supports the topic sentence. At least one research fact supports each statement.	Strong research supports the topic sentence. Two research facts support each statement.
Conclusion	Thesis is restated. No additional conclusions are drawn.	Thesis is restated. Feeble attempts are made to draw general conclusions on the topic.	Thesis is restated. Good closing remarks are made; however, they show no additional perspective.	The essay closes with a restatement of the thesis and insightful closing remarks.
Spelling and Grammar	Essay contains 7 or more spelling or grammatical errors.	Essay contains 5-6 spelling or grammatical errors.	Essay contains 3-4 spelling or grammatical errors.	Essay contains 0-2 spelling or grammatical errors.
Footnotes and Bibliography	Footnotes are not used and/or bibliography is not included.	Some supporting evidence is not footnoted or included in bibliography. OR footnotes and bibliography are in incorrect form.	Attempts are made to footnote all evidence. All sources are included in the bibliography.	All supporting evidence is correctly footnoted and included in bibliography.
Pre-writing Work	Most pre-writing work is missing or none exists; little or no editing on rough draft.	One piece of pre-writing work is missing; rough draft shows brief editing.	All pre-writing work is complete; rough draft shows some editing.	All pre-writing work is complete; rough draft shows close editing.

---

21 Johanna Kroenlein and Diana Assereto, *Persuasive Essay Rubric*, San Francisco, unpublished, 2002. Reprinted with permission of Johanna Kroenlein.

Chapter Nineteen

How can I work with teachers?

"Please, would you tell me—" she began, looking timidly at the Red Queen.

"Speak when you're spoken to!" the Queen sharply interrupted her.

"But if everybody obeyed that rule," said Alice, who was always ready for a little argument, "and if you only spoke when you were spoken to, and the other person always waited for you to begin, you see nobody would ever say anything, so that—"

"Ridiculous!" cried the Queen.

—Through the Looking-Glass

Attitudes: Obedience or access for learning?

Many teachers truly try to make learning accessible to all their students. Many other teachers believe that accommodating students compromises academic standards. And many are not trained to work with students with LD. You will be dealing with them all. Ideally, a cooperative teacher-parent partnership can avoid and alleviate many learning and disciplinary problems both in school and at home. Discretion is the better part of valor, when possible. Be forewarned, however well-intentioned, that academic failure among students with disabilities is not uncommon and requires persistence to solve.

All too often, you will find teachers overwhelmed and oblivious to the problems of students with LD, blaming both your child and you for poor performance. This can be a trying situation in which both you and the teacher regard each other as *difficult*. Stanley Milgram, who found that 65% of ordinary adults were willing to deliver even lethal shocks to *help* others learn word pairs better, wrote "for many persons obedience may be a deeply ingrained behavior tendency, indeed, a prepotent impulse overriding training in ethics, sympathy, and moral conduct."[1] Beware of such situations with authoritarian undertones. In *Educational Care*, Levine contrasts the attitudes of two teachers:[2]

"Teacher A (moralistic and accusatory):

Susan is performing very poorly, yet I know she can do the work when she makes up her mind to succeed. There are days when she decides to put forth effort and accomplish things in class. On other days, she fails to hand in work, she is unwilling to study, and she seems more interested in her friends and what is going on outside the classroom than she is in learning anything. I am sure Susan has potential, but she will not reach it until she changes her attitude and chooses to become motivated.

Teacher B (observant and supportive):

Susan is puzzling to me. Some days she comes to class and is very alert and productive. On other days, she is distractible and appears tired or 'burnt out.' On her tired days she is fidgety and restless and accomplishes very little. She has shown that she has a great deal of ability, but somehow it is very hard for Susan to make use of this ability consistently. She needs to try hard to become more consistent. I know how much Susan would like to succeed. She and I will have to find ways to work on this problem."

Certainly, children need to take responsibility for their actions. Parents need to acknowledge that problems need to be fixed. Still, some children are more difficult to raise and teach than others. Academic excellence should be one goal, but forgotten is that the overall purpose of *universal* education is a functioning adult citizenry.

---

1   Stanley Milgram, "Behavioral Study of Obedience" in *Scientific Psychology and Social Concern*, ed. Leonard W. Schmaltz (New York: Harper & Row, 1971), p. 453. Milgram's experiments used actors, thus no one was actually harmed.

2   Mel Levine, *Educational Care: A System for Understanding and Helping Children with Learning Problems at Home and at School* (Cambridge, Massachusetts: Educators Publishing Service), p. 269. Copyright © 1994 by Melvin D. Levine, M.D.. Reprinted with permission of Educators Publishing Service, Inc.

Good teaching enables universal access for learning. After participating in a program geared to help educators teach children with learning troubles, a teacher reported to Levine that the techniques not only helped these students but the entire class as well; in other words, a child needing intervention may be highlighting an unrecognized problem of instruction.[3] Good teachers learn from their students.

Communication

Putting multiple intelligence theory into practice—assessment and classroom instruction—has brought new thinking into education. In particular, *differentiation* (which one master teacher told me is only a formal restatement of common sense) acknowledges that students learn in different ways and at different rates, in different content areas. That is, students require diverse instructional methods at various levels of depth in each academic subject. (No one said that teaching a classroom of students is easy.) What is important to know is that professional educators have recognized the need for teaching differently those who learn differently. Don't be persuaded into believing that one standard instructional method is appropriate for all students.

For a student with LD, experienced effective teaching in an accepting environment is especially critical. About 30 percent of new U.S. teachers, however, quit within five years.[4] High turnover means that you may be teaching the teacher about learning disabilities.

Parents and teachers: Different assumptions. Part of the problem in discussing a child's educational program is understanding educational thinking, jargon, and methods. Many approaches and techniques are possible, and a teacher should be able to explain the reasons for selecting a particular method.

Unfortunately, according to Claire Smrekar, a professor of education at Vanderbilt University, teachers are usually taught that parents are intimidating and to be avoided; teachers are not taught how "to develop productive relationships with parents. It's not done."[5] In other words, parents in general—much less those whose children have learning difficulties—are adversaries, not partners, in their child's education. Yet parent involvement is more important to higher student achievement than school spending or teachers with master's degrees.[6] Thus, a general comment from a parent may be interpreted as a criticism when none is meant. Many parents sense this and are afraid

---

3   Levine, *A Mind at a Time*, p. 283.
4   Christine Foster, "Why Teach?" p. 52.
5   Lesley Stahl, "Pentagon Schools," *60 Minutes*, CBS broadcast 21 April 2002, Transcript prepared by Burrelle's Information Services, p. 13.
6   Stahl, p. 10.

to talk to teachers who may retaliate against their children. In such an atmosphere, you will have to prioritize problems and pick your battles.

Other communication problems pertain to expectations on assessments. At the elementary school level, many classroom teachers will boost a child's actual grades if the child has shown great effort. This situation changes at the middle-school level when teachers may instruct 180 students daily instead of 30. Grades may easily fall because they now reflect actual scores. Parents and child can end up bewildered at the sudden drop in grades, all other things being equal.

Development presents successive sets of expectations as teachers require more independent functioning[7]

Preschool/Kindergarten	Learning to learn
Grade 1	Learning to read
Grade 4	Reading to learn
Middle School	Learning to organize your learning
High School	Learning to read, organize, and learn on your own
College	Doing it on your own

Learning problems will impede a student's abilities to make these passages to the next level of performance. Be prepared for these transitions.

Many other factors affect whether a cooperative parent-teacher support system for the student develops:
- Different levels of education, personal parenting experiences, and understanding about learning disabilities between parents and teachers
- Divergent perceptions and interpretations of a student's strengths, weaknesses, and behavior
- Bilateral perceptions that the other party is inadequately or inappropriately helping the child
- Teacher's previous experiences with similar students and their families
- Parents' previous experiences with teachers and school policies
- Parents' current stage of adjustment to their child's learning problems
- Personal attitudes toward learning disabilities
- Manner of treating each other: condescension, hostility, dignity, empathy.

The late Jean Augur, herself a teacher and a mother of boys with reading disabilities, wrote about a lack of real communication despite her own efforts with other teachers:

---

7   Jan Baumel, "Academic Stress Points in Education" [Internet], posted 14 November 2000 and updated 6 September 2001, available from: http://www.schwablearning. org/articles.asp?r=34. © Copyright 2001, 2002 SchwabLearning.org. Reprinted with permission of Schwab Learning. For more information please visit www. schwablearning.org.

"What makes the matter even more aggravating and frustrating is that the school may have been repeatedly informed of the problem and the various ways in which it [reading disability] can manifest itself. In spite of these repeated efforts on my part, some teachers, particularly those new to the staff, are evidently not informed and fail to perceive the signs of dyslexia. The most frequent offenders seem to be teachers of English and other languages. Obviously they have found written language so easy it is impossible for them to comprehend the difficulties of this boy. These are the lucky people who, one assumes, must have reliable auditory and visual perception, good sequential ability and memory span."[8]

Meeting the new teacher. While teachers will develop their own professional appraisals of your child's abilities, you can show your concern by proactively meeting the teacher or sending in a brief note at the beginning of the academic term. A well-prepared special educator may also disseminate to teachers a one-page summary on the student's specific difficulties and accommodations and modifications that can make learning more accessible. You should not wait for the results of the first midterm report before presenting your impressions and any relevant information. Many teachers appreciate a *heads up* discussion of a student's strengths and weaknesses. A brief note may be especially helpful at the beginning of a new middle or high school year, when teachers may not know which specific children have learning issues because the files may still be in the counselor's office awaiting adjustments to class schedules. Some topics that you might address:
•   Main problem(s) and past and present measures to improve the situation
•   Strengths, child's methods of dealing with the problem(s), and other interests
•   Assignment concerns
•   Child's temperament, feelings about himself or herself, classmates, and school in general
•   Best times or ways of reaching you, and any other persons involved in helping your child.

Examples of specific problems, learning strategies, and relevant side issues can accelerate a teacher's own learning curve in working with the student. Because teacher training usually does not include

---

8   Jean Augur, *This Book Doesn't Make Sense: Living and Learning with Dyslexia*, (London: Whurr Publishers, 1995), pp. 45-46. Copyright © 1981 by Jean Auger. Reprinted with permission of Whurr Publishers Ltd. All rights reserved.

course work in learning disabilities, teachers may not fully comprehend the child's academic and social frustrations in school. For example, one history teacher better appreciated requests for advanced notice of reading assignments after a parent showed him an atlas mapping historical events and how the student required extra time to tie the text and visual material together.

Many teachers themselves seek information to alleviate learning problems. Before actually meeting the teacher to discuss problems, you may want to establish a wide-ranging neutral base of information from which you and the teacher may proceed. One parent purchased *The Educator's Manual* for her child's school, highlighted relevant portions, and kept it in her son's file as a reference guide for each successive teacher.[9] Another format is provided by Mel Levine's *Educational Care*, which organizes information to recognize and solve problems both at school and at home in nontechnical language. Schwab Learning's 36-page *Educator's Guide to Learning Differences* can be downloaded for free at www.schwablearning.org/articles.asp? r=433&g=4. Whatever you use, alert the teacher to portions that you found relevant, and the teacher can do likewise. Meet to discuss similarities and differences of opinion, and then establish solutions that usually have both school and home components.

Of course, this all presupposes that the teacher is open to suggestions in the first place. If the teacher is unwilling to work with you, meet the child's special education teacher or the school counselor to see if they can intervene. If this proves unsuccessful, see the principal to discuss your views. If you are still having trouble, contact one of the information centers to see if you have grounds for filing a formal complaint. Don't let a year go by because of passive-aggressiveness.

Conferences. Conferences may be formal or spontaneous. Generally, teachers try to establish a rapport with the parents, if only to more successfully deal with the child's difficulties. More sensitive teachers realize that parents are trying to help as best they can while emotionally adjusting to their child's problems. Beware of teachers who have already determined that your child's future is dim and so are reluctant to help. Still, you must try to work in good faith with each teacher unless experience proves otherwise. One teacher acknowledged to me that many parents have developed aggressive stances from years of "fighting" uncaring educators, only to realize later that their child's teacher truly understands the problems and is all too willing to do all that is possible.

Teachers can easily reduce these potential conflicts. From my experience on back-to-school nights, several teachers have signaled their

---

9   Deborah Faber, "Proactive Parenting," *LD Matters*, Spring 2000, p. 4.

willingness to work with parents on learning issues. One special education teacher greeted incoming high school parents by announcing that he would ensure completion of all necessary paperwork. Positive support systems require confidence-building and follow-through.

Formal parent-teacher conferences can end up feeling like a bum's rush. When teachers are scheduled to meet dozens of parents over the course of a week, you will have little time to digest unexpectedly troubling information, probe a teacher's appraisal methods or experiences with similar children, nor develop a specific plan for dealing with the issues. It may be best in these situations to set up another meeting to understand the teacher's practices, review your child's IEP and progress, and explore additional solutions and IEP amendments to any unaddressed or worsening problems. An educator, Lydia Spinelli, presents some general ideas for talking to the teacher during these conferences in "Parent-Teacher Conferences: Working as a Team," available at www.aboutourkids.org/articles/parent-teacher.html.

Frequency of reports. Parents are often unaware of their child's school performance until any possible opportunities for remedies has expired. In particular, by the time the first progress report appears, the student with learning disabilities might be unable to salvage his or her grades. In the fifth grade, my son was about giving up on school. He was even not turning in assignments that I helped him complete. He didn't give me notes from the teacher and he hid his tests. Although this behavior is not unusual, it needed to be squelched quickly. To obviate this problem in the future, I made a point of letting teachers know that if they heard no response from me within 48 hours, I did not receive the message sent home. Telephone calls and email may help, providing your child does not erase incoming messages from the teacher. Bear in mind that students with LD are motivated to beat a system that makes them miserable.

Some areas should be monitored daily like homework completion. Planners or organizers are similar to weekly appointment books such as the two-page format pictured in Figure 19.1. These booklets can provide daily communication between you and the teacher. The teacher just initials the day's written assignments as having been copied correctly and completely, and adds any special remarks. When the assignments are done, the parent initials the planner and notes any difficulties; the time spent on each assignment should be included for any future adjustments in assignments. The *expectation* of receiving the planner literally puts the teacher, the child, and the parents on the same page. This expectation is important because a child, with some practice, can forge a parent's handwriting, leaving you out of the communication loop.

Figure 19.1

LE DS	LE DS	LE DS	LE DS		
Monday MM/DD	Tuesday MM/DD	Wednesday MM/DD	Thursday MM/DD	Friday MM/DD	Saturday MM/DD
———	———	———	———		
———	———	———	———		
———	———	———	———		
———	———	———	———		
———	———	———	———		Sunday MM/DD
———	———	———	———		
———	———	———	———		———
———	———	———	———		———
———			———		

The frequency of progress reports should be established so as to gather a good representative sample of the child's performance, and let the student and parents know if ongoing measures are appropriate. Daily reporting may be too cumbersome and have nothing much to say; biweekly reports may be irrelevant to what the child is currently studying. Relying on a child to show papers to a parent underestimates children's ingenuity because initials can be forged and test papers hidden. The constant vigilance over all imaginable aspects in every subject area is exhausting. Some schools have established websites to provide homework assignments and confidential reports. You may be experimenting a while, but try to develop a system that's effective in helping you monitor your child's progress.

Trust: Required for positive relationships

Young human beings must rely on the integrity, reliability, competence, and judgment of their adult custodians. From trust springs hope and a confidence that work will be rewarded. In contrast, a *gotcha* environment is more about power and politics.

The importance of trust between administrators, teachers, parents, and students is reviewed in "'Trusting' School Community Linked to Student Gains," by Catherine Gewertz, available at www.ldonline.org/news/trusting.html. With respect to students with learning disabilities, trust means that someone will try to do their best to effectively solve problems, and can help support someone over the rough spots. As much as possible, seek constructive and trusting environments for your child. Life is hard enough without having to watch your back.

Chapter Twenty

How can I help motivate my child?

My son was labeled by the teachers as unfocused, stupid, and a problem for not sitting still in his seat. Very quickly he lost his self-esteem and believed he was incapable of learning. The demands made of him in front of his classmates raised his anxiety level to the point that it affected his whole personality. The friendly, outgoing, enthusiastic student withdrew from class participation and peer society.

Through tremendous family support, private tutors, and endless hours of sheer determination and work on our son's part, he began to succeed. The school district testing confirmed the presence of learning disabilities. They changed educational methods, but had very limited resources available. We found as parents we had to be very involved to help steer our son in the right direction.

Most of my son's success stems from his personal character to never give up. He is very tenacious and works unbelievably hard to succeed. I feel one of the most important factors in his success was finding his self-esteem again and gaining respect from his peers.

Our son joined his high school's cross-country team. The couch turned out to be one of the greatest influences in our son's life. He reinforced our son's work ethic and gave him praise not only privately but also in front of the team. Soon the success we saw in his sports transferred to academics. The determination and ability was always there—he just needed to believe in himself to make his success happen.

He graduated from high school with academic high honors. His application was accepted at every university engineering program to which he applied. My son now struggles in college, but he has learned the most valuable lesson: to cope with what he has and to never give up on his dream to be a success. He surmounts the obstacles in his path with determination.

If only the teacher who told me my son was "illiterate and nonteachable" could see him now. I'm sure it would change how she feels about children with LD. It troubles me to know that our educators are so influential over our children and yet many of them are lacking the skills, training, sensitivity, or understanding they need to help children with learning disabilities.

Improving motivation: How to get the ball rolling

The motivation to succeed influences intellectual development.[1] For example, a child's persistent attempts to solve puzzles and overcome obstacles is active learning. Motivation, in turn, is determined by "the extent to which people feel competent, capable, and believe they can succeed at a task."[2]

Unfortunately, a child with learning disabilities will have trouble with academic assignments, and the school can compound the problem by calling the child a failure. In this situation, no bridge exists between what the child can do and what needs to be done. The child perceives external factors beyond his control as setting him up for failure and so stops trying to learn. Bender calls this perception a psychological survival mechanism because "… an external locus of control [see Chapter 7] allows the student the hope that such a message may be a mistake. Understanding the lack of motivation in many students is relatively easy when one considers the responsibility of the school system in fostering such an uncaring attitude."[3]

You will have to counteract such damage. Eliminate the debilitating influences as best you can. Try to improve motivation by building a stronger internal locus of control, self-esteem, or self-confidence in your child. (These terms will be used interchangeably in this chapter.) This personal belief in one's abilities is affected by the choice of activities, identified role models, and positive feedback that reduce self-doubts, according to Dale Schunk, a professor of educational psychology at the University of North Carolina at Chapel Hill.[4] Often, indirect flexible approaches are worth trying, as discussed by Robbie Fanning in "Motivating Kids with Learning and Attention Problems" available at www.schwablearning.org/articles.asp?g=2&r=633.

---

1   Bruce Bower citing 2001 Hauser-Cram study, "Disabilities Develop as Family Affair," p. 276.
2   Robert Brooks, "Islands of Competence," p. 1.
3   Bender, *Learning Disabilities*, p. 187.
4   Schunk, "Self-Efficacy and Cognitive Achievement," p. 140.

Being good at something is so basic to human happiness that it has many equivalents, from *identify your core competency* to *follow your bliss*. Rather than peripheral participation, integral involvement of up to 20[5] hours per week in one or two extracurricular activities is strongly correlated with satisfaction in life, though not with academics.[6] Success drives people to work harder, persist longer, and become more self-reliant in order to overcome difficulties. Students performing well at one level will likely believe that they are capable of learning at the next level,[7] or even in another area.

Students with learning disabilities often show frustration and unhappiness in academics. However, these same students can sustain effort, analyze, actively solve problems, and make deep commitments in nonacademic activities that are meaningful to them.[8] Thus a curriculum fully absorbed in a back-to-basics approach may not be entirely appropriate because your child's better skills—which could lead to adult independence—lie elsewhere.

Identifying an activity. You may have to go far afield if your child has not demonstrated a special knack or interest in the immediate classroom environment. Look outside the school if it cannot financially support an activity that would benefit your child or if your child wants a break from an established pecking order at school. The idea here is to develop confidence and motivation in your child, not to reinforce any ongoing school pessimism about your child's potential. Strong parental involvement is required to find something, *anything*, that will enable your child to be a meaningful part of society. This is not an easy task, especially if your child has poor social skills, for whatever reason. A child who has no stake in mainstream society can grow to become a risk to himself or herself, and perhaps a risk to others as well.

Find an activity in which your child's strengths are valued. For example, if your child is among the last to be chosen for playground ball teams, then look for individualized activities not involving rapid

---

5 The 20-hour figure cited in many media reports today was noted in a 1995 study of data from the National Longitude Study of Adolescent Health, "Adolescent Time Use, Risky Behavior and Outcomes: An Analysis of National Data" [Internet], by Nicholas Zill, Christine Winquist Nord, and Laura Spencer Loomis, 11 September 1995, available from: http://aspe.hhs.gov/hsp/cyp/xstimuse.htm. As true with most statistics, a single figure does not capture all the information in the related study. This particular study also had implications for *school-connectedness* which appeared in a later analysis of the National Longitudinal data, and is discussed in Chapter 17.

6 Light, *Making the Most of College*, p. 26.

7 Schunk, "Self-Efficacy and Cognitive Achievement," p. 143.

8 Baum, Owen, and Dixon, *To Be Gifted & Learning Disabled*, p. 19.

hand-eye-object coordination. If your child is attractive and likes acting, visit some casting directors. Children with LD can succeed in many areas including athletics, crafts, science and technology, and the fine arts. Complex thinking and problem solving *in* the physical world is as much of an intellectual discipline as reading and writing *about* it. "LD and the Arts," by the National Center for Learning Disabilities, available at www.schwablearning.org/articles.asp?r=713, highlights other ways of learning virtually untapped by basic school curriculums. Search for opportunities for your child to successfully complete tasks and have positive social interactions. Naturally, the best activities are those in which your child can shine among peers. Nancy Firchow offers some ideas in "Success Outside of School," available at www.schwab learning.org/articles.asp?g=2&r=76.

Adapt, when possible, any instructional course as part of a developmental program toward lifetime enjoyment. For example, supplement classical music studies with ear-training (perfect pitch can be acquired with ear-training before age seven or eight; thereafter children acquire relative pitch) and improvisational or compositional studies. Much personal satisfaction is thus possible in just playing what one has heard as well as polishing a piece toward perfection.

At least for your child's long-term health, find a physical activity that he or she enjoys. Many high schools offer opportunities in track, wrestling, and swimming. Students on varsity sports teams are "among the happiest students on campus," because friendships are developed through a shared interest, coaching is individualized, and members bond to the institution.[9] Little League offers adolescents umpiring jobs with training and pay. Numerous groups provide martial arts, skiing, sailing, dance, fishing, bird watching, and bicycling activities. Shops that sell equipment in the child's area of interest may have suggestions for participation. Consider time demands of the activity as well, or the child may be too tired to do schoolwork.

The performing arts give children a chance to have a whole audience applaud for *them*. Civic and religious organizations sponsor children's choir groups. Schools as well as professional companies offer many opportunities. Theater is also a good way to gain a first-hand understanding of character and setting, often necessary for studying literature. For example, my children have been extras in several San Francisco Opera productions; one favorite role was shooting arrows in *William Tell*. Be sure to investigate productions not under the direct auspices of school authorities. In California, child labor laws unique to the entertainment industry require an on-site state-certified studio teacher whose role is to advocate for the child's welfare, against overzealous or exploitive adults. Like modeling, the performing arts

---

9   Light, *Making the Most of College*, p. 29.

require intense parental involvement for obtaining entertainment work permits, auditions, and more. Children are expected to be on time, alert, respectful, cooperative, and well-behaved for these jobs. The positions are best understood as slots for team players, a role not usually offered by other children to a child with learning difficulties.

Many civic organizations have developed volunteer programs for adolescents with supervising adults bridging the gap between school and the workplace. Moreover, by helping others, people often help themselves. To illustrate, the San Francisco Zoo offers teenage volunteers summer positions to work with small animals; volunteers are expected to be on time, follow instructions, learn facts about animals, and responsibly present animals to visitors. One student found peace and serenity while working with zoo animals, unlike the peer torments endured at school. Similar programs for older teens may provide some income as well.

Sometimes, commitment must be taught. In this day and age, it can be challenging to instill the value of honoring commitments and promises. For example, a parent must encourage proper attitudes and ensure that the child appears on time for practices and team functions. Only then can a coach work with a child to develop skills, build teamwork, and facilitate a work ethic for continued improvement. Receiving a team's *most improved* award is a great honor. Some people, however, only learn task commitment the hard way. For example, military experience transformed an indifferent college dropout into a serious student who graduated in two and one-half years with a double major *summa cum laude* and attended graduate school thereafter.

In selective programs, many will try, but few are chosen. Find out whether your child will actually participate or be relegated to bench-warmer status. Also, many activities may involve a lot of waiting around such as for a cue to go on stage, or for the ball to come to the child. Evaluate whether your child can handle these long stretches of down time without much ado.

Once I was able to get my son past the title, he liked reading *The Complete Idiot's Guide to Cool Jobs for Teens* by Susan Ireland. Another useful guide is *The Complete Idiot's Guide to Volunteering for Teens* by Preston Gralla. These and similar books are good ways for them to absorb information at their own pace, learn what to expect, rehearse anticipated situations, and refer back to certain topics again. (Alternatively, if your child objects to the title, you could peruse the book yourself for ideas.) Of course, parents should be available to answer questions. Other general self-help guides for teens are found on www.idiotsguides.com (click on the *Teens* icon).

Perceived difficulty of the activity and adult expectations. The difficulty of an assigned goal sends a message about ability. Too easy a goal, and the child senses that that others believe him to have little ability.[10] A more difficult goal communicates that the teacher believes the student to have the right stuff. Accomplishing the more difficult goal improves the student's belief in his or her abilities.

Trust is also an issue. Persuading someone to adopt new activities, interests, or strategies can be tough, especially when a young person has tasted too many failures in too many situations, and interprets anything novel as tantamount to more failure. Children with learning disabilities may have been told what *to do* all their lives, fail, and then build a wall of mistrust and resistance. One method to overcome resistance is for the instructor to establish a program of intermediate steps. A child with a disability may not be able to immediately progress from what may seem like 0 to 60 in his or her eyes, but may be able to move from 0 to 30 instead. By accomplishing the intermediate step, the child will then be able to focus on getting to 60. My son's coach was able to overcome resistance ("bellyaching") by breaking down goals into achievable steps. By seeing life through the prism of the learning disability, the coach understood the issue not as insubordination but as anxiety, a fear of the unknown.

There are times when you will need to make clear that resistance is futile, and then actively confront the situation in order to get the child on track. For best results, the child must also absolutely trust the adult: the child must feel that you are on his side, and that he has some control over the venture. Irrelevant advice or inappropriate discipline will only backfire. (Robin Goodman and Anita Gurian offer some thoughts "About Discipline - Helping Children Develop Self-Control," available at www.aboutourkids.org/articles/discipline.html.) For example, getting my son to go to a high school dance, fraught with teenage social pressures, was impossible. Finally, I dragged him to the school's annual parent-child dance with the understanding that he had no obligation to dance with me. I knew that he would ditch me as soon as we entered the gymnasium, which was fine because he then socialized with his friends and even tried some line dances with them. In the end, he decided that he had a good time, brought me soda from the bar, munched some hors d'oeuvres with me, and even thought that taking some ballroom dance classes at the school would be okay. Mission accomplished.

Help your child establish a meaningful goal. Recognize, reinforce, and respect your child's interests. Photograph, videotape, or assemble a scrapbook of important memories. Ensure that the student receives appropriate instruction, materials, and/or assessments to enable achievement of that goal. Be open to the possibility that your expectations may be misplaced if the child is unhappy in an activity, or more precisely, if he is as unhappy leaving as he was going to the activity.

---

10   Schunk, "Self-Efficacy and Cognitive Achievement," p. 149.

Learning environment. Don't assume that the child will be a self-starter in even the most *enriched* situations; in fact, your child may resent being in a situation not of his or her own choice. Rather, investigate whether the learning environment emphasizes *achievement* or *mastery*, for each of these has been linked to behavioral tendencies:[11]

ACHIEVEMENT FOCUS: Peer competition through "correct" answers, bell-curve grading, and results publicly displayed
* Procrastination and avoidance behaviors
* Excuses for unfulfilled expectations, even as early as fifth grade
* Self-defeating behaviors such as substance abuse and acting out

MASTERY FOCUS: Expertise emphasized through understanding and incremental improvements
* Less procrastination and resistance to novelty
* More effort, persistence, and requests for help.

You may want to look for activities that provide individualized guidance in a supportive atmosphere, such as a child working with the director on stage. Sometimes knowledge can be absorbed by viewing a videotape as opposed to reading a manual. Find out what works and use it. Small-scale environments do not benefit only those with LD either. Harvard students identified small-group tutorials, small seminars, and one-to-one supervision as some of the best undergraduate experiences[12] because, by knowing a student reasonably well, a professor can engage that person in a way that is difficult to do in large classes.[13]

Instructional methods. The pace of instruction must be examined with respect to your child's learning difficulty. A highly structured format organizes and may set time limits on material that is to be mastered. You must assess whether your child can progress with a program's normal course schedule, or if the program makes allowances for individual progress. A good program monitors progress and offers many opportunities to mark proficiency levels in order to sustain interest, such as a karate program that signals advancement with many belt colors: white, yellow, orange, purple, blue, green, brown, black, and striped combinations. (Traditionalists favoring few belt colors may frown, but six months in any of the beginning belt levels is a long time for a child.) Explicit near-term performance goals, established by either the instructor or the student, helps maintain task motivation; distant goals or platitudes do not improve motivation.[14]

The better a teacher teaches, the more competent the student will feel about his ability to learn.[15] Thus, a good teacher is one who can

---

11 Debra Viadero, "Studies Illuminate Self-Defeating Behavior by Students" [Internet], 26 March 2003, available from http://www.ldonline.org/news/self_defeating.html.
12 Light, *Making the Most of College*, p. 9.
13 Light, p. 47.
14 Schunk, "Self-Efficacy and Cognitive Achievement," p. 148.
15 Schunk, p. 145.

organize the presentations and convey them effectively. Students highly regarded for their intellectual ability perform much better than students less regarded; in fact, this latter group may show intellectual declines.[16] Teachers may also perceive compliant female students as working harder than boys although no difference may actually exist.[17] Another issue may be learning style. While an adult teacher will verbally instruct and link the information to other topic areas, a peer tutor will limit instruction to just explaining the problem with nonverbal demonstrations. Thus, the person who is teaching your child can make all the difference in the world.

Learning takes time, usually cycling through three stages: instruction, practice, and review. In addition, instruction for students with learning disabilities should include explicit strategies to integrate and organize various thought processes for task completion.[18]

Instructors should assist to avoid frustration, but not to the point where students believe they are incapable of performing unassisted.[19] Mastery doesn't just happen but takes effort and patience, which some children may not completely grasp in this day of instant gratification. Some instructors may believe that they are challenging their students by telling them that they have no ability—an elitist approach that is more likely to destroy the motivation to execute a mainstream achievement ("… So why am I here?"). This may work in the movies or in volunteer Marine Corps units, but not necessarily with underage students having esteem issues already.

Another version of instructional tough-love is to begin a course by assigning an *F* grade to all students; conversely, I have seen my son work harder when he begins a course with a couple of easy *As*, then try to maintain the A grade during the semester. Too many people forget that hope is an invitation to at least try one's best. Counseling the student to look at the bigger picture, to see that an activity can be ultimately rewarding, despite drudgery or disability, can help a student develop persistence and patience.

Identify appropriate role models

A role model can make children believe that they are capable of the same achievements. Peer models are better than teacher models or no models at all.[20] Children with learning disabilities performed better if

---

16   Bruce Bower citing studies of the Pygmalion effect first described by Rosenthal at Harvard University in 1968, "Fighting Stereotype Stigma," *Science News*, 29 June 1996, p. 409.

17   Bower citing Jussim and Eccles study, "Fighting Stereotype Stigma," p. 409.

18   Swanson, "Information Processing," p. 140.

19   Schunk, "Self-Efficacy and Cognitive Achievement," p. 145.

20   Schunk, p. 147.

exposed to a role model who overcame self-doubt and incompetence or to many role models of varying ability, than if exposed to a peer who was successful from the very beginning.[21] Finding a good role model is not easy. Some role models are offered in Chapter 6.

One junior ROTC student designated herself to be a classmate's social guardian during a volunteer activity. She not only smoothed relationships between other adolescents and him, but also explained to him how to handle situations better, in a way no parent could.

Be deliberate in your feedback: Increasing self-esteem

The type and amount of feedback about performance your child receives is another indicator of ability. Feedback is verbal and nonverbal. There are many aspects to feedback.

Accurate perceptions of feedback. Feedback is not always accurately interpreted. It's common for people to have a false sense of their competence or incompetence. Generally, patterns of performance influence perceptions of ability, not a single success or a single failure.[22] Environment can also affect perceptions of ability: a tough program may be discouraging, an easy program may breed overconfidence.

Commend effort or ability? Schunk found higher motivation, self-confidence, and skill if mastery and effort are commended ("You've been working hard") than if greater mastery and effort are suggested ("You need to work hard"). Self-confidence and skill are increased even more if success is attributed to ability ("You're good at this") instead of ability *and* effort.[23] Conversely, feelings of incompetence develop if a child with LD is still receiving praise for unsuccessful efforts at a late stage of learning or must work harder than those around him.[24] Self-confidence declines if effort is praised for a task perceived as easy because the student will conclude that others doubt his or her ability.[25]

Barkley suggested a general payment plan to improve grades received on papers and tests. His teenage sons received $1 for an *A*, 50 cents for a *B*, and 25 cents for a *C*.[26] He found that he saw schoolwork more often, and the monetary incentives helped drive the grades upward. For some children, however, rigorous enforcement of this payment plan would be unrealistically demanding. For example, not all individuals are capable of getting an *A* in physics, no matter how hard they try. The bar may be set too high, and your child may give up out of frustration. Adjust as the situation requires.

---

21 Schunk, p. 148.
22 Schunk, p. 143.
23 Schunk, p. 149.
24 Schunk, p. 150.
25 Schunk, p. 149.
26 Barkley, "ADHD: Theory, Diagnosis, and Treatment," p. 117.

Quantity of feedback. Having multiple opportunities to make midcourse corrections is much preferred to a summary judgment in which no improvements toward an achievement are possible. Students have reported learning significantly more if feedback was constant and immediate during the learning process such as numerous quizzes and short assignments, rather than after the end of the course as in a high-stakes final exam or paper.[27] In particular, a student with LD may have difficulty managing a large quantity of material with one assessment in a self-paced course, compared to more limited quantities of material with a series of tests in a highly structured course.

Comparing performance to others. Young children compare performances. With maturity, children compare underlying abilities. Social comparisons stem from perceptions of which individuals have higher or lower ability. Students with LD may see their abilities as between those of normal students and other students with disabilities.[28]

In the school environment, academic ability is valued. The flip side of the coin equates poor academics with insignificance. Your child will have to learn much earlier than her classmates that someone will *always* be better than someone else in a given activity, and that no one can excel in everything. This is a hard lesson at a young age when other children are being told that their world is full of unlimited possibilities. Beware of a teacher who openly diminishes individual students by comparing them to others: Humiliation is a method of control and social dominance, not academic instruction.

Nevertheless, peer comparisons are hard to avoid. One solution is comparing an individual's different performances. The YMCA competitive swim program not only awards ribbons for first, second, or third place finishes in a race, but also for swimmers surpassing their own individual records, or *personal best*. This same idea can be extended to school competitions. For example, it's one thing for your child to know that he came in dead last in a race. It's another thing to tell him that he didn't lose by much in his first varsity event, that the other contestants were older, and that he beat his own individual record by a full second. Same result but a different perception of reality. In this case, the child was given encouragement and hope with the knowledge that he could be competitive at this level. This is not just spin, not just saving face.

Expertise or credibility of the person giving feedback. Hearing that one is capable from a knowledgeable source raises self-esteem; comments from sources having less expertise or little information about the conditions surrounding the performance are discounted.[29]

---

27 Light, *Making the Most of College*, p. 8.
28 Schunk, "Self-Efficacy and Cognitive Achievement," p. 152.
29 Schunk, p. 144.

The best advisors help a student connect learning with a personal motivation for learning.[30] For example, many individuals entered the field of special education because they had relatives with disabilities, and wanted to learn more or help others. Help your child recognize supportive teachers and encourage him or her to get to know such individuals better.

Physiological responses to an activity. On one hand, people regarded as having natural ability often exude confidence. On the other hand, discomfort in an activity, like sweating or trembling, are often interpreted as being incapable of performing well.[31] Many acting professionals, however, suffer from stage fright. Anxiety, then, does not necessarily mean incompetence, but is commonly felt when one is inexperienced. In life, it's difficult to distinguish when to attend to your fears and when to ignore them.

Rehearsing anticipated situations can build confidence, much like a professional football team scripting the first 15 offensive plays for the next game. Actual simulations are best, such as scouting out a bus route to school during the morning rush hour. The next best method is practicing *what if* scenarios, as for a job interview. As much as possible, physically introduce your child to new situations with backup strategies and ways to handle pressure.

Well-chosen words are another way to blunt fear. Churchill inspired Great Britain to "never surrender" to the "servitude and shame" of Nazi Germany. Other examples are not difficult to find. Inspirational movies and music can also reduce fear as well as meditation, rituals, or even good luck charms.

An anxious child may be reacting to an environment providing little support and respect for him as a person. Children, like anyone else, want to feel valued and appreciated. One Boston College study demonstrated that children with learning disabilities improved "in all areas" if interactions with adults were consistently warm and responsive.[32] Anxiety reduces a person's capabilities to learn and socialize. Schools in particular, as a child's first nonfamily social unit, often fail to ensure that each child is truly accepted by others, and don't understand the damage they are causing (see Chapter 8). One troubled student with LD transferred to a more accepting environment and within a year made the honor roll and lettered in a sport. Bullying, from teachers as well as other students, makes learning harder than it needs to be.

Linking rewards to achievement. Self-confidence, skill levels, and the speed of problem-solving are increased when actual accomplishments are recognized, not when everyday tasks are rewarded

---

30   Light, *Making the Most of College*, p. 88.
31   Schunk, "Self-Efficacy and Cognitive Achievement," p. 140.
32   Bower, "Disabilities Develop as Family Affair," p. 276.

(such as *participating* in an activity).[33] Furthermore, rewards not dependent upon performance at all may actually decrease self-esteem, because the student senses that others believe him or her as incapable.[34]

Penalties are the opposite of rewards. One father paid for his son's weekend ski lift tickets contingent on school work well done. Had the less expensive season pass been purchased, the father would have been perceived as punishing his son for poor work by taking away the ski pass instead of rewarding him weekly. Mind the perceptions and keep a positive relationship with your child.

In instances of academic probation, try to find alternatives to athletic activity restrictions, especially if your child draws self-esteem from athletic skills. Perhaps join a sports organization unaffiliated with the school such as the YMCA. Be creative and alert to effective reward systems. Some legal issues affecting your child's participation in extracurricular activities despite unhappy academics are reviewed in "Leveling the Playing Field or Leveling the Players?" by Kathleen Sullivan, Patricia Lantz, and Perry Zirkel, available at www.ldonline. org/ld_indepth/legal_legislative/leveling_the_playing_field.html.

Applying extracurricular lessons to academic work

The confidence and work ethic learned in nonacademic activities can be transferred to academics as did the student at the beginning of this chapter. By learning that they are actually good at something, children with disabilities can develop optimism, hope, and persistence.

As with coaching, both parents and teachers can help the academic learning process by clarifying acceptable standards. One high school goes one step further and passes out lists of evaluation standards for research assignments as shown in Figures 18.2 and 18.4. Ideally at some point and with adult guidance, students with LD will pull their own act together. *They* must decide what they want to do and how to achieve their goal. This will not happen overnight. What is important is that you help your child recognize activities that can make life meaningful and rewarding. LD Online posts many articles for parents and teachers (go to its homepage at www.ldonline.org, type in "self-esteem" in the white box, then click on the button *SEARCH LD ONLINE*). Schwab Learning offers "The Expert Answers: Dr. Robert Brooks on Self-Esteem and Resilience," at www.schwablearning.org/articles.asp?g=3&r=491.

---

33 Schunk, "Self-Efficacy and Cognitive Achievement," p. 150.
34 Schunk, p. 150.

Chapter Twenty-One

What are some ways of managing AD/HD?

One of the administrators at the school became the first person who lis-
tened, understood, and did not blame me for my daughter's behavior.
She recommended that Tessa be pulled out of class and relocated to a
nearby public school for special help. My instincts said no. My daughter
had enough trouble tracking the usual classroom routine. The distrac-
tions would have been too much for her. There was also the stigma of
having to leave class. The administrator had alternatives.

So I had specialists in learning disabilities provide my daughter
in-house tutorials. But it was not enough. The sympathetic administra-
tor then suggested a local instructor of the Slingerland method. This
seemed to work. Tessa began developing coping mechanisms and tech-
niques. She entered third grade and had the best experience of her life.
Her devoted teacher was structured and consistent. She was the defini-
tion of fairness and competence. We began to make progress with
teaching tools, private tutorials two to three times a week, and a great
class environment. I begun to have hope for a solution. I was still not
recognizing that a series of challenges still lay ahead.

I helped out in my daughter's fourth grade as much as I could.
I saw her pair herself with the brightest child in the class; they were fast
friends. However, Tessa noticed that her friend's assignments were
early and perfect. Then she began comparing herself to others and
found differences. I was very concerned for my daughter's self-esteem.
My instincts were to try and protect her, which of course would have
been useless. The school administrator gave me emotional support.
Together, we visited a local information center for help. I began to

grow up. Tessa did too. Her tolerance for private tutorials waned sometime before fifth grade.

Nighttime was very important. If I filled the nights with activities, my Tessa would collapse. If I kept the evenings quiet and simple, she was able to cope. No noise or distractions during the homework effort could occur. I didn't learn until later that taking a break was a good thing. I continued to learn that my own issues greatly affected my perceptions of my daughter's issues.

Sixth grade was a serious year. Evenings were for school. Not that the entire evening was filled with study, but rather each required homework assignment took so long that we needed the night to complete what others might have done in one hour. I cannot stress enough that keeping things simple is a must. Parenting a child that is easily distracted means structuring things as often as possible. I myself hate structure, as I am the grownup version of this child. The only possible way of accomplishing schoolwork was simplicity. It worked.

I had kept in contact with the Slingerland instructor. She told me about her daughter who played in the junior symphony and later received her master's degree. She regrets not having taken medication for her attention deficit disorder before college though, because the work would not have been so hard and frustrating. Upon hearing this, I scheduled my child to see the doctor, and she received a prescription.

Tessa took a morning dose before her classes. The school had a lunchtime line of students waiting for their second doses; my young adolescent girl found this unacceptable. We agreed that since her afternoon classes were lighter, she only was required to take the morning dose. This system worked for some time. She became familiar with the drug and got used to its side effects. She does not take it on weekends nor over vacation periods.

My daughter became the star of the school musical. She had a ball. She was acknowledged and fulfilled. It also helped her in her work because she felt the pressure to use her time more efficiently. She could not have done this any earlier than that year. Progress continued. Tessa was accepted into the top private high school in the city. The process was grueling. She was given extended time on the admissions exam which reduced her anxiety. I was quite mindful of the deadlines and essays, but she remained somewhat blasé about the entire process. I believe it was because I had done so much for her in the past, that she never really got the impact of how important it was to do this well.

My daughter is about to begin her sophomore year. Her freshman year was hard. I felt like I was a nag. Her school counselor suggested that I discontinue this. I have to a certain degree and our relationship has improved. She is maintaining about a C+ average, not great, but not impossible. What I have noticed is a marked increase in personal responsibility. We still have esteem issues, but the causes are blurred somewhere in normal adolescence and her learning disability. Tessa loves her school, her friends, her activities, and her life.

Treatment guidelines

An appropriate treatment program of medication and behavioral management can reduce impulsive behavior and improve working memory, academic productivity, and self-control. Such improvements can lead to better relationships, fewer punishments, and a better self-image.

In 2001, the American Academy of Pediatrics (AAP), in collaboration with other organizations—including the American Academy of Family Physicians, the American Academy of Child and Adolescent Psychiatry, the Child Neurology Society, the Society for Pediatric Psychology, the Society for Developmental and Behavioral Pediatrics, and the Society for Developmental Pediatrics—published a set of physician guidelines for managing AD/HD. These guidelines, "Clinical Practice Guideline: Treatment of the School-Aged Child With Attention-Deficit/Hyperactivity Disorder," are a follow-up to the AAP's diagnostic guidelines published a year earlier and are available at www.aap.org/policy/s0120.html. The flowcharts that accompanied these guidelines are not included online however. With respect to treatment, the AAP guidelines state that:[1]

• AD/HD should be recognized as a chronic condition requiring treatment

• Desired goals should determine the treatment program

• The clinician should recommend appropriate therapies and be prepared to reevaluate any recommendations if goals are not met

• The child should be monitored with respect to progress.

The AAP treatment guidelines also state that *behavior therapy*, defined as "a broad set of specific interventions that have a common goal of modifying the physical and social environment to alter or change behavior," is more effective than *psychological therapy*, defined as "interventions directed to the child and designed to change the child's emotional status (eg, play therapy) or thought patterns (eg, cognitive therapy or cognitive-behavior therapy)."[2] Underlying this AAP recommendation is that cognitive therapy seems ineffective for students with AD/HD. According to Barkley, cognitive therapy—also known as self-control training—presumes that an individual can internalize language in order to guide his or her behavior; individuals with AD/HD have trouble internalizing language.[3]

---

1   American Academy of Pediatrics, "Treatment of the School-Aged Child with Attention-Deficit/Hyperactivity Disorder," p. 1033.
2   American Academy of Pediatrics, p. 1039.
3   Barkley, "ADHD: Theory, Diagnosis, and Treatment," p. 86.

Because AD/HD is a chronic condition—ranging from mild to severe—many experts warn that behavioral and environmental interventions and complex medication schedules will become a way of life. The disorder requires task reminders and incentives at the point of performance—not skills instruction—to help keep the student on track. Parents and teachers must anticipate events and increase accountability for behavior. Establish rules and consistent consequences, but provide a positive environment. A system of immediate rewards and swift punishments is more credible than grand rewards and severe punishments delivered after many delays and warnings. This is why a child with AD/HD can quickly learn the intricacies of a videogame in which each movement is immediately rewarded or penalized, as opposed to a literature assignment which is quite complex and entails a delayed appraisal from the teacher. Tips for managing behaviors are:

- Distractible — Minimize diversions in the work area. Establish time limits and rewards.

- No follow through — Divide the task into smaller steps. Post lists of steps to be executed at the task's location. Monitor and encourage work progress.

- Unsustained interest — Make succinct rather than discursive communications. Engage rather than command. Plan activity breaks. Offer a wide variety of incentives that change periodically.

- Impulsive — Work on self-reflecting and self-monitoring behaviors. To illustrate, students with AD/HD are more productive in front of a mirror because they can monitor themselves, whereas normal students will be distracted.[4] Barkley suggests monitoring devices available from A.D.D. WareHouse (800/ 233-9273 or http://addwarehouse.com).

- Disorganized — Promote organization with structured routines, planners, clocks, and reward charts.

All this can be draining for adult caregivers. You may wish to inquire about parent training programs, which, according to the AAP treatment guidelines, are typically 8–12 weekly group sessions with a trained therapist. For information about programs in your area, contact

---

4   Barkley, p. 115.

your physician, resource specialist, or the specialized parent information centers listed at the end of this book.

School accommodations should address the 30% lag in self-control characterizing children with AD/HD when compared to their peers. The workload can be adjusted downward to what would be expected of a student 30% younger, an 11-year-old instead of a 16-year-old, for example.[5] Scheduling the most difficult subjects at the beginning of the school day will avoid many problems caused by fatigue later in the day. Incomplete class work, which may require further instructions, should not be sent home as the parent may already be dealing with a tired child off medication, a poor appetite, and hours of homework. Says Barkley, "There's plenty to deal with at home besides class work."[6]

Steven Kurtz offers resources and interventions for classroom behavioral problems in the May/June 2002 *Child Study Center Letter* "Treating Attention-Deficit/Hyperactivity Disorder (ADHD) in School Settings," available at www.aboutourkids.org/letter/mayjun02.pdf. "Targeting Home-School Collaboration for Students with ADHD," by Candace Bos, Maria Nahmias, and Magda Urban, illustrates specific real-life communication strategies, and is available at www.ldonline. org/ld_indepth/add_adhd/tec_home_school_collab.html. Silver devotes two chapters to AD/HD behavioral management in *The Misunderstood Child*. He offers more information in *Dr. Larry Silver's Advice to Parents on Attention Deficit Hyperactivity Disorder* (Times Books, 1999). Barkley offers many specific interventions (beginning on page 65) in his candid lecture, *ADHD: Theory, Diagnosis, and Treatment*, the 123-page transcript downloadable for free from www.schwablearning. org/pdfs/2200_7-barktran.pdf. His other books for parents are *Taking Charge of AD/HD: The Complete, Authoritative Guide for Parents* (Guilford Press, 2000); *Your Defiant Child: Eight Steps to Better Behavior* (Guilford Press, 1998); and *Attention Deficit Hyperactivity Disorder: A Handbook for Diagnosis and Treatment* (Guilford Press, 1998).

One mother worked alongside her daughter in the evenings, thereby creating a studious atmosphere. Some professionals help parents implement the recommendations provided in *Homework Success for Children with ADHD*, by Thomas Power, James Karustis, and Dina Habboushe (Guilford Press, 2001). The 30% rule may also apply when choosing a college: Select a very small program with a strong accommodations program.[7] Another mother found the local community college an excellent transition between high school and a four-year program, and the instructors were deeply committed to teaching.

---

5   Barkley, p. 109.
6   Barkley, p. 109.
7   Barkley, p. 138.

Medications can temporarily control hyperactivity, distractibility, and impulsivity linked to AD/HD. They do not treat LD, anxiety, depression, conduct disorders or other problems that might exist with or be misdiagnosed as AD/HD. Medications do not cure AD/HD, but can make it easier for an individual to complete a task. One young girl thanked her mother for giving her medicine to help her "think better." If the child is only being treated during school hours, then homework, weekends, and vacations can be trying. Not all people, however, respond to medications. The anatomy and biochemistry underlying the mechanisms and treatment of AD/HD is beginning to be understood.

The decision to medicate a child makes many parents uncomfortable. Nevertheless says the AAP, "At least 80% of children will respond to one of the stimulants if they are tried in a systematic way,"[8] with 38% showing normal behavior in a year.[9] Many clinicians stop medications when a child reaches puberty although about 60% to 80% of children continue to have AD/HD symptoms into adolescence.[10] One study of teens with AD/HD found that schoolwork and social skills improved with low medication levels and behavioral training.[11] Current research is studying the effects of long-term medication and the appropriateness of medication on very young children. Especially for little ones, physician Bernadine Healy recommends that parents become activists, insisting that the healthcare team include a specialist and psychological and family therapy.[12]

Before any medications are dispensed, a physician should evaluate the child's medical health and family history. Follow-up visits should monitor the child's health during treatment. Some people with specific genes do not respond to specific types of medications though; further research may soon ease the process of identifying an appropriate treatment program based on an individual's genetic makeup.[13]

Taken orally as prescribed, stimulants are not addictive.[14] Adhering to a medically prescribed regimen is associated with a decreased risk of illegal drug or alcohol abuse in adolescence and

---

8   American Academy of Pediatrics, "Treatment of the School-Aged Child with Attention-Deficit/Hyperactivity Disorder," p. 1038.

9   American Academy of Pediatrics, p. 1037.

10   American Academy of Pediatrics, p. 1036.

11   Bruce Bower citing 2001 Evans study, "Teens' ADHD Treatment Gets Low-dose Boost," *Science News*, 2 June 2001, p. 343.

12   Bernadine Healy, "Toddlers in Turmoil," *U.S. News & World Report*, 16 December 2002, p. 52.

13   Bruce Bower citing 1999 Winsberg and Comings study, "Gene May Alter Ritalin's Effects in ADHD," *Science News*, 4 December 1999, p. 359.

14   Silver, *The Misunderstood Child*, p. 276.

adulthood.[15] Joseph Biederman of Massachusetts General Hospital conducted a four-year study, and found that boys taking stimulants were three times less likely to develop substance abuse compared to boys who were not given therapeutic medications.[16] Another concern is the safety and efficacy of prescribing medications—for problems such as depression or intense hostility—to children already on stimulants.[17]

Many students feel embarrassed to leave class to take a *chill pill*, although this can be handled discreetly. One teacher assigned a child needing noontime medication the pre-lunchtime responsibilities of turning out the lights and closing the door; he and the teacher would then be at the end of the line from where he could go to the office for his treatment unnoticed by classmates.[18] Some new medications last longer than the usual four hours. This still leaves many medicated children not hungry during lunchtime.

A Duke University Medical Center three-year longitudinal study of 1,422 students demonstrated that AD/HD is both overdiagnosed and undertreated. Of the students receiving stimulants, about 75% of the cases were being medicated based on the behavioral reports from parents. Researchers reevaluated all students. Over half of the 168 9- to 16-year-olds receiving stimulant medications did not have AD/HD symptoms after all. Conversely, over half of the students with AD/HD received no medication. Furthermore, since a greater part of the group receiving medication were boys and 9- to 12-year-olds of both genders, researchers suspected that girls and teenagers may be undertreated. For children without AD/HD, those living in households above the federal poverty line were twice as likely to be given stimulants than those living below the poverty line.[19]

Another study by Stephen Hinshaw of the University of California at Berkeley looked at four types of AD/HD treatments, all lasting 14 months. He found that the greatest behavioral improvements occurred in children receiving carefully calibrated dosages of medications and an elaborate program of behavioral therapy. A close second was the group receiving only the calibrated medication program. The other two groups of children in the study improved as well. The study

---

15   Reuters, "No Abuse Risk in Hyperactivity Drugs, Study Says" [Internet], 6 January 2003, p. 1, accessed 14 January 2003 from http://news.lycos.com/news/story.asp?section=Health&storyId=617272

16   Catherine Arnst, "Attention Deficit: Is It In the Genes?," *Business Week*, 22 November 1999, p. 74.

17   Bruce Bower citing 2000 Guevara study, "Med Use Widens in Kids with ADHD," *Science News*, 1 June 2002, p. 350.

18   Schwab Foundation for Learning Staff, "Classroom Strategies," *LD Matters*, Spring 2000, pp. 6-7.

19   Bruce Bower citing 2000 Angold study, "Study of Stimulant Therapy Raises Concerns," *Science News*, 29 July 2000, p. 69.

noted that the third group, treated by community mental health practitioners, took larger doses than those receiving the carefully calibrated medications. Two-thirds of a fourth group receiving only the elaborate behavioral therapy (psychotherapy, 35 parental training sessions, a summer camp to teach social skills, and 10–16 meetings between a therapist and the child's teacher to plan classroom strategies) did not use medication during the study.[20] To replicate the study's extensive behavioral therapy, however, would be quite expensive and extraordinary given today's common practices.

More information on medication can be found at www.aboutour kids.org, www.chadd.org, and www.ldonline.org. Some specific resources on medications are:

• "Managing AD/HD with Medication—An Overview," by Annie Stuart provides useful terminology, classes of drugs, and brand names. The website, available at www.schwablearning.org/articles.asp?r=340, also links to related resources.

• "Medication Chart to Treat Attention Deficit Disorders," by A.D.D. WareHouse and originally summarized by Harvey Parker, covers the dosages, effectiveness, and comparative advantages of brand name medications. The chart is available at www.ldonline.org/ld_indepth/add_adhd/add_medication_chart.html.

• "Guide to Psychiatric Medications for Children and Adolescents," by Sabine Hack and Brian Klee, is posted on www.aboutourkids.org/articles/guidetopsychmeds.html. The chart lists brand names of medications, benefits, and common side effects.

• Silver reviews in *The Misunderstood Child* his method of determining types of medications, dosage amounts, and medication schedules. He also covers side effects and problems requiring treatment changes. He provides new information on the website, "Update on ADHD Medications," available at www.ldonline.org/ld_indepth/add_adhd/adhd_medications_update.html.

• *Straight Talk about Psychiatric Medications for Kids*, by Timothy E. Wilens (Guilford Press, 2002), reviews many child psychiatric disorders as well as medications. The book also discusses whether to medicate your child, including medication alternatives, safety, efficacy, and abuse. Excerpts of this book appear on www.amazon.com.

• *Practitioner's Guide to Psychoactive Drugs for Children and Adolescents* (Plenum Publishing, 1999), edited by John Werry and Michael Aman, provides technical information about psychiatric medications.

• *The Physicians' Desk Reference (PDR)*, an annual technical manual published by the Medical Economics Company, is found in medical libraries or you may ask your physician about its listings. *PDR*'s online

---

20 Bruce Bower, "Kids' ADHD Care Gets a Wake-Up Call," *Science News*, 18 & 25 December 1999, p. 388.

information on medications is limited to health professionals. For consumers, *PDR* does offer links to general information at www. gettingwell.com or www.pdrhealth.com.

Other treatments

Interactive Metronome trains individuals to coordinate repetitive limb movements to a metronome beat. Treatment requires proficiency in 13 exercises over 15 one-hour sessions. A controlled study published in the March/April 2001 issue of the *American Journal of Occupational Therapy* found significant improvements in overall coordination, concentration, impulse control, and language processing in boys with AD/HD. No similar peer-reviewed studies have been reported. The study has been criticized as being too small for any final conclusions, and the treatment may only be effective for children characterized as having trouble coordinating and sequencing thoughts and actions.[21] More information and demonstrations are available at www.interactive metronome.com.

Martial Arts may improve behavior because continuous physical exercise, discipline, and colored belts denoting individual achievement are all part of the instructional program. One instructor, who remembers being schooled in an institution, told me that he used martial arts discipline to help him gain more self-control. Different kinds of martial arts exist. A good teacher is critical not only for the skills training, but also for maintaining the child's interest. Years of training is required to attain the level of a black belt. Group, semi-private, and private arrangements differ in cost and in variety of sparring partners. Effectiveness seems anecdotal at this time, helping some but not all.[22]

Summer Camps are accessible in many locations around the country and are often publicized through parent information centers. Bear in mind, however, that many of the newly learned behavioral skills may not transfer to your child's school environment. More information about selecting an appropriate summer program is available in "Summer Places for Children with Attention Deficit Disorders," by Steven Kurtz, available at www.aboutourkids.org/articles/summer_ adhd.html. Links to other information sites about specific camps are available through an article by Nancy Firchow, "Summer Camps for Kids with Learning Differences," at www.schwablearning.org/articles. asp?r=285.

---

21 Katy Kelly, "They've Got Rhythm: Clapping Away Attention Deficits?" *U.S. News & World Report*, 16 April 2001, p. 50.
22 Caroline Knorr, "Fighting ADD in the Dojo: Children with Attention Deficit Disorder Find Discipline and Focus with Martial Arts," *San Francisco Chronicle* (27 January 2002) p. E3.

Biofeedback. In biofeedback, basic body functions such as breathing, heart rate, and blood pressure are monitored, while the patient is trained to relax or use mental imagery in order to alter these functions. Anxiety, hypertension, headaches, chronic pain, asthma, and hypertension are sometimes treated by biofeedback. Sensors connected to a machine are attached to an individual, and sensory readings are displayed on a monitor. The individual is taught control techniques to alter the monitor's readings to a more desirable pattern. Eventually, the individual learns how to properly use these techniques without requiring a monitoring machine.

Many physicians remain unsure about the efficacy of biofeedback for all patients. More studies will be needed for a widespread consensus. The director of certification at the Biofeedback Certification Institute of America (BCIA) has warned that the field is unregulated, and that therapy claims should be investigated.[23] A list of certified practitioners is available through www.bcia.org or 303/ 420-2902.

Neurofeedback, a variant of biofeedback, uses EEG brain wave patterns to treat anxiety and AD/HD. Joel Lubar, a psychology professor at the University of Tennessee, has found that individuals with AD/HD normally show low-frequency electroencephalogram (EEG) brain waves; better concentration causes higher frequency brain waves to appear. After a 10-year follow-up study, Lubar reported lasting improvements in attention spans, better school and work performance, and lower dependency on medications.[24] Some other practitioners use a child's software program in which a man moves though a maze only when the child successfully concentrates. The National Institutes of Health, however, lists biofeedback among other treatments not having been "scientifically shown to be effective in treating the majority of children or adults with AD/HD."[25] The parent information center, CHADD (Children and Adults with Attention-Deficit/Hyperactivity Disorder) advises caution on this "expensive, unproven approach."[26] Barkley has observed that no controlled research studies have demonstrated neurofeedback to be a compelling treatment for AD/HD.[27]

---

23 Susan Garland, "Patient Heal Thyself," *Business Week*, 16 October 2000, p. 200E6.

24 Garland, p. 200E5.

25 National Institutes of Mental Health, "Attention Deficit Hyperactivity Disorder" [Internet], p. 17, updated 1 July 1999, available at http://www.nimh.nih.gov/publicat/adhd.cfm#adhd7

26 CHADD, "Assessing Complementary and/or Controversial Interventions - CHADD Fact Sheet #6" [Internet], first posted Spring 2000 as "CHADD Fact Sheet No. 6," accessed 1 September 2002 from: http://www.chadd.org/fs/fs6.htm

27 Barkley, "ADHD: Theory, Diagnosis, and Treatment," p. 86.

Chapter Twenty-Two

How can technology help my child?

What is "assistive technology?"

> "... *Assistive technology device* means any item, piece of equipment, or product system, whether acquired commercially off the shelf, modified, or customized, that is used to increase, maintain, or improve functional capabilities of a child with a disability."
>
> —*34 CFR § 300.5*

> "... *Assistive technology service* means any service that directly assists a child with a disability in the selection, acquisition, or use of an assistive technology device. The term includes evaluation ... [p]urchasing, leasing ... [s]electing ... customizing ... maintaining, repairing ... replacing ... and ... training."
>
> —*34 CFR § 300.6*

Assistive technology can be provided as a special education service or related service, and is required when it will enable your child to receive an appropriate education. An analogy would be eyeglasses or hearing aids to improve neurological functioning. For example, calculators are invaluable for students who cannot recall math facts. Spellcheckers help those who have a hard enough time decoding words when reading much less coding up new ones when writing. The adoption of an appropriate device or service will allow your child to function better in the general environment. To ensure that your child has access to these devices or services when needed, they—and any circumstances of concern—must be specified in your child's IEP or 504 plan. An essay generated by a laptop for an exam appears in Appendix 6.

Make a good faith effort with the teacher, however, to reduce any disruptions that the technology may cause. Using the device may be embarrassing for the child with LD and may cause envy in some other students. This chapter will review many technologies to assist your child's learning.

Assistive technology ranges from low-tech items like pencil grips, highlighter pens, and planners to high-tech wonders such as laptops, talking calculators, and text-to-speech software. High-tech *utility* software, which improves functioning in order to learn, is more likely to be included in an IEP or a 504 plan than educational *content* software, such as early math and reading programs, which may be perceived as less effective teaching methods or as ancillary curriculum enrichment exercises. This latter type of software, sometimes called *edutainment software* because academic material is presented in a game format, is discussed in Chapter 24.

A 1998 Amendment of the Rehabilitation Law, Section 508 (or 29 U.S.C. § 794 (d)), mandates that federal agencies, when purchasing new electronic technology, install information systems accessible to individuals with disabilities. This means that computer manufacturers must produce assistive technology and devices if they are to sell products to the government. As this market develops, you should find more options available. States and local governments generally follow federal guidelines. This law can be read at www.section508.gov. Shelly Brisbin provides a discussion on software and compatible devices on pages 69–73 in the May 2002 issue of *Macworld*.

Many equipment manufacturers and vendors target professionals and so service providers are good sources of information for what may be particularly useful for your child. Special educators, for example, receive many brochures and catalogs of specialized curriculum resources from companies such as Super Duper Publications (www. superduperinc.com or 800/ 277-8737 or 864/ 288-3536). Libraries and booksellers also carry manuals listing resources for special education. Other sources of information are:

•   *Assistive Technology Guide* by Schwab Learning is free and downloadable from www.schwablearning.org/articles.asp?r=488.

•   The nonprofit Alliance for Technology Access (ATA) has published a book, *Computer and Web Resources for People with Disabilities* (2000). It identifies types of devices that could be suitable for specific situations, and presents case studies of people using assistive technology successfully. This comprehensive guide also explains computer terminology, applicable laws, funding, product features, and alternatives to consider when purchasing items. Lists of vendors and Internet addresses ease procurement. ATA's website, www.ataccess.org (voice 415/ 455-4575 or TTY 415/ 455-0491), has information about local information centers and service providers who can help you with your individual needs.

• The Center for Applied Special Technology (www.cast.org or voice 781/ 245-2212 or TTY 781/ 245-9320) offers information, Family Learning Centers, and summer camps (type "family" or "camp" in the *Search* box, then click on the *Go* button).

• Riverdeep Interactive Learning 800/ 825-4420 or www.riverdeep.net, click on *Special Needs*) offers devices and technical support for people with disabilities.

• CNET.com (www.cnet.com) and ZDnet.com (www.zdnet.com) are two Web portals which gather present and some past product reviews.

Reading assistants: Transforming text into speech

Many individuals have trouble comprehending reading material, because so much effort is invested into decoding individual words that fluency and meaning are lost. Poor readers may also skip unfamiliar words or lose their place on the page. For these students, a reader would be analogous to a foreign language translator. Parents, however, can't always be available to read text on demand.

One solution is providing prerecorded audiotapes produced either by professionals or parents themselves. Some students prefer the independence and convenience of "reading" alone. Moreover, reading along with a recording is a form of *paired reading*, in which the student practices word recognition, pronunciation, and reading fluency with another reader. With increased proficiency, a desire to read may develop. However, as one of my son's resource specialists noted, parents must monitor reading progress or be ready to parachute into the situation to explain passages that the child may not fully understand. Public library collections offer some recordings, but I have found most to be abridged versions.

The National Library Service for the Blind and Physically Handicapped (NLS) at the U.S. Library of Congress provides free prerecorded audio cassettes through their Talking Books program. Although catalogs are available, you can call the participating library in your area and order the available recordings from your child's class reading list. Sometimes, it might take a few weeks to obtain a specific recording. The four-track tapes require a specially designed playback cassette machine, but this can also be provided by the library with certain conditions, such as use restricted to the home. (Alternatives are presented in the next paragraph.) Several standards of program eligibility exist but generally depend on a person's inability to read standard "printed material in a normal manner." The application requires U.S. residency and confirmation of an existing learning disability from a professional such as a physician, therapist, or special education teacher. The cassettes, encased in small green or blue plastic boxes, are delivered and returned for free through the U.S. Post Office. (The NLS at the time of this writing is studying its options for providing CDs and associated playback technologies.) For more information on eligibility, available resources, and phone number of the participating library in your area, the web address is http://lcweb.loc.gov/nls or www.loc.gov/nls, or telephone 800/ 424-8567 or TDD: 202/ 707-0744. Figure 22.1 shows a typical mailer with an audiocassette.

Figure 22.1

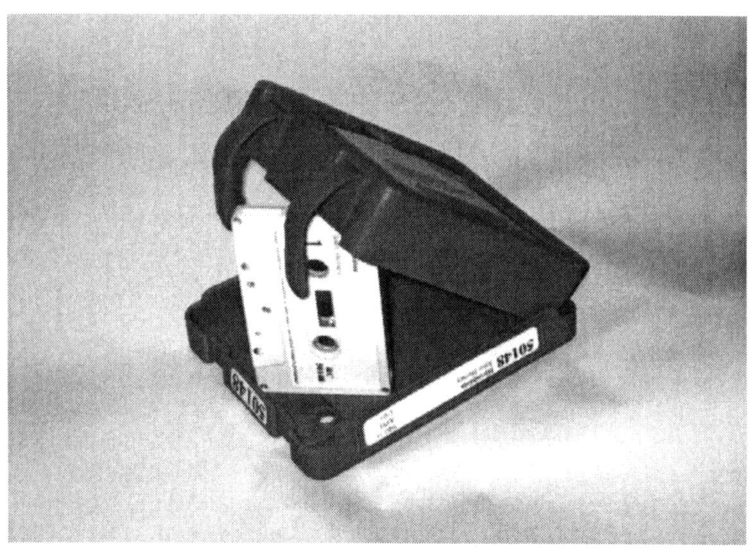

Recording for the Blind & Dyslexic (RB&D) at www.rfbd.org or 800/ 221-4792 provides tape and CD recordings of school textbooks and classic literature such as *Around the World in 80 Days*. The tapes and CDs require specially designed playback technologies. RB&D offers a variety of compatible machines—including portable devices for use outside the home—or PC software for purchase. Alternatively, you can use at home the audiotape machine available through the NLS (see paragraph above). A textbook can require a good number of audiotapes, which arrive in small cardboard cartons. The CD format is far easier to ship. Mailing costs are free through the U.S. Post Office. As with all mail, if the package weighs more than one pound, the Post Office requires that the return shipment be taken to the post office counter.

Initial membership is $75 and annual renewals are $25. The website has more information, including branch locations and applications for membership.

Voice-synthesis or *speech-synthesis* is really the combination of two different computer technologies. For example, reading assignments can be digitized (scanned or otherwise encoded) into the computer with optical character recognition (OCR) software, then "read" using speech synthesis software. Students with *severe* difficulties in silent reading have improved comprehension with a machine having OCR and speech imitation capabilities.[1] More proficient readers may find this method of phonological decoding inefficient. You must determine which technologies work best for your child and under what circumstances. Several options exist:

• The Kurzweil 3000 for either Windows or Macintosh environments (www.kurzweiledu.com or 800/ 894-5374, extension 603) is specifically designed for people with reading difficulties.

• OCR and speech synthesis software are commonly included in scanners and Mac computers respectively.

• ScanSoft (www.scansoft.com) offers OCR and text-to-speech capabilities in its software products, OmniPage Pro and RealSpeak.

Computerized remediation: Building phoneme awareness

A "strong consensus" now exists that an auditory perceptual deficit is involved in most reading difficulties.[2] Paula Tallal of Rutgers University estimates that at least 80 percent of children with language problems have reading troubles in school.[3] A high-tech approach to auditory perceptual training developed over the last decade (VAKT approaches are presented in Chapter 23) has enabled children to more efficiently process phonemes into meaningful thoughts.

A computer program can produce more opportunities for repetitious phoneme practice with greater control (speech clarity, variety of sounds, pronunciation speed, and pace of presentation) than is possible for any human speech therapist. While some clinicians remain skeptical because of few control studies, one Finnish control study in 2001 demonstrated that phoneme awareness drills—in the form of

1   Eleanor L. Higgins and Marshall H. Raskind, "The Compensatory Effectiveness of Optical Character Recognition/Speech Synthesis on Reading Comprehension of Postsecondary Students with Learning Disabilities," *Learning Disabilities*, Spring 1997, p. 75.

2   Torgesen, "Instructional Interventions for Children with Reading Disabilities," p. 202.

3   John Travis, "Let the Games Begin," *Science News,* 17 February 1996, p. 106.

audiovisual computer games—can not only substantially improve reading speed, reading comprehension, and spelling skills, but also lead to brain imaging patterns associated with efficient sound processing.[4]

Fast ForWord. Since the 1970s, Tallal noticed that 5–8% of children had normal intelligence but also had "great difficulty mastering oral language, often displaying an inability to understand or properly speak simple phrases."[5] Although standard hearing tests identified no abnormalities, the children could not distinguish basic speech sounds, or phonemes (as discussed in Chapter 3). In particular, the children could not process rapid streams of consonant and vowel sequences into meaningful language.

In the 1990s, Michael Merzenich of the University of California at San Francisco demonstrated that intensive training could reorganize neural connections in monkey brains and enhance identification of specific sounds. The combination of these two lines of scientific investigation resulted in Fast ForWord.

Using a computer game format to retain the subject's interest, modified speech sounds are piped into headphones. In the games, the sounds are modified by increasing the volume slightly and lengthening the normal duration by 50 percent. Some games work on identification of difficult phonemes. One game requires identification of which sound came first, such as *ba-da* or *da-ba*. As competence is attained, the duration of the sound units or the interval between two different sounds are shortened gradually, until normal speech speed is reached. Computers can repeat sounds rapidly, doggedly, and unerringly, thus providing an intensive drill-and-practice session. One study demonstrated a two-year gain in language skills with a month of Fast ForWord therapy versus a six-month gain in a control group.[6] This and other studies have shown that plasticity of the post-childhood brain indeed exists. ("Survival of the Busiest," by Sharon Begley, a *Wall Street Journal* article published 11 October 2002 on page B1, provides more general information on brain plasticity.)

This *practice-makes-perfect* therapy emphasizes phonological awareness, not reading skills. However, since phonological deficits are associated with low reading skills, improving auditory skills can enable better reading skills. Specially trained professionals provide this therapy at licensed centers. More information on Fast ForWord is available at www.scilearn.com or 888/ 358-0212.

---

4   Bruce Bower citing 2001 Kujala study, "Audiovisual Aids May Lessen Dyslexia," *Science News*, 8 September 2001, p. 155.

5   Travis, "Let the Game Begin," p. 104.

6   Travis, p. 105.

Earobics. A software product for home use is *Earobics* (www. earobics.com or 888/ 328-8199). Like Fast ForWord, *Earobics* teaches sound discrimination skills through games, and has developed programs for children ages 5–10 or adolescents and adults. Designed by Cognitive Concepts for both PC and Mac platforms, the software has won a Parent's Choice Award. The May/June 2001 issue of *Children's Software & New Media Revue* (*CSR*) generally praised *Earobics Step 2* but had a couple of reservations. For more details contact *CSR* at www.childrenssoftware.com or 800/ 993-9499).

Waterford Early Reading Program. The Waterford Institute (www.waterford.org) has designed computerized instruction for phonological awareness, reading fluency and comprehension, math, and science. These multimedia lessons are provided in schools. Pearson Digital Learning (www.pearsondigital.com/EE_Home.php or 888/ 977-7900) also carries information on Waterford programs.

Writing devices: Increasing labor efficiency

Taking notes in the upper grades—which requires a student to comprehend speech, identify important points, then write it all down as the teacher continues speaking—may be impossible for some students. Voice recorders are useful but playback is time-consuming and often indistinct. Computer laptops, AlphaSmart word processors, or a combined *personal data assistant* (*PDA*) like a Palm Pilot (www.palm.com or www.palmgear.com) and a keyboard can ease simultaneous input-output writing tasks. Ideally, letter-formation labors are eliminated, allowing a student to focus more on oral comprehension. Cost, durability, possible hours of (rechargeable) battery life, ease of handling, portability, available locker space, likelihood of theft, and teacher preferences are some factors to consider.

Many manufacturers offer various configurations of laptops, so investigate alternatives before purchasing one. A primary concern should be compatibility with the school's operating system. Apple's iBook laptop is specifically designed for student use.

Some *mobile accessories* may prove useful also. Some backpacks (www.tenba.com, www.targus.com, www.spireusa.com, www.codi direct.com, and www.ebags.com among others) are constructed with a protective laptop pocket and provide a low profile for your child against thieves. Belkin (www.belkin.com) makes a variety of keyboards. Macally (www.macally.com) produces a 3" USB MicroMouse® and a 5" 4PortMiniHub. Kensington (www.kensington.com) offers a long-neck LED Flylight™ for working in dark environments. Many companies manufacture laptop security cables with key, combination, or alarmed motion-detector locks, such as Kryptonite (www.kryptonite. com). Figure 22.2 shows an iBook with a Flylight and security cable.

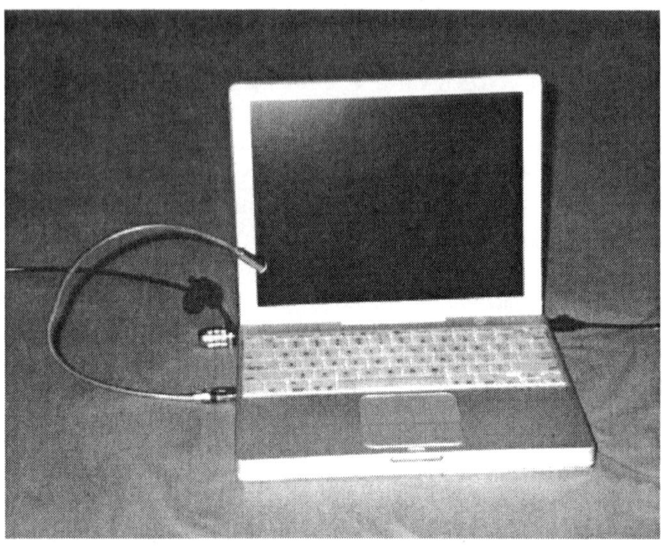

AlphaSmart (www.alphasmart.com or 888/ 274-0680) produces portable kid-friendly word processors that can be used for note-taking and writing. The AlphaSmart 3000, for example, uses three AA batteries for, according to the manufacturer, 500+ hours of use. It comes in four different configurations and is less expensive than a laptop. Text written on it can be easily downloaded to your PC or Mac. It is simple to use (kindergartners and first graders can use it), lightweight, and durable. Additional models and optional equipment are also available. AlphaSmart's Dana is a hardy word processor and incorporates PDA applications.

Some PDAs—also called *handhelds*—can beam information to each other. It is possible for a student to receive notes from a teacher this way, download the notes onto a computer, and then use a speech synthesizer to "read" the notes aloud. Files can be downloaded into a PC or Mac. A digital recorder module may be snapped into the upper Handspring bay, enabling hours of simultaneous voice recording and keyboarding. One high school student has taken notes with an 8MB Handspring Deluxe Visor plugged into a compatible fold-up Targus Stowaway Portable Keyboard (seen in Figure 22.3) or clamshell-style LandWare GoType! Keyboard (www.landware.com). The PDA and Targus keyboard combination fit into his khaki pants pocket. Once, he tripped and damaged the screen to his Visor. Within two days,

Handspring sent him a refurbished replacement unit (in exchange for the damaged unit and at a cost of less than a new unit) which has worked fine since. This example of the possible capabilities of even an older PDA illustrates that your child need not have the most expensive model available on the market.

Figure 22.3

Voice recorders capture not only lectures for playback, but also clue parents into how to better assist a child with a lesson. Many analog devices exist. Olympus (www.olympus.com) has engineered hand-size digital voice recorders that download recorded speech to a computer. A fundamental problem of environment still exists, however. Speech must be inputted directly from a built-in microphone for best results, making these devices questionable for classrooms with background noise and mediocre acoustics.

Overall, a *coolness* factor may determine whether a child will employ a particular technology, assuming that school authorities encourage its use. Continued use must be promoted as new ways are sometimes hard to adopt. While a parent will emphasize the utilitarian nature of the technology and its cost, a child—especially one with low self-esteem—will focus on whether the technology seems acceptable to others. My son was reluctant to use prerecorded tapes until he saw the actor John Malkovich use recordings in the movie *Places in the Heart*. A third-grade girl was happy when she found out that her AlphaSmart fit perfectly into a *Hello Kitty* bag, and felt quite grown-up carrying her "lap" to school.

Many students successfully write by dictating fluent thoughts into a voice recorder, then playing back the recording to help them commit the words to paper. Word-processing, spellchecker, and thesaurus software speed the mechanics of writing. Use of these computer aides, however, requires recognition of their limitations. Spellcheckers may not correct for homophones (*here* and *hear*), word variations (*paper-clip* the verb versus *paper clip* the object), or words spelled incorrectly but resembling other words (*conversation* instead of *conservation*). Word processing programs can review word repetitions, phrase usage, sentence structure, and grammar mechanics but may flag nonexistent problems. Thus, despite all of the available software, human beings remain the best editors on the planet.

Writing requires a purpose, concepts and details, and a logical flow. Writing, like house painting, requires preparation. *Kidspiration* for elementary students or *Inspiration* for older students, both by Inspiration Software (www.inspiration.com or 800/ 877-4292) help tame an ideation cascade into an ordered sequence of thoughts. A student enters keywords and phrases, links related concepts, and the software generates an outline or work plan for writing. A simple example appears in Appendix 10; more complex demonstrations are on the website. (Additional suggestions to help your child with writing are presented in Chapters 18 and 24.)

Speech recognition software enables *voice writing*, in which a person produces text by speaking into a computerized device. Students can speak their thoughts into a microphone connected to a computer with voice-to-text software, edit the text, and then listen to the playback using text-to-voice software. For tasks such as short messages or verbatim court-reporting, this system can work well. Longer pieces of original writing take forethought and rounds of editing. Some people with visual-dysphonetic reading disorders could consider using this type of software. The main drawback, however, is that accuracy of translating speech into text lies in the 90–95% range, even if the software is acoustically customized or trained to the user's speaking habits.[7] Other drawbacks include:[8]

- No automatic punctuation of sentences
- Difficulty with accents
- Trouble with the high-pitched voices of women and children.

Accuracy in speech-recognition software is still evolving. A program's vocabulary size, accuracy of homophone selection, and capacity

---

7   Michael J. Martinez, "Speak Easy," *Kiplinger's*, October 2002, p. 120.
8   Faith Keenan, "PCs and Speech: A Rocky Marriage," *Business Week,* 9 September 2002, p. 64.

to disregard extraneous sounds are critical features. If your child uses this type of software, you should monitor its performance because the printed form of the spoken word can differ markedly from what was intended. The following list of erroneous computer transcriptions[9] can seemingly echo the writing of many students with auditory processing difficulties:

__Words Spoken__	__Computer Transcription__
number of variations	number of very Asians
there was no	therewith snow
more along the lines	Maura Long the lines
Motorola	motor roll a
modem port	mode import
breakable	break a bull
a procedure	upper seizure
and then stick it in the mail	and dense thicket in the mail
movie clips	move eclipse
I might add	I my dad
a paramedic	up aromatic
minority	my nor it he
a nameless feeling	an aimless feeling
inscrutable	in screw double
oxymoron	ax a moron

While the list is amusing, it underscores the need for parental oversight of student assignments.

Although many voice-to-text products exist, two seem to lead the pack: IBM's *ViaVoice* (www-3.ibm.com/software/speech) and ScanSoft's *Dragon Naturally Speaking* (www.scansoft.com). *Kiplinger's* compared the two products in its October 2002 issue. "Let's Talk," by Janet Rae-Dupree (*U.S. News & World Report*, 12 May 2003), presents some tips for proficient computer dictation. Look for product reviews and demonstrations in order to evaluate practicality and ease of use.

---

9   David Pogue, "Listen Up," *Macworld*, June 2000, p. 70. Excerpt adapted with permission from *Macworld*.

Chapter Twenty-Three

How much homework should I expect my child to do and who should help my child with it?

By the third grade, Max was pulled out of class to work with a private reading specialist who visited the school at an extra cost. She was a speech therapist and my son seemed to be making progress with her. She was replaced in the fourth grade by someone much less knowledge-able and unable to refund or reschedule sessions that we had to miss due to an out-of-town family wedding. Meanwhile, the regular teacher went out on maternity leave. Although she had mentioned something about referring him for testing at the parent-teacher conference, testing was forgotten during her absence.

I spent a good deal of the evenings tutoring Max so that he could get through exams. I found that by drawing diagrams, he understood many concepts. I was elated when my son understood time as a series of events, thus making history a possible undertaking. I helped him figure out important ideas in his assigned reading. He began working with a private educational therapist after school on gross and fine motor skills. He wrote very slowly, and had odd methods of forming cursive letters. His switch-hitting ability in baseball turned out to be an unde-veloped right-hand dominance; most children have a preference for their right or left hand by age six. His phonological processing ability improved immensely with a month-long auditory perceptual training program recommended by the educational therapist.

In middle school, Max was tutored weekly by one of his former teachers. She was able to obtain prospective test information from his other instructors in order to teach him to each test. The tutor understood his capacity to absorb material and developed study guides. She alerted me to troublesome academic areas and other obstacles hindering his development. I still tutored him the rest of the week, and experimented with strategies to increase his awareness of what he needed to do in order to learn better. By the eighth grade, I held Max responsible for knowing factoids; I would then help him generalize them into the broader themes presented in his textbook. We worked on assignments until nearly bedtime. His special education class worked on conceptual development.

Some years were harder than others, depending on the teacher's attitude or style of teaching. Looking back, I realize that the long hours of homework and level of assignments given were way too much to expect for even a normal child, and did not contribute to his high school performance. In fact, he learned more as a high school freshman with less homework. Some math methods taught in the middle-school classroom as ways to solve problems confused more than helped; in high school these ways had to be unlearned in order for real progress to be made.

Homework: How much is enough?

The recommended length of homework assignments varies by grade and by each school. Some schools have no homework, and others initiate homework as early as kindergarten. Some teachers let students begin homework in class and are thus available to guide them if help is needed.

Note whether your child is spending inordinate amounts of time on homework. Children should have time to do chores, attend to other responsibilities, and relax. Homework should not become nightly battles of frustration destroying family relationships. But today, parental unhappiness with long nights of homework is an open secret, and has appeared even in *The Wall Street Journal*, for example, "'The Dog Ate Her Paper': How Parents Help Get Their Kids Out of Homework," by Sue Shellenbarger (12 September 2002, page D1) or "Schools Face Up to Reality: Mom is Doing the Homework," by Anne Marie Chaker (29 October 2002, page D1). One rule of thumb for daily homework is 10 minutes multiplied by the grade level such as 20 minutes of homework for a second grader. Harris Cooper, Professor and Chair of the Department of Psychology at the University of Missouri, has extensively studied the effects of homework and recommends moderation and flexibility:[1]

---

1   Harris Cooper, "Homework for All—In Moderation" [Internet], 2001, pp. 3-8, available from: http://www.bryan.k12.oh.us/teachresource/hmwrkmoder.doc; and Westchester Institute for Human Services Research, "The Balanced View: Homework" [Internet], June 2002, pp. 3-4, available from: http://www.sharing success.org/code/bv/homework.pdf

ELEMENTARY SCHOOL
*   Homework may only minimally affect the achievement of normal elementary school students, unlike homework-like assignments completed in class which do improve performance.
*   Homework can show parents the material being taught in class.
*   Homework should result in successful experiences and not be used as punishment.
*   Homework can demonstrate that learning occurs outside the classroom but should not crowd out the learning that happens in other after-school activities.
*   1st through 3rd Grades: 1–3 assignments per week, each assignment requiring up to 15-minutes to complete.
*   4th through 6th Grades: 2–4 assignments per week, each assignment lasting 15–45 minutes.

JUNIOR HIGH SCHOOL
*   Homework somewhat improves performance until assignments exceed 1–2 hours.
*   7th through 9th Grades: 3–5 assignments per week, each assignment totaling 45–75 minutes.

HIGH SCHOOL
*   Homework substantially improves performance with no point of diminishing returns observed.
*   10th through 12th Grades: 4–5 assignments per week, each assignment being 75–120 minutes in duration.

All children need a routine and a quiet, well-lit, organized work space. This does not necessarily mean desk space as some fidgety students work better lying on their bellies with little gizmos to keep fingers occupied. Keep work materials neatly available. Some parents purchase a second set of books for the student to highlight and write notes in. Another solution is to use paper stickies for notes that can be fastened to the relevant page. Children with learning disabilities (and children who are disorganized in general) often have a hard time keeping track of homework assignments; even if they do them, they may forget to turn them in. Teachers sometimes make it easier by posting assignments and due dates on the school website. Absent this, parents should express their concerns to teacher(s) about their child's assignments. Some other guidelines will promote homework success:[2]
*   Assignments should not be busywork but essential for learning.
*   Homework objectives should be clear, such as greater proficiency of a specific skill.
*   A reasonable amount should be assigned.

---

2   Mercer, *Students with Learning Disabilities*, pp. 228-229.

- Homework difficulty should be appropriately matched to the student's abilities.
- The student should understand the assignment.
- Homework should have high success rates, 70% or above.
- Homework should not be used to teach complex skills.
- Parents should foster conditions encouraging homework. (Parents with night-shift employment demands may enlist the help of an after-school program.)
- Teachers should discuss or review homework.

More research information on homework can be found in the references cited in the first footnote of this Chapter and at "Homework Guidelines," by Tuscarora School District, available at www.tus.k12.pa.us/central/homework%20guidelines.htm, which compares research on homework in different developed countries.

If you find that your child is often struggling for three hours on an assignment that should have taken 30 minutes, discuss the situation with the teacher. Working harder is not necessarily learning. A learning disability can easily compound homework overload into a burnout situation. Homework assignments can be modified. Some accommodations that you can request include:

- Regular teacher assistance during office hours
- Shorter assignments
- More time to complete assignments
- Receiving assignments before the rest of the class or obtaining the entire week's homework at the beginning of the week
- Establishing a homework confirmation procedure: The teacher acknowledges correct homework instructions by signing off on the student's daily assignment notebook. The parent countersigns when the homework is completed noting any difficulties (see Chapter 19)
- Establishing a work plan for long-term assignments, with action steps and completion dates.

Additional measures for parents or teachers to ease learning and homework are available at www.ldonline.org. Enter "strategy" or "strategies" into the *SEARCH LD ONLINE* box.

Tutoring arrangements

Home tutoring. Before taking on home tutoring, make sure you are the best tutor for your child, and don't feel bad if you conclude you are not. Some professionals recommend that parents of children with learning disabilities not help their children because of the frustrations that inevitably occur. Not every parent is a natural tutor. Unfamiliarity with the subject material, a parent's lack of confidence, personality traits (impatience for example), child resistance or simply an emotionally charged parent-child relationship can cause home tutoring to backfire. Still, it is your choice whether to help your child with homework.

Research studies are mixed on the effectiveness of home tutoring. The best results occurred when the child's teacher was involved and the parent received some training.[3] Several guidelines to help you:[4]

- Give simple precise instructions.
- Adjust the length of a tutoring session according to the student's ability to concentrate.
- Log observations and inform the teacher of homework difficulties.
- Take breaks.
- Establish a good time and place to work with your child.
- Challenge but do not overwhelm the student; tutoring should be positive and success-oriented.
- For up to the sixth grade, limit sessions to 15 minutes; for older students, limit sessions to 30 minutes.
- Make the work interesting. Give encouragement and praise effort.

As the academic demands increase past elementary school, consider delegating specific tutoring duties to the most capable adult in terms of background knowledge, ability to tutor the subject, and time available. For example, a father who majored in journalism tutored his son in reading, writing, and vocabulary. Meanwhile, the mother who is more knowledgeable in math, science, and social studies, tackled those subjects.

Some books provide methods to address certain problems. A reissued publication, *This Book Doesn't Make Sense*, by Jean Augur, discusses visual perceptual problems in reading and offers tips on identifying and remediating these types of problems. A good source of ideas for tutoring elementary-level math is *Mathematics for Dyslexics: A Teaching Handbook*, by Stephen Chinn and J. Richard Ashcroft. Parent information centers and www.ldonline.org (type in "tutor" in the white box then click on the button *SEARCH LD ONLINE*) also will have many specific suggestions. One forward-thinking publisher, CPM Educational Program, supplements its textbook lessons with extra practice problems that parents can download for free or purchase in booklet form. Additional tutoring materials are presented in Chapter 24.

Peer Tutoring. Students tutoring each other in either regular classes or special education settings can be effective; my son buddied up with a few classmates and together they obtained some of the highest grades in their algebra class. Light found that students were more engaged in the subject, better prepared, and learned significantly more if they independently did the homework before meeting in discussion

---

3   Mercer, p. 115.
4   Mercer, p. 116.

groups of four to six people, than if they worked by themselves.[5] Students with AD/HD may learn better from a peer group than from the teacher.[6] Students with specific learning disabilities, however, may require specialized professional help in certain areas.

Teacher Tutoring. During regular class time, a student usually needs only three to five minutes of individualized instruction for encouragement or to clarify directions or a concept.[7] A teacher may schedule individual time for a student to get extra help every day. Outside of class, teachers can provide extra help before, during lunchtime, or after school. (Many schools do not want students eating in classrooms, posing problems for those required to participate in before- and after-school practices or activities.)

Hiring your child's current teacher as your child's tutor would be an awkward situation for you, the teacher, the child, and the rest of the class. Later on when your son or daughter has graduated to another teacher, you may then wish to engage the former teacher as the tutor. Be aware that schools may not allow private tutoring arrangements to occur on their premises.

Professional Tutoring. Your child's IEP may specify tutoring, which can be given within the school. Tutoring expenses can also be paid through other programs such as Title I for low-income families. Absent school tutoring, private individuals and nonprofit and commercial organizations offer help. Schools, colleges of education, and parent information centers knowledgeable about LD should be able to provide you with appropriate candidates. (To be prudent you may wish to ask for references and do a background check of any stranger who will be working alone with your child.)

Regardless of your arrangements though, you should find a tutor with a successful track record in managing children with learning disabilities; tutoring is often more than getting help with academics. Many tutors are not necessarily experienced in managing a child with behavioral and motivational problems as well as various types of learning disabilities. For this reason, some parents have privately hired individuals known in the local community to have successfully worked with students with learning problems, such as a credentialed special educator, a psychologist licensed in psychoeducational testing, or someone certified in a nationally known method of instruction. This type of tutoring is quite expensive but can offer individuals of all ages compensating strategies to help them learn and work better.

At the elementary-school level, a child's teacher can provide some help before or after school. Alternatively, a child's former teacher will

---

5   Light, *Making the Most of College*, p. 52.
6   Barkley, "ADHD: Theory, Diagnosis, and Treatment," pp. 109-110.
7   Mercer, *Students with Learning Disabilities*, p. 224.

not only have a good understanding of how to work with your child in content areas but—in the absence of a special educator on campus—may also act as a central liaison between you and other teachers at the school. Teachers are sometimes willing to let a colleague know areas of emphasis and types of test questions. This is especially valuable if the tutoring is in a subject in which you do not feel knowledgeable or have communication difficulties with your child's current instructors.

At higher-grade levels, your child can set up sessions with teachers or visit the school's tutoring program open to all students. It took my son a while to identify which instructor in such a program was best suited at helping *him* understand a course better. This person may or may not be your child's instructor. If your child's grades improve, you will know that your child is finding effective help on his or her own.

Online tutoring for a fee is available through eSylvan (www.esylvan.com). Tutor.com (www.tutor.com) will charge fees after an initial trial subscription. A list of online math lessons, tutoring services, and quizzes and worksheets is found at Purplemath (www.purplemath.com). Solutions to frequently asked homework questions are available at HomeworkSpot (www.homeworkspot.com).

The business of education has become a growth industry today. Many companies are developing new products and services to enhance school performance. Some may be perfectly fine. Others may aggressively advertise and raise false hopes. In a bad scenario, a company may develop an initial in-house assessment, teach according to that assessment, then claim success based on an in-house follow-up exam, all the while the items taught are irrelevant to the child's school program; if the child fails, then more lessons are needed. It will be your job to scrutinize the pros and cons of whether any product or service will be able to truly help your child. Check in with your child's teacher to see if such tutoring has been effective, as evident in improved work, attitude, self-confidence, class participation, or homework well-done and timely. Make the best use of your time and money. *Caveat emptor.*

Tutoring reports. Be sure you talk to the tutor a few weeks into the process. One mother thought her 14 year-old daughter would relate better to young college-age tutors, but found out (through the tutors' written evaluations several months later) that her daughter was so intrigued by the tutor's blue hair and nose rings that she had trouble concentrating. The mom changed to a ("boring") adult tutor who worked for a university's special ed program with much better results.

A weekly report card, like the one illustrated in Figure 23.1, can be a tool to elicit cooperation from your child. The tutor can simply gauge the child's effort on a simple scale of 1–5 or 0–100 for example. (A cell can be divided for twice weekly sessions.) If the child obtains a score below 70, he or she can be grounded until the next session. For example, videogame privileges can be removed. If the score is above 100 for extraordinary effort, a small special treat can be arranged. The key to this report card is parental follow through on rewards and punishments, unless extenuating circumstances exist. If the next session is not scheduled until another month, the child must learn that he or she blew it big time: no videogames for a month. Ensure that the tutor understands the system so that grading will be appropriate and humane. Eventually, the tutoring sessions will focus less on behavior management and more on academics.

Figure 23.1

MONTH	AUG	SEP	OCT	NOV	DEC	JAN	FEB	MAR	APR	MAY	JUN	JUL
WEEK 1												
WEEK 2												
WEEK 3												
WEEK 4												
WEEK 5												
NOTES												

Professional tutoring and remediation programs

Reading. Some children learn to read without much instruction. In contrast, children with reading disorders need instruction that is explicit, intensive, thorough, and supportive.[8] Remediation promotes *overlearning* through considerable repetition and reinforcement to ensure that material is embedded into the student's memory. Remedial programs also have a sequential progression, emphasizing decoding skills (matching sounds to letter symbols, also known as phonics) before moving on to vocabulary, reading comprehension, and written expression. Some individuals, however, may not master word recognition skills and may never advance to reading comprehension. Often, reading difficulties persist despite all efforts.

---

8   Torgesen "Instructional Interventions for Children with Reading Disabilities," pp. 205-206.

If one approach seems ineffective, try another. For example, reading fluency may not increase through decoding, but through more intensive practice that distinguishes subtle sound differences (phonological awareness is explained in Chapter 3). Combinations of approaches might also be tried. One student's reading and writing improved with Fast ForWord in conjunction with intensive basic skills remediation. Cognitive reading models are presented in Chapter 18. Assistive technology is reviewed in Chapter 22.

Many reading studies are available today. However, you still need to review which measures would work best for your child. Not every child will thrive with a particular method. You will need to sift out relevant facts, consider material consequences, scrutinize the sources of various opinions, and compare other options. Determine whether your child's special education program is providing what your child needs. Be aware that many studies on reading instruction provide information on younger, not older children. As reviewed in Chapter 3, reading involves much more than the mechanical process of matching symbols and sounds. The goal of reading should be to understand the writer's intended meaning. The relationship between the instructor and the child is also important for learning to occur. You can find much information about reading instruction from Schwab Learning's *E-ssential Guide on Reading Basics*, available at www.schwablearning.org/pdfs/ EG_ReadingBasics.pdf.

Programs may or may not combine phonological awareness and reading remediation. Many options exist, from low-tech to high-tech. Low-tech methods can require years of individual instruction. High-tech methods (see Chapter 22) may seem more costly, but because they are much shorter in duration, may be less expensive overall. School districts have offered both of these types of services.

The most popular reading approach is the VAKT method. Research results are mixed and it's not clear what type of sensory instruction works best with certain types of students.[9] VAKT is an acronym for *visual, auditory, kinesthetic,* and *tactile* instruction. This *hear-it, say-it, see-it, write-it* method has many variations: Orton-Gillingham, Gillingham and Stillman, Slingerland, Alpha to Omega, Alphabetic Phonics, Hickey Multisensory Language Course, Recipe for Reading, Teaching Reading through Spelling, and Wilson Reading System. The Bangor Dyslexia Teaching System was designed for teachers and speech therapists to teach both young children and secondary students. Project Read and Letterland have been adapted for classroom use. The method common to all these programs introduces sounds as separate units, then blends them into syllables, then into words. Word

---

9   Bender, *Learning Disabilities*, p. 306.

attack skills move onto reading, spelling, dictionary, and handwriting skills. Two books, *Dyslexia* (1998) by Gavin Reid and *Dyslexia* (1996) by Carol Sullivan Spafford and George S. Grosser present more information about these instructional methods. A search engine can also locate information and reviews on most of these reading remediation programs. LD Online offers research findings on reading programs:

•   "A Scientific Approach to Reading Instruction," by Barbara Foorman, Jack Fletcher, and David Francis, 1997, www.ldonline.org/ld_indepth/reading/cars.html

•   "Report of the [2000] National Reading Panel: Teaching Children to Read," by Susan Hall, www.ldonline.org/ld_indepth/reading/teaching_children_to_read.html

•   "'Reading Disability' or 'Learning Disability': The Debate, Models of Dyslexia, and a Review of Research-validated Reading Programs," by Kathleen Ross-Kidder, 2003, www.ldonline.org/ld_indepth/reading/reading_approaches.html

The Academy of Orton-Gillingham Practitioners and Educators (www.ortonacademy.org or 845/ 373-8919) and Slingerland (www.slingerland.org or 425/ 453-1190) can provide local instructors in your area. *The Gillingham Manual: Remedial Training for Students with Specific Disability in Reading, Spelling, and Penmanship*, written by Anna Gillingham and Bessie W. Stillman, was reissued in 1997 by Educators Publishing Service (www.epsbooks.com or 800/ 435-7728). The book has detailed lesson plans, some of which require additional materials, which are also available from the publisher. Educators Publishing Service also offers Slingerland Teaching Materials. (At the web site, click on the arrow next to *choose a subject…*, scroll down the list and click on either *Learning Differences: Programs* or *LD: Materials and Assessments*.

Joseph Torgesen, a professor of psychology at Florida State University, created an experimental poor-reading prevention program for kindergartners with phonological awareness problems, who most likely would have otherwise gone on to perform at the bottom 10% of their class. After two and one-half years of over 80 hours of one-to-one instruction, two methods improved performance in comprehension skills (word attack and word identification) to near normal levels. The Lindamood-Bell (www.lindamoodbell.com or 800/ 233-1819) PASP VAKT method (mouth movements, hearing sensitizing, tactile representations of phoneme sequences) was better, but not significantly better, than a less-intensive phonics reading-writing program. Both methods were better than regular classroom reading instruction or no instruction at all.[10] Within the PASP VAKT group, 24% of the students

------

10   Torgesen, "Instructional Interventions for Children with Reading Disabilities," pp. 207-212.

did not improve significantly. Torgesen did not conduct his study using computer phonological perceptual training, however. Nevertheless, the study—along with others—demonstrated the promise of early intervention.

Direct Instruction is a published series of scripted instructional exercises beginning with preschool to improve decoding, reading comprehension, spelling, and arithmetic skills. Commercially available programs are *Reading Mastery* for grades 1–6 and *Corrective Reading Program* for students in grades 4–12 who are weak in decoding and comprehension skills. For example, the *Corrective Reading Program* provides teacher scripts for shaping thinking skills necessary for higher-level reading such as analogies, deductions, classification, similarities, and inferences. Highly trained teachers, not teacher aides nor parent volunteers, are to give this type of instruction. Although Direct Instruction has improved the reading comprehension of students with learning disabilities,[11] many students may be unable to keep pace even in a small group, and so will require individualized instruction. The senior author of this reading program is Siegfried Engelmann, a professor of special education at the University of Oregon at Eugene. Many websites carry information about Direct Instruction; you may wish to begin with www.uoregon.edu/~bgrossen/aftdi.htm and www.adihome.org/who-we-are.html.

Some reading remediation methods exist that do not include phonics instruction. In the neurological impress method, the student follows along while the teacher reads or an audiocassette plays: Words are seen and heard simultaneously. The Fernald method emphasizes sight-word and whole-word recognition.

Reading Recovery is an individualized reading and writing program designed for children who failed reading at the end of first grade. Specially trained teachers work 30 minutes a day with children over 12–20 weeks. Rather than progress through a highly structured series of skills, Reading Recovery instruction uses an approach in which new words are learned by sight and within a reading context, often referred to as *whole-word reading*. The effectiveness of this program has been questioned as reported in "Researchers Urge Officials to Reject Reading Recovery," by David Hoff at www.ldonline.org/ld_indepth/research_ digest/reading_recovery.html.

Getting help in many areas. Sylvan Learning Center (www. educate.com or 888/ 338-2283) offers online, individual, and group remediation; teachers are state-certified, screened, and trained. Your child will be formally assessed with Sylvan's own test battery even

---

11 Sara Tarver, "Direct Instruction," in *Controversial Issues Confronting Special Education: Divergent Perspectives*, ed. William Stainback and Susan Bray Stainback (Needham Heights, Massachusetts: Allyn and Bacon, 1992), p. 147.

though you may have a thick file of past evaluations on hand. The usual program is 50–100 hours of instruction, with two to four hours per week. The company guarantee of a one-grade improvement within 36 hours of instruction does not hold for children with learning disabilities. Sylvan offers reading instruction from word recognition through comprehension, analysis, and critical thinking. It also offers assistance in other areas such as math and test preparation. While one mother liked the group sessions for her son because the other group members helped each other develop a desire to read, she added that a lot depends on the teacher's ability to work with your child. Sylvan Learning Center is part of Sylvan Learning Systems, Inc., which operates a network of franchised instructional facilities in the U.S. and around the world.

Kumon (www.kumon.com or 800/ 222-6284) offers math and reading tutoring at well over a thousand franchised centers in North America. The program begins with an achievement assessment to determine the current level of proficiency. Individualized instruction occurs in two 30-minute sessions per week, with 15 minutes of homework expected on the other five days of the week. Instruction emphasizes success and self-confidence, with the philosophy that practice builds conceptual understanding. The child cannot progress to the next level of difficulty until mastery of skills is demonstrated at the current level. This program may be trying for students whose processing difficulties cannot be accommodated by the timed proficiency assessments.

An alternative to at-home computer-based learning is *Score!* (www.escore.com or 800/ 497-2673), which offers interactive computer instruction in reading and math and is offered at the preschool through tenth-grade levels. *Score!*'s one-hour classes are twice a week on a drop-in basis, seven days a week. Breaks are given as needed. Specially trained coaches monitor, assist, and encourage students. The first month of the program assesses the child's appropriate placement level. *Score!* and its software publisher, Computer Curriculum Corporation, are subsidiaries of Kaplan, famous for its college entrance exam preparation courses. Kaplan (www.kaplan.com) itself is a subsidiary of *The Washington Post*, which also publishes *Newsweek* magazine. (While there is nothing wrong with these corporate relationships, parents should be aware of who is operating the business when investigating the quality and appropriateness of a product or service for the child, especially any reviews of a product published by a related organization. At the time of this writing, consolidations of companies in the education, textbook, and testing businesses are occurring. Thus, some products and services will be shuttered, but the ones remaining will have better financial support.)

$$\overline{}$$

Chapter Twenty-Four

How can I help my child with assignments?

Max was not identified as requiring special education until almost the sixth grade. His academic outlook looked grim. My son could neither read nor write well, but was observant and could draw better than most adults. He received therapy and tutoring and participated in community activities. He did every extra credit project to boost his grades and absorbed information from TV documentaries, videos, and picture books. I helped him with his long homework assignments every night. We were relieved when he was accepted into a small college preparatory high school with a highly regarded learning disabilities program and a wide variety of sports.

In his freshman year, his performance was uneven but at least a B-average. During the next year after some intensive reading and writing practice at school, my son started getting his act together. He earned an A from a very demanding English teacher who assigned 80 vocabulary words and an essay each week. The earlier visual learning seemed to pay off at this time in a history class now that he was better able to write. His biology teacher recommended him for next year's chemistry class. His English and social studies teachers recommended him for honors and AP classes. His classmates don't believe that he has LD, but they don't know how hard he works. Doing this well was unimaginable only five years before.

General areas requiring assistance

Often, a child's difficulties are not just limited to a specific academic area. Trouble with any of the following skills affect school performance:

- Prioritizing and monitoring work (executive function)
- Applying facts and procedures to new contexts (memory)
- Reading and understanding inferences (input)
- Organizing and integrating information (abstraction)
- Oral and written expression (output).

You will need to experiment with materials and methods in order to identify how best to help your child. Levine's *Educational Care* suggests some approaches for many types of problems. Be wary of inappropriate instructional materials that can cause frustration, failure, and erroneous learning. Calculators, workbooks with answer keys, and educational software are some examples of self-correcting materials which provide immediate feedback. These same materials, however, are not open-ended creative activities but are designed to train thinking according to certain rules. Bear in mind as your child matures, that his or her strengths may not necessarily be developed within the confines of an elementary or secondary academic school curriculum.

When students with LD are explicitly instructed to use cognitive strategies, performance improves.[1] Eight guidelines for successful strategy instruction are:[2]

- Use different strategies for different purposes. Some strategies are better for remembering facts, some are better for learning procedures, and some are better for comprehending concepts.
- Teach a few strategies well rather than teach many superficially.
- Good strategies for normal students may not be effective for those with LD.
- Instruction must consider the student's knowledge base and processing abilities.
- Productivity can be enhanced by improving strategies, that is, working smarter.
- Don't expect strategy use to necessarily eliminate inherent processing difficulties.
- Don't assume that similar performances between students mean that similar strategies were used.
- Don't expect that comparable use of strategies between students will equalize performances if the individuals have different abilities.

Anticipating priorities and scheduling work

Help your child organize in advance as much as possible. Purge unnecessary papers from his backpack or binder; you will find corrected tests and assignments while doing this (and maybe assignments that have

---

1   H. Lee Swanson, "Learning Disabilities and Memory," in *A Cognitive Approach to Learning Disabilities*, 2nd Edition, ed. D. Kim Reid, Wayne P. Hresko, and H. Lee Swanson (Austin, Texas: PRO-ED, 1991), p. 170.
2   Swanson, pp. 171-176.

not been turned in). Have a few extra school supplies just in case your child forgets to tell you that graph paper, a composition book, or poster board is needed for school that morning. Keep extra pens, pencils, batteries, lunch money, etc. handy. Assemble clothes the night before. Color-code binders and book covers for each subject, for example, science is red and history is blue; you can use colored circle labels. (Clear packing tape ensures that these labels stick.) Figure 24.1 illustrates coded book covers: The number of circle labels corresponds to the class-period number; other labels identify the subject and the class location. Teachers can provide reading lists, lecture outlines, visual material, work plans, and study guides to direct what is important to learn. Use an organizer or planner to keep track of assignments.

Figure 24.1

Try to do the more demanding homework tasks first and the easy tasks last—like coloring maps—when mental energy wanes. Reduce resistance to transitions between activities with routines, so that getting tasks done won't involve a battle at each step along the way. Structure or pace the workflow to reward execution of the less desirable portions with the more enjoyable parts.

When your child gets older, independence will become an issue. The *me do it!* refrain you heard 10 years ago may now be recast as no notice given to you of upcoming quizzes, papers, or projects, *even if you inquire about it.* Your adolescent is setting himself or herself up for frustration if help is required for getting the work done. True independence has its responsibilities. Sometimes a bad grade is the only way to get the point across.

Learning information for later recall

Teaching to the teacher's test. There are many ways of determining what's important to learn and what school projects may be assigned. Talk to parents of students in the previous year's class. Work with your child's teacher on what topics will be covered. See if you can borrow a textbook to work from during the summer before class begins. Previewing material can ease processing and memory demands later in the school year, build a base for reinforcing the information when formal instruction occurs, and perhaps create some confidence since the student may be better able to follow class discussions of the material.

Constructing acronyms can strengthen memory, for example, *HOMES* cues the names of the five Great Lakes: Huron, Ontario, Michigan, Erie, and Superior. Often, learning course material may require a physical, not just mental, rehearsal of the information. One student memorized the quadratic equation by singing it to the tune of *Row, Row, Row Your Boat*. Recopying and reorganizing class notes can help a visual learner distinguish salient points from supporting facts and remember the lecture material better. Another student found that if she prepared written summaries—thereby rehearsing names, unique terms, significance of events, and so on—the night before history tests, she was better able to recall the specific names and terms in order to receive full credit on her essay exams. Drawing a picture can enhance understanding of relationships between parts of a system; one anatomy student sketched schematic diagrams as a way of learning the circulation system. Constructing historical time lines demand awareness of people and events. To learn vocabulary, a copy of a list of words and definitions can be cut apart then physically rejoined. Whenever possible, act out new vocabulary words. Once, to explain *mollify*, I jabbed my son unexpectedly with my elbow, then apologized, thus *mollifying* his irritation. The type of activity chosen may determine whether learning really occurs; Pasteur, for example, understood the physics of acoustics better by taking a singing class—which also gave him more self-confidence and improved his diction and voice projection.[3] Be creative. Above all, try to foster a love of learning.

In the upper grades, students are expected to understand abstract concepts. Work on study skills. Identify what your child doesn't know; too often, you will not discover your child's deficits of understanding until after the test. Such is the world of academics but the game is far from over, for life is full of *late bloomers*. Review homework problems

---

3   Debré, *Louis Pasteur*, pp. 23-24.

and tests with your child. Help your child integrate all the reading material and class notes into an organized summary. If necessary, make flashcards or audiotapes of material that needs more rehearsal. When studying textbook material, develop some test questions. Work at a steady pace, don't try to learn everything all at once. Take breaks with physical activity. Improve task performance by getting a good night's sleep, as it appears to enhance memory.[4]

If a student is having trouble in a particular course, it may be worthwhile to go back to the beginning of the course and review material. Sometimes key concepts may have been missed, previous lessons may require a bit more practice, or an alternative learning strategy may exist. A workbook matching your child's course of study can quickly identify the gaps in your child's learning. Demand of your child, as much as possible, to spend time with a teacher before, during or after school for some tutoring; done often enough these visits can evolve into a matter of routine. One retired high school teacher with decades of experience found that the students who needed the most help were those least likely to seek it.

Bear in mind that any pressure you exert on your child to visit a teacher has several caveats. Teacher office hours may conflict with an after-school activity from which your child draws much self-esteem. Your child may not consistently visit the teacher during office hours. An accommodation might be necessary because the learning problem may significantly limit progress, as seen in the profile of the student with dyscalculia. The teacher must be able to address your child's needs in a suitable positive manner; sometimes another instructor may be more helpful than your child's actual teacher. A bullied child may need more immediate help with safety issues than schoolwork. Until your child learns what needs to be done in order to do well and can follow through on execution, you may find yourself working through each of these issues to ensure that your child receives real help. It took a while, but now my son thinks nothing of making the time to see any teacher whenever he needs assistance.

Workbooks: Pencil work practice. Workbooks provide extra practice, but don't often match exactly what is taught in class. Your child's teacher may have recommendations. Absent this, you can purchase generic workbooks. They range from booklets containing sample problems, to brief course reviews with problem sets, to full instructional manuals. Find something that realistically works with the time constraints of both you and your child. Many local retailers offer the workbooks suggested here, but not all vendors may be listed in a publisher's Internet *store locator* search feature. (For example, a school

---

4   Bruce Bower citing Stickgold and Gais studies, "Certain Memories May Rest on a Good Sleep," *Science News*, 2 December 2000, p. 358.

supply store frequented by teachers will probably be listed, but maybe not the family-owned business in an ethnic neighborhood.) These workbooks have book identification codes, or ISBNs, and can also be ordered through many booksellers. Many publishers also have customer service representatives that can provide product information not available on their websites.

• *Homework Booklet* mathematics series is supplementary math practice for grades 1–8, prealgebra, algebra, geometry, precalculus, and trigonometry. Published by McGraw-Hill, each $3 booklet has examples, problems, and solutions. The series can be viewed at McGraw-Hill's website, www.mhkids.com/cgi-bin/searchcat.cgi and enter into the *Search by keyword(s)* box at the bottom of the website:

> "Homework Booklets: Mathematics" · for grades 1 through 8
> "Homework Booklets: Pre-Algebra" · · for prealgebra
> "Homework Booklets: Algebra" · · · · for beginning algebra and
>   algebra II
> "Homework Booklets: Geometry" · · · for beginning geometry
> "Homework Booklets: Precalculus" · · for precalculus and trigonometry.

McGraw-Hill also offers workbooks on the U.S. Constitution useful for previewing or reinforcing this middle-school social studies requirement. These books can be viewed by entering "constitution" into the *Search by keyword(s)* box at www.mhkids.com/cgi-bin/searchcat.cgi. You can order a catalog of McGraw-Hill product offerings, including the Spectrum series (discussed next) from the website, at www.mhkids.com or by calling 800/ 417-3261.

• The *Spectrum* series, published by McGraw-Hill, provides enrichment for the following areas and grade levels:

Preschool letters, math readiness, and basic concepts	Spelling 1–8 Writing K–6
Phonics K–6	Language Arts K–6
Reading K–6	Vocabulary 3–6
Math K–8	Geography 3–6

The *Spectrum* product line also includes flashcards. One mother rewards her son with a videogame cartridge each time he completes a workbook. To view these workbooks, go to www.mhkids.com/cgi-bin/searchcat.cgi, and type in "spectrum" in the *Search for keyword(s)* box.

• Zaner-Bloser Educational Publishers (www.zaner-bloser.com or 800/ 421-3018), a unit of the publisher Highlights for Children, offers elementary school workbooks in reading, handwriting, writing, and spelling. The study skills series, for students in grades 6–8, practices many strategies for better learning. A comparison of handwriting curricula is found at www.zanerbloser.com.

- *CliffsQuickReview* covers the essential topics of various high school or college courses, and adds some sample questions. These workbooks and other Cliffs Notes products can be found on the website, www.cliffsnotes.com or bookstores.
- *Schaum's Outlines* are fairly comprehensive workbooks for high school students and up in many subjects. These workbooks are published by McGraw-Hill, and are available at many retailers or at http://books.mcgraw-hill.com/cgi-bin/pbg/schaums-home.html. The customer service phone number is 800/ 262-4729. The website also offers shortened versions of these workbooks, user-friendly math and science instruction manuals, and parent guides to help children in social studies.

Computer resources: Games of knowledge. For parents willing to work with their children using educational computer software, choices abound in stores and in the many catalogs. Math facts and spelling seem to be good candidates for a drill-and-practice method disguised as an arcade game. Some computer simulation games, such as *Oregon Trail 5*, provide a taste of times long gone. The key element, then, in software selection is the identification of the skill to be learned. Some programs will require more parental involvement than others, from using the program to monitoring perseverance under conditions of repetition and increasing skill difficulty.

Excellent software should be easy to use and set up, meet its educational goals, retain the child's interest, and have multiple levels of play. My personal favorites are Riverdeep's *Thinkin' Things*, Broderbund's *Logical Zoombinis*, Sanctuary Woods' *NFL and Major League Math* (difficult to find today), Sierra's Hoyle card and board games, and Microprose's *Civilization*. Many software programs teach keyboarding skills. Beware of purchasing *shovel ware*, which is software containing piles of indifferent material on CD-ROMs. Two free catalogs with a great variety of K–12 educational titles are:

Educational Resources	Learning Services
Phone: 800/ 860-7004	Phone: 800/ 877-9378 (West)
Website: www.edresources.com	800/ 877-3278 (East)
	Website: www.learnserv.com

Children's Software & New Media Revue or *CSR* (800/ 993-9499 or www.childrenssoftware.com) publishes every other month comprehensive and current reviews and articles for parents and teachers on selecting titles and managing their use. Experienced educators, with testing information from children, families, and schools, write reviews of specific software titles and electronic gizmos, comprehensive articles on technology topics relevant to students, and updates to an ongoing list of highly-regarded titles on the market for preschool through high school. Although *CSR* does not usually make specific recommendations for students with LD because each child has different needs and preferences, its March/April 2002 issue discusses mainstream software that might be helpful towards solving learning problems in areas such as math, reading, writing, and organizing. A subscription comes with a password for online access to past articles and review summaries.

LeapFrog Enterprises (www.leapfrog.com or 800/ 701-5327) offers educational interactive books and toys. Their Phonics Learning System™ was developed with a Stanford emeritus professor of education. LeapPad™ is a phonemic awareness platform on which specially prepared book titles can be mounted. *Children's Software & New Media Revue* has examined many of the company's products such as My First LeapPad, LeapPad Pro, Explorer II and Odyssey Globes, Turbo Twist Spelling, Turbo Twist Vocabulator, Turbo Twist Math, and Turbo Twist BRAIN QUEST. Contact *CSR* for their detailed reviews.

The Internet is the ultimate research tool. Investigate your public library as well as its access to subscription resources. "Writing Tools," by Leah McGrath Goodman (*The Wall Street Journal*, 16 June 2003, p. R11), reviews four such services: MSN Learning and Research, Britannica.com, eLibrary.com, and Questia.com. Some other websites:

• Motivated or curious students can find activities on HomeworkSpot (www.homeworkspot.com), Yahooligans! (www.yahooligans.com), DiscoverySchool.com (http://school.discovery.com) and the Family Education Network (www.learning network.com or http://fen.com).

• The Library of Congress offers America's Story (www.americas library.com), a social studies website for children.

• *The New York Times* supports the Learning Network, an online newspaper for middle-school students and up (www.nytimes.com/ learning).

• Interactive activities and ideas for science and technology experiments are available at the Exploratorium (www.exploratorium.edu), HowStuffWorks (www.howstuffworks.com), and North Carolina State University's The Science House (www.science-house.org).

• San Francisco Symphony's website, www.sfskids.org, offers musical activities for grade-school experimentation.

Just the facts: Minimized reading. Illustrated summaries distill the verbiage down to the essentials. BarCharts (www.barcharts.com or 800/ 226-7799) offers laminated two- to six-page QuickStudy summaries in over 200 subject areas, prepared by college professors. Permacharts (www.cram.com or 800/ 387-3626) also carries laminated page summaries in over 300 titles and in different format sizes.

SparkNotes (www.sparknotes.com or www.sparknotes.com/ guides) provides free online study guides popular with many high school students. The study guides cover a myriad of subjects from ancient Greek history to the theory of relativity, and are written by academically successful university graduates. Begun by Harvard students in 1999, SparkNotes was purchased by Barnes & Noble (www.barnes andnoble.com or www.bn.com).

CheatBooks.com (www.cheatbooks.com), in association with Amazon.com (www.amazon.com) offers study guides published by *Cliffs Notes*, *Barron's Book Notes*, *Bloom's Notes*, *MAX Notes*, and *Bloom's Review*. These book overviews, organized at the website by the title of the book being studied, are roadmaps for students totally lost in a long literature assignment. Tying these summaries with supporting details from the story helps the student integrate the material better.

Have on hand good reference materials to fill in gaps of information that inevitably occur during homework assignments, such as a CD-ROM encyclopedia, thesaurus, and dictionary. Other helpful books are the *Scholastic Rhyming Dictionary*, by Sue Young and *Scholastic Dictionary of Idioms*, by Marvin Terban. *The Encyclopedia of World History*, edited by Peter Stearns (Houghton Mifflin), is much pricier, but has maps, genealogies, and brief summaries of events.

Increasing knowledge with alternatives to books. Having a strong knowledge base will make school learning easier. Keep your child learning despite reading difficulties. Though it is a limitation, there is nothing morally wrong if someone really cannot manage long reading comprehension passages. It is just a fact of life. Wrote Accardo, "Reading is merely a technology, a technique to store and transfer information. It is one technology among others, and now an eminently replaceable one."[5] Many alternatives to reading exist.

Illustrated books: A picture is worth a thousand words. Libraries and bookstores offer a wide variety of well illustrated books that are as informational as they are beautiful. DK Publishing produces illustrated *Eyewitness Travel Guides* of various geographical locations, as well as other illustrated children's books. For example, the *Travel Guides* contains maps, chronologies, photographs, architectural cross-sections, and important historical facts. Borders Press in association with HarperCollins publishes *Atlas of World History* replete with chronologies and maps showing the cultural, economic, and political trends shaping major events. Larry Gonick has authored or co-authored many illustrated books on technical subjects as well as *The Cartoon History of the Universe* and *The Cartoon History of the United States*. David Macaulay has illustrated many technical subjects, many of them animated and carried on PBS. *Usborne Essential Guides* (www. usborneworld.com) contains key facts for basic biology, chemistry and physics courses. (At this Usborne web page, click on *Science* listed under the *Books by Categories* heading. At the next screen under the

---

5   Pasquale Accardo, "Reading Dyslexia," in *Specific Reading Disability: A View of the Spectrum*, ed. Bruce K. Shapiro, Pasquale J. Accardo, and Arnold J. Capute (Timonium, Maryland: York Press, 1998), p. 259.

Secondary heading, click on *Essential Guides*.) One student, with a parent, previewed the conceptual material for a high school chemistry class by reading two to four pages a day of Usborne's amply illustrated *Essential Chemistry* during the summer before school. He later completed the course successfully, and thought the drawings helped his understanding.

Many periodicals also have informational illustrations. *National Geographic* (www.nationalgeographic.com 800/ 647-5463 or TDD 800/ 548-9797) is well-known for excellent productions and publications. *Kids Discover* www.kidsdiscover.com or 212/ 677-4457 is an award-winning 20-page monthly magazine for elementary school children on various topics like *20th Century*, *Microbes*, *George Washington*, or *Australia*; a collection of their titles makes a nice illustrated reference library for many assignments. *Highlights for Children* (www. highlights.com or 800/ 603-0349) has expanded its product line beyond the puzzles, creative activities, and early reading experiences of its familiar flagship magazine.

Films and videos. DVDs, videos, movie rentals, and prerecorded television broadcasts of high quality programs can provide pictures that thousands of words can't describe nearly as well. At the very least, good visual materials can add general background knowledge, which may help with a school assignment. *The Civil War* TV documentary by Ken Burns is a good example. While I don't think my son understood everything, and watching it in one-hour segments over the December holidays was a small discipline, the effort paid off. My son loved being knowledgeable in his eighth-grade class about the details of this time period. Videos can teach the lessons of history, explore unfamiliar environments, and demonstrate principles of science and technology. Videos can also make literature better understood with period costumes and sets, and skillful actors to dramatize abstract concepts such as irony, diplomacy, and duplicity.

As when reading a book, watching a home video with your child provides opportunities to ask about character behavior and how the story will end. Critical thinking can be enhanced by pointing out implausible portions of the show. Bear in mind that some confusion can arise from differences between the screen interpretation of a particular novel and the literary work itself, or the historical details in a movie and what is being taught in class. Older titles can be found in public libraries, in independent video stores, or through video search services.

Shakespeare, now 400 years old, is almost foreign to the average adolescent both in terms of language and culture. Plays, in particular, are meant to be performed by actors who have studied the script and understand its background. In this age of easily accessible videos, I am mystified why students are still required to learn Shakespeare through script-reading alone. (To me, a better appreciation would come from watching a traditional performance of the play while studying the script, then viewing not only the play again, but also comparing it to another production's interpretation of the same play and then another production's interpretation of the same plot—such as *Romeo and Juliet* versus *West Side Story*, or *King Lear* versus Akira Kurosawa's movie *Ran*.) While I am no Shakespeare scholar, some videos can make the plays more accessible to today's audiences:

- Franco Zeffirelli's production of *Romeo and Juliet*
- *The Taming of the Shrew* with Elizabeth Taylor and Richard Burton
- *Twelfth Night* with Helena Bonham Carter
- *Richard III* with Ian McKellen
- *King Lear* with Laurence Olivier
- Kenneth Branagh's *Hamlet*, *Henry V*, or *Much Ado About Nothing*.

Knowing that my son would eventually run into a study of Shakespeare, I had been exposing him over the years to videos as well as free performances in local parks and a Renaissance Faire. At least, until his sophomore year, he had a positive reaction to Shakespeare; he especially liked watching Kenneth Branagh's *Henry V*. Due to time constraints, however, his English instructor did not have time to show in class *The Merchant of Venice* (itself a controversial work) as planned. Had I known that this would happen, I would have shown the play to my son at home before the exam. (Talk to your child's teacher as he or she may have preferences on video interpretations. Absent any recommendations, peruse online reviews. For example, productions may be lavish or bare-bones, full-length or truncated, with brilliant actors or miscast celebrities.) The lesson here is to let the teacher know how important it is to see a video of the play being studied and somehow work it out accordingly, or a poor mark in the Shakespeare portion of the course can sharply diminish any further interest in one of the world's greatest writers.

Hands-on learning. With the demise of home economics, wood shop, and auto mechanics from high school programs, many opportunities to improve hand-eye coordination, planning, organization, and math through physical measurement were lost. Possible alternatives today are activities such as stage crew, in which carpentry and costuming skills are needed. Cooking is not only a basic survival skill but also can bring understanding of weights, measures, and time.

Make learning fun when possible. Dividing (soft) cookies can help with fractions. Field trips can make narrative descriptions come alive. Songs like *Ten Green Bottles* or the matching game *Memory* reinforce memory skills. Lego building kits require the child to translate nonverbal two-dimensional directions into three-dimensional constructions.

Bingo practices visual perception skills. Mazes and picture puzzles help visual memory. Card games, *Set*, *Uno*, and dominoes can strengthen addition and classification skills. Puzzles and board games challenge spatial skills—for example, *Chutes and Ladders* involves location, sequence, and progression—and sometimes have a critical-thinking element like *The a Maze ing Labyrinth*. Chinese checkers and battleship are strategy games. Rhyming and pig-Latin games work on language skills. (*Scrabble* may not be fun for children with poor spelling and vocabulary skills.) Throwing, catching, skipping, and jumping games work on gross motor skills. In general, much learning occurs through play, often denied to children socially neglected or rejected by other children. Educational therapists use many of these *play* activities in their work with children.

Museums and zoos offer hands-on activities. The Cornell Lab of Ornithology (http://birds.cornell.edu) seeks individuals to send them information about local bird populations. Some other sources of general educational materials can be found at museum shops and college bookstores. Parents' Choice (www.parents-choice.org or 410/ 308-3858) recommends high-quality products for children. Check out hobby shops and art supply and craft stores. Other retailers you might peruse are:
• The Discovery Channel Stores: 800/ 627-9399 or www.discovery store.com
• Edmund Scientific: 800/ 728-6999 or www.scientificsonline.com
• Exploratorium Museum: 415/ 397-5673 or www.exploratorium store.com
• Lego Shop At Home: www.lego.com
• MindWare: 800/ 999-0398 or www.mindwareonline.com
• Orion Telescope & Binoculars: 800/ 447-1001 or www.telescope.com
• Scientific Explorer: www.scientificexplorer.com
• Wild Goose: 888/ 621-1040 or www.wildgoosescience.com.

Understanding math. Math instruction progresses from concrete experiences to generalized concepts. Counters (a great number of any small items), coins, and tape measures are convenient materials. A specialty item is Cuisenaire rods, which are of different lengths and colors, each rod representing a certain number; for example, a *two* rod and a *three* rod placed end-to-end would be as long as a *five* rod. Flash cards, some math computer software programs, using an analog clock, and experiences with kitchen recipes can supplement classroom learning. (It would also help many students if the metric system were universally adopted in the U.S. for linear and volume measurement.)

Although students with LD commonly receive math instruction in the regular classroom, teachers may not necessarily employ methods to overcome your child's difficulties. Some suggestions are presented in Chapter 3. Practice workbooks are mentioned earlier in this Chapter. Additional approaches can be found in these articles:

• "Adapting Mathematics Instruction in the General Education Classroom for Students with Mathematics Disabilities," by Robin Lock, available at www.ldonline.org/ld_indepth/math_skills/adapt_cld.html
• "Developing Fluency with Basic Number Facts: Intervention for Students with Learning Disabilities," by Katherine Garnett, available at www.ldonline.org/ld_indepth/math_skills/garnett_ldrp.html
• "Mathematics Instruction for Secondary Students with Learning Disabilities" by Eric Jones, Rich Wilson, and Shalini Bhojwani, available at www.ldonline.org/ld_indepth/math_skills/math_jld.html
• *Mathematics for Dyslexics: A Teaching Handbook*, by Stephen Quinn and J. Richard Ashcroft (Whurr Publishers, 1993)
• "Videos Show Best Math Teaching Practices from Other Countries," by Cara Branigan, available at www.eschoolnews.com/news/Alert unreg.cfm?ArticleID=4316&ul=%2Fnews%FshowStory%2Ecfm%3F ArticleID%3D4316.

Many difficulties in math may result from language comprehension problems. Word problems can be especially troublesome, especially if the child must work through a multi-step solution process involving the simultaneous retention of different numerical amounts. Explaining a math word problem in pictures can improve understanding, and is a skill the student should develop. Sometimes the best short-term school solution to alleviate utter frustration is to request that the child not be graded on word problems. When language skills improve, word problems can be revisited.

• *Prealgebra: Getting comfortable with alphanumeric symbols.* Algebra begins the study of higher math, required for solving problems in science and technology. In algebra, the use of letters to conceptualize arithmetic quantities is unsettling for many students. You should anticipate this shift of math instruction from numerical certainty to universal algorithms. "Low X-pectations: Here's Y the Teaching of Algebra in the U.S. Has Been Such a Flop," by June Kronholz (*The Wall Street Journal*, 16 June 1998, page A1) examines many of the reasons why U.S. students *in general* have trouble making this shift—attitudes toward math, textbook content, instructional methods, teacher preparation, and parents' inability to tutor their children in higher math. These problems have various solutions. For example, if algebra becomes an eighth-grade instead of a ninth-grade curriculum requirement, then the elementary-school teaching credential may be an insufficient professional prerequisite as compared to the secondary-school credential.

For students with language difficulties, algebra becomes a critical course if only because it unlocks a wide range of career possibilities. It may be tough to excite your student over the study of numbers after years of mind-numbing calculations. Higher math, however, may offer your child a second chance and may even be easier than arithmetic for some students because procedures take precedence over math facts. For example, an uncle taught a young Albert Einstein that algebra was a hunt for an unknown x, and, when the prey was caught, it was given the appropriate name.[6] Understanding the language of math can lead to creative discoveries such as Einstein's elegant equation that a certain amount of energy equals a certain amount of matter.

You need not wait until middle school to get your child comfortable with mathematical abstractions; indeed, Stanford's EPGY math program infiltrates its elementary math instruction with simple prealgebra problems. When my children were young, I prepared them by having them add apples: 2 apples + 2 apples = 4 apples. From here, the lesson became 2 a + 2 a = 4 a, or in writing "$2a + 2a = 4a$". (Other letters should be used as well: bananas can be used with b, cars can be used with c, and so on.) From here, the next lesson could explain *substitution*. To illustrate: given $4a = ?$, if $a = 3$, then 4 times 3 = 12; if a = 4, then 4 times 4 = 16. On paper, these substitutions would be written as "4(3) = 12" or "4(4) = 16." Subtraction and division—using easy-to-remember numbers as the emphasis should not be on math facts—can proceed in similar ways.

• *Simplifying algebra: Multiplying polynomials.* With so much to remember I prefer methods that work in every situation. Some tasks are unnecessarily complex, frustrating, and discouraging. For example, long ago, disposable diapers were sold in pink or blue designs and by the child's weight; stockouts routinely occurred in boy toddler sizes but not in the girl sizes because girls typically toilet-train earlier than boys. Similarly, algebraic multiplication problems require students to first identify the problem type being posed—e.g., squaring or a difference of squares—before applying the appropriate algorithm to solve that problem. To avoid this need for problem identification, my ninth-grade algebra teacher taught his students a generic trick. My children now employ this strategy—which they call the *box method*—for all situations involving multiplication of polynomials. One high school student found it easy to use because *middle terms* are clearly visualized, as opposed to the traditional FOIL method, which relies on memory. His mother, a teacher, wishes she had known about this method as a student herself for it would have given her the confidence to pursue math or science studies in high school.

To multiply $(2a^2 + 3b - 5)(4a - 3)$, a student could quickly draw a table three cells across by two cells down, write the multipliers across the top and down the left side, perform the multiplication, and finally line up the terms:

---

6   Clark, *Einstein*, pp. 29-30.

	$2a^2$	$+\ 3b$	$-\ 5$
$4a$	$8a^3$	$+\ 12ab$	$-\ 20a$
-3	$-6a^2$	$-\ 9b$	$+\ 15$

$$= 8a^3 - 6a^2 - 20a + 12ab - 9b + 15$$

Some *like* terms in problems will add together when squaring $(3x + 4)$:

	$3x$	$+\ 4$
$3x$	$9x^2$	$+\ 12x$
$+\ 4$	$+\ 12x$	$+\ 16$

$$(3x + 4)^2 = 9x^2 + 12x + 12x + 16$$
$$= 9x^2 + 24x + 16$$

or cancel each other when multiplying a difference of squares $(4x - 5y)(4x + 5y)$:

	$4x$	$-\ 5y$
$4x$	$16x^2$	$-\ 20xy$
$+\ 5y$	$+\ 20xy$	$-\ 25\ y^2$

$$(4x - 5y)(4x + 5y) = 16x^2 - 20xy + 20xy - 25y^2$$
$$= 16x^2 - 25y^2$$

Being able to conjure up simple boxes instead of remembering several situation-specific formulas not only avoids memory problems but also provides an understanding of how the quantities combine together. This box method in reverse can also be applied to factoring *simple* polynomials. (Algebra courses will usually teach other methods of factoring such as the quadratic equation.)

Improving text comprehension

To read is to actively extract meaning from text. Your child's teacher should be able to offer ideas to help you help your child with reading assignments. Often, these problems are typical of those observed in younger students. Yuill and Oakhill (see Chapter 3), suggest many ideas to improve reading comprehension:
- Linking pronouns, noun phrases, and word substitutes to their antecedents
- Paraphrasing, clarifying, discussing, predicting, and summarizing text passages for conceptual recall
- Detecting and making inferences from one or a few words of text (e.g., *He used a stolen key to enter the house.* Question: *How do you know that the man should not be in the house?*)
- Studying how conjunctions, prepositions, and inferences construct relationships between characters, events, and ideas

• Applying relevant informational clues in the text and personal experiences outside the text
• Stating the main idea of the text and subsidiary details
• Self-questioning to monitor comprehension with such words as *who, what, where, when, why, how*
• Learning reading comprehension approaches from skilled peers
• Age-appropriate riddles and jokes to improve comprehension of the non-literal uses of language
• Illustrations that integrate the text rather than depictions of isolated characters or events for conceptual understanding and recall
• Keywords and titles to cue main ideas.

Some concepts may not be understood until adolescence, for example, riddles with ambiguous grammar and stories involving deception. Yuill and Oakhill strongly urge that students be taught explicit strategies to improve their comprehension skills; indeed many fluent decoders may not recognize that their comprehension is poor.

Little things add up. Reading instruction is not easy because vigilance is required over a good number of areas such as those identified by Yuill and Oakhill. Other measures can facilitate reading as well. If your child can decode and understand with some fluency, a bookmark or flexible plastic ruler can help him or her read down the page without skipping lines. If you know your child will have trouble comprehending a work of literature for example, read along with him or her (with or without a prerecording) so you can fill in any gaps of comprehension. Heighten interaction with the text such as assigning certain character parts to be read by your child or having your child supply missing dialog as in this example of a one-sided phone conversation: "Hello, Mrs. Smith? ... This is Jaime. Will you let me talk to Chris, please? ... Yes, it is. ... Thanks." Encourage your child to take notes and review unknown vocabulary words with you. Fasten little paper stickies on important pages as bookmarks for later study or for writing papers. Some parents purchase a second set of textbooks for highlighting and annotating. By the time a student reaches secondary school, reading strategies should encompass compensation strategies to comprehend and learn the material better.

Students with learning disabilities may have trouble visualizing objects and situations from long narratives in the absence of concrete visual materials. For literature assignments, my son and I would diagram relationships between characters; translate descriptive passages into what was seen, felt, heard, left unsaid, etc.; pause to summarize plot; discuss concepts; and predict the rest of the storyline. This is time-consuming, but such is the nature of a disability.

Beyond school assignments, you can find many resources that may help with reading comprehension. A few suggestions:

• Edcon Publishing Group offers reading comprehension workbooks based on classic literature for reading levels 1 through 5. A speech therapist has worked with students using these materials. Titles include *White Fang*, *The Prince and the Pauper*, *War of the Worlds*, *Gulliver's Travels*, and *Adventures of Sherlock Holmes*. The Shakespeare series consists of *The Tempest*, *As You Like It*, *Macbeth*, *Othello*, *Hamlet*, and *Romeo & Juliet*. To view these on the Internet, visit www.edcon publishing.com, click on *Reading Comprehension*, then click on *High Interest Classics*. The phone number is 888/ 553-3266.

• *Aesop's Fables* remains one of the best methods to teach idioms and abstract concepts.

• *Classic Brainteasers*, by Martin Gardner (Sterling Publications, 1995), and *Whodunit Math Puzzles*, by Bill Wise (Sterling Publications, 2002), have logic and math puzzles for older children and up.

• *Quick-to-Solve Brainteasers*, by J. J. Mendoza Fernández (Sterling Publications, 1998) require out-of-the box problem-solving skills, sometimes needed for exams, extra-credit problems, and life in general. The booklet is available through retailers or www.us.mensa.org/ products/books.php3.

• Age-appropriate detective stories can sharpen inferential skills.

• *Vocabulary Workshop*, a series of vocabulary workbooks for grades 3–12, is published by Sadlier-Oxford (www.sadlier-oxford.com or 800/ 221-5175). Two versions are available, a basic 1996 edition and an enhanced 2002 edition (which uses the same 1996 words but with more activities). A teacher's certificate or homeschooling verification is required to obtain the answer keys, which cost extra. A customer service representative suggested that a teacher could order a workbook for you provided that the delivery address is that of the school. Alternatively, you could refer to your dictionary for answers. Sadlier-Oxford also offers instructional series for reading, writing, and arithmetic.

• *1100 Words You Need to Know*, by Murray Bromberg and Melvin Gordon (2000) covers vocabulary and idioms, and has an answer key. The workbook is published by Barron's, and is available at retailers. You can peruse the contents of this book at the www.amazon.com or www.borders.com websites.

Background information. Because children with learning disabilities must be taught so explicitly in order to obtain depth of understanding, they sometimes miss breadth of background knowledge. A series of K–6 books systematically provides material "that can reasonably be expected to make up about *half* of any school's curriculum," according to its editor and author of *Cultural Literacy*, E. D. Hirsch, Jr. This *Core Knowledge* program includes readings and activities to use when teaching language arts, social studies, fine arts, mathematics, and natural sciences. The titles are:

What Your Kindergartner Needs to Know
What Your First Grader Needs to Know
What Your Second Grader Needs to Know
What Your Third Grader Needs to Know
What Your Fourth Grader Needs to Know
What Your Fifth Grader Needs to Know
What Your Sixth Grader Needs to Know.

Extracurricular activities help as well. For example, if your child spends much time in science, try other new activities, such as the fine arts. One child who excels in math loves performing in theatrical productions. Sports provide social connections, especially for boys. Reading to your child can have unexpected benefits too. George Patton's extensive knowledge of classic literature, the result of family members reading to him in his childhood, helped him understand how battles were won or lost over the millennia.

Sorting and relating facts to concepts

Before a student can solve a problem or begin a writing assignment, information must be gathered, evaluated for its relevancy, and organized into a useful sequence of facts. In contrast to acquiring a myriad of facts to establish a base of knowledge, organizing requires the application of common procedures to rearrange the knowledge for some purpose. Some methods to organize information include:

Storyboards. Storyboards are pictures showing a sequence of events. A comic strip is an example of a storyboard. Students can use a storyboard to depict historical events.

Flowcharts. Flowcharts are diagrams detailing the successive steps of a process. For students with learning disabilities, diagraming a series of linear events showing their relationships and consequences has applications in logic, history, logistics, and more. An example of a flowchart is presented in Appendix 10.

Syllogisms. A syllogism *explicitly* links logical ideas and clarifies hidden assumptions. In this example, the first sentence states the hidden assumption:

> *All dogs have tails.*
> *Lassie is a dog.*
> *Lassie has a tail.*

As a sentence, the syllogism could appear as *Lassie has a tail because Lassie is a dog.* An illogical sentence would be *Lassie has a tail because she is happy.* More on syllogisms is found in *The World Book*

Encyclopedia (existing in many school and public libraries) under the subject heading *Logic*.

Webbing. Ideas do not necessarily develop in an orderly fashion, especially while brainstorming. *Story webbing*, *story mapping*, or *mind mapping* is a form of visual thinking in which a main idea leads to other ideas which, in turn, create even more ideas, and so on. Many students with LD, however, have trouble identifying a main idea from supporting evidence. Papers become tough to organize as logical sequences of thought because the ideas are not clearly arranged in a hierarchy such as an outline. *Inspiration* (presented in Chapter 22) can solve this organizing dilemma by taming a cascade of thoughts into a sequence of thoughts to guide writing. Students can brainstorm ideas then, with everything in front of them, establish appropriate linkages between keywords or phrases. With a click of a button, *Inspiration* will generate an outline. The student is thus free to do the more important task of thinking up the ideas and how they relate to one another. How to use *Inspiration* as part of the overall writing process is presented in "Using Inspiration to Organize Reading and Writing," by Kristin Kight, available at www.ldonline.org/ld_indepth/technology/inspiration.html.

Venn diagrams. Schematic pictures can help compare, contrast, categorize, and generalize facts and data into broader concepts. In the first diagram, U is the universal set of all trees, B is the set of all types of broadleaf trees, and N is the set of all types of needleleaf trees. While B and N are both trees, the trees are defined as being either broadleaf or needleleaf, not both simultaneously, and so B and N are separate sets:

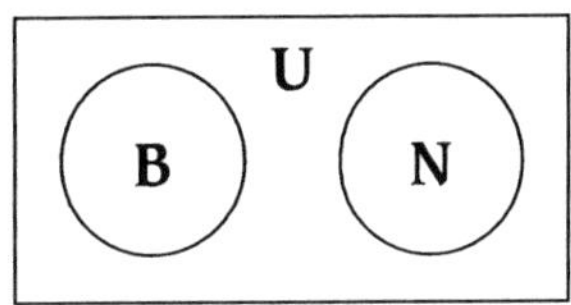

In the second diagram, P is the set of all types of palm trees, N is the set of all types of trees producing edible nuts, and C is the set of palm trees producing coconuts:

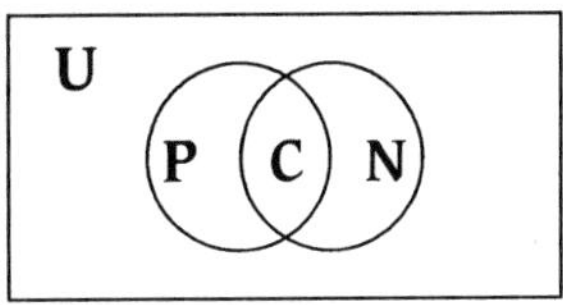

In the third diagram, F is the set of flowering trees, and N is the subset of trees producing edible nuts:

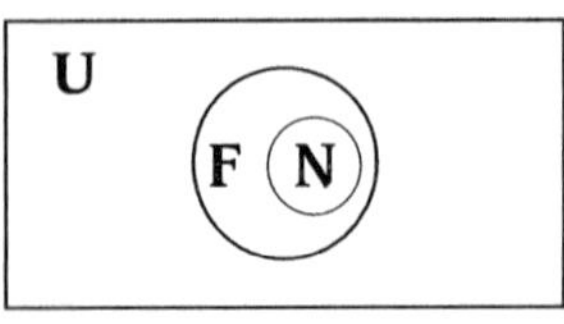

This type of reasoning is part of mathematical set theory, which is further explained in *The World Book* under the subject heading *Set Theory*.

Expressing information for assessments

Oral presentations. In the performing arts, preparation and rehearsal are crucial for a good result. Help your child prepare a script either in writing or on tape, with any props required for the assignment. As the speech becomes better committed to memory, the script may be reduced to notecards. Finding a subject that generates enthusiasm will help carry the day. For dramatic interpretations, audiotape and make a transcript of a speech from a favorite movie if possible; the student can then mimic a favorite actor or actress. As with any homework assignment, don't just ask whether the talk is ready to be presented to the teacher—ask to see a performance. Gently offer suggestions to improve the presentation. Review the teacher's comments about the speech with your child. Expertise and self-confidence will come with experience.

Adjusting for neurodevelopmental problems in writing. An awkward pencil grip slows the speed of writing. Some children try so hard that they break the pencil lead and tear a hole in the paper. Many children would rather print than use cursive handwriting. Wordprocessors can bypass many of these problems.

A child with language problems but excellent visual skills may find writing easier than speaking, because writing can be edited whereas speaking often demands improvisation. Children with sequencing or memory problems may dictate thoughts into a tape recorder or input keywords into *Inspiration* software, before organizing the written content. A child with visual problems may prefer to dictate into a tape recorder or computer loaded with reliable voice-recognition software. The important task is to get down some ideas for later editing.

Writing: Connecting ideas not mechanical production. Similar to the educational assumptions in which decoding leads to reading comprehension and arithmetic generalizes to higher mathematical principles, traditional writing instruction assumes that exercises in mechanics and grammar result in compositions with accuracy and of substance. In this model, students work in isolation on a production deadline; are expected to supply the ideation, substantiation, and presentation strategies; initiate rounds of editing themselves; and teachers mark mistakes and assign grades. Typical of back-to-the-basics instruction, the critical issues of *what* to write and *how* to express the content are not explicitly conveyed to students. Figure 18.3 is an example of such instruction.

Over the past decade, new approaches to writing instruction have emerged in schools. You may see hints of this when teachers try to introduce concepts from *the Writing Workshop* on back-to-school nights for parents. Essentially, specific strategies are taught for the writing stages of planning, execution, and revision—in addition to writing mechanics. An example of this approach is reviewed in "Every Child Can Write: Strategies for Composition and Self-Regulation in the Writing Process," by Karen Harris, Tanya Schmidt, and Steve Graham, available at www.ldonline.org/ld_indepth/writing/harris_writing.html. Other resources on writing instruction are:

• "Simple Ways to Assess the Writing Skills of Students with Learning Disabilities," by Stephen Isaacson, available at www.ldonline.org/ld_indepth/writing/isaacson_assessment.html, presents evaluation worksheets for measuring the writing proficiency of a child with LD.

• "Prevention and Intervention of Writing Difficulties for Students with Learning Disabilities," by Steve Graham, Karen Harris, and Lynn Larsen, available at www.ldonline.org/ld_indepth/writing/prevention_intervention.html, provides six principles for improving the writing process for students with LD.

• "All Children Can Write," by Donald Graves, available at www.ldonline.org/ld_indepth/writing/graves_process.html, is the 1985 article that initiated the current changes in writing instruction.

• *The Writing Dilemma: Understanding Dysgraphia* (RET Press, 1998, www.retctrpress.com), by Regina Richards, offers many solutions for a wide variety of problems, from holding a pencil to writing appropriate responses on essay exams. This book is out of print but may exist in libraries.

• For writing fundamentals, one of the most enduring and popular guides is *The Elements of Style*, by William Strunk, Jr. and E. B. White.

Research papers. The most important step is defining the topic. In life, one writes because there is a reason to write; an interesting topic can provide motivation. You can provide some written material to spark ideas and model a level of writing appropriate to the assignment. Teachers should provide format requirements, approach, and methods. Too often, parents are tacitly delegated the task of teaching their children how to write a paper.

Sometimes, topics are determined by what resources are available. If your child has trouble reading, you may need to direct the research effort. The scope of the assignment is also crucial in determining how much help your child will require. For example, a junior high student with difficulties in reading or staying on track will need much less research assistance if a topic is about General Washington's victory at the Battle of Trenton than a topic about Hessian involvement during the entire Revolutionary War. Discuss with the teacher whether the higher project goal is the process of producing a paper or the original scholarship resulting from research. A teacher may be unfamiliar with how your child's learning issues affect his or her productivity. Work with the teacher to set realistic time and work demands.

As the facts are gathered, a general organization evolves. Some people fill in the facts from a predetermined outline, others develop outlines as information builds. Rubrics for writing papers and executing research projects are presented in Chapter 18. One common research practice is to use index cards when making a note from reference materials. Later, when organizing points and ideas for the paper, the cards can be easily sorted and resorted as needed. Each card should identify the source of the reference such as book title, author, page number, and publisher. Alternatively, each card can be coded with the title, author, and publisher from a master list.

A variation of this card method was necessitated by a teacher's insistence of including copies of notes in the report. So my son used a different sheet of paper with each reference. The top of each page would indicate the reference used, and each entry would include the page number where the material was found. When he was through with his research, each page of notes was photocopied on one side. He then assigned each book a different marker color (green, yellow, blue) and ran an appropriate color-coded stripe or two down each page copy. (The original pages of notes remained unmarked as they were to be included in the final draft report.) He also kept a master list identifying which stripe(s) went with which book. He next cut the color-coded notes apart (dotted lines in Figure 24.2), physically sorted the strips into subtopics according to a rough outline, determined the order of ideas and statements by physically lining up each note item (as seen in Figure 24.3),

Figure 24.2

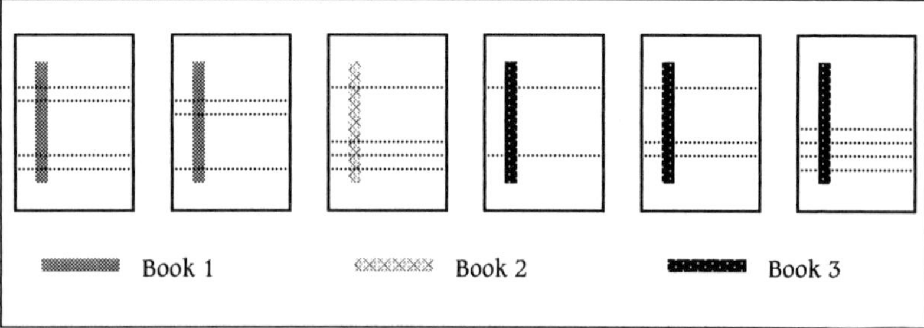

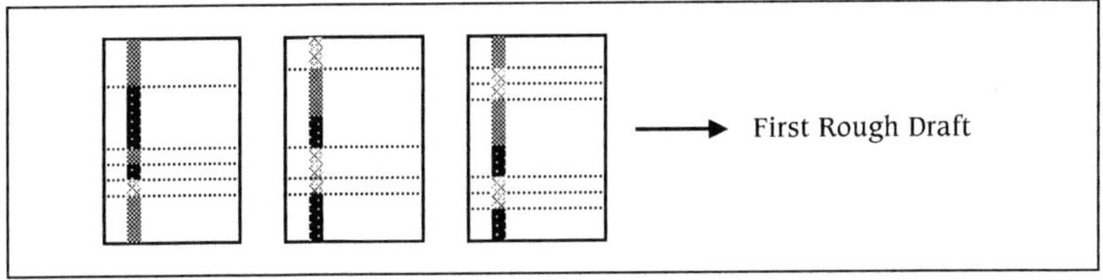

and then typed everything up in this sequence. With the material thus pulled together, writing and editing subsequent drafts became easier.

Plagiarism can be an unintended occurrence if the child struggles to find the words to express ideas. Encourage your child to use a thesaurus. It is essential for students to write their own papers. Teachers have access to online services that can identify Internet files that have been reformatted as a student's own work.

Exams. Recognize the advantages and disadvantages of various types of tests. Weekly tests prevent a student from falling far behind, and lessen the effect of an unusually bad test result. Weekly tests, however, made it harder to rescue a grade if a poor performance pattern is well-established. Essay tests can be frustrating for students who do not write well and have trouble recalling words from memory. Multiple-choice and true-false tests may confuse students.

Many tests are exercises of pattern recognition and can be rehearsed. Some teachers offer practice tests. Help your child understand the teacher's evaluation system. Determine whether your child's essay exams are being graded for language ability or spelling errors as well as concepts. Nancy Firchow offers many tips in "Test-Taking Strategies," available at www.schwablearning.org/articles.asp?r=375&g= 2&d=2. For students planning to take AP or SAT II standardized exams, purchase one of the many test preparation books and teach to the test during the related course as well as to the instructor's material.

Practice test tactics with your child. Some workbooks offer help in studying and taking tests such as those offered by Zaner-Bloser Educational Publishers. Have your child get into the habit of reading the directions carefully, then quickly skimming the test to see what's required. Remind the child to flip the test paper over to see if there are more questions. Some questions can be answered quickly, while others should be flagged and answered later. Many students will make the mistake of rushing at the end of the test and make many careless errors. Urge the child to check answers if time allows.

Accommodations for tests. Accommodations can be crucial to determining a student's academic program. For example, some schools use standardized tests to determine whether students may enroll in honors courses. To disallow a particular accommodation—such as a spellchecker for a dyslexic—state officials must provide evidence of undue advantage, according to a 2001 U.S. District Court ruling in Portland, Oregon.[7] Section 309 of the 1990 Americans with Disabilities Act requires that exams affecting high school, postsecondary, professional, or vocational outcomes be given in an accessible place and manner, or through an alternative arrangement; this includes standardized testing services and licensing boards.[8]

Generally, accommodations do not modify test content but do modify the circumstances surrounding an evaluation. For example, a reader or mechanical device can be used to overcome *proven* areas of disability. Often lost in the controversies of establishing performance standards is that tests need not demonstrate again what is already evident in the student's school record. If so, they are tests of disability, not of achievement. Specific examples of accommodations allowed in many states and promulgated by the U.S. Department of Education Office for Civil Rights include, and are not limited, to:[9]

MODIFICATIONS OF PRESENTATION FORMAT:

- Large-print test editions
- Reordering of items
- Use of spell checker
- Use of word lists/dictionaries
- Templates to reduce visual field
- Short-segment testing booklets
- Key words highlighted in directions

MODIFICATIONS OF ADMINISTRATION PROCEDURES:

- Oral reading of questions
- Use of magnifying glass
- Explanation of directions
- Repeating of directions
- Enhanced lighting
- Use place marker
- Student wears noise buffers
- Administrator faces student
- Read questions aloud to self
- Colored transparency
- Extended testing time
- More breaks
- Audiotape directions or test items
- Individual administration
- In small groups
- At home with appropriate supervision
- In a separate room
- Alone in study carrel
- Off campus
- Assist student in tracking by placing student's finger on item
- Typewriter device to screen out sounds
- Extending sessions over multiple days
- Altered time of day that test is administered

---

7   Daniel Golden, "Disabled Students Gain More Aid on Test," *The Wall Street Journal*, 1 February 2001, p. B2.

8   Laura F. Rothstein, "Legal Issues," in *Success for College Students with Learning Disabilities*, ed. Susan A. Vogel and Pamela Adelman (New York: Springer-Verlag, 1993), p. 29.

9   U.S. Department of Education Office for Civil Rights, "The Use of Tests as Part of High-Stakes Decision-Making for Students," pp. 82-83.

MODIFICATIONS OF RESPONSE METHODS:

- Mark response in booklet
- Use template for recording
- Point to response
- Answers recorded on audiotape
- Use typewriter/computer/word processor
- Alternative response methods, use of scribe
- Lined paper for large script printing
- Administrator checks to ensure that student is placing responses in correct area

A study of the available data of the types of accommodations used by states showed that the ones most frequently allowed—large print, Braille, and reading directions—are not the ones most frequently used.[10] The reason says Martha Thurlow—author, Director of the National Center on Educational Outcomes, and co-Editor of the journal *Exceptional Children*—is that "Most students have learning disabilities, speech and language impairments, emotional or behavioral disabilities, and mental retardation, *not* visual disabilities as the most frequently allowed accommodations might suggest."[11] An odd trend found in this study was that the percentage of students using accommodations diminished as the grade level increased. The study offered some hypotheses: the students may no longer require accommodations, the students may be embarrassed to use them in the higher grades, more restrictions were placed on their use in the higher grades, or the students who used them in lower grades are no longer in school in the higher grades. Conclusions require further studies.

An IEP or 504/ADA accommodations plan details specific measures available to your child in test situations. If your child is allowed extended time or other accommodations on tests, ensure that you or the child follow procedures so that appropriate arrangements can be made by the teacher. Some students will be too timid in requesting accommodations for tests. Should this be the case, you will need to discuss this problem with the teacher, rehearse the child in making this request, or both. If the conventional test format compromises the child's ability to demonstrate mastery of the material, request an alternative format and amend the IEP if necessary.

Standardized testing: No single correct answer. Special education students must be included in statewide or district-wide standardized tests, according to 1999 IDEA regulations:

> "… (a) Children with disabilities are included in general State and district-wide assessment programs, with appropriate accommodations and modifications in administration, if necessary;

---

10   Martha Thurlow, "Use of Accommodations in State Assessments: What Databases Tell Us About Differential Levels of Use and How to Document the Use of Accommodations" [Internet], p. 12, August 2001, available from: http://www.ldonline.org/ld_indepth/special_education/nceo_technical_report30.html
11   Thurlow, p. 3.

(b) As appropriate, the State or LEA [local educational agency, i.e., public school]—

(1) Develops guidelines for the participation of children with disabilities in alternate assessments for those children who cannot participate in State and district-wide assessment programs;

(2) Develops alternate assessments in accordance with paragraph (b)(1) of this section; and

(3) Beginning not later than July 1, 2000, conducts the alternate assessments described in paragraph (b)(2) of this section."

—34 CFR § 300.138

Before this amendment took effect, several states improved reading scores by excluding special education students from testing. School performance can have *financial* or *restaffing* consequences (euphemisms meaning bonus payments or replacing all school personnel). Thus, this amendment is a double-edged sword. While schools should be encouraged to improve the reading of *all* of its students, some students may receive a message that their presence in school is unwanted because they pull down test scores. Schools, however, are also being evaluated on their dropout rates.

Testing itself may not be so straightforward. Standardized tests measuring performance may not be aligned to your state's mandated curriculum standards—which themselves may differ from your child's actual instruction. Thus, students may be tested on material that has not been taught in school. In addition, school reforms, such as increased curriculum and testing requirements, are often developed without considering the special needs of many students. The U.S. Department of Education reports public confusion over the use of modifications and accommodations when students with learning disabilities participate in large-scale assessments.[12] Although prohibited from causing undue advantage and unreasonable corrective actions, modifications and accommodations are generally regarded by the public as unfair, difficult to implement, and expensive, "resulting in students not receiving appropriate accommodations."[13] Finally, almost half the states permit parents to withdraw their children from participation in standardized tests measuring school performance, thus skewing results. These issues are covered in the following articles:

---

12 Department of Education, "Twenty-third Annual Report to Congress," p. IV-25.

13 Department of Education, *Twenty-third Annual Report to Congress on the Implementation of the Individuals with Disabilities Education Act* [Internet], p. I-22, 2001, available from: http://www.ed.gov/offices/OSERS/OSEP/Products/OSEP 2001 AnlRpt/Section_I.pdf

- "Why Johnny Can't Fail," by Alexandra Starr (*Business Week*, 25 November 2002, page 72), reviews general test mandates of the No Child Left Behind Act and the states' responses to this new law.
- "Teaching to the Test: The Good, the Bad, and Who's Responsible," by Nancy Kober (published by the Center on Education Policy, June 2002, available at www.schwablearning.org/schwablearning.asp?id=1309 or www.cep-dc.org/pubs/testtalk.html), discusses a chicken-and-egg phenomenon now applying to curricula and tests.
- "What Tests Can and Cannot Tell Us," by Nancy Kober (published by the Center on Education Policy, October 2002, available at www.schwablearning.org/schwablearning.asp?id=1309 or www.cep-dc.org/pubs/testtalk.html), suggests caution on being overly reliant on test results.
- "More Schools Rely on Tests, but Study Raises Doubts," by Greg Winter (28 December 2002, available at www.nytimes.com/2002/12/28/education/28EXAM.html) raises concerns found in an Arizona State University study that using standardized testing may be self-defeating: teaching-to-the-test is replacing more comprehensive curricula and increasing school drop-out rates, instead of raising academic standards and increasing school accountability.
- "Standardization and Its Unseen Ironies," by Peter Cookson (22 January 2003, available at www.edweek.org/ew/ewstory.cfm?slug=19cookson.h22) questions whether the drive to shape learning for test-measurement purposes compromises original or critical thought so necessary for a tolerant democracy with multiple opportunities for success.
- "Pros Debate Whether Standardized Tests Should Be Timed," by June Kronholz (*The Wall Street Journal*, 20 November 2002, page B1), reviews the issues of knowledge mastery versus speed of recall.
- In 2000, the U.S. Department of Education Office for Civil Rights documented its testing concerns in "The Use of Tests as Part of High-Stakes Decision-Making for Students," (available online at www.ed.gov/offices/OCR/testing/TestingResource.doc).
- "Standard Deviation: Student's Dream, Principal's Dread: The Test Not Taken," by Daniel Golden (*The Wall Street Journal*, 24 December 2002, page A1) reviews not only the conflicting interests of parents and schools regarding tests on school performance, but also the possible consequences of a parent withdrawing their child from participating in standardized assessments.
- "States Cut Test Standards to Avoid Sanction," by Sam Dillon (22 May 2003, accessed from www.nytimes.com/2003/05/22/education/22EDUC.html?th), found states are revisiting their decisions on implementing test requirements.

High school exit exams. State exit exams, required in over half the states for graduation, may add more fuel to the controversy. You should monitor whether laws, school policies, and instructional quality will affect your child's test performance. The federal No Child Left Behind Act of 2001 mandates assessments of students' abilities as a way to measure school competence; it is the states that determine execution of this new law and whether tests are required for graduation. A student not passing the required high school exit exam will not receive a diploma but a certificate of completion or another alternative. Not having a diploma may limit opportunities for employment and further education. In other words, your child may be paying the penalty for the poor performance of the school or for any institutional restrictions on test modifications. (Private schools remain outside government requirements for state-wide assessments.) Moreover, you may be dealing with public officials who misunderstand yet decide the issues of LD. For example in 2001, the California State Board of Education made a policy decision to forbid testing "modifications" on the California High School Exit Exam (CAHSEE), a 2004 graduation requirement.

In January, 2002, a U.S. District Court in San Francisco affirmed federal laws requiring states to provide "any accommodations or modifications their IEP or Section 504 plan specifically provides for" regarding the high school exit exam, even if these documents address only standardized or classroom testing in general (*Juleus Chapman et al., v. California Department of Education et al.*, p. 16). Evidently, this decision was not the last word. On August 14th of the same year in San Francisco, a three-judge panel of the Ninth Circuit Court of Appeals did not change the lower court order requiring California to provide test accommodations and modifications but created the possibility for confusion over which devices are permissible for any one person. (In practice, any federal court decision affects other jurisdictions throughout the country.)

To understand this case, two California-specific definitions must be understood. California defined *accommodations* as changes in the circumstances of taking the test (such as format, student response, or timing) and are therefore allowed because these measures do not invalidate the score achieved. In contrast, *modifications* are defined as changes that obviate what the test is supposed to measure and thus are disallowed because they invalidate the student's test score. Modifications would include calculators and spellcheckers. (The federal District Court decision did not identify any definitive distinctions between accommodations and modifications in federal law.)

Thus, the Ninth Circuit will allow the State of California to challenge the use of modifications (i.e., *prove it*) because students "have alleged a real and immediate injury" of not being able to receive a high school diploma without modifications. The decision states, "However, though this right to participate in statewide testing requires that participation must be meaningful ... it does not require us to prohibit the state from exercising its traditional authority to set diploma requirements." Somehow, a state that bases *high school* graduation requirements on *elementary school* skills such as spelling and arithmetic is missing the point of secondary education, critical thought and logic as examples. For individuals with LD, this decision portends the loss of function over an unrelated matter of form, akin to requiring the lame to walk to their destinations. Students not passing the CAHSEE will have to find another way to fulfill graduation requirements, alternate testing being yet unavailable at the time of this writing.

Other problems are illustrated in the high rates of failure on 2002 high school exit exams in two states. Massachusetts was sued on the grounds that its exit exam covered material not presented to thousands of students, and that the exam was discriminatory because about half of the students who are African American, Latino, vocational, non-native English speakers, or with LD did not pass it; much lower percentages of white and Asian students flunked this exam.[14] California flunked almost 90% of students with disabilities. The lawsuit filed by Disability Rights (*Juleus Chapman et al., v. California Department of Education et al.*, see above) requested that modifications be allowed, an alternate exam be provided, and exam material be taught before the exam. A survey of California's principals showed that 45% thought that students with disabilities had not been prepared for the math section and 36% thought the same applied to the language arts section.[15] Another study linked test failure with uncredentialed teachers—a situation overwhelmingly found in schools with low-income students.[16] (At the time of this writing, California may yet decide to postpone its high school exit exam requirement until 2006 due to potential lawsuits over inadequate instruction and a statewide budget crisis.[17]) "The Great Divide," by Lynn Olson (9 January 2003, available at www.edweek.org/sreports/qc03/templates/article.cfm?slug=17divide.h22) shows the magnitude of these problems. "Spec. Ed. Tech Sparks Ideas," by Lisa Goldstein (8 May 2003, available at www.edweek.org/sreports/TC03/

14 Anand Vaishnav and Michele Kurtz, "Lawsuit to Allege MCAS is Widely Discriminatory" [Internet], 19 September 2002, accessed 20 September 2002 from: http://www.boston.com/dailyglobe2/262/metro/Lawsuit_to_allege_MCAS_is_widely_discriminatory+.shtml

15 Nanette Asimov, "90% of Disabled Kids Flunk Exit Exam," *San Francisco Chronicle*, 27 September 2002, p. A22.

16 Nanette Asimov, "More Uncredentialed Teachers' Students Fail," *San Francisco Chronicle*, 11 December 2002, p. A17.

17 Nanette Asimov, "School Exit Exams Need Warnings, Attorneys Says," *San Francisco Chronicle*, 4 January 2003, p. A13.

article.cfm?slug=35speced.h22), presents experimental evaluation methods of special education students.

Practice tests for state proficiency exams are offered through The Princeton Review (www.princetonreview.com). Test-taking skills at the elementary school level and up are found in McGraw-Hill's Spectrum book series (800/ 417-3261 or www.mhkids.com/cgi-bin/searchcat.cgi —enter "spectrum" into the *Search by keyword(s)* box and click on the *Search* button). Check with the school's principal on any changes in the upcoming state exams.

College entrance exams. For students given accommodations on undergraduate and graduate admissions exams, test scores may be *flagged*. For example, SAT I score reports will have an asterisk appended to relevant test dates, indicating "Non-Standard Administration" such as additional time or a separate testing room. In 1978—after passage of the 1973 Rehabilitation Act—the Department of Education allowed testing services to flag nonstandard test scores as an interim policy, thus creating a preadmissions inquiry of a disability for colleges and universities that receive the flagged test scores.[18]

In 2001, the Educational Testing Service (ETS) agreed to stop flagging several tests—such as the Graduate Record Examinations (GRE) and the Graduate Management Admission Test (GMAT) as examples—after settling a lawsuit charging that this practice violated antidiscrimination laws.[19] (A Stanford graduate born without hands used a computer with a trackball, was given extra time on the GMAT, and was later rejected by business schools.) In another court settlement, the College Board decided to discontinue flagging all score reports—regardless of test date—sent to colleges and universities beginning October 1, 2003, which would affect 2% of the total test takers, mostly for extra time due to learning disabilities. Similarly, flags will be dropped on all ACT Assessment reports issued after September 1, 2003. Some college admission officials fear that an end to flagging will encourage widespread inequitable test situations and specious demands for test accommodations.[20] Conversely, one medical school professor told me that his main concern would not be the presence of a learning disability, but rather what accommodations that person would be requiring.

The elimination of flagged nonstandard test scores is, in effect, a return to a previous situation. Section 504 prohibits preadmissions inquiries about a disability unless:

---

18 Rothstein, "Legal Issues," p. 25.

19 Ben Wildavsky, "Helping or Hurting? A New Test-Score Policy," *U.S. News and World Report*, 19 February 2001, p. 57.

20 Wildavsky, p. 57.

• The response is voluntary and useful to the discloser (such as obtaining assistance), and
• The applicant is advised that refusing to provide information will not adversely affect the application.

Any information obtained in a preadmissions inquiry is to remain confidential.

Determining whether test accommodations will help you. Students with unremarkable test scores can be admitted to many "good" colleges providing the rest of the application is strong. Still, applying to college is a rite of passage requiring applicants to improve their test-taking skills.

Teenagers can simulate a nonstandard administration by taking old exams in *10 Real SATs* and *Real SAT II: Subject Tests* (published by the College Entrance Examination Board and Educational Testing Service) with and without accommodations. If accommodations help, then use them. Another source of general information is "Summary of Test Accommodations for the SAT and ACT for Students Who Are Learning Disabled 1999–2000 School Year," by Earl Hishinuma available at www.ldonline.org/ld_indepth/transition/hishinuma_actsat.html. In 2003, nonstandard exam formats included larger print exams, readers, and computers for writing (such as the SAT II Writing and AP exams).

The College Board provides a list of the types of *nonstandard accommodations* available at www.collegeboard.com/disable/counsel/html/accom.html. *Extended time* is either up to 50% extra time or more than 50% but not more than 100%. (Feed your teenager a good breakfast before an exam with extended time; a three-hour exam with 50% extra time may last four and one-half hours.)

The Educational Testing Service (ETS) administers *center testing* of standard College Board tests and accommodations like 50% extended time. Non-ETS or *school-based testing* occurs for such accommodations like use of a computer for essay-writing. Both of these types of testing may take place at the same location but, because different test administrators are required, school-based testing is scheduled on different days from center testing. You will know that school-based testing is required because your child's College Board admission ticket will state that you must "see the test coordinator at your school" to arrange the test(s). Do this as soon as possible because your child's testing materials need to be shipped to the appropriate person who will administer the test(s).

Students eligible for College Board testing with accommodations can apply online beginning in August 2003. Applications that are mailed in should include an *Accommodations Request Form for the SAT* which previously would have arrived with a College Board letter approving accommodations for your teenager. Contact the College

Board for a test application form if you are unable to obtain one locally in schools or public libraries. A cashed check is proof that the College Board received your child's application. More information on college admission tests appears in Chapter 26 or from the College Board Services for Students with Disabilities, available at www.collegeboard.com/ssd or voice 609/ 771-7137 or TTY 609/ 882-4118. Otherwise visit www.collegeboard.com, click on *SEARCH*, then at the *Site Search* page, type in "accommodations" in the *Keyword(s)* box and click on the *search* button, and a menu of topics will appear.

ACT at its website, www.act.org/aap/disab/index.html, advises students to work through their high school guidance counselors and not contact ACT directly. ACT has its own process for establishing accommodations. Be forewarned that every ACT test administration does not allow accommodations, for example, October but not June.

Before committing to a test preparation program, consider how your child learns best in addition to time and cost factors. Practice workbooks from many publishers are widely available in bookstores. These books vary in degree of difficulty, presentation of content, date of publication, and number of practice tests. Peruse the candid reviews of students available from online booksellers. Kaplan's test preparation software for the SAT, ACT, and PSAT—recommended by *Children's Software Revue*—drills and tracks individual progress. Contact the school for information on prep courses or tutors.

Additional information about standardized tests and the college application process can be found on the ETS (www.ets.org), College Board (www.collegeboard.com), ACT (www.act.org) websites. A *Wall Street Journal* article, "To Prep for Saturday's Test, an SAT I Primer" by June Kronholz, discusses test preparation, strategies, and scoring (January 23, 2003, page B1). The U.S. Department of Education website also has topics pertaining to the standardized-testing and the college application process.

Chapter Twenty-Five

What other treatments exist?

The educational therapist completed her work with my son in about a year. He actually had improved in several areas, but now the remaining problem was auditory processing. He could hear better than I but often couldn't understand what was said. My husband and I inquired at a local university medical center about an experimental therapy published in several scientific journals as having phenomenal results in improving phonological awareness. But we received no response. I later learned that I was not alone in my direct inquiries; a psychiatrist had the same experience when seeking help for her son.

Then a miracle happened. The educational therapist learned that the researchers of the experimental therapy were seeking children with auditory processing problems for national beta testing, that is, to see if newly developed computer software was effective for many children across the U.S. having the same exact problem as our son. A respected nonprofit clinic offered the free services under its auspices though we would be responsible for the cost of the before and after evaluations. Candidates were screened to determine if they would be suitable subjects. No invasive procedures were involved and I could watch the proceedings through a one-way mirror. Our son would be required to play computer games for two hours every weekday, over four weeks.

We applied immediately, our son was accepted into the test program, and one month later, his auditory processing skills had risen three grade levels to that of a normal fifth grader. I remember making a joke to my children soon afterward, and this time all of them laughed together. It was wonderful.

Still, not all my son's language problems evaporated. He learned to compensate for a poor auditory memory. Over time, better reading and writing skills have come with practice.

Some other parents I know have not seen the same dramatic benefit in their children as I saw in my son. The lesson here is that treatments have different therapeutic benefits in each person.

Evaluating experimental or alternative treatments

Learning problems and associated stigmas have been around for a long time, accounting for the wide variety of remedies. Parents need to evaluate the limits of standard treatments and the efficacy of nonstandard ones. If the therapy has been available for a while, be wary if control studies or endorsements from a reputable professional group don't exist. Bender has offered the following warning about purported cures:

> "… [Y]ou can find written testimonials for almost any proposition, and such testimonials do not replace research treatment studies that have been recognized as acceptable research by other researchers in the field. Further, parents who are desperate enough to seek help for a child with learning disabilities when acceptable special education treatments have not shown promise will often investigate alternative treatments, even though there may not be strong evidence in support of them."[1]

Many treatments are *controversial*, because little independent peer-reviewed research is available to verify the claims of treatment results. Many nontraditional treatments commonly have four characteristics:[2]

- Discrepancies with contemporary science
- Claims of success over a wide range of applications
- Information campaigns directed at consumers, instead of research findings subjected to peer review at reputable professional forums
- Endorsements from nonspecialists rather than a reputable body of informed professionals.

This is not a world of perfect knowledge. One well-meaning professional sent me literature on products—now regarded with some suspicion—that she had been using for her daughter. It is sometimes difficult to differentiate between a promising experimental therapy and a slickly promoted dream. In everyday life, if the cost is little, people are willing to take chances. A bigger commitment of time and money

---

1   Bender, *Learning Disabilities*, p. 302.
2   Mercer citing work by Golden in 1984 and Shaywitz and Shaywitz in 1988, *Students with Learning Disabilities*, p. 79.

though is serious business. Still, consider the following questions when evaluating a prospective nonstandard treatment:

- Is the treatment plausible given current concepts about the disorder?
- How will the treatment help my child's specific problem?
- What evidence of efficacy exists? Is the treatment significantly better than no treatment at all or placebo treatment (usually identified in a properly controlled study)? Have these results been duplicated by other field investigators?
- What are the alternatives? Can my child's time and my money be better spent elsewhere?

You may see offers to participate in research studies. The Centers for Disease Control and Prevention (CDC) has suggested raising several issues before you take part in any clinical trial:[3]

- What is the purpose of this study?
- Who are the researchers and supporters of this study?
- What quality controls are built into this study?
- Who can participate in this study?
- What are the anticipated benefits for me personally?
- Can I be harmed?
- How is my privacy to be protected?
- What must I do in this study?
- What happens to the information used and found in the study?

The CDC brochure, *Taking Part in Research Studies: What Questions Should You Ask?* (www.cdc.gov/hiv/pubs/brochure/unc3bro.htm or call the CDC National Prevention Information Network at 800/ 458-5231) elaborates further on these inquiries. Some other resources about clinical trials are available for your review:

- General information and definitions are found online at a National Institutes of Health website, www.clinicaltrials.gov/info/resources, and in a New York University Medical Center article, "Participating in Research: Frequently Asked Questions," by Stephanie Irby Coard, at www.aboutourkids.org/articles/participatingresearch.html.
- Some personal experiences with clinical trials are reviewed in two articles in the April 11, 2002 *The Wall Street Journal*, "Clinical Trials Want You, But Is It Worth the Risk?" by Laura Landro (pages D1-D2) and "The Biggest Concern of All for Research Volunteers: Am I Going to Be Stuck With a Placebo?" by Vanessa Fuhrmans (page D2).
- Questions to ask before participating in a pediatric study are presented in the May 29, 2002 *Wall Street Journal* article, "Desperately Seeking Kids for Clinical Trials," by Rachel Zimmerman (page D1).

---

3   Centers for Disease Control and Prevention, "Taking Part in Research Studies: What Questions Should You Ask?" [Internet], last updated 13 August 1998, available from: http://www.cdc.gov/hiv/pubs/brochure/unc3bro.htm

In science, truth is distilled through duplication of results, not by advertisements, promotions, or just by repeating an assertion often enough. A website, www.quackwatch.com is dedicated to health fraud and quackery (use the *Search* feature on the homepage). Be suspicious of a prospective treatment that uses strange or odd terms and concepts, seems illogical in its workings, is not developed through years of peer-reviewed research, or in which a single service provider both diagnoses and treats a problem. I found one research study that observed whether insurance would pay for the experimental therapy. This study had inconsistent methods of treatment and evaluation. Those participants who were deemed *successful* after 20 weeks of treatment were asked to undergo another 20 weeks of treatment. This is just one study with irregular practices. Lately, much attention has been focused on paid product endorsements and drug trials supported by manufacturers. It's a jungle out there.

You need not feel alone in trying to evaluate the efficacy of a treatment. Given the growing number of researchers investigating learning disorders today, any new significant concepts or therapies will be not be secret for long. Your job, however, is to keep current with new developments and contrasting views pertaining to your child's disorder. By doing so, you will be better able to evaluate the many opinions of field specialists should news of a new treatment emerge. An excellent information source is physician-author Larry Silver, renowned for his investigations of alternative nonstandard therapies, and widely quoted in many academic publications.

"When you say 'hill,'" the Queen interrupted, "I could show you hills, in comparison with which you'd call that a valley."

"No, I shouldn't," said Alice, surprised into contradicting her at last: "a hill ca'n't be a valley, you know. That would be nonsense—"

The Red Queen shook her head. "You may call it 'nonsense' if you like," she said, "but I've heard nonsense, compared with which that would be as sensible as a dictionary!"

—Through the Looking-Glass

Controversial skills treatments

Social skills treatments. By improving peer acceptance, some parents hope to improve their child's academic performance. The hard truth, though, is that improved academics generally improves peer acceptance. Still, many parents want their children to have friends.

Play therapy does not improve behavior in individuals diagnosed with AD/HD, conduct disorders, or oppositional disorders in controlled studies with placebos.[4] Researchers agree that social skills training outside the normal peer environment, like in a clinic or at a summer camp, does not necessarily improve acceptance when the child returns to his normal social groups. Continuous social skills training in the normal peer environment might help.

Auditory perceptual training. Auditory-perceptual problems have been associated with language deficits which, in turn, cause reading problems. Various treatments assume that training can diminish auditory-perceptual disorders.

Auditory Integration Training (AIT), as developed by Guy Bernard, remedies auditory perceptual defects by reorganizing the auditory cortex, strengthening the muscles controlling the three ear bones, and normalizing hearing. An AudioKinetron first assesses the frequencies of a person's overly sensitive or insensitive hearing, then amplifies or filters out problem frequencies when it plays selected compact disks or audiotapes over 20 half-hour treatments of two per day. AIT is used to treat learning disabilities, autism, AD/HD, and depression.

The website, www.tomatis.com/English/index.htm states that the Tomatis Method will help reduce the symptoms of AD/HD, learning delays, autism, dyslexia, balance and coordination problems, sensory integration and motor skill difficulties, Asperger's syndrome, pervasive development disorder, and Down's syndrome. Silver investigated Bernard's AIT and listening training, developed by Albert Tomatis, which uses specialized equipment to teach sound discrimination. He reported that a review of these two treatments by the Edmonton Canada Public School System and the Manitoba Canada Speech and Hearing Association advised caution, because no research has validated the underlying theory or demonstrated treatment benefits.[5]

Other commercial sound therapies have been developed. For example, the July 2002 website of Sound Therapy, www.superlearning.com/ pr_sound_therapy.htm, stated that its treatment could cure LD, AD/HD, and autism: *Ultra high* frequency sounds of 5000 – 8000 hertz delivered brain-altering sounds through an Electronic Ear device at a Sound Therapy Center or a personal audiotape player. In truth, however, these *ultra high* frequency sounds exist well within the 20 – 20,000 hertz range of normal human hearing. How these sounds remedy problems is also unclear.

Real *ultrasound*, according to *The World Book Encyclopedia*, lies above the range of human hearing, and is considered safe enough to diagnose diseases and monitor fetal development. Knowing, however, whether you were receiving any ultrasound *therapy* would be difficult, because you would not be able to hear it. Moreover, specific

---

4   Barkley, "ADHD: Theory, Diagnosis, and Treatment," p. 85.
5   Silver, *The Misunderstood Child*, pp. 320-321.

applications of such devices using real ultrasound—therapeutic or otherwise—must meet the approval of the Food and Drug Administration with regard to safety and effectiveness.

An Internet search in September 2002 did not find the Sound Therapy website. A quick check at eBay found some Sound Therapy equipment for sale. Among these items were two cassette tapes for 95 cents, discounted from $345 for six tapes seen back in July.

Other types of auditory exercises require listening before writing what was spoken; completing the last syllable of a multiple-syllable word then pronouncing the entire word; and discriminating words from background noise. These auditory training methods have not effectively helped children with learning disabilities.[6]

In the 1990s, university research studies led to a computerized phonological training program, which does appear to have real benefits. It and other phonological programs are discussed in Chapter 22.

Optometric visual training. Reading problems like perception of letters and word skipping have been theorized to have been caused by ineffective muscular control of the eyes or visual interpretation.[7] Some optometrists believe vision training is effective.[8] Children with learning disabilities, however, are no more likely to have visual difficulties than normal peers, including the optometric measures of convergence, accommodation, or binocular vision.[9] The National Institute of Mental Health (NIMH) regards eye training as not having been "scientifically shown to be effective in treating the majority of children or adults with AD/HD."[10] (In all cases, medical vision problems, like nearsightedness, should be treated.)

Then again, there may be a kernel of truth in optometric visual training. A review of the records of 1,700 children diagnosed with AD/HD found that 16% have convergence insufficiency, an eye disorder usually treated with simple eye exercises.[11] Thus, misidentification may underlie professional experience. The restlessness of a young child with a vision problem—misdiagnosed as a learning disorder—could be corrected by an optometric treatment. This is not the same as saying that ocular malfunctioning causes or has anything to do with learning

---

6   Bender, *Learning Disabilities*, p. 305.

7   Bender, *Learning Disabilities*, p. 302.

8   Mercer, *Students with Learning Disabilities*, p. 80.

9   William Feldman, *Learning Disabilities: A Review of Available Treatments*, (Springfield, Illinois: Charles C Thomas, 1990), p. 96.

10   National Institute of Mental Health, "Attention Deficit Hyperactivity Disorder" [Internet], p. 17, updated 1 July 1999, available from: http://www.nimh.nih.gov/publicat/adhd.cfm#adhd7

11   Jay Dixit citing a finding by Granet, "An Eye on ADHD" [Internet], *Psychology Today*, accessed 31 August 2002 from: http://www.psychologytoday.com/HTDocs/prod/PTOhome/home.asp

disorders. Still, like any other discovery, these results need to be verified through the peer-review process.

Nevertheless, a wide variety of vision training and visual-perceptual exercises have been recommended for individuals with LD. Many of these exercises require fine motor skills such as stringing beads, drawing lines between closely spaced lines, solving mazes, or finding hidden objects in a drawing. Other treatments use specialized training equipment, lenses, prisms, filters, nutritional counseling, family counseling, and more.[12] Not clear from this list is what constitutes an appropriate vision training program. No evidence supports vision training for learning disorders.[13]

Controversial neurological treatments

Colored lenses. *Scotopia* is vision in dim light. White light is the sum of various wavelengths from red to violet. Helen Irlen postulated that *scotopic sensitivity syndrome*—identified by symptoms of light sensitivity, eyestrain, and impaired, visual resolution, depth perception, span of focus, and sustained focus—is corrected by identifying specific wavelengths of light causing vision problems, then either wearing colored lenses (not corrective lenses) or covering reading material with colored transparencies. A similar approach using blue-gray lenses and transparencies has been theorized to work something like a computer-monitor screen saver by preventing sustained afterimages, so that the eyes can focus on something new. Research on the Irlen and blue-gray lenses "casts some doubt"—though not "definitively"—on these treatments;[14] The NIMH reports on its website at www.nimh. nih.gov/publicat/adhd.cfm#adhd7 that special colored glasses remain unproven as an effective treatment for AD/HD.[15]

Vestibular dysfunction. The vestibular system provides a person with a sense of balance. Harold Levinson has associated physical awkwardness with dyslexia, and so has hypothesized that inner-ear problems cause reading troubles. However, no differences in vestibular function have been found between normal children and children with learning disabilities, nor has any correlation been found in measures of vestibular function and academic performance.[16] Still, motion-sickness medication has been prescribed for dyslexia despite a lack of scientific evidence verifying these treatment claims.[17] With respect to AD/HD, the

---

12 Feldman, *Learning Disabilities*, p. 97.
13 Feldman, p. 99.
14 Spafford and Grosser, *Dyslexia*, p. 62.
15 National Institute of Mental Health, "Attention Deficit Hyperactivity Disorder," p. 17.
16 Feldman, *Learning Disabilities*, p. 84.
17 Feldman, p. 113.

NIMH states that medicines to correct problems in the inner ear are scientifically unproven treatments.[18]

Sensory integration treatment stimulates the vestibular system in premature infants and in children with cerebral palsy and mental retardation. With respect to children with learning disabilities, sensory integration therapy does not improve vestibular functioning, perceptual processing, or academic achievement.[19] With respect to children with AD/HD, the exercises do not involve the parts of the brain associated with the disorder.[20]

Hypnosis. No control studies exist showing improved recall and learning when under hypnosis. Flawed studies reduce the significance of any reports of impressive gains.[21]

Patterning. While the child lies passively, adults manipulate the head and limbs so as to replicate developmental sequences like rolling over, crawling, standing, and walking. This technique, described by Glenn Doman and Carl Delacato in 1968, is supposed to *repattern* the brain's neural connections by repeating the developmental stage not yet mastered. Then, the reorganized brain would allow learning to occur. Treatments can take 10–15 hours a day, every day, for years; require four or more adults to move the child's arms, legs, and head simultaneously; and charge "a considerable fee" for specialized assessment and therapy.[22] The American Academy of Pediatrics states that treatment is unproven and onerous enough to be counterproductive. A summary of the AAP's findings is available at www.aap.org/policy/re9919.html entitled "The Treatment of Neurologically Impaired Children Using Patterning (RE9919)".

Applied kinesiology. Carl Ferreri postulated that skull bones shift out of position and put pressure on the brain. Neural organization technique (NOT), a variation of applied kinesiology, manipulates the bones of the skull, especially around the eyes and so theoretically remedies dyslexia, AD/HD, allergies, and Down's Syndrome. Silver has found no standard anatomical basis for the theory, no published research supporting the therapy, nor any published documentation on the results of treatment.[23] Barkley has also found no anatomical evidence for this theory.[24] The NIMH reports that chiropractic adjustment and bone realignment have "not been scientifically shown to be effective in treating" AD/HD.[25] *Consumer Reports* has advised parents to be skeptical of

---

18   National Institute of Mental Health, "Attention Deficit Hyperactivity Disorder," p. 17.
19   Feldman, *Learning Disabilities*, p. 85.
20   Barkley, "ADHD: Theory, Diagnosis, and Treatment," p. 84.
21   Feldman, *Learning Disabilities*, p. 41.
22   Bender, *Learning Disabilities*, p. 308.
23   Silver, *The Misunderstood Child*, p. 319.
24   Barkley, "ADHD: Theory, Diagnosis, and Treatment," p. 85.
25   National Institute of Mental Health, "Attention Deficit Hyperactivity Disorder," p. 17.

chiropractic treatment claims that applied kinesiology can cure learning disabilities.[26]

Vigorous exercise has also been studied for any effects on learning disabilities. Aerobic exercise improved physical fitness and self-concept, but not academic achievement; a trampoline-reading program improved self-esteem but reported no results on reading achievement.[27]

Controversial biochemical treatments

Harmful Substances. Doris Rapp suggested identifying then eliminating possible environmental allergens (mold or chemicals) and food allergens (such as dairy, wheat, chocolate, or peanuts) to diminish aggressive, oppositional, or hyperactive behavior. William Crook reported that allergies and yeast infections are related to problem behaviors associated with LD or AD/HD. Benjamin Feingold recommended a diet eliminating artificial food colorings, artificial flavors, and natural salicylates—which would include many fruits, nuts, beverages, candies, condiments, cereals, and bakery goods—to improve learning, memory, motor coordination, mood, and behavior. Silver found no evidence showing that allergies, yeast infections, or food additives cause learning disabilities or AD/HD.[28] The NIMH states that the effectiveness of restricted diets, allergy treatments, and treatment for yeast infection as being scientifically unproven for AD/HD.[29]

Sugar. One study found no behavioral differences when boys with AD/HD were given drinks with sucrose or aspartate.[30] Another study did not confirm parental reports of hyperactiveness following glucose and fructose intake.[31] In a follow-up study, however, some children became relatively more active if given refined sugar after a high-carbohydrate breakfast, as opposed to a high-fat or high-protein breakfast followed by refined sugar, fruit sugar, or placebo.[32]

Megavitamins. Massive doses of vitamins, especially the B vitamins, have been recommended to treat learning disabilities and AD/HD. Studies using randomized, double-blind, placebo-controlled trials found that megavitamins are ineffective treatments for learning disabilities and AD/HD; more troubling was that megavitamins resulted in a 25% increase in disruptive classroom behavior, and that 42% of the children had abnormal liver function tests from taking large doses of

---

26   "Chiropractors," Joel Gurin, Editor, *Consumer Reports*, June, 1994, p. 387.
27   Feldman, *Learning Disabilities*, p. 113.
28   Silver, *The Misunderstood Child*, pp. 323, 324, and 326.
29   National Institute of Mental Health, "Attention Deficit Hyperactivity Disorder," p. 17.
30   Feldman, *Learning Disabilities*, p. 74.
31   Silver, *The Misunderstood Child*, p. 327.
32   Silver, p. 327.

B vitamins.[33] Other possible side effects of megavitamins are cardiac arrhythmias, headaches, and fatigue.[34] The NIMH,[35] American Academy of Pediatrics, and American Psychiatric Association do not recommend megavitamin treatment for learning disabilities.[36] Still, if you are concerned about vitamin supplements, consult your pediatrician or pharmacist on appropriate dosage amounts.

Trace elements. Trace elements are extremely small amounts of certain chemicals required by the body's normal physiology. Many are listed on a typical bottle of vitamin tablets, each tablet containing less than a few milligrams (abbreviated as *mg*, meaning a thousandth of a gram) or micrograms (abbreviated as *mcg*, meaning a millionth of a gram) of trace chemical elements. No formal published studies have confirmed that deficiencies in trace elements either cause learning disabilities or, if given in a replacement therapy, effectively improve performance.[37] In contrast, a deficiency of a more common element, iron, has been correlated with lower math achievement.[38] The FDA provides updated information in "Dietary Supplements," available at www.cfsan.fda.gov/~dms/supplmnt.html.

Herbs. The Mayo Clinic website "Herb-buying Tips" (www.mayo clinic.com/invoke.cfm?id=sa00044) offers information on dietary supplements. The website also cautions that some claims may be too good to be true. When seeking supporting evidence from manufacturers that herbs effectively treat learning disabilities (including AD/HD), Silver received advertisements with undefined technical jargon and three job offers to be a product spokesman.[39] The information also implied that parents not providing the product to their child were impeding their child's development.[40] Similarly, Barkley has advised that antioxidants, minerals, St. John's wort, and Ginkgo biloba are useless in treating AD/HD.[41]

More information is available on the Medline Plus website, "Herbal Medicine" at www.nlm.nih.gov/medlineplus/herbalmedicine.html.

---

33   Feldman, *Learning Disabilities*, pp. 77-78.
34   Mercer, *Students with Learning Disabilities*, p. 81.
35   National Institute of Mental Health, "Attention Deficit Hyperactivity Disorder," p. 17.
36   Mercer, *Students with Learning Disabilities*, p. 81.
37   Silver, *The Misunderstood Child*, p. 322.
38   Jill S. Halterman, Jeffrey M. Kaczorowski, C. Andrew Aligne, Peggy Auinger, and Peter G. Szilagyi, "Iron Deficiency and Cognitive Achievement Among School-aged Children and Adolescents in the United States," *Pediatrics* [Internet], 6 June 2001, p. 2, available from: http://www.biwa.ne.jp/~mccshiga/anemia3.html
39   Silver, p. 328.
40   Silver, p. 328.
41   Barkley, "ADHD: Theory, Diagnosis, and Treatment," p. 84

Chapter Twenty-Six

How can I help my child move into the workplace?

"What do you mean by 'If you really are a Queen'? What right have you to call yourself so? You ca'n't be a Queen, you know, till you've passed the proper examination. And the sooner we begin it, the better."

"I only said 'if'!" poor Alice pleaded in a piteous tone.

The two Queens looked at each other, and the Red Queen remarked, with a little shudder, "She says she only said 'if'—"

"But she said a great deal more than that!" the White Queen moaned, wringing her hands. "Oh, ever so much more than that!"

"So you did, you know," the Red Queen said to Alice. "Always speak the truth—think before you speak—and write it down afterwards."

"I'm sure I didn't mean—" Alice was beginning, but the Red Queen interrupted her impatiently.

"That's just what I complain of! You should have meant! What do you suppose is the use of a child without any meaning? Even a joke should have some meaning—and a child's more important than a joke, I hope."

—Through the Looking-Glass

What is "transition?"

Elementary school children receive the most attention in LD identification, services, and research. However, the teenage years present new challenges: spurts in physical and mental development, social pressures, and grades. About half of the states do or will require students to pass a high school exit exam in order to receive a diploma. In many states, your teenager will reach majority at age 18. And perhaps more than most other parents, you are concerned about your child's ability to live independently as an adult.

With respect to special education, *transition* refers to activities during the time your child passes from adolescence to adulthood. Appendix 11 flowcharts secondary school curriculum decisions. This chapter will first cover postsecondary outcomes, then review the high school transition process.

Developing a vision of your child's adult outcome

The period after high school can be especially trying for adults with learning disabilities who have lower academic achievements, self-esteem, self-confidence, social skills, and personal satisfaction than normal high school graduates. (Augusta Gross offers tips in maintaining an emotional even keel in "Young Adults with Learning Disabilities in Post-secondary Educational Settings: Meeting the Challenges of Maintaining Confidence as a Learner" available at www.ldonline.org/ld_indepth/postsecondary/maintaining_confidence.html.) Employers and college instructors may not be aware of or sensitive to the needs of adults with LD. Furthermore, although IDEA covers individuals through age 21, postsecondary institutions are not required to continue the special education services provided through the public school district. Thus, Section 504 and the ADA provide the basis for modifications and accommodations after high school. (Parents who wish to explore financial support measures for their adult children can find some suggestions in the April 2000 *Kiplinger's* article, "Very Special People," by Jane Bennett Clark.)

Help your child identify some careers and vocations that can provide a crucial path to success in life. (Many job concerns are covered in "Put Your Experiences to Work," by Robert Gregory, available at www.ldonline.org/ld_indepth/abilities/ experiences.html.) The fact that individuals with learning disabilities can have successful careers and fulfilling lives (see Chapter 6) offers hope that discouraging grade-school academics need not result in poor adult outcomes. Because teachers and administrators often underestimate the *overall* capabilities of students with LD and have low expectations for them,[1] these students are not challenged in areas of their strengths. This is getting back to the idea of multiple intelligences, in which everyone learns at different rates in different areas. If you have really been observing your child's development all these years, then you should know his or her strengths and preferences, and can *suggest* (no nagging please!) some directions in life. At times, it may feel like tossing

---

1   Trapani, *Transition Goals for Students with Learning Disabilities*, p. 90.

your teenager a life raft, but it is at least something to think about for the time being. After high school, the choices are continued education, employment, or both simultaneously:

- Employment right after high school — Private competitive or supported employment
  Military service, AmeriCorps (www.americorps.org or 800/ 942-2677 or TTY 800/ 833-3722)
- Vocational school — Community college, trade, or technical schools
  Work-study programs, Job Corps (www.jobcorps.org or 800/ 733-5627)
- College — Continuing and adult education
  2-year junior or community college program
  4-year college or university baccalaureate degree
  Postgraduate masters, professional, and doctorate degrees

Your child is preparing for adulthood like any other young person. Use the expertise available at your adolescent's high school. Other websites offer help:

- "Parenting Teens with AD/HD, Made Simple," by Mary Fowler, available at www.ldonline.org/ld_indepth/parenting/parenting_teens.html

- "Auxiliary Aids and Services for Postsecondary Students with Disabilities: Higher Education's Obligations Under Section 504 and Title II of the ADA," by the U.S. Department of Education Office for Civil Rights, available at www.ldonline.org/ld_indepth/technology/auxiliary_aids.html

- "ERIC Clearinghouse for Community Colleges," available at www.gseis.ucla.edu/ERIC/find.htm, provides search engines to help identify postsecondary institutions of interest—technical schools, 2- and 4-year colleges, and universities—by such factors as location, academic disciplines, cost, and special programs.

Because your teenager may not want *your* advice alone, assemble an informal advisory team to help your student make the right choices:

Team Member	Ongoing K–12 School Duties	Additional High School Duties
Parent	identifies strengths & preferences encourages interests & activities	oversees transition process teaches independent living skills
Psychologist	tests and evaluates capabilities	suggests adult range of possibilities
Counselor	plans course schedule monitors at-risk students	tests vocational preferences suggests career & college options
Resource specialist	provides support services facilitates exam accommodations monitors progress	supports transition & self-advocacy skills, prepares documents for postsecondary accommodations
Regular teachers	instructs academics tutors during office hours	suggests curriculum & career ideas writes letters of recommendation

Begin a resume for your child during the freshman year of high school. Include school-related honors and activities; academic activities at other institutions; extracurricular sports, fine arts, and volunteer activities; and other hobbies and interests. This information resource will not only be useful for IEPs, counselors, and job and college applications, but may also remind your child of his or her achievements and activities for autobiographical assignments or scholarship applications. JobStar Central suggests resume tips online at http://jobstar.org/tools/resume/index.cfm.

Employment

Employers generally expect a willingness to work; good reading, writing, math, and interpersonal skills; and no personal distractions. Low salaries, little potential for advancement, underemployment, and unemployment are readily found among high school graduates with LD who have trouble not only with academic and social skills, but also with workplace skills like handling criticism, making suggestions to co-workers, and explaining concerns to supervisors.[2] Many adults with learning disabilities continue to live with parents and rely on them for advocacy and job contacts. Help your child identify a job with a strong employee development program or good on-the-job training. This could avoid many of the following personnel issues identified in a survey of business owners:[3]

- Disciplining workers
- Correcting errors
- Executing the work of others
- Teaching skills that should already have been learned.

Look for a good fit between your offspring and a potential employer. Find out how easily the job skills learned at one place can be transferred to another place. The right job is crucial for success and happiness.

Vocational training

Vocational assessments can be the basis for determining:

- Eligibility for particular vocational programs and services available through schools or rehabilitation agencies

---

2   Trapani, pp. 91-92.
3   The results of the study by a management consulting firm, George S. May International Company of Park Ridge, Illinois were presented in "Owners Identify Time-Wasters," *Business Advisor*, a Wells Fargo publication, March/April 2001, p. 33.

• Preferences for certain types of careers which may launch further exploration into specific jobs

• Abilities and aptitudes in particular areas, leading to in-depth curriculum planning. For example, "A New Blue-Collar World," by Clare Ansberry (*The Wall Street Journal*, 30 June 2003), mentions fifth graders with good Lego construction skills being recruited by a Cleveland high school to potentially fill a looming U.S. shortage of machinists.

The ideal vocational assessment includes standardized tests, work samples, and behavioral observations. Still, an assessment is only one considered opinion, not an irrevocable determination of your child's future. Under Section 504, students cannot be advised to restrict their career options due to learning disabilities[4] but they may be informed about job requirements and the specific difficulties that they may encounter. The authors of *Negotiating the Special Education Maze* urge parents to be proactive:

> "… [E]mployers and adult service providers recognize that vocational training alone seldom fully prepares a person for a job. If you wait until a young person is 'ready' for a job; if you wait until he has learned in school all the requirements for a job; if you wait until some service provider has prepared him to move from a sheltered, segregated job to a job in the community; the day may never come. It is now widely acknowledged that young people with disabilities are able to get and to keep jobs for a longer period of time if they are placed in jobs that interest them, are trained on the job, and then are given the supports they need to keep the job."[5]

For many individuals with learning disabilities, vocational training during secondary school brought success after graduation.[6]

> "*Vocational education* means organized educational programs that are directly related to the preparation of individuals for paid or unpaid employment, or for additional preparation for a career requiring other than a baccalaureate or advanced degree."
>
> *—34 CFR § 300.26*

---

4   Rothstein, "Legal Issues," p. 27.

5   Excerpted from *Negotiating the Special Education Maze*, 3rd Edition, by Winifred Anderson, Stephen Chitwood, and Deidre Hayden, p. 154. Copyright © 1997 by Winifred Anderson, Stephen Chitwood, and Deidre Hayden. All rights reserved. Published by Woodbine House, Inc., Bethesda, MD. Reprinted with permission of Deidre Hayden.

6   Bender, *Learning Disabilities*, p.355.

Different types of vocational programs exist. Auto mechanics and carpentry are rare class offerings today; schools are more likely to offer computer and multimedia courses. Traditional high school programs require regular academic instruction leading to a high school diploma. Some high school vocational programs go a bit further with hands-on classroom training, paid work experiences, and a vocational certificate. Charter schools may have trade-school themes.[7] Programs integrating training within the local community place students in a protected environment to learn business etiquette and technical skills. One magnet program in San Francisco, John A. O'Connell Technical High School, combines high-school and community-college classes with work experience, paid internships, and mentors in areas promising employment such as construction, health sciences, auto mechanics, and food service.

Before placing your teenager in a high school vocational program, consider whether it is a good match for his or her skills and interests. If so, then investigate your child's long-term prospects in this field.

• Talk to the program's graduates. Instructors may be quite successful in their field, but unsuccessful in communicating the material and motivating the students. The curriculum may proceed at too rapid a pace or be outdated. The equipment may be inadequate. The overall program may not be able to deliver all that it promises.

• Talk to companies in the field. Learn which programs or courses they would recommend. Ask whether they have and/or would hire graduates of the prospective program. Identify accredited programs.

• Compare alternatives, for example private institutions versus public schools and community colleges. Weigh financial costs against potential job earnings. Determine whether getting that first job would require additional training after graduation such as an internship.

Vocational training after high school graduation focuses on technical skills. Community colleges work with local employers to train students for hard-to-fill job positions and offer support for students with disabilities. (The American Association of Community Colleges' website, www.aacc.nche.edu, can locate a community college near you.)

Private schools offer training as well, but thoroughly investigate the school's professional practices, accreditation, and continuing operation. Private high-tech companies, local colleges, and private training centers offer certificates in computer technology. Culinary academies have menu specialties. Good jobs, however, usually require at least two years of experience in addition to certification.

---

7   Carlos Tejada, "These Students Wear Hardhats and Learn How to Cut Tiles," *The Wall Street Journal*, 28 May 2002, p. B1.

Purpose of education. Almost all colleges and universities receive some form of federal financial assistance, and so are subject to Section 504 as well as ADA requirements. At the graduate school level, administrators are "less responsive" to students with disabilities, especially those with learning disabilities than at the undergraduate level.[8] Community colleges offer open enrollment, inexpensive tuition, disability services and accommodations, and courses easily transferable to four-year colleges. Some community colleges offer bachelors and graduate programs to disadvantaged students. Two books which may be useful are *College Students with Learning Disabilities: A Handbook*, by Susan A. Vogel, and *College and Career Success for Students with Learning Disabilities*, by Rosyln Dolber. The student also needs to learn specific strategies to overcome problems commonly found in college:

- Mediocre reading skills impede execution of assignments.
- Word retrieval difficulties, limited vocabulary, or expressive-language sequencing problems reduce participation in class discussions.
- Poor writing skills cause evaluation difficulties.
- Lecture material, which may draw on state-of-the art research, may not be otherwise available in a convenient form like a textbook, and thus problematic for poor note takers.
- Time-management or self-monitoring troubles can result in unfinished assignments and unbalanced academic and extracurricular activities.
- Social awkwardness leads to negative student and faculty interactions or misunderstanding of advice and suggestions.
- Self-awareness deficits or immaturity, that is, not knowing one's capabilities and limitations, can result in overconfidence or denial.

Many academicians question the worthiness of students with disabilities at the highest academic levels. In particular, while students with LD often synthesize new concepts and interpretations, professors and classmates value oral and written skills more.[9] Essentially, this debate is really a question about the purpose of education.

As noted in Chapter 5, while language is important, it isn't the sole measure of intelligence. Words alone can't land a man on the moon, compose a symphony, create a sense of well-being through design and architecture, or give visual realism to cinematic worlds. From another perspective, while many fear lowered standards in oral discourse and writing proficiency, others decry junk science, technical illiteracy, and poor imagination. In truth, society demands all kinds of skills. In the

---

8   Vogel, "Postsecondary Education for Adults with Learning Disabilities," p. 7.
9   Trapani, *Transition Goals for Students with Learning Disabilities*, p. 99.

real world, people specialize in what they do best, try to be educated as best as possible, and life moves on. One college instructor labeled as *old style* the debate over whether to provide college opportunities to students with LD.

Accommodations. Under Section 504, colleges cannot deny admission based on the presence of a disability if the individual has fulfilled the requisite technical and academic standards of the program. Admissions tests or criteria that disproportionately or adversely affect applicants with a disability or a specific type of disability are prohibited, "unless these tests have been validated as a predictor of success and alternate tests are not available."[10] Colleges are prohibited from noting accommodations on the transcripts of only these students with disabilities, unless accommodations and waivers are noted on the transcripts of all students.[11]

Students need not disclose their learning disabilities to colleges, but if they don't they will not have access to critical services and accommodations such as:
- Extended time for testing and degree completion
- Note taking services
- Taped recordings of lectures and required texts
- Study guides
- Time-management and advocacy assistance
- Counseling
- Waivers of foreign language requirements
- Assessment services
- Reduced class loads.

Institutions cannot limit participation of those with learning disabilities; for example, a complete prohibition on tape recorders could be unacceptable, although—in cases of the instructor's intellectual property—use of the recordings could be restricted to study purposes only.[12] In another example, a court invalidated an athletic ineligibility ruling for an overage student with LD who was held back earlier in school.[13] (The NCAA website, "Frequently-Asked Questions on Students with Disabilities," available at www.ncaa.org, reviews the formal process for submitting the documentation necessary for receiving accommodations in NCAA activities. At the home page click on *Site Index*; at the next screen entitled *NCAA Alphabetical Site Index* click on the letter *D*; then under the *D* listings click on *Disabilities, students with*.) Some

---

10 From *Success for College Students with Learning Disabilities*, ed. Susan A. Vogel and Pamela B. Adelman, "Legal Issues" by Laura F. Rothstein, p. 25. Copyright © 1993 by Springer-Verlag New York, Inc. All rights reserved. Reprinted with permission of Springer-Verlag GmbH & Co.KG and Susan A. Vogel.
11 Rothstein, "Legal Issues," p. 33.
12 Rothstein, pp. 26-27.
13 Osborne, *Legal Issues in Special Education*, p. 24.

legal issues affecting your child's participation in extracurricular activities despite unhappy academics are reviewed in "Leveling the Playing Field or Leveling the Players?" by Kathleen Sullivan, Patricia Lantz, and Perry Zirkel, available at www.ldonline.org/ld_indepth/legal_legislative/leveling_the_playing_field.html.

Accommodations that fundamentally change the nature of a program are not required, often for reasons of safety,[14] such as surgery, which demands excellent hand-eye coordination. Thus a course element, if demonstrated to be an essential part of the instructional program, does not have to be modified. A college that has demonstrated that quick responses are essential in a debate class does not need to give extra time to a student with learning disabilities; a law school does not have to simplify complex exam questions if lawyers need to understand legal analysis and applications.[15]

Colleges offer student-support services through one of three types of programs:[16]

• *Partially segregated resource programs* offer tutors, readers, note-takers, counselors, advocates, basic skills remediation, and strategy training to a limited number of students. This type of program usually has a separate admissions process, an extra fee, and a summer orientation to review basic skills and familiarize students with services and the college's physical layout.

• *Walk-in programs* provide LD assessments, minimal tutoring, and advocacy assistance. Many graduate students first learn of their disability through this type of program.

• *General service programs* provide assistance to all students with disabilities, including physical, visual, and hearing disabilities. Note-taking, tutoring, counseling referral, and student advocacy services may be available to students with learning disabilities.

Getting to college. A high school freshman with LD, competent in math and reading skills at least at the fifth or sixth grade level, should be encouraged to take college preparatory classes but with a special educator to assist with any skill deficits.[17] High school preparation for college demands strategy, planning, vigilance, and patience.

• *Freshman:* Begin assessments and secondary program planning before the ninth grade, because most introductory courses are offered in the first two years of high school.[18] Initiate career exploration. Continue appropriate remediation and learn new compensation strategies.

14　Rothstein, "Legal Issues," p. 24.
15　Rothstein, pp. 25-26.
16　Trapani, *Transition Goals for Students with Learning Disabilities*, pp. 97-98.
17　Sara Cowen, "Transition Planning for College-Bound Students with Learning Disabilities," in *Success for College Students with Learning Disabilities*, ed. Susan A. Vogel and Pamela B. Adelman (New York: Springer-Verlag, 1993), p. 43.
18　Trapani, *Transition Goals for Students with Learning Disabilities*, p. 94.

Implement classroom modifications and accommodations. Develop new extracurricular activities, interests, self-advocacy and independent functioning. Get to know teachers who can help with career advice and letters of recommendation. Begin working with self-paced SAT I or ACT preparation workbooks or software during weekends, holidays, and summers when school matters are less pressing. The College Board recommends that schools submit *Students with Disabilities (SSD) Student Eligibility* application forms in the spring of the freshman year. A student with a history of using accommodations for schoolwork is much more likely to receive accommodations for college entrance tests than a student without one. The College Board assigns an SSD number for their testing. Only one form need be submitted for each student, but a current evaluation (at least every three years) must be on file for the student to be eligible for testing accommodations. If your teenager plans to take an AP or SAT II test in May, you may wish to submit the SSD form before February. An SSD Timeline is available at www.college board.com/disable/students/html/time.html. You will know whether an SSD application is being completed because parents must sign it. Make sure your teenager returns the form to the school; one student thought he could avoid college entrance exams by not turning in his SSD form. Many colleges require three SAT II tests in addition to the SAT I. Consider taking SAT II subject tests after the related high school course, such as the SAT II Biology test in June. Study the course along with an SAT II test preparation book as best as possible; the school's curriculum may not match the material to be tested. Or work on the subject test over the summer and take it in the fall. Some colleges specifically require the SAT II Math and SAT II Writing tests. One major university may soon require five SAT II tests in math, writing, science, social science, and foreign language. Try to finish SAT II testing before the senior year. A student is not limited in the total number of SAT II tests and may take up to three SAT II exams in one day. SAT II exams are not offered every month during the testing season (October–June) and cannot be taken the same day as the SAT I. Moreover, not all SAT II Subject Tests are available at SAT II testing sessions. (Given that many colleges require more tests or have earlier deadlines than a generation ago, it is surprising that SAT schedules provide only monthly SAT I *or* SAT II testing and no summer testing or at all. See Chapter 24 for test accommodations.)

• *Sophomore:* Continue activities begun in the freshman year. Evaluate student performance and further hone career prospects. Plan future classes to satisfy high school graduation requirements, college admission requirements, and any math or science requirements if a science or engineering degree seems possible. Take a career preferences test if not done in the freshman year. Begin to explore college campuses. The

Independent Educational Consultants Association offers "Top Ten Ways to 'Test Drive' a College" at www.educationalconsulting.org/parents_testdrive.html. Review your high school record to see if any course deficiencies exist; repair any transcript problems in summer school. AP exams occur in May of each year. AP courses require specially trained instructors and thus may be the closest approximation to a national curriculum. Use an AP test preparation book during the course.

- *Junior:* Given the developmental progress of first two years of high school, begin evaluating specific college options, a tentative career objective, prospective areas of study, and types of services required after high school. Peruse your local library or online book recommendations for guides on college selection. (L. Scott Lissner offers advice in "Choosing a College" available at www.ldonline.org/ld_indepth/post secondary/lissner_choosing_college.html.) Visit college campuses. The October PSAT is a practice test for the SAT I, both of which are rooted in verbal-math aptitude tests. Unsatisfying results may require tutoring, stress reduction, adjusted accommodations, or taking the ACT as well as the SAT I. While many counselors advise taking the SAT I in the spring (particularly for students applying for early college admissions) *then* fixing any identified problems, please note that any score improvements above 350 trigger an ETS inquiry. Thus, your teenager may wish to delay SAT I testing until the fall, after a summer of preparing for the initial exam. This is assuming that test preparation will greatly improve an abysmal PSAT performance; single-digit percentile rankings for students with LD is not uncommon. Moreover, *all* scores are now reported to colleges, not just the "best" ones. Instead, finish taking SAT II *content* exams in the spring, especially the SAT II writing test in May and June when writing practice may be at its most developed state. Send for college applications or study online application requirements. Many books offer advice on the application process itself. Begin writing prospective essays with the counselor's guidance; colleges are more interested in what makes the student tick than irrelevant hard-luck stories. Review your high school record and repair deficiencies.

- *Senior:* Continue personal and academic development. Colleges may withdraw acceptances if grades slip even through the last semester of high school. Wrap up standardized testing and take the SAT I or the ACT or both. Observe application deadlines; college admissions officers note with regret that a surge of last-minute online applications inevitably crashes their computer systems. Give teachers recommendation forms with stamped envelopes addressed to admissions offices. Visit prospective campuses, perhaps meeting faculty members of departments of interest. Depending on the decision to self-disclose during the application process (or perhaps to be submitted after admission), a transition packet can be assembled containing a recent (within the past three years) psychoeducational report, the IEP, writing samples, a letter of recommendation from the resource specialist, and any other relevant documents. Ensure that the final high school transcript will be sent to the college on time.

High school: Almost an adult

Adolescents with learning disabilities may not be fully capable of managing all the academic, social, motivational, and cognitive demands of high school. High school requires abilities in many areas (ranked from highest to lowest according to teacher expectations):[19]

1. Independent work habits, including time and materials management to complete assignments, and requesting help only when needed

2. Social skills, including teamwork, respect for authority, and acceptance of criticism

3. Communication skills, including oral and written

4. Study skills, including lecture note-taking, library usage, and testing ability

5. Mastery of subject content.

Students with LD must also learn how to advocate for themselves. This is a particularly difficult task since teenagers would rather not call attention to any disability. (Deborah Stern offers suggestions on self-advocacy in "Building the Bridge between Community College and Work for Students with Learning Disabilities," available at www. ldonline.org/ld_indepth/postsecondary/building_the_bridge.html). All too often, the reasons for a student exiting a special education program have more to do with chronological age than self-sufficiency. During the 1998–99 school year, 299,457 U.S. students with specific learning disabilities age 14 and older left special education programs for the following reasons:[20]

Graduated with a diploma	33.6%
Received a certificate	4.6%
Reached the maximum age covered by IDEA	0.3%
Returned to regular education	12.6%
Moved and continued special education elsewhere	22.7%
Moved but unknown if special education was continued	11.7%
Dropped out	14.4%
Died	0.2%

---

19 Mercer citing 1983 Knowlton study, *Students with Learning Disabilities*, p. 354.

20 Figures were calculated from data in Table AD1, U.S. Department of Education, "Twenty-third Annual Report to Congress," p. A-254. (Additional statistics are available on the website for each state and other categories of disability. AD/HD and Asperger's syndrome are not separately broken out.)

The *DSM-IV-TR* estimates that nearly 40% of students with LD drop out of school.[21] Any academic and motivational problems of elementary school generally continue in high school. Adolescents with learning disabilities generally do not form positive attachments to school, usually participate less than normal peers in extracurricular activities, and can be withdrawn or disruptive.[22]

Transition planning: Moving from adolescence to jobs and careers

As the child grows, he or she needs to shoulder more responsibility for his or her actions. In the adult real world, few accommodations (roughly being those not too onerous to an employer) are provided to alleviate the difficulties underlying LD. The question is whether one can do the work. Thus, growing children should not expect to use learning disabilities as an acceptable excuse for substandard job performance. However, failing to educate anyone today is condemning someone to a life of failure, because agricultural, factory assembly, and clerical jobs continue to disappear. IDEA, according to the U.S. Congress is "an opportunity to prepare children with disabilities better in order to make a successful transition to adult life."[23]

Transition planning identifies the desired situation for a student with learning disabilities following high school graduation, and then constructs a program to prepare the student toward this goal. The student must be invited to any meeting involving his or her transition planning to help decide his or her future.

> "... [T]ransition services means a coordinated set of activities for a student with a disability that—
> (1) Is designed within an outcome-oriented process, which promotes movement from school to post-school activities, including postsecondary education, vocational training, integrated employment (including supported employment), continuing and adult education, adult services, independent living, or community participation;
> (2) Is based upon the individual student's needs, taking into account the student's preferences and interests; and
> (3) Includes—
> (i) Instruction;
> (ii) Related services;

---

21 *Diagnostic and Statistical Manual of Mental Disorders*, p. 50.
22 Trapani, *Transition Goals for Students with Learning Disabilities*, pp. 50-51.
23 U.S. Department of Education, "Twenty-third Annual Report to Congress," p. IV-29.

(iii) Community experiences;
(iv) The development of employment and other post-school adult living objectives; and
(v) If appropriate, acquisition of daily living skills and functional vocational evaluation.
(b) Transition services for students with disabilities may be special education, if provided as specially designed instruction, or related services, if required to assist a student with a disability to benefit from special education.

—34 CFR § 300.29

It is critical that appropriate transition services be secured for your adolescent while he or she remains eligible under IDEA and before high school graduation. In 1999–2000, less than half of the students receiving IDEA services were in middle school and high school:[24]

Ages 6–11 years· · · · 52.7%
Ages 12–17 years· · · · 42.0%
Ages 18–21 years· · · · · 5.3%

Although many students learn to compensate and will require no services as teenagers, "twice as many children with disabilities drop out as compared to children without disabilities."[25] After high school graduation, young adults with disabilities effectively have nowhere to go for continued support services. A summary of a 2002 study, "High School Programs as Perceived by Youth with Learning Disabilities," by Larry Kottering and Patricia Braziel, highlights the best and worst aspects of school, changes which could help prevent drop outs, and is available at www.ldonline.org/ld_indepth/research_digest/high_school _perceptions.html.

Transition services. Beginning at age 14, or younger if appropriate, the child's IEP team is required to identify his or her prospective transition *needs* for programming purposes (*34 CFR § 300.347*). Thus, by the freshman year of high school, postsecondary employment, vocational, or college options may have already been determined. For example, to be an engineer, one must not only plan on attending an engineering college, but also plan on taking math and science courses in high school. A vocational assessment for determining appropriate placement "can be considered a related service and written into your child's IEP when he reaches middle school or early high school years."[26] Either the school system itself conducts vocational assessments, or

---

24   U.S. Department of Education, "Twenty-third Annual Report to Congress," p. II-25.
25   U.S. Department of Education, "Twenty-third Annual Report to Congress," p. IV-12.
26   Anderson, Chitwood, and Hayden, *Negotiating the Special Education Maze*, p. 153.

they may engage an outside agency. (Community colleges may also provide these assessments.)

Beginning at age 16, the IEP team must identify actual transition *services*. The IEP for a 16-year-old examines his or her prospective adult functioning in society, and determines services, opportunities, and experiences required to prepare the student for life after high school (*34 CFR § 300.347 (b)*). For some students, these transition services can be incorporated into their IEP even by age 14 or younger, if appropriate, as in potential drop out cases. Some researchers have identified several drop out warning signs, among them:[27]

- Low academic achievement
- Weak social integration
- At least one grade retention
- Poor extracurricular participation
- At least one transfer between schools within a district
- Overt dislike for school
- High absenteeism and tardiness
- Suspensions and expulsions
- Inadequate accumulation of high school credits
- Substance abuse.

Transition services must be reconsidered annually, and specified at IEP meetings whether they are needed. (For students held in correctional facilities, IDEA has specific regulations.) Transition planning should address several problems commonly found in many students:[28]

- No understanding of their individual disability, demonstrated by a lack self-confidence, a focus on weaknesses and not on strengths, and little motivation to succeed academically
- Inadequate academic preparation for life after high school, particularly if the goal is college
- No exploration of career possibilities, which can provide a reason for staying in school
- Undeveloped independent living skills like social skills and flexibility in changed circumstances
- Insufficient guidance in selecting suitable and interesting postsecondary programs with support services.

Instructional options. The most aggressive efforts to improve academic and social skills, as well as to help develop career goals, should

---

27 Gary M. Clark and Oliver P. Kolstoe citing 1987 studies by Jay and Padilla; deBettencourt, Zigmond, and Thornton; and Blackorby, Kortering, Edgar, and Emerson, *Career Development and Transition Education for Adolescents with Disabilities*, (Needham Heights, Massachusetts: Allyn and Bacon, 1990), pp. 380-381.
28 Cowen, "Transition Planning for College-Bound Students with Learning Disabilities," pp. 39-40.

be in high school.[29] To satisfy the diverse needs of students with learning disabilities, at least five types of instructional options exist:[30]

- Skills remediation
- Cognitive strategies instruction
- Regular course work with tutorial support
- Career-related programs
- Independent living skills.

Not all schools will have all options. For example, a college prep school is unlikely to offer a functional living skills program. Also, any single student can require different types of services during transition, such as learning strategies during the freshman year, career-related instruction during the senior year, or any combination at any time. Summer school presents another opportunity to receive specialized help or to ease the following year's schedule by taking a required course. James McAfee and Christopher Greenawalt review legal decisions involving transition in "IDEA, the Courts, and the Law on Transition," available at www.ldonline.org/ld_indepth/transition/law_of_transition.html.

An adult at last. If necessary before the student leaves high school, the transition team should prepare a plan with public and/or private arrangements. In states that transfer rights at the age of 18, you will no longer have access to your adult child's records unless your child signs a waiver, so inquire about getting one. A child who began formal schooling *late* or was held back will be at least 18 during at least part of the senior year of high school. The law requires that the student be notified at least one year before the age of majority, 17 in this case, of this impending transfer in the IEP:

> "... [B]eginning at least one year before a student reaches the age of majority under State law, the student's IEP must include a statement that the student has been informed of his or her rights ... that will transfer to the student...."
>
> *—34 CFR § 300.347 (c)*

Follow-up. IDEA does not provide for continued services after high school graduation. This is unfortunate. Not only can students miss opportunities for assistance as eligibility is possible until the 22nd birthday under federal law, but there is no feedback to the high schools on the efficacy of any transition efforts utilized. Ideally, an IEP should clearly identify appropriate services past high school graduation for successful vocational or collegiate transitions.

---

29 Trapani, *Transition Goals for Students with Learning Disabilities*, p. 6.
30 Mercer, *Students with Learning Disabilities*, p. 363.

Conclusion

Of all the strange things that Alice saw in her journey Through The Looking-Glass, this was the one that she always remembered most clearly. Years afterwards she could bring the whole scene back again, as if it had been only yesterday—the mild blue eyes and kindly smile of the [White] Knight—the setting sun gleaming through his hair, and shining on his armour in a blaze of light that quite dazzled her—the horse quietly moving about, with the reins hanging loose on his neck, cropping the grass at her feet—and the black shadows of the forest behind ....

—Through the Looking-Glass

In the preface to this book, I alluded to the seven blind men who each had a different description of an elephant. Learning disabilities is like an elephant in another way—it's a problem in the room with no common resolution. What has surprised me in gathering the material for this book is that much useful information is already available which could go a long way towards appropriately managing the problems.

Until the public understands that most learning difficulties have solutions, you are left with the immediate problem of helping your child as the White Knight helped Alice. Teachers and service providers may come and go, but *you* are the parent of this developing individual. For this reason you are very important to your child, more than you may realize. Your child's trust in you may be the only hope he or she may have for the future. Learn how your child learns and where your child's strengths and interests lie. Keep in touch with informational networks and support groups. Connect your child with mainstream society in some way. Know your child's rights but understand that the goal must be to integrate your child into society as best as possible. The individuals mentioned in Chapter 6 may have been challenging children to raise, but in the end, have brought something wonderfully unique to this world. While you must be realistic, have hope. You may be pleasantly surprised.

References

• Abercrombie, Sharon. "Going Extra Mile: Riordan Program Reaches Out to Kids with Special Needs." *Catholic San Francisco*, 26 January 2001.

• Accardo, Pasquale J. "A Developmental Pediatric Perspective on Neurologically Based Specific Learning Disabilities," in *Learning Disabilities: Lifelong Issues*, ed. Shirley C. Cramer and William Ellis. Baltimore: Paul H. Brookes Publishing Co., 1996.

• Accardo, Pasquale. "Learning Disabilities Just Don't Add Up," *The Journal of Pediatrics*, September 1998.

• Accardo, Pasquale. "Reading Dyslexia," in *Specific Reading Disability: A View of the Spectrum*, ed. Bruce K. Shapiro, Pasquale J. Accardo, and Arnold J. Capute. Timonium, Maryland: York Press, 1998.

• Almanac of Policy Issues, "U.S. Education Spending: 1999-2000" [Internet]. Accessed 16 January 2003 from: http://www.policyalmanac.org/education/archive/doe _education_spending.shtml

• Alonso, Connie and Anita Gurian. "Youth Suicide," *Child Study Center Letter* [Internet]. May/June 2001. Available from: http://www.aboutourkids.org/letter/mayjun 01.pdf

• American Academy of Pediatrics, Subcommittee on Attention-Deficit/Hyperactivity Disorder and Committee on Quality Improvement. "Clinical Practice Guideline: Treatment of the School-Aged Child with Attention-Deficit/Hyperactivity Disorder," *Pediatrics*, 4 October 2001.

• American Association for the Advancement of Science. "Study Examines Impact on Dyslexia of English, French and Italian Spelling" [Internet]. 2002. Available from: http://www.aaas.org/news/releases/dyslexia/shtml

• Anderson, Winifred, Stephen Chitwood, and Deidre Hayden. *Negotiating the Special Education Maze: A Guide for Parents and Teachers*, 3rd Edition. Bethesda, Maryland: Woodbine House, 1997.

• Arnst, Catherine. "Attention Deficit: Is It In the Genes?" *Business Week*, 22 November 1999.

• Asimov, Nanette. "90% of Disabled Kids Flunk Exit Exam," *San Francisco Chronicle*, 27 September 2002.

• Asimov, Nanette. "Effect of Smaller Elementary Classes Unclear, Study Says," *San Francisco Chronicle*, 28 June 2002.

• Asimov, Nanette. "More Uncredentialed Teachers' Students Fail," *San Francisco Chronicle*, 11 December 2002.

• Asimov, Nanette. "School Exit Exams Need Warnings, Attorneys Says," *San Francisco Chronicle*, 4 January 2003.

• Augur, Jean. *This Book Doesn't Make Sense: Living and Learning with Dyslexia*. London: Whurr Publishers, 1995.

• Barkley, Russell. "ADHD: Theory, Diagnosis, and Treatment" [Internet]. 17 June 2000. Available from: http://www.schwablearning.org/pdfs/2200_7-barktran.pdf

• Barkley, Russell A. "Attention Deficit Hyperactivity Disorder (ADHD)," *LD Matters*, a Schwab Learning Publication. Spring 2000.

• Barkley, Russell A. "Critical Issues in Research on Attention," in *Attention, Memory, and Executive Function*, ed. G. Reid Lyon and Norman A. Krasnegor. Baltimore: Paul H. Brookes Publishing Co., 1996.

• Barkley, Russell A. and others. "International Consensus Statement on ADHD" [Internet]. January 2002. Available from: http://www.chad.org/webpage.cfm?cat_id=10 &subcat_id=67&sec_id=0

• Baum, Susan M., Steve V. Owen, and John Dixon. *To Be Gifted & Learning Disabled*. Mansfield Center, Connecticut: Creative Learning Press, 1991.

- Baumel, Jan. "Academic Stress Points in Education" [Internet]. Posted 14 November 2000 and updated 6 September 2001. Available from: http://www.schwablearning.org/articles.asp?r=34
- Begley, Sharon. "Genes May Determine Which Abused Kids Will 'Grow Up Bad,'" *The Wall Street Journal*, 20 September 2002.
- Begley, Sharon. "Survival of the Busiest," *The Wall Street Journal*, 11 October 2002.
- Bender, William N. *Learning Disabilities: Characteristics, Identification, and Teaching Strategies*, 2nd Edition. Needham Heights, Massachusetts: Allyn and Bacon, 1995.
- Bower, Bruce. "A Tip of the Tongue to the Brain," *Science News*, 8 September 2001.
- Bower, Bruce. "Audiovisual Aids May Lessen Dyslexia," *Science News*, 8 September 2001.
- Bower, Bruce. "Biology of Rank," *Science News*, 26 January 2002.
- Bower, Bruce. "Boys Take a Tumble," *Science News*, 11 May 2002.
- Bower, Bruce. "Certain Memories May Rest on a Good Sleep," *Science News*, 2 December 2000.
- Bower, Bruce. "Disabilities Develop as Family Affair," *Science News*, 3 November 2001.
- Bower, Bruce. "Dyslexia Gets a Break in Italy," *Science News*, 31 March 2001.
- Bower, Bruce. "Fighting Stereotype Stigma," *Science News*, 29 June 1996.
- Bower, Bruce. "Findings Puncture Self-Esteem Claims," *Science News*, 7 June 2003.
- Bower, Bruce. "Gene May Alter Ritalin's Effects in ADHD," *Science News*, 4 December 1999.
- Bower, Bruce. "Growing Up in Harm's Way," *Science News*, 25 May 1996.
- Bower, Bruce. "IQ's Evolutionary Breakdown," *Science News*, 8 April 1995.
- Bower, Bruce. "Kids' ADHD Care Gets A Wake-Up Call," *Science News*, 18 and 25 December 1999.
- Bower, Bruce. "Language Mastery Goes Native in the Brain," *Science News*, 23 November 1996.
- Bower, Bruce. "Math Fears Subtract from Memory, Learning," *Science News*, 30 June 2001.
- Bower, Bruce. "Med Use Widens in Kids with ADHD," *Science News*, 1 June 2002.
- Bower, Bruce. "Plight of the Untouchables: Stigmas Harm Public Health in Unexplored Ways," *Science News*, 27 October 2001.
- Bower, Bruce. "Popular Boys Show Their Tough Side," *Science News*, 22 January 2000.
- Bower, Bruce. "Study of Stimulant Therapy Raises Concern," *Science News*, 29 July 2000.
- Bower, Bruce. "Teens' ADHD Treatment Gets Low-dose Boost," *Science News*, 2 June 2001.
- Bower, Bruce. "Words Get In the Way: Talk Is Cheap but It Can Tax Your Memory," *Science News*, 19 April 2003.
- Brooks, Robert. "Islands of Competence," *LD Matters*, a Schwab Learning Publication. Winter 1997.
- Bull, George. *Michelangelo: A Biography*. New York: St. Martin's Press, 1995.
- Cannell, Stephen J. "A Writing Fool," *Newsweek*, 22 November 1999.
- Cantu, Norma V. and Judith E. Heumann. "Dear Colleague" Letter to educators that harassment based on disability is wrong and illegal [Internet]. 26 July 2000. Available from: http://www.ed.gov/offices/OCR/docs/disabharassltr.html
- Carle, Eben. "ADHD For Sale," *Psychology Today* [Internet]. May/June 2000. Accessed 31 August 2002 from: http://www.psychologytoday.com/HTDocs/prod/PTOhome/home.asp
- Carroll, Lewis. *Through the Looking-Glass* [Internet]. 1872. Accessed 26 May 2003 from: http://www.4literature.net/Lewis_Carroll/Through_the_Looking_Glass

• Centers for Disease Control and Prevention. "Taking Part in Research Studies: What Questions Should You Ask?" [Internet]. Last updated 13 August 1998. Available from: http://www.cdc.gov/hiv/pubs/brochure/unc3bro.htm

• CHADD. "Assessing Complementary and/or Controversial Interventions - CHADD Fact Sheet #6" [Internet]. Previously posted as "CHADD Fact Sheet No. 6," Spring 2000. Accessed 1 September 2002. Available from: http://www.chadd.org/fs/fs6.htm

• Chervin, Ronald D., Kristen Hedger Archbold, James E. Dillon, Parviz Penahi, Kenneth J. Pituch, Ronald E. Dahl, and Christian Guilleminault. "Inattention, Hyperactivity, and Symptoms of Sleep-Disordered Breathing," *Pediatrics*, 3 March 2002.

• Chinn, Stephen J. and J. Richard Ashcroft. *Mathematics for Dyslexics: A Teaching Handbook*. London: Whurr Publishers, 1993.

• Clark, Gary M. and Oliver P. Kolstoe. *Career Development and Transition Education for Adolescents with Disabilities*. Needham Heights, Massachusetts: Allyn and Bacon, 1990.

• Clark, Ronald W. *Einstein: The Life and Times*. New York: Avon Books, 1971.

• Cline, Starr and Diane Schwartz. *Diverse Populations of Gifted Children: Meeting Their Needs in the Regular Classroom and Beyond*. Upper Saddle River, New Jersey: Prentice-Hall, 1999.

• Cohen, Matthew. "Legal Briefs from Matt Cohen, Esq." [Internet]. Accessed 11 October 2002 from: http://www.ldonline.org/legal/index.html

• Compton, Carolyn. *A Guide to 85 Tests for Special Education*. Belmont, California: Fearon/Janus/Quercus, 1990.

• Cooney, John B. "A Cognitive Theory of Learning: Implications for Learning Disabilities," in *A Cognitive Approach to Learning Disabilities*, 2nd Edition, ed. D. Kim Reid, Wayne P. Hresko, and H. Lee Swanson. Austin, Texas: PRO-ED, 1991.

• Cooper, Harris. "Homework for All—In Moderation" [Internet]. 2001. Available from http://www.bryan.k12.oh.us/teachresource/hmwrkmoder.doc

• Cowen Sara. "Transition Planning for LD College-Bound Students," in *Success for College Students with Learning Disabilities*, ed. Susan A. Vogel and Patricia Adelman. New York: Springer-Verlag, 1993.

• Critchley, H.D., E.M. Daly, E.T. Bullmore, S.C. Williams, T. Van Amelsvoort, D.M. Robertson, A. Rowe, M. Phillips, G. McAlonan, P. Howlin, and D.G. Murphy. "The Functional Neuroanatomy of Social Behaviour: Changes in Cerebral Blood Flow When People with Autistic Disorder Process Facial Expressions," *Brain* [Internet]. November 2000. Available from: http://www.ncbi.nlm.nih.gov/entrez/query.fcgi?cmd=Retrieve&db=PubMed&list_uids=11050021&dopt=Abstract

• Crossen, Cynthia. "Think You're Smart? Then Just Try to Sell a New Kind of IQ Test," *The Wall Street Journal*, 5 June 1997.

• Darwin, Charles. *The Autobiography of Charles Darwin*, ed. Nora Barlow. New York: W.W. Norton & Company, 1958.

• Dawson, Jodie. "Successful People with LD and AD/HD" [Internet]. Created 22 January 2001 and updated 22 January 2003. Available from: http://www.schwablearning.org/articles.asp?r=258

• Debré, Patrice. *Louis Pasteur*, English translation by Elborg Forster. Baltimore: The Johns Hopkins University Press, 1998.

• D'Este, Carlo. *Patton: A Genius for War*. New York: HarperCollins Publishers, 1995.

• *Diagnostic and Statistical Manual of Mental Disorders*, 4th Edition, Text Revision. Washington, D.C.: American Psychiatric Association, 2000.

• Dixit, Jay. "An Eye on ADHD" [Internet], *Psychology Today*. Accessed 31 August 2002 from: http://www.psychologytoday.com/HTDocs/prod/PTOhome/home.asp

• Downey, D.M., L.E. Snyder, and B. Hill. "College Students with Dyslexia: Persistent Linguistic Deficits and Foreign Language Learning," *Dyslexia* [Internet]. July-September 2000. Available from: http://www.ncbi.nlm.nih.gov/entrez/query.fcgi?cmd=Retrieve&db=PubMed&list_uids=10840510&dopt=Abstract

- Duenwald, Mary and Denise Grady. "Young Survivors of Cancer Battle Effects of Treatment" [Internet]. 8 January 2003. Available from: http://www.nytimes.com/2003/01/08/health/08CANC.html
- Ehrenberg, Ronald G., Dominic J. Brewer, Adam Gamoran and J. Douglas Willms. "Does Class Size Matter?" *Scientific American*, November 2001.
- Epstein, Joseph. "Going without the Flow: Inarticulacy, uh, Reconsiderated." *The Wall Street Journal*, 26 January 2001.
- Epstein, Joseph. *Snobbery: The American Version*. New York: Houghton Mifflin, 2002.
- Ewers, Justin. "No Room at State U.? Here Are Some Things You Can Do," *U.S. News & World Report*, 23 September 2002.
- Ewers, Justin, Ulrich Boser, and Rachel Hartigan Shea. "Getting In: What's New, What's True," *U.S. News & World Report*, 23 September 2003.
- Faber, Deborah. "Proactive Parenting," *LD Matters*, a Schwab Learning Publication. Spring 2000.
- Federal Register. *Part II Department of Education: 34 CFR Parts 300 and 303 Assistance to States for the Education of Children with Disabilities and the Early Intervention Program for Infants and Toddlers with Disabilities, Rules and Regulations*. Washington D.C.: U.S. Government Printing Office, 12 March 1999.
- Feldman, William. *Learning Disabilities: A Review of Available Treatments*. Springfield, Illinois: Charles C Thomas, 1990.
- Fisher, Gary and Rhoda Cummings. *When Your Child Has LD (Learning Differences): A Survival Guide for Parents*. Minneapolis: Free Spirit Publishing, 1995.
- Fletcher, Jack M. and Bennett A. Shaywitz. "Attention-Deficit/Hyperactivity Disorder," in *Learning Disabilities: Lifelong Issues*, ed. Shirley C. Cramer and William Ellis. Baltimore: Paul H. Brookes Publishing, 1996.
- Fletcher, Michael A. "Connectedness Called Key to Student Behavior" [Internet]. Accessed 12 April 2002 from: http://www.washingtonpost.com/ac2/wp-dyn?pagename=article&node=&contentId=A34686-2002April11
- Foster, Christine. "Why Teach?" *Stanford Magazine*, September/October 2001.
- Foster, R.F. *W.B. Yeats: A Life*. New York: Oxford University Press, 1997.
- Ganschow, Lenore and Richard Sparks. "'Foreign' Language Learning Disabilities: Issues, Research, and Teaching Implications," in *Success for College Students with Learning Disabilities*, ed. Susan A. Vogel and Pamela Adelman. New York: Springer-Verlag, 1993.
- Gardner, Howard. *Multiple Intelligences: The Theory in Practice*. New York: BasicBooks, 1993.
- Garland, Susan. "Patient Heal Thyself," *Business Week*, 16 October 2000.
- Geary, David C. "Mathematical Disabilities: What We Know and Don't Know" [Internet]. Accessed 24 February 2002. Available from: http://www.ldonline.org/ld_indepth/math_skills/geary_math_dis.html
- Gloeckler, Lawrence C. "It's Time to Simplify and Focus on Performance," in *Rethinking Federal Education Programs for Children with Disabilities* [Internet]. January 2002. Available from: http://www.ctredpol.org/specialeducation/timelyidea2002.pdf
- Golden, Daniel. "Disabled Students Gain More Aid on Test," *The Wall Street Journal*, 1 February 2001.
- Goodman, Robin F. Bullies: "More Than Sticks, Stones, and Name Calling" [Internet]. Posted 1 March 2000 and updated 28 December 2000. Available from: http://www.aboutourkids.org/articles/bullies.html
- Goodman, Robin F. "Children with a Chronic Illness: The Interface of Medicine and Mental Health," *Child Study Center Letter* [Internet]. March/April 2001. Available from: http://www.aboutourkids.org/letter/marapr01.pdf
- "Chiropractors," *Consumer Reports*, ed. Joel Gurin, June, 1994.

•   Hack, Maureen, Daniel J. Flannery, Mark Schluchter, Lydia Cartar, Elaine Borawski, and Nancy Klein. "Outcomes in Young Adulthood for Very-Low-Birth-Weight Infants," *The New England Journal of Medicine*, 17 January 2002.

•   Hales, Dianne. "Is Your Child At Risk?" *Ladies Home Journal*, November 1999.

•   Haller, Mary Cathryn. *Learning Disabilities 101: A Primer for Parents*. Highland City, Florida: Rainbow Books, 1999.

•   Halterman, Jill S., Jeffrey M. Kaczorowski, C. Andrew Aligne, Peggy Auinger, and Peter G. Szibgyi. "Iron Deficiency and Cognitive Achievement Among School-aged Children and Adolescents in the United States," *Pediatrics* [Internet]. 6 June 2001. Available from: http://www.biwa.ne.jp/~mccshiga/anemia3.html

•   Hayden, Thomas. "The Inner Einstein," *U.S. News & World Report*, 9 December 2002.

•   Healy, Bernadine. "Toddlers in Turmoil," *U.S. News & World Report*, 16 December 2002.

•   Hehir, Thomas. "An Opportunity to Improve Educational Results for Students with Disabilities," in *Rethinking Federal Education Programs for Children with Disabilities* [Internet]. January 2002. Available from: http://www.ctredpol.org/specialeducation/timelyidea2002.pdf

•   Higgins and Eleanor L. and Marshall H. Raskind. "The Compensatory Effectiveness of Optical Character Recognition/Speech Synthesis on Reading Comprehension of Postsecondary Students with Learning Disabilities," *Learning Disabilities*, Spring 1997.

•   Hoffman, Banesh. *Albert Einstein: Creator and Rebel*. New York: Plume, 1972.

•   Home School Legal Defense Association. "Answers to Frequently Asked Questions about HSLDA" [Internet]. Accessed 17 March 2003. Available from: http://www.hslda.org/docs/faqs/default.asp

•   Horgan, John. "Playing Past Learning Disabilities," *Scientific American*, November 1996.

•   Johnson, Jean, Ann Duffett, Steve Farkas, and Leslie Wilson. *When It's Your Own Child: A Report on Special Education from the Families Who Use It*. New York: Public Agenda, 2002.

•   Johnston, Theresa. "Charles Schwab's Secret Struggle," *Stanford Magazine*. March/April, 1999.

•   Kandel, Eric R., James H. Schwartz, and Thomas M. Jessell. *Principles of Neural Science*, 2nd Edition. New York: McGraw-Hill, 2000.

•   Keegan, John. "His Finest Hour," *U.S. News & World Report*, 29 May 2000.

•   Keenan, Faith. "PCs and Speech: A Rocky Marriage," *Business Week*, 9 September 2002.

•   Kelly, Katy, "They've Got Rhythm: Clapping Away Attention Deficits?" *U.S. News & World Report*, 16 April 2001.

•   Knorr, Caroline. "Fighting ADD in the Dojo: Children with Attention Deficit Disorder Find Discipline and Focus with Martial Arts," *San Francisco Chronicle*, 27 January 2002.

•   Koerner, Brendan I. "Where the Boys Aren't," *U.S. News & World Report*, 8 February 1999.

•   Koppel, Ted. "The Messenger," *Nightline*, ABC broadcast 4 January 2001. Transcript prepared by Burrelle's Information Services.

•   Kroenlein, Johanna and Diana Assereto. *Persuasive Essay Rubric*. San Francisco. Unpublished, 2002.

•   Kurzweil, Ray. "Artificial Intelligence" [Internet]. Accessed 14 April 2002 from: http://www.kurzweilai.net/brain/frame.html

•   Lauren, Jill. *Succeeding with LD: 20 True Stories About Real People with LD*. Minneapolis: Free Spirit Publishing, 1997.

•   Lauricella, Tom. "Your Kid Your Choice," *Offspring*, September/October 2000.

•   Leslie, Mitchell. "The Vexing Legacy of Lewis Terman," *Stanford Magazine*, July/August 2000.

• Levine, Melvin D. *Developmental Variation and Learning Disorders*. Cambridge, Massachusetts: Educators Publishing Service, 1987.

• Levine, Mel. *Educational Care: A System for Understanding and Helping Children with Learning Problems at Home and in School*. Cambridge, Massachusetts: Educators Publishing Service, 1994.

• Levine, Mel. *A Mind at a Time*. New York: Simon & Schuster, 2002.

• Levine, Melvin D. "What's Riding on Writing," Foreword to *The Writing Dilemma: Understanding Dysgraphia* by Regina G. Richards. Riverside, California: RET Center Press, 1998.

• Lewkowicz, Marc. "Helping Children Through Juvenile Court: The Youngster with Learning Disabilities," *The GRAM*, September 1995.

• Light, Richard J. *Making the Most of College: Students Speak Their Minds*. Cambridge, Massachusetts: Harvard University Press, 2001.

• Liptak, Adam. "Judging a Mother for a Crime by Someone Else" [Internet]. Accessed 29 November 2002 from: http://www.nytimes.com/2002/11/27/national/27MURD.html

• Little, L. "Middle-class Mothers' Perceptions of Peer and Sibling Victimization Among Children with Asperger's Syndrome and Nonverbal Learning Disorders," *Issues in Comprehensive Pediatric Nursing* [Internet]. January-March 2002. Available from: http://www.ncbi.nlm.nih.gov/entrez/query.fcgi?cmd=Retrieve&db=PubMed&list_uids=11934121&dopt=Abstract

• Lyon, Reid. "Developing Reading Skills in Young Children," *LD Matters*, a Schwab Learning Publication. Winter 1998.

• Lyon, G. Reid. "The State of Research," in *Learning Disabilities: Lifelong Issues*. ed. Shirley C. Cramer and William Ellis. Baltimore: Paul H. Brookes Publishing Co., 1996.

• Marcus, David L. "One Class, and 20 Learning Styles," *U.S. News & World Report*, 9 April 2001.

• Marsh, Ann. "When the Alphabet is a Struggle," *Forbes*, 6 September 1999.

• Martinez, Michael J. "Speak Easy," *Kiplinger's*, October 2002.

• McAlonan, G.M., E. Daly, V. Kumari, H.D. Critchley, T. Van Amelsvoort, J. Suckling, A. Simmons, T. Sigmundsson, K. Greenwood, A. Russell, N. Schmitz, F. Happe, P. Howlin, and D.G. Murphy. "Brain Anatomy and Sensorimotor Gating in Asperger's Syndrome," *Brain* [Internet]. July 2002. Available from: http://www.ncbi.nlm.nih.gov/entrez/query.fcgi?cmd=Retrieve&db=PubMed&list_uids=12077008&dopt=Abstract

• McCormick, Marie C. and Douglas K. Richardson. "Premature Infants Grow Up," *The New England Journal of Medicine*, 17 January 2002.

• McKinney, James D. "Longitudinal Research on the Behavioral Characteristics of Children with Learning Disabilities," in *Cognitive and Behavioral Characteristics of Children with Learning Disabilities*, ed. Joseph K. Torgesen. Austin, Texas: PRO-ED, 1990.

• McLaughlin, Margaret J. "Issues for Consideration in the Reauthorization of Part B of the Individuals with Disabilities Education Act," in *Rethinking Federal Education Programs for Children with Disabilities* [Internet]. January 2002. Available from: http://www.ctredpol.org/specialeducation/timelyidea2002.pdf

• McLynn, Frank. *Carl Gustav Jung*. New York: St. Martin's Press, 1997.

• Mercer, Cecil D. *Students with Learning Disabilities*, 4th Edition. New York: Macmillan Publishing Company, 1992.

• Milgram, Stanley. "Behavioral Study of Obedience" in *Scientific Psychology and Social Concern*, ed. Leonard W. Schmaltz. New York: Harper & Row, 1971.

• Moats, Louisa Cook. "Implementing Effective Instruction, in *Learning Disabilities: Lifelong Issues*. ed. Shirley C. Cramer and William Ellis. Baltimore: Paul H. Brookes Publishing Co., 1996.

• Morris, Betsy. "Overcoming Dyslexia," *Fortune*, 13 May 2002.

• Mulrine, Anna. "Are Boys the Weaker Sex?," *U.S. News & World Report*, 30 July 2001.

• Museum of Paleontology, University of California at Berkeley. "Leonardo da Vinci (1452-1519)" [Internet]. Accessed 29 January 2003 from: http://www.ucmp.berkeley.edu/history/vinci.html

• Nadeau, Kathleen G., Ellen B. Littman, and Patricia O. Quinn. *Understanding Girls with AD/HD*. Silver Spring, Maryland: Advantage Books, 1999.

• Nansel, Tonja R., Mary Overpeck, Ramani S. Pilla, W. June Ruan, Bruce Simons-Morton, and Peter Scheidt. "Bullying Behaviors Among US Youth," *JAMA*, 25 April 2001.

• National Institutes of Mental Health. "Attention Deficit Hyperactivity Disorder" [Internet]. Updated 1 July 1999. Available at http://www.nimh.nih.gov/publicat/adhd.cfm#adhd7

• Navarrette, Ruben Jr. "In Special Ed, Accountability Is Left Behind," *Los Angeles Times*, 17 April 2002.

• Novick, Barbara Z. and Maureen M. Arnold. *Why Is My Child Having Trouble at School?: A Parent's Guide to Learning Disabilities*. New York: Villard Books, 1991.

• Ochert, Ayala. "The Mathematical Mind," *California Monthly*, April 2002.

• Orey, Michael." Bipolar Disorder Is a Physical Ill, U.S. Judge Rules," *The Wall Street Journal*, 12 March 2002.

• Osborne, Allan G., Jr. *Legal Issues in Special Education*. Needham Heights, Massachusetts: Allyn & Bacon, 1996.

• Osman, Betty B. and Henriette L. Blinder. *No One to Play With: Social Problems of LD and ADD Children*. Novato, California: Academic Therapy Publications, 1995.

• "Owners Identify Time-Wasters," *Business Advisor*, a Wells Fargo Publication, March/April 2001.

• Perry, Bruce D. "First Experiences," *Scholastic Parent & Child*. September 2000.

• Pogue, David. "Listen Up," *Macworld*, June 2000.

• Procaccio, Martin. *Making Modifications in the Classroom: A Collection of Checklists*. Unpublished, 2001.

• Procaccio, Martin. *Special Education Referral Form*. Unpublished, 2001.

• Recording for the Blind & Dyslexic. *Impact*. Spring/Summer 2000 newsletter.

• Reinhardt, Andy. "Meet Mr. Internet," *Business Week*, 13 September 1999.

• Reuters. "No Abuse Risk in Hyperactivity Drugs, Study Says" [Internet]. 6 January 2003. Accessed 14 January 2003 from: http://news.lycos.com/news/story.asp?section=Health&storyId=617272

• Roper Starch Worldwide. *Measuring Progress in Public & Parental Understanding of Learning Disabilities* [Internet], March 2000. Available from: http://www.ldonline.org/news/roper_poll_2000.pdf

• Rose, Ernest. "Faculty Development: Changing Attitudes and Enhancing Knowledge About Learning Disabilities," in *Success for College Students with Learning Disabilities*, ed. Susan A. Vogel and Pamela B. Adelman. New York: Springer-Verlag, 1993.

• Rothstein, Laura F. "Legal Issues," in *Success for College Students with Learning Disabilities*, ed. Susan A. Vogel and Pamela Adelman. New York: Springer-Verlag, 1993.

• Rumsey, Judith M. and Guinevere Eden. "Functional Neuroimaging of Developmental Dyslexia: Regional Cerebral Blood Flow in Dyslexic Men," in *Specific Reading Disability: A View of the Spectrum*, ed. Bruce K. Shapiro, Pasquale J. Accardo, and Arnold J. Capute. Timonium, Maryland: York Press, 1998.

• Sands, Stephen A. and Susan J. Schwartz. "Nonverbal Learning Disabilities," *Child Study Center Letter* [Internet]. May/June 2000. Available from: http://www.aboutourkids.org/letter/mayjun00.pdf

• Schevitz, Tanya. "SAT is to Achievement as …," *San Francisco Chronicle*, 13 May 2001.

• Schevitz, Tanya. "SATs Gain an Essay, Lose the Analogies," *San Francisco Chronicle*, 28 June 2002.

• Schoch, Russell. "UC to SAT: RIP." *California Monthly*, April 2001.

• Schultz, R.T., I. Gauthier, A. Klin, R.K. Fulbright, A.W. Anderson, F. Volkmar, P. Skudlarski, C. Lacadie, D.J. Cohen, and J.C. Gore. "Abnormal Ventral Temporal Cortical

Activity During Face Discrimination Among Individuals with Autism and Asperger Syndrome," *Archives of General Psychiatry* [Internet]. April 2000. Available from: http://www.ncbi.nlm.nih.gov/entrez/query.fcgi?cmd=Retrieve&db=PubMed&list_uids=10768694&dopt=Abstract

• Schunk, Dale H. "Self-Efficacy and Cognitive Achievement: Implications for Students with Learning Problems," in *Cognitive and Behavioral Characteristics of Children with Learning Disabilities*, ed. Joseph K. Torgesen. Austin, Texas: PRO-ED, 1990.

• Schwab Learning. "Educator's Guide to Learning Differences" [Internet]. 2002. Available from: http://www.schwablearning.org/articles.asp?r=433&g=4

• Schwab Learning. "Navigating the LD Journey: A Study on the Experiences and Needs of Mothers of Children with Learning Differences" [Internet]. January 2002. Available from: http://www.schwablearning.org/articles.asp?g=4&r=452

• Schwab Foundation for Learning Staff. "Classroom Strategies." *LD Matters*, Spring 2000.

• Schwartz, Susan. "Promote or Retain? Questions About Tougher School Standards" [Internet]. Posted 1 October 1999 and updated 5 December 2000. Available from: http://www.aboutourkids.org/articles/promoteretain.html

• Science Faculty of Archbishop Riordan High School, San Francisco. *Physical Science Moon Lab Grades*. Unpublished, 2001.

• Szegedy-Mazak, Marianne. "The Sound of Unsound Minds," *U.S. News & World Report*, 13 January 2003.

• Shalev, R.S., J. Auerbach, O. Manor, and V. Gross-Tsur. "Developmental Dyscalculia: Prevalence and Prognosis," *European Child & Adolescent Psychiatry* [Internet]. 2000. Available from: http://www.ncbi.nlm.nih.gov/entrez/query.fcgi?cmd=Retrieve&db=PubMed&list_uids=11138905&dopt=Abstract

• Shalev, Ruth S., Orly Manor, Judith Auerbach, and Varda Gross-Tsur. "Persistence of Developmental Dyscalculia: What Counts?" *The Journal of Pediatrics*, September 1998.

• Shaywitz, Sally E. "Dyslexia," *Scientific American*, November 1996.

• Shaywitz, Sally E. "Dyslexia," *The New England Journal of Medicine*, 29 January 1998.

• Shaywitz, Sally E. and Bennett A. Shaywitz. "Unlocking Learning Disabilities: The Neurological Basis," *Learning Disabilities: Lifelong Issues*, ed. Shirley C. Cramer and William Ellis. Baltimore: Paul H. Brookes Publishing Co., 1996.

• Shea, Thomas M., and Anne M. Bauer. *Parents and Teachers of Children with Exceptionalities: A Handbook for Collaboration*, 2nd Edition. Needham Heights, Massachusetts: Allyn and Bacon, 1991.

• Shore, Milton F., Patrick J. Brice, and Barbara G. Love. *When Your Child Needs Testing: What Parents, Teachers, and Other Helpers Need to Know About Psychological Testing*. New York: The Crossroad Publishing, 1992.

• Siegel, Linda S. "The Discrepancy Formula: Its Use and Abuse," in *Specific Reading Disability: A View of the Spectrum*. ed. Bruce K. Shapiro, Pasquale J. Accardo, and Arnold J. Capute. Timonium, Maryland: York Press, 1998.

• Silver, Larry B. "Introduction," *The Assessment of Learning Disabilities: Preschool Through Adulthood*, ed. Larry B. Silver. Austin, Texas: PRO-ED, 1989.

• Silver, Larry B. *The Misunderstood Child: Understanding and Coping with Your Child's Learning Disabilities*, 3rd Edition. New York: Three Rivers Press, 1998.

• Silver, M. and P. Oakes. "Evaluation of a New Computer Intervention to Teach People with Autism or Asperger Syndrome to Recognize and Predict Emotions in Others," *Autism: The International Journal of Research and Practice* [Internet]. September 2001. Available from: http://www.ncbi.nlm.nih.gov/entrez/query.fcgi?cmd=Retrieve&db=PubMed&list_uids=11708589&dopt=Abstract

• Simmons, F. and C. Singleton. "The Reading Comprehension Abilities of Dyslexic Students in Higher Education," *Dyslexia* [Internet]. July-September 2000. Available from: http://www.ncbi.nlm.nih.gov/entrez/query.fcgi?cmd=Retrieve&db=PubMed&list_uids=10989566&dopt=Abstract

- Sobel, Rachel K. "Hope for the Learning Disabled," *U.S. News & World Report*, 14 May 2001.
- Solomon, Maynard. *Beethoven*. New York: Schirmer Books, 1977.
- Spafford, Carol Sullivan and George S. Grosser. *Dyslexia*. Needham Heights, Massachusetts: Allyn and Bacon, 1996.
- Stahl, Lesley. "Pentagon Schools," *60 Minutes*. CBS broadcast 21 April 2002. Transcript prepared by Burrelle's Information Services.
- Swanson, H. Lee. "Information Processing: An Introduction," in *A Cognitive Approach to Learning Disabilities*, 2nd Edition, ed. D. Kim Reid, Wayne P. Hresko, and H. Lee Swanson. Austin, Texas: PRO-ED, 1991.
- Swanson, H. Lee. "Learning Disabilities and Memory," in *A Cognitive Approach to Learning Disabilities*, 2nd Edition, ed. D. Kim Reid, Wayne P. Hresko, and H. Lee Swanson. Austin, Texas: PRO-ED, 1991.
- Symonds, William C. "How to Fix America's Schools," *Business Week*, 19 March 2001.
- Szegedy-Maszak, Marianne. "The Melancholy Body," *U.S. News & World Report*, 16 December 2002.
- Szegedy-Maszak, Marianne. "The Sound of Unsound Minds," *U.S. News & World Report*, 13 January 2003.
- Tam, Pui-Wing. "From Chips to Neurons: Palm's Inventor Sets His Sights on the Brain," *The Wall Street Journal*, 20 November 2001.
- Tarver, Sara. "Direct Instruction," in *Controversial Issues Confronting Special Education: Divergent Perspectives*, ed. William Stainback and Susan Bray Stainback. Needham Heights, Massachusetts: Allyn and Bacon, 1992.
- Tejada, Carlos. "These Students Wear Hardhats and Learn How to Cut Tiles," *The Wall Street Journal*, 28 May 2002.
- Thurlow, Martha. "Use of Accommodations in State Assessments: What Databases Tell Us About Differential Levels of Use and How to Document the Use of Accommodations" [Internet]. August 2001. Available from: http://www.ldonline.org/ld_indepth/special_education/nceo_technical_report30.html
- Torgesen, Joseph K. "A Model of Memory from an Information Processing Perspective: The Special Case of Phonological Memory," in *Attention, Memory and Executive Function*, ed. G. Reid Lyon and Norman A. Krasnegor. Baltimore: Paul H. Brookes Publishing, 1996.
- Torgesen, Joseph K. "Instructional Interventions for Children with Reading Disabilities," in *Specific Reading Disability: A View of the Spectrum*, ed. Bruce K. Shapiro, Pasquale J. Accardo, and Arnold J. Capute. Timonium, Maryland: York Press, 1998.
- Trapani, Catherine. *Transition Goals for Students with Learning Disabilities*. Boston: College-Hill Press, 1990.
- Travis, John. "Gene Change Linked to Poor Memory," *Science News*, 23 November 2002.
- Travis, John. "Let the Games Begin," *Science News*, 17 February 1996.
- USA Today Editorial/Opinion. "Paperwork Pushes Patience of Special-ed Teachers" [Internet]. Accessed 25 June 2002 from: http://www.usatoday.com/news/commentary/2002/06/19/nceditf.htm
- U.S. Commission on Civil Rights. "U.S. Commission on Civil Rights Recommendations for the Reauthorization of the Individuals with Disabilities Education Act" [Internet]. May 2002. Available from: http://www.usccr.gov/pubs/idea/recs.htm
- U.S. Department of Education. "Goals 2000: Implementing Standards-Based Reform," *Goals 2000: Reforming Education to Improve Student Achievement* [Internet]. 30 April 1998. Available from: http://www.ed.gov/pubs/G2KReforming/g2ch3.html
- U.S. Department of Education, "Twenty-second Annual Report to Congress on the Implementation of the Individuals with Disabilities Education Act" [Internet]. 2000. Available from: http://www.ed.gov/offices/OSERS/OSEP/Products/OSEP2000AnlRpt

* U.S. Department of Education. "Twenty-third Annual Report to Congress on the Implementation of the Individuals with Disabilities Education Act" [Internet]. 2001. Available from: http://www.ed.gov/offices/OSERS/OSEP/Products/OSEP2001AnlRpt

* U.S. Department of Education Office for Civil Rights. "The Use of Tests as Part of High-Stakes Decision-Making for Students: A Resource Guide for Educators and Policy-Makers" [Internet]. December 2000. Available from: http://www.ed.gov/offices/OCR/testing/TestingResource.doc

* Vail, Priscilla. "Detecting Problems," *The Expert Answers: Priscilla Vail on Learning Styles and Emotions* [Internet]. 22 March 2002. Available from: http://www.schwablearning.org/pdfs/expert_vail.pdf

* Vail, Priscilla L. *Words Fail Me: How Language Works and What Happens When It Doesn't*. Rosemont, New Jersey: Modern Learning Press, 1996.

* Vaishnav, Anand and Michele Kurtz. "Lawsuit to Allege MCAS is Widely Discriminatory" [Internet]. 19 September 2002. Accessed 20 September 2002 from: http://www.boston.com/dailyglobe2/262/metro/Lawsuit_to_allege_MCAS_is_widely_discriminatory+.shtml

* Vergason, Glenn and M.L. Anderegg. "Preserving the Least Restrictive Environment," in *Controversial Issues Confronting Special Education: Divergent Perspectives*, ed. William C. Stainback and Susan Bray Stainback. Needham Heights, Massachusetts: Allyn and Bacon, 1992.

* Viadero, Debra. "Public or Private, Study Finds Schools Similar" [Internet]. 22 January 2003. Accessed from: http://www.edweek.org/ew/ewstory.cfm?slug=19private.h22

* Viadero, Debra. "Studies Illuminate Self-Defeating Behavior by Students" [Internet]. 26 March 2003. Available from: http://www.ldonline.org/news/self_defeating.html

* Vogel, Susan A. "A Retrospective and Prospective View of Postsecondary Education for Adults with Learning Disabilities," in *Success for College Students with Learning Disabilities*, ed. Susan A. Vogel and Pamela Adelman. New York: Springer-Verlag, 1993.

* Wagner, Richard K. "From Simple Structure to Complex Function: Major Trends in the Development of Theories, Models, and Measurements of Memory," in *Attention, Memory and Executive Function*, ed. G. Reid Lyon and Norman A. Krasnegor. Baltimore: Paul H. Brookes Publishing, 1996.

* Waldie, Karen and Otfried Spreen. "The Relationship Between Learning Disabilities and Persisting Delinquency," *Journal of Learning Disabilities*, June/July 1993.

* Westchester Institute for Human Services Research. "The Balanced View: Homework" [Internet]. June 2002. Available from: http://www.sharingsuccess.org/code/bv/homework.pdf

* Wildavsky, Ben. "Helping or Hurting? A New Test-Score Policy," *U.S. News and World Report*, 19 February 2001.

* Wisconsin Legislative Audit Bureau. "97-18 Correction Costs, Department of Correction [Internet]. 1997. Available from: http://www.legis.state.wi.us/lab/Reports/97-18summary.htm

* Wodrich, David L. *Children's Psychological Testing: A Guide for Nonpsychologists*, 3rd Edition. Baltimore: Paul H. Brookes Publishing Co., 1997.

* Worthington, Marjorie. *Miss Alcott of Concord*. Garden City, New York: Doubleday & Company, 1958.

* Yuill, Nicola and Jane Oakhill. *Children's Problems in Text Comprehension: An Experimental Investigation*. Cambridge: Cambridge University Press, 1991.

* Zill, Nicholas, Christine Winquist Nord, and Laura Spencer Loomis. "Adolescent Time Use, Risky Behavior and Outcomes: An Analysis of National Data" [Internet]. 11 September 1995. Available from: http://aspe.hhs.gov/hsp/cyp/xstimuse.htm

Appendix 1

Some Brain Anatomy

The left hemisphere of a male right-handed human brain has regions that largely constitute a language implementation system for hearing, speaking, and reading. Females and left-handed individuals have different brain organizations.

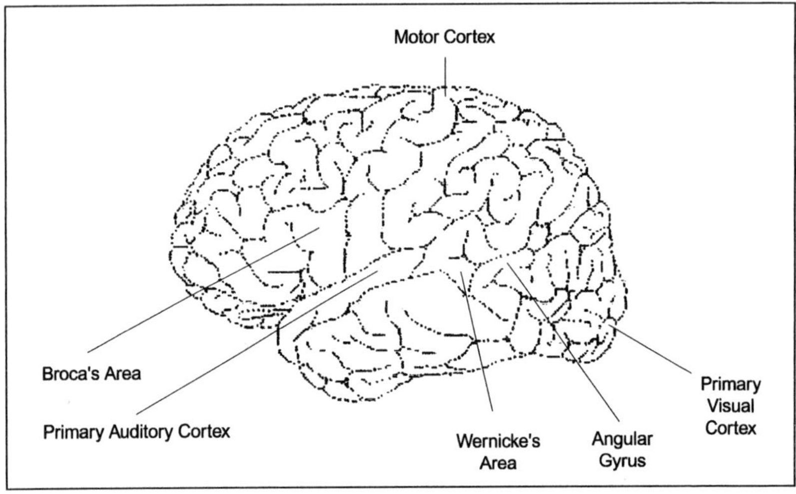

- Hearing is received by the primary auditory cortex, then processed in Wernicke's Area for language comprehension.
- The signal for speaking begins in Wernicke's Area, is transmitted to Broca's Area, which then triggers the nearby motor cortex for speech.
- Reading begins with visual patterns in the primary visual cortex, which are then transmitted to the angular gyrus, which connects with the auditory word representations in Wernicke's Area.

Injury to Broca's Area hinders speech production. Injury to Wernicke's Area impedes language comprehension, speech, reading, and writing. Injury to the angular gyrus inhibits reading and writing.

Researchers continue to locate regions and structures controlling word and image recognition, quantity perception, visual motion perception, memory, and behavior. Such regions are organized into a conceptual knowledge system and a mediational system connecting the knowledge and language implementation systems. More information is available in *Principles of Neural Science*, edited by Eric Kandel, James Schwartz, and Thomas Jessell, and published by McGraw-Hill.

Appendix 2

Is Your Child At Risk? (by Dianne Hales)

Almost daily, we're bombarded with shocking headlines about violent kids. Horrific episodes, such as the Littleton and Jonesboro shootings, have been replicated across the country. Emotional problems, such as depression, are on the rise in children and adolescents. What's a parent to do?

To find out, we went to Harold S. Koplewicz, M.D., a renowned child and adolescent psychiatrist and the director of the New York University Child Study Center, in New York City. He is also the co-editor of a new book, *Childhood Revealed: Art Expressing Pain, Discovery & Hope* (Harry N. Abrams, Inc.), a compilation of drawings and thoughts that offers a glimpse into the world of children dealing with emotional and psychological problems. Koplewicz talked to the *Journal* about the state of our nation's children.

Q Why are so many children today in trouble?

A Actually, most American children are normal kids. They have friends, they're doing well at school. But at least 12 percent of the population under age eighteen—somewhere between eight million to ten million children and teenagers—have a diagnosable psychiatric illness. These children may suffer from something as mild as a learning disorder, or as serious as depression. In these cases, their lives are much more stressful than the average child's, and their parents' job is much more challenging.

Unfortunately, because of the misconceptions about psychiatric illnesses, we don't give these children's symptoms the same respect or attention we would if they were physical symptoms. Fewer than 20 percent of these kids get the treatment they need.

Q Is it harder to be a child now than it ever was before?

A Yes, I definitely think it's harder. Parents are working, and their time is very limited. Children are watching more TV and being exposed to more violent material. That's not good for any kid, but it's especially problematic, even dangerous, for children with psychiatric illnesses, particularly those who are aggressive or impulsive to begin with.

"Is Your Child At Risk?" by Dianne Hales from the *Ladies Home Journal*, November 1999, pp. 102-107. Copyright © 1999 by Dianne Hales. Reprinted with permission of Dianne Hales.

We also have too many guns. When I went to school, a bully might have threatened to beat you up. Today the bullies have guns.

But what I see as the biggest threat to kids now is illicit drugs. They're bad for everyone, of course, but for mentally-ill children, drugs are a double whammy. Often these kids end up with a substance-abuse problem as well as a psychiatric problem.

Q Is it harder to be a parent than ever before?

A Yes. The most important element of parenting is time, and there's a real shortage of it today. You have to spend a quantity of time with your children before you can spend quality time. Working eight or ten hours a day doesn't really make a difference, as long as you can find twenty to thirty minutes for your child. But it has to be time for just the two of you—reading, chatting, playing a game, preparing dinner together.

Spending time with a child is like putting money in a bank: Interest grows. So if there's a problem, you know your child so well that you can tell something's wrong.

Q Are there critical ages in childhood that parents should be aware of?

A First grade is difficult because children learn that play is over. They have to sit in their seats. There's a schedule, and less freedom to do what they'd like to do. Third grade is the time when learning differences show up. By then, kids are supposed to know how to read. If they're struggling with reading, a teacher can say, "Nine out of ten kids have picked it up. Your child hasn't."

An American invention, which turns out to be a rather stupid one, is middle school, which usually is fifth grade to eighth grade—another critical period. Moving from one class to another with six or seven teachers instead of one can be hard for any child, but it's especially difficult for one who has an attention-deficit or learning disorder. If a child who was a B student becomes a C or D student in middle school, there may be a problem.

The last critical period is adolescence, when depression increases. Normal teens may dye their hair orange or purple, but they still get up in the morning. They attend school. They have friends. They love their mom and dad, even though they might not like them. They're sleeping and eating normally. Massive change is a warning sign of depression.

Q Do boys have it tougher today than girls?

A Before puberty, boys have more difficulty. They have trouble sitting still; they tend to have more learning problems. Lots of boys struggle through school, although they catch up in adolescence. Boys are also more aggressive. Look at the school violence episodes. We keep saying it's children killing children, but it's really boys killing other kids.

During adolescence, girls have more eating disorders. Boys and girls have the same incidence of anxiety disorders and depression. But girls are much more willing to talk about their feelings and to get help. Our society still sees this as a weakness in boys.

Parents face different issues in raising sons and daughters. With boys, parents have to encourage them to express their feelings and be better communicators. They need to teach girls not to be afraid of competition nor ashamed of winning.

Q What are the most common psychological problems kids suffer from?

A The most common psychiatric disorders fall into two categories: The disruptive disorders—including attention-deficit disorder, with or without hyperactivity, and conduct disorders—and internalizing disorders, which include anxiety and mood disorders. One group of kids distracts and disrupts other people; the others are pathologically self-conscious or shy or have terrible worries, but they suffer silently. They're the ones who very often get missed. Depression comes on much more frequently in adolescence than in any other time of childhood. I've read reports stating that there are at least two million kids and teenagers who suffer from depression and probably three million who suffer from anxiety disorders. About 5 percent of all youngsters have learning problems.

Unfortunately, many people still have the misconception that these problems are a sign of weakness. Psychiatric illnesses are as real as physical illnesses. They run in families and often have a physiological basis. If properly identified and diagnosed, the good news is that we have treatments, whether psychosocial interventions or medications, that are effective and safe and that literally can change lives.

Q How can parents distinguish between a child's moodiness and a real emotional problem?

A Two of the things you should look at are your child's school life and his or her play or recreational life. Just because children are inattentive or sad doesn't mean they have attention-deficit disorder or depression. The number-one cause of inattention, in my view, is a boring teacher.

Depression is very different from demoralization, when bad things happen and a kids feels crummy. Depression is a change in mood, attitude, the ability to enjoy things, sleep, appetite, concentration. Most often, depressed adolescents are very irritable. The duration and severity of these changes are what differentiate clinical depression from normal adolescent moodiness.

With anxiety disorders, kids may develop obsessive-compulsive symptoms. For instance, they can't stop washing their hands. Other kids have separation anxiety. If you can't take a child to birthday parties because he clings to you or he doesn't want to leave the house, you should be somewhat concerned.

Q What is the typical mistake mothers and fathers make when it comes to troubled kids?

A Denial. Parents tell themselves, "It's just a phase. He'll outgrow it." Parents should trust their gut feelings. If they're worried, they should get a diagnosis.

The first person to turn to is your pediatrician or family practitioner. Parents should ask the doctor, "Is this depression or just moodiness? Is this a shy child or is it social phobia?" Getting the answers may require evaluation by a mental-health professional—a child and adolescent psychiatrist or a clinical psychologist with a specialization in children.

After getting a diagnosis, parents should explore prognosis and treatment options. If the doctor suggests medication, find out the cost-benefit ratio of taking the medicine and, just as critical, of not taking the medicine. Ask: What risks does my child face by taking or not taking this medicine? What are the side effects? How many studies have been done to show that it's effective? How long does my child have to take it? Will it interfere with his normal growth and development? What kind of monitoring will have to be done? How will we know my child is getting the right dosage?

Q How can parents tell if their child is getting the best treatment?

A Parents should ask for a treatment plan that they understand. If, after six months, they see that their child is not significantly better, they should get a second opinion. The best place to go for this is a university-affiliated hospital with a medical school. Call the department of psychiatry and ask for a referral to a child and adolescent psychiatrist or an expert in child mental health. Or call the American Academy of Child and Adolescent Psychiatry at 800-333-7636. [The web site offers resources at www.aacap.org.]

Appendix 3

July 25, 2000

Dear Colleague:

On behalf of the Office for Civil Rights (OCR) and the Office of Special Education and Rehabilitative Services (OSERS) in the U.S. Department of Education, we are writing to you about a vital issue that affects students in school - harassment based on disability. Our purpose in writing is to develop greater awareness of this issue, to remind interested persons of the legal and educational responsibilities that institutions have to prevent and appropriately respond to disability harassment, and to suggest measures that school officials should take to address this very serious problem. This letter is not an exhaustive legal analysis. Rather, it is intended to provide a useful overview of the existing legal and educational principles related to this important issue.

Why Disability Harassment Is Such an Important Issue

Through a variety of sources, both OCR and OSERS have become aware of concerns about disability harassment in elementary and secondary schools and colleges and universities. In a series of conference calls with OSERS staff, for example, parents, disabled persons, and advocates for students with disabilities raised disability harassment as an issue that was very important to them. OCR's complaint workload has reflected a steady pace of allegations regarding this issue, while the number of court cases involving allegations of disability harassment has risen. OCR and OSERS recently conducted a joint focus group where we heard about the often devastating effects on students of disability harassment that ranged from abusive jokes, crude name-calling, threats, and bullying, to sexual and physical assault by teachers and other students.

We take these concerns very seriously. Disability harassment can have a profound impact on students, raise safety concerns, and erode efforts to ensure that students with disabilities have equal access to the myriad benefits that an education offers. Indeed, harassment can seriously interfere with the ability of students with disabilities to receive the education critical to their advancement. We are committed to doing all that we can to help prevent and respond to disability harassment and lessen the harm of any harassing conduct that has occurred.

We seek your support in a joint effort to address this critical issue and to promote such efforts among educators who deal with students daily.

What Laws Apply to Disability Harassment

Schools, colleges, universities, and other educational institutions have a responsibility to ensure equal educational opportunities for all students, including students with disabilities. This responsibility is based on Section 504 of the Rehabilitation Act of 1973 (Section 504) and Title II of the Americans with Disabilities Act of 1990 (Title II), which are enforced by OCR. Section 504 covers all schools, school districts, and colleges and universities receiving federal funds. Title II covers all state and local entities, including school districts and public institutions of higher education, whether or not they receive federal funds. Disability harassment is a form of discrimination prohibited by Section 504 and Title II. Both Section 504 and Title II provide parents and students with grievance procedures and due process remedies at the local level. Individuals and organizations also may file complaints with OCR.

States and school districts also have a responsibility under Section 504, Title II, and the Individuals with Disabilities Education Act (IDEA), which is enforced by OSERS, to ensure that a free appropriate public education (FAPE) is made available to eligible students with disabilities. Disability harassment may result in a denial of FAPE under these statutes. Parents may initiate administrative due process procedures under IDEA, Section 504, or Title II to address a denial of FAPE, including a denial that results from disability harassment. Individuals and organizations also may file complaints with OCR, alleging a denial of FAPE that results from disability harassment. In addition, an individual or organization may file a complaint alleging a violation of IDEA under separate procedures with the state educational agency. State compliance with IDEA, including compliance with FAPE requirements, is monitored by OSERS' Office of Special Education Programs (OSEP).

Harassing conduct also may violate state and local civil rights, child abuse, and criminal laws. Some of these laws may impose obligations on educational institutions to contact or coordinate with state or local agencies or police with respect to disability harassment in some cases; failure to follow appropriate procedures under these laws could result in action against an educational institution. Many states and educational institutions also have addressed disability harassment in their general anti-harassment policies.

Disability Harassment May Deny a Student an Equal Opportunity to Education under Section 504 or Title II

Disability harassment under Section 504 and Title II is intimidation or abusive behavior toward a student based on disability that creates a hostile environment by interfering with or denying a student's participation in or receipt of benefits, services, or opportunities in the institution's program. Harassing conduct may take many forms, including verbal acts and name-calling, as well as nonverbal behavior, such as graphic and written statements, or conduct that is physically threatening, harmful, or humiliating.

When harassing conduct is sufficiently severe, persistent, or pervasive that it creates a hostile environment, it can violate a student's rights under the Section 504 and Title II regulations. A hostile environment may exist even if there are no tangible effects on the student where the harassment is serious enough to adversely affect the student's ability to participate in or benefit from the educational program. Examples of harassment that could create a hostile environment follow.

o Several students continually remark out loud to other students during class that a student with dyslexia is "retarded" or "deaf and dumb" and does not belong in the class; as a result, the harassed student has difficulty doing work in class and her grades decline.

o A student repeatedly places classroom furniture or other objects in the path of classmates who use wheelchairs, impeding the classmates' ability to enter the classroom.

o A teacher subjects a student to inappropriate physical restraint because of conduct related to his disability, with the result that the student tries to avoid school through increased absences.

o A school administrator repeatedly denies a student with a disability access to lunch, field trips, assemblies, and extracurricular activities as punishment for taking time off from school for required services related to the student's disability.

o A professor repeatedly belittles and criticizes a student with a disability for using accommodations in class, with the result that the student is so discouraged that she has great difficulty performing in class and learning.

o Students continually taunt or belittle a student with mental retardation by mocking and intimidating him so he does not participate in class.

When disability harassment limits or denies a student's ability to participate in or benefit from an educational institution's programs or activities, the institution must respond effectively. Where the institution learns that disability harassment may have occurred, the institution must investigate the incident(s) promptly and respond appropriately.

Disability Harassment Also May Deny a Free Appropriate Public Education

Disability harassment that adversely affects an elementary or secondary student's education may also be a denial of FAPE under the IDEA, as well as Section 504 and Title II. The IDEA was enacted to ensure that recipients of IDEA funds make available to students with disabilities the appropriate special education and related services that enable them to access and benefit from public education. The specific services to be provided a student with a disability are set forth in the student's individualized education program (IEP), which is developed by a team that includes the student's parents, teachers and, where appropriate, the student. Harassment of a student based on disability may decrease the student's ability to benefit from his or her education and amount to a denial of FAPE.

How to Prevent and Respond to Disability Harassment

Schools, school districts, colleges, and universities have a legal responsibility to prevent and respond to disability harassment. As a fundamental step, educational institutions must develop and disseminate an official policy statement prohibiting discrimination based on disability and must establish grievance procedures that can be used to address disability harassment. A clear policy serves a preventive purpose by notifying students and staff that disability harassment is unacceptable, violates federal law, and will result in disciplinary action. The responsibility to respond to disability harassment, when it does occur, includes taking prompt and effective action to end the harassment and prevent it from recurring and, where appropriate, remedying the effects on the student who was harassed.

The following measures are ways to both prevent and eliminate harassment:

o Creating a campus environment that is aware of disability concerns and sensitive to disability harassment; weaving these issues into the curriculum or programs outside the classroom.

o Encouraging parents, students, employees, and community members to discuss disability harassment and to report it when they become aware of it.

o Widely publicizing anti-harassment statements and procedures for handling discrimination complaints, because this information makes students and employees aware of what constitutes harassment, that such conduct is prohibited, that the institution will not tolerate such behavior, and that effective action, including disciplinary action, where appropriate, will be taken.

o Providing appropriate, up-to-date, and timely training for staff and students to recognize and handle potential harassment.

o Counseling both person(s) who have been harmed by harassment and person(s) who have been responsible for the harassment of others.

o Implementing monitoring programs to follow up on resolved issues of disability harassment.

o Regularly assessing and, as appropriate, modifying existing disability harassment policies and procedures for addressing the issue, to ensure effectiveness.

Technical Assistance Is Available

U.S. Secretary of Education Richard Riley has emphasized the importance of ensuring that schools are safe and free of harassment. Students can not learn in an atmosphere of fear, intimidation, or ridicule. For students with disabilities, harassment can inflict severe harm. Teachers and administrators must take emphatic action to ensure that these students are able to learn in an atmosphere free from harassment.

Disability harassment is preventable and can not be tolerated. Schools, colleges, and universities should address the issue of disability harassment not just when but before incidents occur. As noted above, awareness can be an important element in preventing harassment in the first place.

The Department of Education is committed to working with schools, parents, disability advocacy organizations, and other interested parties to ensure that no student is ever subjected to such conduct, and that where such conduct occurs, prompt and effective action is taken. For more information, you may contact OCR or OSEP through 1-800-USA-LEARN or 1-800-437-0833 for TTY services. You also may directly contact one of the OCR enforcement offices listed on the enclosure or OSEP, by calling (202) 205-5507 or (202) 205-5465 for TTY services.

Thank you for your attention to this serious matter.

Norma V. Cantu,   Judith E. Heumann,
Assistant Secretary for   Assistant Secretary
  Civil Rights   Office of Special Education
                                        and Rehabilitative Services

---

"Dear Colleague" Letter available from http://www.ed.gov/offices/OCR/docs/disabharass ltr.html

Appendix 4

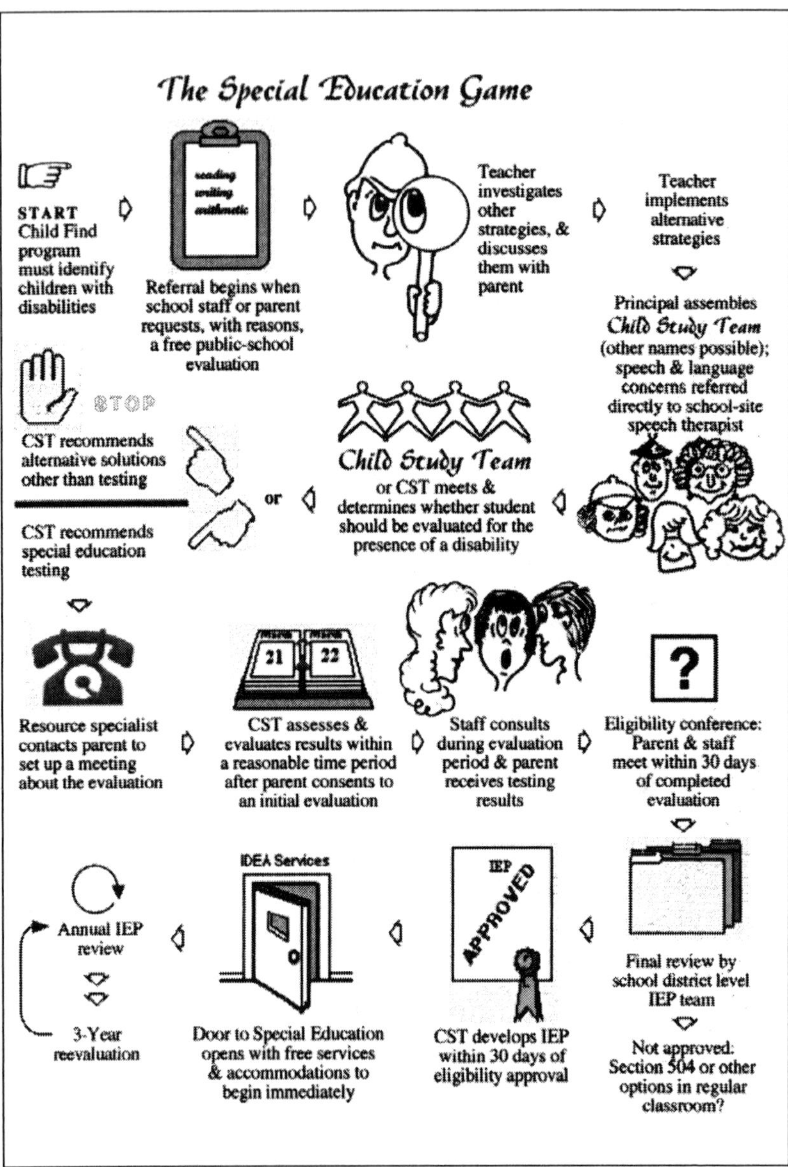

Adapted from *The Special Education Game* by Martin Proccacio. 2001. Unpublished. Reprinted with permission of Martin Proccacio.

Appendix 5

Where to Find Information about a Psychological Test

A psychoeducational report will include test results. Usually parents are provided little information to help them understand the meaning and implications of results, and to evaluate the strengths and weaknesses of a particular test. Moreover, tests are available in different editions and for various age groups. Further confusion may arise when a test administrator uses only subsections of a test. Often the reason for the use of a specific test is the administrator's familiarity with that test.

You might feel uncomfortable asking for information about the tests from the test administrator because 1) understanding the test concepts will take time to digest, and 2) you may have no basis for appraising the test administrator's unbiased judgment, training, and field expertise. To prepare yourself, ask which tests will be used and why they will be used. Parent centers can refer you to independent sources of information, as well as specialists who can help you analyze test results.

Below is an alphabetic list of *school-age* psychological tests with common variations of acronyms and abbreviations. This is the alphabet soup that parents encounter when looking at a psychoeducational report. This is not a complete list, but those explained and critiqued in four books dedicated to this subject. These books vary in depth of explanation, price, and availability—either for purchase or in a public library.

Some sample test questions may appear in these books for illustrative purposes, not for preparing your child. The test administrator should be trained in providing all the information that your child needs during the evaluation. In this list, letters on the left side indicate where you will find information about a particular test:

• C = *A Guide to 100 Tests for Special Education* by Carolyn Compton (1999). A lower case *c* indicates that only a brief summary of the test is given. This author's earlier works have included *A Guide to 85 Tests for Special Education*, *A Guide to 75 Tests for Special Education*, and *A Guide to 65 Tests for Special Education* over the past 20 years. Her books carry examples of test questions.

• P = *Special Educator's Complete Guide to 109 Diagnostic Tests: How to Select & Interpret Tests, Use Results in IEPs, and Remediate Specific Difficulties* by Roger Pierangelo and George Giuliani (1998). The book discusses symptoms and diagnostic methods.

• S = *Assessment*, Eighth Edition by John Salvia and James E. Ysseldyke (2001). A lower case *s* indicates that the test is only briefly summarized or statistically compared to other tests. This is the most comprehensive of these books, exploring issues of classroom and standardized testing as well as those of individual psychological testing.

• W = *Children's Psychological Testing: A Guide for Nonpsychologists*, Third Edition, by David L. Wodrich (1997). A lower case *w* indicates that only a brief summary of the test is given. The book presents case studies.

P,S	AAMD (or AAMR) Adaptive Behavior Scale: Residential and Community, Second Edition (ABS-RC2)
P,S,W	AAMD (or AAMR) Adaptive Behavior Scale—School 2 (ABS-S2)
C	Academic Performance Rating Scale (APRS)
C,s,W	ADHD Rating Scale
P,S	Adaptive Behavior Evaluation Scale—Revised (ABES-R)
S	Adaptive Behavior Inventory (ABI)
C	Aprenda: La Prueba de Logros en Español (APRENDA)
C	Arizona Articulation Proficiency Scale, Second Edition (AAPS)
C	Assessing Semantic Skills Through Everyday Themes (ASSET)
C	The Assessment of Phonological Processes—Revised (APP-R)
C	Attention Deficit Disorders Evaluation Scale (ADDES)
S	Attention Deficit Disorders Evaluation Scale, Home Version (ADDES-HV)
P	Attention Deficit Disorders Evaluation Scale—Revised (ADDES)
S	Attention Deficit Disorders Evaluation Scale—Second Edition, School Version (ADDES-2 SV)
w	Auditory Discrimination Test
P	Auditory Perception Test for the Hearing Impaired (APT/HI)
S	Autism Screening Instrument for Educational Planning, Second Edition (ASIEP-2)
C,s,w	Basic Achievement Skills Individual Screener (BASIS)
P	The Battelle Developmental Inventory (BDI)
s	Battelle Screening Test
C	Beery Picture Vocabulary Screening (Beery PVS)
C	Beery Picture Vocabulary Test (Beery PVT)
S,W	Behavior Assessment System for Children (BASC)
S,w	Behavior Evaluation Scale—2 (BES-2)
S	Behavior Evaluation Scale—2 Home Version (BES-2HV)
S	Behavior Rating Profile, Second Edition (BRP-2)
C,P,S,W	Bender Visual Motor Gestalt Test (BVMGT)
C	Bilingual Syntax Measures (BSM I and II)
C	The Boder Test of Reading-Spelling Patterns
c,P,W	Boehm Test of Basic Concepts—Preschool Version
C,P,S,W	Boehm Test of Basic Concepts—Revised (Boehm-R or BTBC-R)
P,w	Bracken Basic Concept Scale (BBCS)
C	Brigance Inventory of Early Development—Revised
C,P	Brigance Inventory of Basic Skills
C	Brigance Diagnostic Inventory of Essential Skills
C	Brigance Diagnostic Comprehensive Inventory of Basic Skills
C	Brigance Life Skills Inventory
C	Brigance Diagnostic Inventory of Basic Skills, Spanish Edition
C,P	Bruininks-Oseretsky Test of Motor Proficiency
w	The Bzoch-League Receptive-Expressive Emergent Language Scale (REEL)

W   California Verbal Learning Test—Children's Version (CVLT-C)
P   Carolina Picture Vocabulary Test for Deaf and Hearing Impaired (CPVT)
W   Category Test
C,P,S,W   Child Behavior Checklist (CBCL)
W   Childhood Autism Rating Scale (CARS)
P,w   Children's Apperception Test (CAT)
C   Clinical Evaluation of Language Fundamentals—Preschool (CELF-Preschool)
C   Clinical Evaluation of Language Fundamentals—Revised (CELF-R)
C   Coloured Progressive Matrices (CPM)
P,w   Columbia Mental Maturity Scale (CMMS)
S   Cognitive Abilities Test (CogAT)
S   Cognitive Assessment System (CA)
C,P,S   Comprehensive Receptive and Expressive Vocabulary Test (CREVT)
s   Comprehensive Scales of Student Abilities
S   Comprehensive Test of Basic Skills (CTBS)
P,S   Comprehensive Test of Nonverbal Intelligence (CTONI)
S   Comprehensive Test of Phonological Processing (CTOPP)
w   Conners continuous performance test
C,P,s,w   Conners Parent Rating Scale (CPRS)
s   Conners Self-Report of Personality (CSRP)
C,P,s,w   Conners Teacher Rating Scale (CTRS)

C,P   Decoding Skills Test (DST)
P   Degangi-Berk Test of Sensory Integration (TSI)
C,P   Denver Developmental Screening Test—Revised (Denver II)
P   Denver Handwriting Analysis (DHA)
C,s   Detroit Tests of Learning Aptitude—Primary, Second Edition (DTLA-P2)
C,W   Detroit Tests of Learning Aptitude—Third Edition (DTLA-3)
P,S   Detroit Tests of Learning Aptitude—Fourth Edition (DTLA-4)
S   Developmental Indicators for the Assessment of Learning—Third Edition
          (DIAL-3)
P   Developmental Profile II (DP-II)
C   Developmental Test of Visual Motor Integration—Third Edition (VMI-3R)
P,S,w   Developmental Test of Visual Motor Integration—Fourth Edition (VMI-4)
C,S   Developmental Test of Visual Perception—Second Edition (DTVP-2)
w   Devereaux Behavior Rating Scales—School Form
w   Devereaux Scale of Psychopathology
C,S   Diagnostic Achievement Battery—Revised (DAB-2)
C   Diagnostic Reading Scales—Revised (DRS-81)
S,W   Diagnostic and Statistical Manual of Mental Disorders-IV (DSM-IV)[1]
S,w   Direct Observation Form (DOF)
P,W   Draw-a-Person: Screening Procedure for Emotional Disturbance (DAP-SPED)
C,P   Durrell Analysis of Reading Difficulty (DARD)

S   Early Childhood Behavior Scale (ECBS)
S   Early Screening Inventory—Revised (ESI-R)
s   Early Screening Profile
C,P   Enright Diagnostic Inventory of Basic Arithmetic Skills (Enright)
P   ESL Literacy Scale (ESL)
C,S   Expressive One-Word Picture Vocabulary Test—Revised (EOWPVT-R)
C   Expressive One-Word Picture Vocabulary Test—Upper Extension
          (EOWPVT-UE)

---

1   More information pertaining to AD/HD in Russell Barkley, "ADHD: Theory,
    Diagnosis, and Treatment" [Internet], 17 June 2000 lecture transcript, pp. 7-20,
    available from: http://www.schwablearning.org/pdfs/2200_7-barktran.pdf

C   The Fisher-Logemann Test of Articulation Competence (Fisher-Logemann)
S   Formal Reading Inventory (FRI)
S   Full-Range Picture Vocabulary Test

C,s   Gates-MacGinitie Reading Tests—Third Edition
P   Gates-MacGinitie Silent Reading Test—Third Edition
C,P   Gates-McKillop-Horowitz Reading Diagnostic Test
P,w   Gilmore Oral Reading Test (GORT)
C,P,S   The Goldman-Fristoe Test of Articulation (GFTA)
P   Goldman-Fristoe-Woodcock Test of Auditory Discrimination (GFW)
w   The Goldman-Fristoe-Woodcock Test of Auditory Discrimination
C,P,s,W   Goodenough-Harris Drawing Draw-A-Person Test (Goodenough-Harris, GHDT
           or Draw-a-Man)
c,W   Gordon Diagnostic System
C,P,S,W   Gray Oral Reading Test—Third Edition (GORT-3)

C   Halstead Neuropsychological Test Battery for Children (HRNB-C)
C   Halstead-Reitan Neuropsychological Test Battery (HRNB or Halstead-Reitan)
W   Halstead-Reitan Neuropsychological Test Battery for Older Children
           (Halstead-Reitan)
w   Hand Test
W   Hart Sentence Completion Test for Children
P,w   Hiskey-Nebraska Test of Learning Aptitude
w   Holtzman Inkblot Technique
C   Home and School Situations Questionnaire (HSQ/SSQ)
W   House-Tree-Person

C,P,S,W   Illinois Test of Psycholinguistic Abilities (ITPA)

C,s,W   Kaufman Adolescent and Adult Intelligence Test (KAIT)
C,P,S,W   Kaufman Assessment Battery for Children (K-ABC)
P,s   Kaufman Brief Intelligence Test (KBIT)
P   Kaufman Survey of Early Academic and Language Skills (K-SEALS)
C,P,s,W   Kaufman Test of Educational Achievement (KTEA)
S   Kaufman Test of Educational Achievement—Normative Updates (KTEA-Nu)
C,P,s,W   Key Math Diagnostic Arithmetic Tests—Revised (Key Math-R)
S   Key Math Diagnostic Arithmetic Tests—Revised—Normative Update
           (Key Math-R-Nu)
P   Kindergarten Readiness Test (KRT)
W   Kinetic Family Drawings
P,W   Kinetic-House-Tree-Person Drawings (K-H-T-P)
W   Kinetic School Drawings
w   Kohn Social Competence Scale

P   Language Proficiency Test (LPT)
S   Leiter International Performance Scale (LIPS)
P,S,w   Leiter International Performance Scale—Revised (Leiter-R)
P   Light's Retention Scale (LRS)
P   Lindamood Auditory Conceptualization Test (LACT)
C   Lindamood Auditory Conceptualization Test, Revised Edition (LACT)
C,W   Luria-Nebraska Neuropsychological Battery—Children's Revision
           (LNNB-C or Luria-Nebraska)

C   Malcomesius Specific Language Disability Test (MSLDT)
C,P,w   Marianne Frostig Developmental Test of Visual Perception (DTVP)

P,w   Matrix Analogies Test—Expanded Form (MAT-Expanded Form)
C,P,S,W   McCarthy Scales of Children's Abilities (MSCA or McCarthy Scales)
           McLean Motion and Attention Test (M-Mat)[2]
S   Metropolitan Achievement Tests 7 (MAT7)
P,S   Metropolitan Readiness Tests—Sixth Edition (MRT-6)
P   Milani-Comparetti Motor Development Test
C,P,w   Miller Assessment for Preschoolers (MAP)
S   Mini-Battery of Achievement (MBA)
s   Minnesota Child Development Inventory
S   Minnesota Functional Vision Assessment (MFVA)
W   Minnesota Multiphasic Personality Inventory—Adolescent (MMPI-A)
s,W   Minnesota Multiphasic Personality Inventory—Second Edition (MMPI-2)
P   Motor-Free Perceptual Test—Revised (MVPT-R)
C,s   Motor-Free Visual Perception Test (MVPT or MFVPT)
S   Mullen Scales of Early Learning (MSEL)
C   Myklebust Picture Story Language Test (PSLT)

S   Naglieri Nonverbal Ability Test
S   Nebraska Test of Learning Aptitude
C,P   The Nelson-Denny Reading Test (NDRT)
w   New Sucher-Allred Reading Placement Inventory
C,P   Norris Educational Achievement Test (NEAT)

S   Oral and Written Language Scales (OWLS)
P   Otis-Lennon School Ability Test (OLSAT)
S   Otis-Lennon School Ability Test, Seventh Edition (OLSAT7)

s   PASS Scales
C   Peabody Developmental Motor Scales (PDMS)
C,P,s,W   Peabody Individual Achievement Test—Revised (PIAT-R)
S   Peabody Individual Achievement Test—Revised — Normative Update
           (PIAT-R-Nu)
C,s,W   Peabody Picture Vocabulary Test—Revised (PPVT-R)
P,S   Peabody Picture Vocabulary Test-III (PPVT-III)
W   Personality Inventory for Children (PIC)
W   Personality Inventory for Youth (PIY)
C   Photo Articulation Test (PAT)
w   Pictorial Test of Intelligence
P   The Picture Story Language Test (PSLT)
w   Piers-Harris Children's Self-Concept Scale (The Way I Feel About Myself)
P   The Politte Sentence Completion Test (PSCT)
P,S   Preschool Evaluation Scale (PES)
C,P   Preschool Language Scale—Third Edition (PLS-3)
C   Preschool Language Scales—Third Edition, (PLS-3), Spanish Edition
w   Progressive Matrices
C   Pruebas de Expression Oral y Perception de la Lengua Española (PEOPLE)
C,P   Purdue Perceptual Motor Survey (PPM)

s   Quay-Peterson Behavior Problem Checklist
P   Quick Neurological Screening Test (QNST)
s,w   The Quick Test

---

2   Tara Parker-Pope reviews this test in "Hyperactive or Just a Kid? New Tests Claim to
     Get Rid of the Guesswork," *The Wall Street Journal*, 10 December 2002, p. D1.

s	Raven's Standard Progressive Matricies
W	Reitan-Indiana Neuropsychological Test Battery for Children (Reitan-Indiana)
S	Responsibility and Independence Scale for Adolescents (RISA)
s	Revised Problem Behavior Checklist (RPBC)
W	Rey-Osterrieth Complex Figures Test
P	Rhode Island Test of Language Structure (RITLS)
s	Richman Behavior Checklist
W	Roberts Apperception Test for Children
P,W	Rorschach Inkblot Technique or Rorschach Psychodiagnostic Test
W	Rotter Incomplete Sentence Blank
S,w	Scales of Independent Behavior—Revised (SIB-R)
P	Screening Instrument for Targeting Educational Risk (SIFTER)
P	Screening Test of Spanish Grammar
C,P	Sensory Integration and Praxis Test (SIPT)
w	Sequential Assessment of Mathematics Inventories
c	Slingerland College Level Screening
c	Slingerland High School Level Screening
C	Slingerland Pre-Reading Screening Procedures
C,P,w	Slingerland Screening Tests for Identifying Children with Specific Language Disability (SST)
C,P,w	Slosson Intelligence Test for Children and Adults—Revised (SIT-R)
P	Slosson Oral Reading Test—Revised (SORT-R)
w	Southern California Sensory Integration Tests
P	Spache Diagnostic Reading Scales (DRS)
P	The Spellmaster Assessment
W	The Stanford-Binet Intelligence Scale: Form L-M (Stanford-Binet L-M)
C,P,S,W	Stanford-Binet Intelligence Scale: Fourth Edition (SB, Stanford-Binet IV))
P	The Steenburgen Diagnostic-Prescriptive Math Program and Quick Math Screening Test (Steenburgen)
C	Structured Photographic Expressive Language Test—Revised (SPELT-II)
C,P	System of Multicultural Pluralistic Assessment (SOMPA)
S	Systematic Screening for Behavior Disorders (SSBD)
W	Teacher's Report Form (TRF)
P	Test of Academic Achievement Skills—Reading Arithmetic, Spelling, and Listening Comprehension (TAAS-RASLC)
C,P,S	Test of Adolescent and Adult Language—Third Edition (TOAL-3)
P,S	Test of Auditory Comprehension of Language, Revised (TACL-R)
P	Test of Auditory Perceptual Skills—Revised (TAPS-R)
P	Test of Early Language Development—Second Edition (TELD-2)
P	Test of Early Mathematics Ability, Second Edition (TEMA-2)
S	Test of Early Reading Ability, Revised (TERA-R)
w	The Test of Early Reading Achievement
s	Test of Early Socioemotional Development
P	Test of Early Written Language—2 (TEWL-2)
P	Test of Gross Motor Development (TGMD)
C,P	Test of Language Development—Intermediate: Second Edition (TOLD-I:2)
S	Test of Language Development—Intermediate: Third Edition (TOLD-I:3)
C,P	Test of Language Development—Primary: Second Edition (TOLD-P:2)
S	Test of Language Development—Primary: Third Edition (TOLD-P:3)
P,S	Test of Mathematical Abilities—2 (TOMA-2)
C	Test of Nonverbal Intelligence—Second Edition (TONI-2)
P,S	Test of Nonverbal Intelligence—Third Edition (TONI-3)

C   Test of Problem Solving—Revised (TOPS-R)
C   Test of Reading Comprehension—Revised (TORC)
P,S   Test of Reading Comprehension—Third Edition (TORC-3)
C   Test of Sensory Integration (TSI)
c,w   Test of Variables of Attention (TOVA)
S   Test of Visual-Motor Integration (TVMI)
C   Test de Vocabulario en Imágenes Peabody (TVIP)
C   Test of Word Finding (TWF)
C   Test of Word Knowledge (TOWK)
C,P   Test of Written Language—Second Edition (TOWL-2)
P,S,w   Test of Written Language—Third Edition (TOWL-3)
C,P   Test of Written Spelling—3 (TWS-3)
S   Test of Written Spelling—4 (TWS-4)
P,W   Thematic Apperception Test for Children and Adults (TAT)
w   Token Test for Children

S   Universal Nonverbal Intelligence Test (UNIT)

P,S,W   Vineland Adaptive Behavior Scale (VABS or Vineland)
S   Vineland Social Maturity Scale (VSMS)
C   The Visual Aural Digit Span Test (VADS)

S   Walker-McConnell Scale of Social Competence and School Adjustment (W-M)
S   Wechsler Abbreviated Scale of Intelligence (WASI)
c,P,s   Wechsler Adult Intelligence Scale—Revised (WAIS-R)
S   Wechsler Adult Intelligence Scale—Third Edition (WAIS-III)
S   Wechsler-Bellevue Intelligence Scale
C,P,S,W Wechsler Individual Achievement Test (WIAT)
C,P,S,W Wechsler Intelligence Scale for Children—Third Edition (WISC-III)
C,P,S,W Wechsler Preschool and Primary Scale of Intelligence—Revised (WPPSI-R)
C,P   Wepman Auditory Discrimination Test—Second Edition (ADT-2)
C,P,S,W Wide Range Achievement Test—3 (WRAT-3)
C,W   Wide Range Assessment of Memory and Learning (WRAML)
s   Wide Range Assessment of Visual Motor Abilities
c,W   Wisconsin Card Sorting Test (WCST)
S   Woodcock Diagnostic Reading Battery (WDRB)
C,P,S,W Woodcock-Johnson Psychoeducational Battery—Revised (WJ-R) Tests of
         Cognitive Abilities and Tests of Achievement
S   Woodcock-Johnson Psychoeducational Battery—III (WJ-III) Tests of Cognitive
         Abilities and Tests of Achievement
C   Woodcock Language Proficiency Battery—Spanish (WLPB-S)
C   Woodcock-McGrew-Werder Mini Battery of Achievement (MBA)
C,P   Woodcock Reading Mastery Tests—Revised (WRMT-R)
S   Woodcock Reading Mastery Tests—Revised, Normative Update (WRMT-Rnu)
C   The Word Test—Adolescent (Word-A)
C   The Word Test—Revised (Elementary) (Word-R)
S   Work Sampling System (WSS)
P   Written Language Assessment (WLA)

S,w   Youth Self-Report Form (YSR)

Students' Writing Samples

Egg Drop was carefully written by a fifth grader with a language disability about student devices that could safely land an egg dropped from the top floor of a building. *Dear E.B. White* was written by a fourth grader who lived in the same household as the fifth grader.

Six years later—and with appropriate instruction, an educational environment built on trust, and the accommodations of extended time and a word processor—the student who had so much writing trouble received full credit for the typed essay which was part of a science exam. (The answer was in response to the premise that "Scientists often build on each other's ideas as new levels of understanding are uncovered.")

Egg Drop

This Monday I saw an egg drop. It was fun when it just got boring when it was sixth grade's turn. Sometimes it gets boring, when I don't like it anymore. Next time I will not get boring anymore.

Student's Writing Samples. Reprinted with permission of anonymous students.

Dear E. B. White,

Recently I read *Charlotte's Web*. My teacher asked me to give you my opinion of your story. I think it wasn't that good because it didn't have much action. It also was to sad. But I did like how Fern could hear the animals talk. I also liked the way that Charlotte and Wilbur relationship grew as they grew, how Charlotte kept her promise and how Fern wanted to keep Wilbur even though he was a runt. I like how the gander always repeated everything it said. I didn't like how Wilbur boasted.

Overall, I'd give this story a 7. I liked it a lot, but it had some weaknesses. Keep up the good work!

Sincerely,

J. J. Thomson began a series of cathode rays experiments in the late 1890s to determine the ratio of its change to its mass. Thomson was able to determine the change-to-mass ratio of the charged particle. Thomson concluded that the mass of the charged particle was much less than that of a hydrogen atom. After this discovery, Thomson proposed a model of the atom that became known as the plum pudding model. It consisted of an spherically shaped atom composed of a uniformly distributed positive charge within which the individual negatively charged electrons existed in.

Ernest Rutherford designed and conducted an experiment to see if alpha particles would be deflected as they passed through a thin piece of gold foil. He was also aware of Thomson's plum pudding model. As he was testing his experiment, he discovered that the alpha particles were being deflected away from the dense center. He concluded that Thomson and his plum pudding model was incorrect because it could not explain the results of the gold foil experiment. Later, he developed a new atomic model based on his findings. He concluded that there was a tiny, dense region called the nucleus, centrally located within the atom. According to Rutherford's new nuclear atomic model, most of an atom consists of electrons moving rapidly trough empty space. The electrons move through the available space surrounding the nucleus and are held within the atom by their attraction to the positively charged nucleus.

The reasons why these developments by Thomson and Rutherford were so radical are because it has allowed modern-day chemists to understand the behavior the nucleus and the electrons surrounding it. Both of these individuals have also allowed us to understand why electrons travel in circular orbits and not in square orbits. They have also allowed modern chemists to discover the atomic mass, the speed, and the rate at which the proton, neutron, and electron travel. Together, both of these individuals have allowed understanding the meanings of the nucleus and its electrons.

Appendix 7

Number of Children and Percentage Based on Estimated Resident Population, Ages 6-17, Served Under IDEA During the 1999-2000 School Year[1]

State	All Disabilities Number	All Disabilities Percentage	Specific LD Number	Specific LD Percentage	SLD/Total Percentage
Alabama	87,165	12.16	39,486	5.51	45.3
Alaska	15,202	11.13	8,732	6.39	57.4
Arizona	80,199	9.19	47,191	5.41	58.8
Arkansas	49,220	11.01	21,243	4.75	43.2
California	556,887	9.45	332,460	5.64	59.7
Colorado	65,638	9.11	32,663	4.53	49.8
Connecticut	63,934	11.33	30,855	5.47	48.3
Delaware	14,106	11.54	8,772	7.18	62.2
District of Columbia	7,995	12.90	3,601	5.81	45.0
Florida	312,174	12.90	151,199	6.25	48.4
Georgia	143,357	10.52	45,581	3.35	31.8
Hawaii	20,312	10.59	10,265	5.35	50.5
Idaho	24,501	10.24	14,378	6.01	58.7
Illinois	251,592	11.87	126,365	5.96	50.2
Indiana	130,656	12.67	54,719	5.31	41.9
Iowa	62,720	12.56	31,468	6.30	50.2
Kansas	50,079	10.48	22,088	4.62	44.1
Kentucky	72,352	11.07	19,897	3.04	27.5
Louisiana	81,881	10.09	33,896	4.18	41.4
Maine	29,558	14.14	12,401	5.93	42.0
Maryland	97,873	10.99	43,655	4.90	44.6
Massachusetts	141,912	14.26	88,123	8.86	62.1
Michigan	183,790	10.39	87,126	4.93	47.4
Minnesota	92,174	10.43	37,625	4.26	40.8
Mississippi	52,759	10.36	25,785	5.06	48.9
Missouri	118,040	12.27	61,659	6.41	52.2
Montana	16,601	10.40	9,294	5.82	56.0
Nebraska	36,943	12.08	15,515	5.07	42.0
Nevada	30,905	9.65	19,695	6.15	63.7
New Hampshire	24,932	11.61	12,326	5.74	49.4
New Jersey	188,375	13.99	104,674	7.78	55.6
New Mexico	44,888	13.31	27,313	8.10	60.8
New York	360,438	12.13	193,340	6.51	53.6
North Carolina	150,403	11.57	65,021	5.00	43.2
North Dakota	11,636	10.33	5,331	4.73	45.8
Ohio	203,326	10.42	78,112	4.00	38.4
Oklahoma	72,865	12.07	40,649	6.73	55.8
Oregon	64,191	11.38	33,109	5.87	51.6
Pennsylvania	198,718	10.00	109,104	5.49	54.9
Puerto Rico	49,204	6.51	26,192	3.47	53.2
Rhode Island	25,856	15.58	15,027	9.05	58.1
South Carolina	88,290	13.55	39,581	6.08	44.8
South Dakota	13,233	9.58	6,875	4.98	52.0
Tennessee	110,113	12.23	52,774	5.86	47.9
Texas	431,984	11.50	249,099	6.63	57.7
Utah	46,998	10.26	27,326	6.02	58.1
Vermont	11,890	11.85	4,599	4.59	38.7
Virginia	140,439	12.52	69,665	6.21	49.6
Washington	99,636	9.80	48,232	4.75	48.4
West Virginia	42,539	15.13	18,239	6.49	42.9
Wisconsin	101,476	10.72	48,385	5.11	47.7
Wyoming	11,054	12.26	5,675	6.30	51.3
50 States and D.C.	5,383,009	11.26	2,716,655	5.68	50.5

1   Population numbers combined respective data from Tables AA3 and AA4; related percentages are from Table AA10; U.S. Department of Education, "Twenty-third Annual Report to Congress on the Implementation of the Individuals with Disabilities Education Act" [Internet], 2001; pp. A-5, A-8, and A-23; available from http://www.ed.gov/offices/OSERS/OSEP/Products/OSEP2001AnlRpt/Appendix_A_Pt1.pdf. The last column of data was derived by dividing the *Specific LD Number* by the *All Disabilities Number*.

Specific Learning Disabilities, During the 1999-2000 School Year
Percentage of Children Ages 6-17, Based on Estimated Resident Population

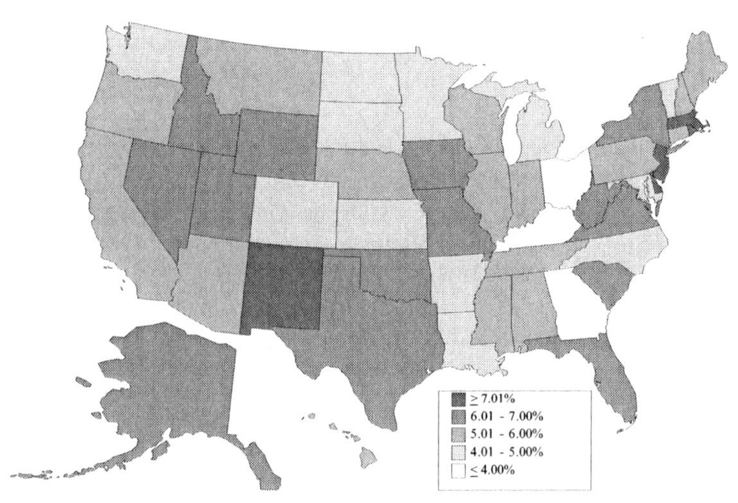

All Disabilities, During the 1999-2000 School Year
Percentage of Children Ages 6-17, Based on Estimated Resident Population

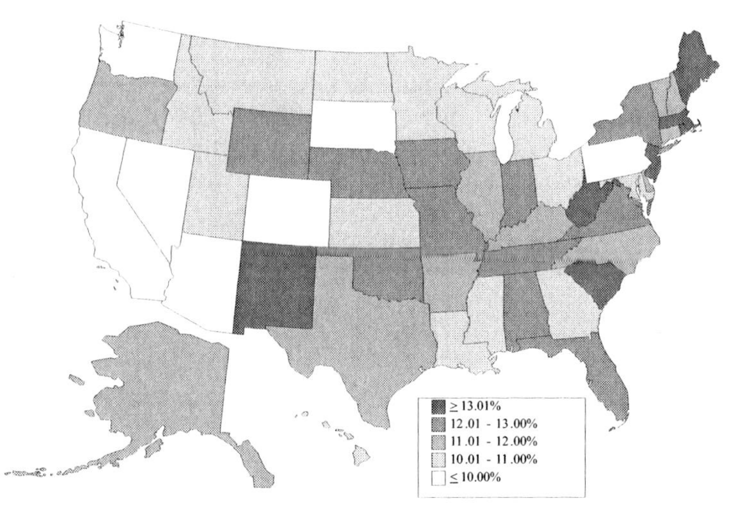

Appendix 8

Study Finds More Disabled Students in Regular Classes (04/12/2000)

Associated Press

Washington – Record numbers of students with disabilities are being educated in regular classrooms but few teachers are specially trained to instruct them, the Education Department said yesterday.

In 1996-97, 46 percent of the nation's 5.9 million special education students spent most of their time in a regular classroom, up slightly from the previous year's 45.9 percent, the department said.

Yesterday, Judith Heumann, assistant secretary of the Office of Special Education and Rehabilitative Service, praised the end of the "days of turning away the students with disabilities at the schoolhouse door."

But, she said, just 330,000 of the nation's 2.2 million teachers are hired to teach special education students.

Among general teachers, 4 out of 5 teachers with special education students in their classes feel ill-prepared to teach them, officials said. General education teachers are not required to have special education certificates, though nearly half of states require some course work in special education.

Heumann said colleges need to focus on training any teacher to instruct special-needs children.

That includes persuading more teacher candidates to choose working with special education children, she said.

Paula Gardner, an associate professor at California State University at Sacramento, which combines special education and regular education training, said school districts are seeing the value of this as a way of educating future teachers," she said. "We can't graduate them fast enough."

The 1975 Individuals with Disabilities Education Act which gives states money to help end discrimination against disabled children, requires that disabled children be schooled with other students whenever possible. Previously, children were often put in institutions or separate programs. The department considered children as included in a regular classroom atmosphere if they spent at least 80 percent of their time in regular classrooms.

Article appeared in *The San Francisco Chronicle*, 12 April 2000, p. A12. Reprinted with permission of The Associated Press.

Appendix 9

Number of Teachers Providing Special Education and Related Services for Students Ages 6-21 During the 1997-98 and 1998-99 School Years[1]

State	Number of Teachers Fully Certified		Number of Teachers Not Fully Certified		Vacant Positions
	1997-98	1998-99	1997-98	1998-99	1997-98
Alabama	5,581	5,704	193	160	76
Alaska	-	1,016	-	48	-
Arizona	3,567	4,001	217	280	121
Arkansas	2,866	2,866	137	137	97
California	21,503	21,827	4,334	5,747	358
Colorado	3,025	3,243	545	664	26
Connecticut	5,173	5,358	0	0	0
Delaware	1,216	1,354	295	218	7
District of Columbia	-	527	-	0	-
Florida	14,530	14,492	1,976	2,303	255
Georgia	8,821	9,982	343	221	64
Hawaii	771	1,102	276	365	26
Idaho	943	976	16	33	157
Illinois	18,846	19,276	806	1,008	430
Indiana	5,498	5,685	603	665	0
Iowa	4,233	4,535	485	603	24
Kansas	3,206	3,341	0	0	75
Kentucky	4,816	4,678	359	557	42
Louisiana	5,498	5,485	2,258	2,601	84
Maine	1,961	2,001	129	184	22
Maryland	6,485	6,545	718	805	89
Massachusetts	9,565	10,156	0	0	134
Michigan	10,472	11,900	554	951	105
Minnesota	6,525	6,428	281	704	19
Mississippi	3,737	3,663	307	357	83
Missouri	7,471	7,911	778	503	92
Montana	824	601	25	59	14
Nebraska	2,140	2,212	39	16	10
Nevada	1,539	1,782	33	30	67
New Hampshire	1,587	1,605	179	255	9
New Jersey	15,246	14,722	0	225	88
New Mexico	3,353	3,439	475	356	0
New York	25,218	27,114	6,781	7,167	178
North Carolina	7,224	7,768	855	1,022	154
North Dakota	700	687	30	40	19
Ohio	14,033	13,556	342	620	259
Oklahoma	3,773	3,898	48	55	17
Oregon	2,661	2,627	82	115	28
Pennsylvania	13,788	13,490	0	19	10
Rhode Island	1,459	1,558	7	13	2
South Carolina	10,679	4,543	349	327	158
South Dakota	812	843	8	9	10
Tennessee	4,609	4,636	21	56	17
Texas	20,728	21,008	3,270	3,495	0
Utah	1,977	2,309	88	102	13
Vermont	785	833	4	6	7
Virginia	9,899	10,038	1,124	1,505	51
Washington	4,489	4,493	43	45	25
West Virginia	2,288	2,329	286	338	25
Wisconsin	6,702	6,831	283	284	68
Wyoming	740	1,226	0	1,237	0
50 States and D.C.	313,562	318,200	29,982	36,510	3,615

1   State data is from Table AC2, U.S. Department of Education, "Twenty-second Annual Report to Congress on the Implementation of the Individuals with Disabilities Education Act" [Internet], 2000, p. A-210, available from: http://www.ed.gov/offices/OSERS/OSEP/Products/OSEP2000AnlRpt/PDF/Appendix-A.pdf; and from Table AC2, U.S. Department of Education, "Twenty-third Annual Report to Congress on the Implementation of the Individuals with Disabilities Education Act" [Internet], 2001, p. A-241, available from: http://www.ed.gov/offices/OSERS/OSEP/Products/OSEP2001AnlRpt/Appendix_A_Pt2.pdf.

Appendix 10

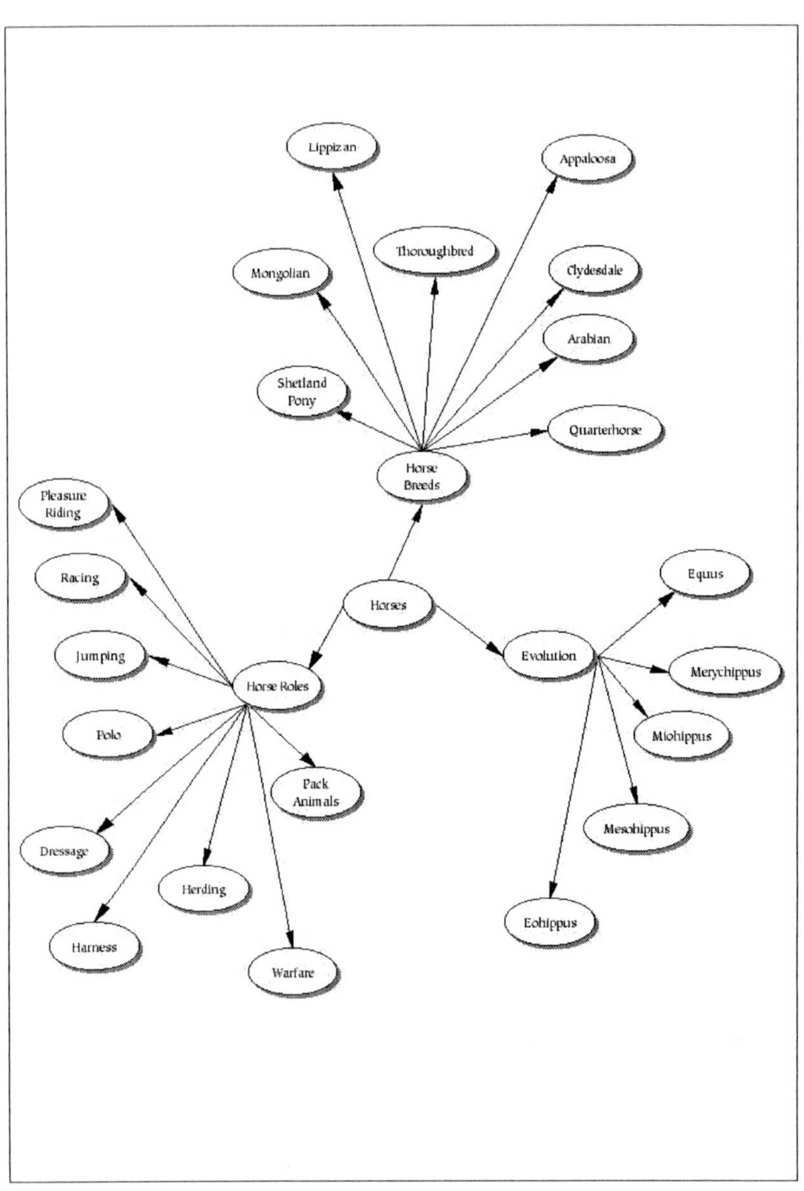

Story Webbing and Outline generated from *Inspiration* software.

Horses

I.   Horse Breeds

    A.   Thoroughbred

    B.   Quarterhorse

    C.   Arabian

    D.   Appaloosa

    E.   Lippizan

    F.   Clydesdale

    G.   Mongolian

    H.   Shetland Pony

II. Horse Roles

    A.   Pleasure Riding

    B.   Racing

    C.   Jumping

    D.   Polo

    E.   Dressage

    F.   Herding

    G.   Harness

    H.   Warfare

    I.   Pack Animals

III. Evolution

    A.   Eohippus

    B.   Mesohippus

    C.   Miohippus

    D.   Merychippus

    E.   Equus

Appendix 11

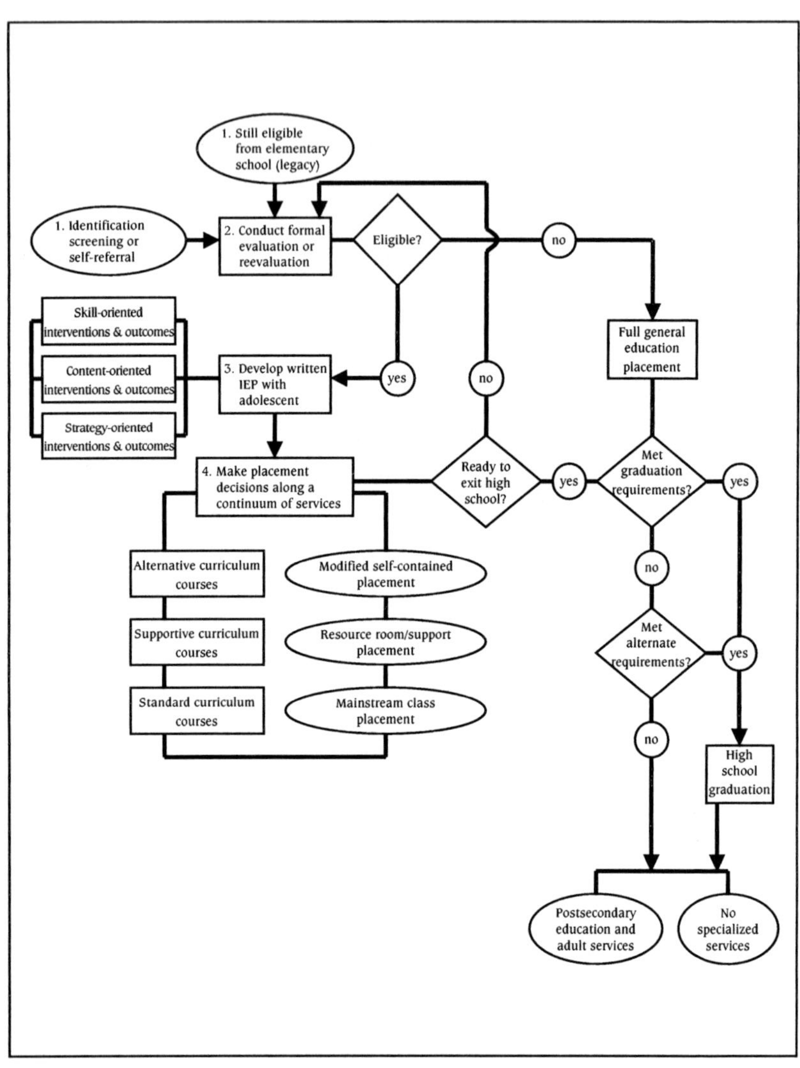

Students with Learning Disabilities, 4/E by Mercer, © 1992 by Macmillan Publishing Company. Reprinted by permission of Pearson Education, Inc., Upper Saddle River, NJ.

Resources

Many resources are listed within the chapter text or footnotes of this book and so may not be repeated here. Your public school district or local parent groups may help you find libraries with specialized information on learning disabilities. Several books are available in audio-cassettes form; many information sources have Spanish translations. Browsing an online bookseller will often pick up information on other books popular with people who have purchased the book you are contemplating. Some bookstores do not carry publications by a competitor. "Bookmarks," an article in the January 2002 issue of *Consumer Reports,* compares booksellers. Harvest Book Company (www.harvestbooks.com or 800/ 563-1222) searches, at no charge, for available out-of-print books.

Typing up key words does not necessarily lead to the best sources of information. Be vigilant for incomplete, inaccurate, and outdated information, as well as new credible discoveries. You can find other resources by visiting chatrooms; precautions are reviewed by Linda Broatch and Scott Moore in "Online Parent Groups: Support at Your Fingertips," available at www.schwablearning.org/articles.asp?g=3&r =62.

Parent Information Centers

The U.S. Department of Education funds many local parent information and support centers through the Office of Special Education Programs:
* *Exceptional Parent Magazine* (www.eparent.com) lists many local support organizations including Parent Training and Information (PTI) Centers (www.eparent.com/resources/directories/pti.html) and Parent to Parent (P-P) Programs (www.eparent.com/resources/directories/p2p info.htm).
* International Dyslexia Association (www.interdys.org or 800/ 222-3123) has branches with support groups, referral services, workshops, and seminars. It offers a learning disabilities simulation kit to promote better understanding; for more information, go to the website "The Disability Simulation" at www.dyslexia-ncbida.org/ simulation.html or www.dyslexia-ncbida.org and click on *simulations*. This organization was formerly known as The Orton Society.
* National Center for Learning Disabilities (NCLD) is an advocacy group with information on resources in each state, such as information and support centers, schools, and other service providers (www.ld.org or 888/ 575-7373 or 212/ 545-7510).

• National Information Center for Children and Youth with Disabilities (NICHCY) is an information and referral center with links to many nonprofit organizations (www.nichcy.org or 800/ 695-0285).

Websites provide information on learning problems and resources. The following organizations do not provide individual parent support. Many offer free periodic newsletters by email subscription.

• LD Online (www.ldonline.org) has an extensive library of informational articles. It has received excellent reviews by *NEA Today* and *USA Today*. This website has won the "Best of the Best Sites of '98" from *Yahoo Internet Life*; the 1998 Clarion Award for the best nonprofit web site; and the 1997 EDI Award from the National Easter Seal Society. WETA, the Washington, D.C. Public Broadcasting Station, supports this website. Dr. Larry Silver takes email inquiries at this website. Matt Cohen, Esq., answers general questions on special education law.

• Schwab Learning (www.schwablearning.org) has informational articles and message boards pertaining to learning disabilities and AD/HD, including state-specific information and links to other related websites. Free downloadable publications are accessible through www.schwablearning.org/resources.asp?g=4&s=1. Lists of local, national, and international service providers are found at www.schwablearning.org/resources.asp?g=4&s=5. Upcoming conferences and workshops are announced at www.schwablearning.org/calendar/index.asp. The website is supported by Schwab Learning, a service of the Charles and Helen Schwab Foundation.

• www.aboutourkids.org provides parenting, treatment, and other mental health information, including psychological and psychiatric issues, from the New York University Child Study Center and the resources of the NYU School of Medicine. If an article proves difficult to access, refer to "When a PDF Document Does Not Display" available at www.aboutourkids.org/pdfinstructions.html.

• Children and Adults with Attention Deficit Disorder (CHADD) is an advocacy group with information for parents (www.chadd.org or 800/ 233-4050).

• National Resource Center on AD/HD (NRC) is a national clearinghouse to disseminate science-based information on AD/HD (www.help4adhd.org or 800/ 233-4050).

• Attention Deficit Disorder Association (ADDA) offers information, resources, and support for adults with AD/HD (www.add.org or 847/ 432-2332).

• Council for Exceptional Children is an advocacy group offering information and professional development (www.cec.sped.org or voice: 888/ 232-7733 or 703/ 620-3660 or TTY 866/ 915-5000).

• Learning Disabilities Association of America (LDA) is an advocacy group supported by the ACLD Foundation. The websites provide infor-

mation on conferences, as well as books and materials of interest to parents (www.ldanatl.org or 412/ 341-1515).
• ERIC Clearinghouse on Disabilities and Gifted Education is a repository of information such as IDEA regulations, disability laws, dual exceptionalities (gifted LD and gifted AD/HD), and databases for further research (http://ericec.org or 800/ 328-0272).

Medicine, psychiatry, and psychology

Diagnostic and Statistical Manual of Mental Disorders, 4th Edition, Text Revision, (American Psychiatric Association, 2000) is the standard for diagnosing many mental developmental disorders. This manual may be on reserve at your public library.

www.medlineplus.gov is a free, reliable, continuously updated, comprehensive website, supported by The National Institutes of Health's National Library of Medicine (www.nlm.nih.gov). It is available for nonprofessionals in both English and Spanish, and neither requires registration nor links to other sites requiring registration. The site includes medical dictionaries, encyclopedias, and directories of health professionals and health care facilities. A copy of the original article can be ordered from medical libraries and journals for a fee.

Much information is available on learning and behavioral disorders with various degrees of technical explanations and some by primary investigators.

Larry Silver's most recent books include *The Misunderstood Child: Understanding and Coping with Your Child's Learning Disabilities* (Times Books or Three Rivers Press,1998), and *Dr. Larry Silver's Advice to Parents on AD/HD* (Times Books, 1999). Dr. Silver's paperbacks offer tips for identification, treatment, and self- advocacy.

Mel Levine has written many books for parents, teachers, other field specialists, and young people, and are available at many booksellers. These books explore problem areas and ways of approaching appropriate solutions. His writings are especially unique for his information about spatial organization and graphomotor troubles. Available from Educators Publishing Service are many books written for different audiences (800/ 435-7728 or www.epsbooks.com; at the website, click on *About the Authors,* click on *Dr. Mel Levine,* then click on *Books for Learning Differences*):
• *Educational Care: A System for Understanding and Helping Children with Learning Problems at Home and in School,* 2nd Edition (2002). This book can be considered a *demystification* manual for parents and teachers concerned about possible learning disorders. The book has taken great pains to present information in a nonjudgmental

fashion. No technical knowledge is required to understand the concepts. Many suggestions for resolving problems are provided as well.

* *Developmental Variation and Learning Disorders,* 2nd Edition (1998) is a comprehensive review of identification, education, and treatment issues at a professional level.

* *All Kinds of Minds* (1993) is written for elementary school children.

* *Keeping A Head in School* (1990) is written for children 11 years and older.

Available from Simon & Schuster are two more publications written by Levine for the general public:

* *A Mind at a Time* (2002)

* *The Myth of Laziness* (2003).

Developing Minds multimedia library is a complete set of 22 videos and 18 guides cover learning disorders, academic challenges, and management strategies. The information is based on the programs used at All Kinds of Minds, a private non-profit institute founded by Mel Levine and affiliated with the University of North Carolina at Chapel Hill. The videos may be ordered separately or as an entire set. For more information, contact WGBH Boston Video at www.pbs.org/wgbh/misunderstood minds/videos.html or 800/ 949-8670. The introductory video, *Misunderstood Minds*, was broadcast on PBS in March, 2002.

* *Overcoming Dyslexia: A New and Complete Science-Based Program for Overcoming Reading Problems at Any Level* by Sally Shaywitz (Knopf, 2003). This book discusses scientific discoveries about reading and dyslexia, and offers tips on diagnosis and treatment.

* *Specific Reading Disability: A View of the Spectrum,* edited by Bruce K. Shapiro, Pasquale J. Accardo, and Arnold J. Capute (York Press, 1998). This collection of papers is technically demanding, but the many contributing authors detail identification and treatment issues.

* *Dyslexia: Research and Resource Guide* (Allyn and Bacon, 1995) by Carol Sullivan Spafford and George S. Grosser, is an overview of LD.

* "Attention-Deficit Hyperactivity Disorder" by Russell Barkley. This article, published in the September 1998 issue of *Scientific American,* pp. 66-71, presents many of his findings, anatomical illustrations of problem areas, and lists of additional resources.

* *Understanding Girls with AD/HD* (Advantage Books, 1999), by Kathleen G. Nadeau, Ellen B. Littman, and Patricia O. Quinn addresses many of the issues faced by girls with AD/HD.

* *Straight Talk About Learning Disabilities* (Facts on File, 1999) by Kay Marie Porterfield offers information and advice for adolescents and adults with LD. The author, who has LD herself, includes self-advocacy, dealing with learning problems, and choosing a direction in life.

• *No One to Play With: Social Problems of LD and ADD Children* (Academic Therapy Publications, 1995), by Betty Osman and Henriette Blinder, explains the social processes affecting a child with LD.

Periodicals report new developments in learning and science. Two magazines for the general public which have reported on LD issues are:

• *Science News* is a 16-page nonprofit, weekly digest of new developments in science and technology, sometimes relating to learning disabilities. The website, www.sciencenews.org, has an archival feature that enables searches for past articles on specific topics. Abstracts are free; complete articles can be purchased for a small fee. For new subscriptions and customer service, call 800/ 552-4412.

• *Scientific American* articles can be viewed at www.sciam.com or downloaded from www.sciamarchive.com for a small fee.

• *The Cartoon Guide to Statistics* (HarperPerennial, 1993) by Larry Gonick and Woollcott Smith explains statistics without the heavy math.

Education

Resources suggesting methods for managing students are:

• *Learning Disabilities: Characteristics, Identification, and Teaching Strategies*, 4th Edition, by William N. Bender (Prentice Hall College Division, 2000) reviews teaching practices.

• *Students with Learning Disabilities,* 5th Edition, by Cecil D. Mercer (Prentice-Hall, 1996) provides the historical background and a review of teaching practices.

• *Dyslexia: A Practitioner's Handbook,* 3rd Edition (John Wiley & Sons, 2003), by Gavin Reid, reviews many educational practices.

• *Handbook of Learning Disabilities* by H. Lee Swanson, Karen Harris, and Steve Graham (Guilford Press, 2003) offers information from authors recognized for their work in memory and reading and writing instruction.

• *Children's Problems in Text Comprehension: An Experimental Investigation* by Nicola Yuill and Jane Oakhill (Cambridge University Press, 1991) provides details of investigations into the types of troubles observed in reading comprehension (not dyslexia).

• WestEd, a national consulting firm in education links to information about *Special Needs & Full Inclusion* from its home page, www.wested.org.

• *To Be Gifted & Learning Disabled* (Creative Learning Press, 1991) by Susan M. Baum, Steve V. Owen, and John Dixon explains many perplexing behaviors seen in twice-exceptional students.

Resources with information on solving school problems are:

Free Spirit Publishing (www.freespirit.com or 800/ 735-7323) offers many paperbacks for students, teachers, and parents.

•   *The Survival Guide for Kids with LD* (2002) by Gary Fisher and Rhoda Cummings offers solutions for school and social problems.

•   *The Survival Guide for Teenagers with LD,* (1993) by Rhoda Woods Cummings and Gary L. Fisher provides advice on a wide variety of topics including self-advocacy, employment, living skills, social life and dating, and planning for life after high school.

•   *When Your Child Has LD (Learning Differences): A Survival Guide for Parents* (1995) by Gary Fisher and Rhoda Cummings offers many ways for coping and helping your child.

•   *Help4ADD@High School* (1998) by Kathleen G. Nadeau has many concrete ideas not only for students with AD/HD but also learning disabilities such as understanding the disability; organizing work, time, and materials; learning and memorizing; improving self-advocacy; and getting expert help.

•   *Succeeding with LD* (1997) by Jill Lauren profiles real-life accounts of people with LD.

•   *Bullies Are a Pain* (1997) by Trevor Romain gives suggestions for 8- to 13-year-olds.

•   *More Than a Label* (2002) by Aisha Muharrar discusses high school stereotyping and what to do about it.

•   *The Gifted Kids' Survival Guide: A Teen Handbook* (1996) by Judy Galbraith and Jim Delisle touches on issues relating to being both gifted and learning disabled.

•   *What Kids Need to Succeed: Proven, Practical Ways to Raise Good Kids* (1998) by Peter L. Benson, Judy Galbraith, and Pamela Espeland offers many concrete suggestions based on research.

•   *Choosing the Right School for Your Child* (Association of Ideas, 1995), by Brandi Roth and Fay Van Der Kar-Levinson, surveys nine instructional approaches found in elementary and secondary schools. The workbook organizes a step-by-step method for identifying optimal school choices, preparing the application, and communicating information during an interview.

•   *Colleges with Programs for Students with Learning Disabilities or Attention Deficit Disorders,* 6th Edition (Peterson's, 2000), by Charles T. Mangrum II and Stephen S. Strichart offers detailed information on specialized programs at over 750 two- and four-year colleges and universities in the U.S. and another 20 in Canada. Program details provided can be quite specific such as the use of personal computers, Franklin Speller, Kurzweil, or Dragon speech recognition program. Information pertaining to admission requirements affected by circumstances of disability are included, as well as tips for boosting a candidate's admission success at a particular institution. Charts provided in the book list schools by state and depth of support services. The book does not address concerns pertaining to general admissions. This guide is best used as an indicator of services available; the schools themselves can provide more details. In the case of public colleges and universities, the guide can suggest available services at unlisted campuses for further investigation.

• *College and Career Success for Students with Learning Disabilities* (VGM Career Horizons, 1996) by Roslyn Dolber is a comprehensive book, written for college-bound and college students. It provides explicit information on types of college environments, tips for college success, choosing a career, and finding employment.

• *Survival Guide for College Students with ADD or LD*, by Kathleen Nadeau (Magination Press, 1994) includes topics such as college selection, types of assistance commonly available on campuses or in the surrounding community, and tactics and strategies to make learning easier. For example, in scheduling classes, a student with a language disability is advised to avoid signing up for many classes with significant reading and writing assignments in one term. Available through booksellers or the publisher at www.maginationpress.com, this is a book for someone who does not want to read a lot.

• *College Students with Learning Disabilities: A Handbook,* 7th Edition, 2000, by Susan A. Vogel offers possible accommodations in academic settings, along with other resources and relevant requirements emanating from Section 504. This inexpensive handbook can be ordered from LDA Bookstore at www.ldanatl.org/store/index.html (click on *Adolescent/Young Adult*), or call 412/ 341-1515.

• The George Washington University HEATH Resource Center (Higher Education and Adult Training for People with Handicaps) is a national information clearinghouse on postsecondary options. Contact www.heath.gwu.edu or 800/ 544-3284 or 202/ 973-0904.

General resources offer additional advice:

• *Making the Most of College: Students Speak Their Minds,* by Richard J. Light (Harvard University Press, 2001) gives practical advice from a Harvard professor to students, parents, and schools on how to use time most effectively for college success. Much of the advice is also useful in secondary settings.

• *Barron's Profiles of American Colleges* categorizes over 1,650 institutions in the U.S. and Canada from "noncompetitive" to "most competitive," as well as specialized and pre-professional programs. This thorough guide offers self-assessments to help the process of matching students with suitable college programs, and provides information on majors, finances, and general profiles of successful candidates.

• *The Fiske Guide to Getting into the Right College*, by Edward B. Fiske and Bruce G. Hammond (Sourcebooks, 2002), highlights schools noted to be strong in certain disciplines or approaches. This guidebook may be more useful than others that discuss colleges primarily seeking students with high verbal aptitude scores.

• *The Public Ivies: America's Flagship Public Universities*, by Howard R. Greene and Matthew W. Greene (Cliff Street Books, 2001), is a mainstream college applications guidebook with suggestions for students with special needs. Like the public school system, large state colleges and universities have some of the best academic support programs.

• "Secrets of the SAT," available at www.pbs.org/wgbh/pages/frontline/shows/sats, examines the college admissions process.

• U.S. Department of Education (www.ed.gov) offers topics on special education (click on *Other preK-12 topics* listed under *Education Resources*, then scroll down to *Special education* where you will find recent news and documents). For information on IDEA, visit the website "IDEA '97" at www.ed.gov/offices/OSERS/Policy/IDEA. The Office of Special Education Programs (OSEP at www.ed.gov/offices/OSERS or 202/ 205-5465) is part of the Office of Special Education and Rehabilitative Services (OSERS at www.ed.gov/offices/OSERS/OSEP or 202/ 205-5507), which is part of the Department of Education. Publications appear on the website www.ed.gov/offices/OSERS/OSEP/Products/comppubs.html.

• Education Week on the Web (www.edweek.org) at the time of this writing is a free repository of news on education, often the basis for media reports. Registration is required.

Career and employment planning

While many resources address the specific issues of students with disabilities, individuals should still investigate whatever interests them. Some general sources of information are:

• *What Color Is Your Parachute?* by Richard N. Bolles, (Ten Speed Press, annually updated) includes Internet resources as well as practical advice for job hunting. The Flower Exercise provides a method for determining an individual's employment preferences. Additional advice from Bolles is available at www.jobhuntersbible.com.

• Periodicals, especially professional publications, examine trends in the current job market. For example, *U.S. News & World Report* publishes its Career Guides in February of each year; the February 18, 2002 issue highlighted prospects with steady employment for individuals in technical fields, security, and special education.

• The U.S. Department of Education's Office of Vocational and Adult Education offers information on transitioning from high school to careers at www.ed.gov/offices/OVAE.

• *Occupational Outlook Handbook,* U.S. Bureau of Labor Statistics. This manual, published by the U.S. Government Printing Office every two years, is usually available through school counselors or public libraries. The website, www.bls.gov/oco/home.htm, provides updated job descriptions, educational requirements, and typical salaries.
• Many websites, like www.salary.com, give local market information on employment and salary. Beware of posting your personal information on websites.

Two places to begin research on federal and state labor laws are:
• "Understanding and Applying Child Labor Laws to Today's School-to-Work Transition Programs" by Dorianne Beyer gives an overview of federal and state child labor laws at http://vocserve.berkeley. edu/CenterFocus/cf8.html. The Child Labor Resource Guide attached to this 1995 article may be outdated however.
• The U.S. Department of Labor offers information on federal labor laws and state labor agencies at www.dol.gov.

Legal

Many books can provide basic information on your child's legal protections and the background for why these laws exist. Most information pertains to children in public schools. Expect new books to be published each time IDEA is amended.
• *The Complete IEP Guide: How to Advocate for Your Special Ed Child,* 2nd Edition (Nolo, 2001), by Lawrence M. Siegel explains the IEP process and what you can do at each step. The book also has portions of IDEA and Section 504 and sample letters to school authorities.
• *Negotiating the Special Education Maze: A Guide for Parents and Teachers,* 3rd Edition (Woodbine House, 1997), by Winifred Anderson, Stephen Chitwood, and Deidre Hayden reviews the IEP process, FERPA, and Section 504. A workbook format can help you analyze your child's needs. Online excerpts are available at www.ldonline.org/ld_indepth/parenting/maze.html.
• *Wrightslaw: Special Education Law* (1999, Harbor House Law Press), by Peter W.D. Wright and Pamela Wright explains laws and court decisions governing special education. The website, "Wrightslaw" at www.wrightslaw.com, links to information on advocacy.
• *Legal Issues in Special Education* (Allyn & Bacon, 1995), by Allan G. Osborne, Jr. reviews the twists and turns of court rulings. Unfortunately, no update of this book has been published.
• *Separation of Church and State* (Harvard University Press, 2002), by Philip Hamburger traces the historical development of this judicial

tradition, not specified in the First Amendment, but with roots in mid-19th Century debates about public education.
• *A Potent Spell: Mother Love and the Power of Fear* by Janna Malamud Smith (Houghton Mifflin, 2003), reviews historical limitations on mothers, thus reducing their ability to effectively advocate for their children.
• www.edlaw.net offers texts of special education statues, regulations, interpretations, and decisions.
• LRP Publications offers legal publications on special education (www.lrp.com/store or voice 800/ 341-7874).
• LD Online offers many articles with legal information, available at www.ldonline.org/ld_indepth/legal_legislative/legal_legislative.html.
• Disability Rights Education and Defense Fund (DREDF) engages in legal reform, litigation, and education to help secure the civil rights of individuals with disabilities (www.dredf.org or 510/ 644-2555).
• The American Correctional Association offers informational books and videos addressing the issues of juveniles and those with disabilities (www.aca.org or 800/ 222-5646).
Government websites provide reliable legal information:
• The updated Code of Federal Regulations (CFR) are available at the government website www.access.gpo.gov/nara/cfr. The laws referred to in this book are identified as follows:

ADA:	Title 28	Volume 1	Chapter I	Parts 35-42
Section 504:	Title 34	Volume 1	Chapter I	Part 104
IDEA:	Title 34	Volume 2	Chapter III	Part 300

Once at the Code of Federal Regulations website, click on *New Code of Federal Regulations Browse Feature*. At the next screen, scroll down and click on the latest revision date of the title(s) you want, then click on the *Continue* button at the bottom of the page. At the next screen:

For Title 28: click on the highlighted *0-42*, then at the next screen scroll down to Parts 35-42.

For Section 504: click on the highlighted *100-199*. At the next screen, click on the highlighted *104*.

For IDEA regulations: click on the highlighted *300-399*. At the next screen, click on the highlighted *300* which will bring up another screen listing all the regulations from 300.1 through 300.756.

(The above terminology from the website may be confusing when seen in other places. *Volume* is also referred to as *Part* when ordering a text publication. *Part* is also referred to as *Section*, often seen as §—or two stylized s's stuck together—when looking at legal citations.)

Alternatively, you can call the Education Publications Center (877/ 433-7827 or TTY/TDD at 877/ 576-7734) to order a copy of these regulations. (Its website at www.ed.gov/pubs/edpubs.html lists its most recent publications. The regulations to IDEA, *Federal Register: Part II 34 CFR, Parts 300 and 303,* had previously been listed online, but no longer). The order will be shipped at no charge.
• The Department of Justice offers "A Guide to Disability Rights Laws" at www.usdoj.gov/crt/ada/cguide.htm. For information about filing complaints, mediation, and other resources, contact www.usdoj. gov/crt/ada/adahom1.htm, 800/ 514-0301, or TDD 800/ 514-0383.
• The Office for Civil Rights (OCR) affiliated with the Department of Education enforces federal laws prohibiting discrimination in education programs and activities receiving federal financial assistance, on the basis of disability—as well as race, color, national origin, sex and age—for complaints filed within 60 days of the "extraordinary circumstance." More information, including that of state and regional offices, is available from http://bcol01.ed.gov/CFAPPS/OCR/contactus.cfm or 800/ 421-3481 or TDD: 877/ 521-2172.
• U.S. Equal Employment Opportunity Commission (EEOC) can provide information on federal laws prohibiting job discrimination (www. eeoc.gov or 800/ 669-4000 or TTY: 800/ 669-6820).

Kim Glenchur graduated from Stanford University with a major in human biology before completing a masters program in medical illustration at The Johns Hopkins University School of Medicine and an MBA from the University of California at Berkeley. She has worked in both business and education, is raising three teenagers, and has been working with one child's learning issues for at least a dozen years—finally seeing him happy being an honors student.